# THE MYSTERY FANCIER
# INDEX

# MORE WILDSIDE CLASSICS

*Dacobra, or The White Priests of Ahriman*, by Harris Burland
*The Nabob*, by Alphonse Daudet
*Out of the Wreck*, by Captain A. E. Dingle
*The Elm-Tree on the Mall*, by Anatole France
*The Lance of Kanana*, by Harry W. French
*Amazon Nights*, by Arthur O. Friel
*Caught in the Net*, by Emile Gaboriau
*The Gentle Grafter*, by O. Henry
*Raffles*, by E. W. Hornung
*Gates of Empire*, by Robert E. Howard
*Tom Brown's School Days*, by Thomas Hughes
*The Opium Ship*, by H. Bedford Jones
*The Miracles of Antichrist*, by Selma Lagerlof
*Arsène Lupin*, by Maurice LeBlanc
*A Phantom Lover*, by Vernon Lee
*The Iron Heel*, by Jack London
*The Witness for the Defence*, by A.E.W. Mason
*The Spider Strain and Other Tales,* by Johnston McCulley
*Tales of Thubway Tham,* by Johnston McCulley
*The Prince of Graustark*, by George McCutcheon
*Bull-Dog Drummond*, by Cyril McNeile
*The Moon Pool*, by A. Merritt
*The Red House Mystery*, by A. A. Milne
*Blix*, by Frank Norris
*Wings over Tomorrow*, by Philip Francis Nowlan
*The Devil's Paw*, by E. Phillips Oppenheim
*Satan's Daughter and Other Tales*, by E. Hoffmann Price
*The Insidious Dr. Fu Manchu*, by Sax Rohmer
*Mauprat*, by George Sand
*The Slayer and Other Tales*, by H. de Vere Stacpoole
*Penrod (Gordon Grant Illustrated Edition)*, by Booth Tarkington
*The Gilded Age*, by Mark Twain
*The Blockade Runners*, by Jules Verne
*The Gadfly*, by E.L. Voynich

*Please see www.wildsidepress.com for a complete list!*

# THE MYSTERY FANCIER

## AN INDEX TO VOLUMES I–XIII

by

## WILLIAM F. DEECK

**WILDSIDE PRESS**

To Guy Townsend, the founder of the fest, and to the contributors and subscribers over the years who made possible thirteen wonderful volumes of The Mystery Fancier.

**THE MYSTERY FANCIER INDEX**

This edition published in 2006 by Wildside Press, LLC.
www.wildsidepress.com

# Reader's Guide

*The Mystery Fancier* began as a bimonthly publication in 1976. Because of a hiatus in publishing, Volume 8 comprises three issues published in 1984, with Steven A. Stilwell as Editor while Guy Townsend continued as Publisher and "Eminence Grise," and three issues published in 1986 with Townsend once again Editor. With Volume 10, TMF ceased being bimonthly and became quarterly. The first two issues of Volume 13 were published in 1991, the second two in 1992.

Each entry in the index includes Volume number, Issue number, and the page number at which the item begins and ends. P indicates the Preview issue, dated November 1976. Ending page numbers on book reviews have sometimes been removed to shorten the length of the index. Occasionally, for the same reason, article titles used in cross references have been condensed.

Alphabetization has been done by the WordPerfect sort program, which has its own way of doing things, with some minor alterations. Purists, I fear, will be distressed to learn that the Mac's and the Mc's are in different places.

Book titles are in caps, as are films and television shows, with the latter two marked as such; short stories are quoted.

Reviews are indexed under title, author, and subject, when the latter is applicable. For example, biographies of Raymond Chandler will be found under his entry. Individual reviews are indexed also under the reviewer, but reviews in columns have not been listed under the column itself. Generally, films will be found under the *Movies* heading, not individually.

Abbreviations: (IAC) It's About Crime; (L:) letters; (M*F) Mystery*File; (MS) comments or reviews in Mysteriously Speaking...; (R) reviews in Verdicts; (RM) Reel Murders; (SSC) Spy Series Characters; (TAR) The Armchair Reviewer; (TBR) The Backward Reviewer; (TCITC) The Curmudgeon in the Corner; (TNSPE) The Not So Private Eye.

Letters (L:) have been indexed for the most part, when my feeble brain was capable of deciding whether and how. If letter writers discussed a book as such rather than the writer, the letter is indexed to that book—well, most of the time. Hey, this is subjective stuff, folks. Read Stephen Leacock's "There Is No Index" if you don't believe me.

My thanks to Charles K. Cook, whose index to TMF Volumes I–V was of great help in compiling this index.

# Checklist of Issues Indexed

| Volume | Issue | Date | Pages |
|---|---|---|---|
| | Preview | November 1976 | 42 |
| 1 | 1 | January 1977 | 48 |
| 1 | 2 | March 1977 | 54 |
| 1 | 3 | May 1977 | 58 |
| 1 | 4 | July 1977 | 60 |
| 1 | 5 | September 1977 | 60 |
| 1 | 6 | November 1977 | 60 |
| 2 | 1 | January 1978 | 60 |
| 2 | 2 | March 1978 | 64 |
| 2 | 3 | May 1978 | 76 |
| 2 | 4 | July 1978 | 62 |
| 2 | 5 | September–October 1978 | 61 |
| 2 | 6 | November–December 1978 | 61 |
| 3 | 1 | January–February 1979[1] | 62 |
| 3 | 2 | March–April 1979 | 62 |
| 3 | 3 | May–June 1979 | 62 |
| 3 | 4 | July–August 1979 | 62 |
| 3 | 5[2] | September–October 1979 | 50 |
| 3 | 6 | November–December 1979 | 50 |
| 4 | 1 | January–February 1980 | 48 |
| 4 | 2 | March–April 1980 | 62 |
| 4 | 3 | May–June 1980 | 50 |
| 4 | 4 | July–August 1980 | 50 |
| 4 | 5 | September–October 1980 | 50 |
| 4 | 6 | November–December 1980 | 50 |
| 5 | 1 | January–February 1981 | 50 |
| 5 | 2 | March–April 1981 | 50 |
| 5 | 3 | May–June 1981 | 46 |
| 5 | 4 | July–August 1981 | 46 |
| 5 | 5 | September–October 1981 | 50 |
| 5 | 6 | November–December 1981 | 54 |

1. The cover date is March–April 1979.
2. Marked as Volume 3, Number 4, on cover.

| Volume | Issue | Date | Pages |
|--------|-------|------|-------|
| 6 | 1 | January–February 1982 | 50 |
| 6 | 2 | March–April 1982 | 50 |
| 6 | 3 | May–June 1982 | 50 |
| 6 | 4 | July–August 1982 | 50 |
| 6 | 5 | September–October 1982 | 50 |
| 6 | 6 | November–December 1982 | 50 |
| 7 | 1 | January–February 1983 | 50 |
| 7 | 2 | March–April 1983 | 50 |
| 7 | 3 | May–June 1983 | 50 |
| 7 | 4 | July–August 1983 | 50 |
| 7 | 5 | September–October 1983 | 50 |
| 7 | 6 | November–December 1983 | 50 |
| 8 | 1[1] | January–February 1984 | 46 |
| 8 | 2 | March–April 1984 | 50 |
| 8 | 3 | May–June 1984 | 50 |
| 8 | 4[2] | July–August 1986 | 50 |
| 8 | 5 | September–October 1986 | 50 |
| 8 | 6 | November–December 1986 | 50 |
| 9 | 1 | January–February 1987 | 50 |
| 9 | 2 | March–April 1987 | 50 |
| 9 | 3 | May–June 1987 | 50 |
| 9 | 4 | July–August 1987 | 50 |
| 9 | 5 | September–October 1987 | 50 |
| 9 | 6 | November–December 1987 | 50 |
| 10[3] | 1 | Winter 1988 | 104 |
| 10 | 2 | Spring 1988 | 104 |
| 10 | 3 | Summer 1988 | 104 |
| 10 | 4 | Fall 1988 | 104 |
| 11 | 1 | Winter 1989 | 104 |
| 11 | 2 | Spring 1989 | 104 |
| 11 | 3 | Summer 1989 | 104 |
| 11 | 4 | Fall 1989 | 104 |

1. First issue with Steven A. Stilwell as editor. Guy Townsend continued as Publisher and "Eminence Grise."

2. With this issue, Guy Townsend resumed his role as editor. The gap in the dates, with the first three issues of Volume 8 published in 1984 and the final three in 1986, is the result of a hiatus in publishing the magazine.

3. With this volume, TMF began quarterly publication.

| Volume | Issue | Date | Pages |
|:------:|:-----:|:----:|:-----:|
| 12 | 1 | Winter 1990 | 104 |
| 12 | 2 | Spring 1990 | 104 |
| 12 | 3 | Summer 1990 | 104 |
| 12 | 4 | Fall 1990 | 104 |
| 13 | 1 | Winter 1991 | 104 |
| 13 | 2 | Spring 1991 | 104 |
| 13 | 3 | Summer 1992 | 104 |
| 13 | 4 | Fall 1992 | 104 |

# Cover Art

My apologies to those whose cover art may not be listed below. Guy Townsend had a strange way of acknowledging artists in the issue following the publication of their art or not mentioning them at all. And for the Doerrer cover on Volume 2, Number 6, Guy graciously attributes it, in Volume 3, Number 1, to "Dave Doerrer's wife."

Volume 4, Number 6, is the first issue to carry the later ubiquitous chap sitting in an armchair and smoking a pipe—anyone we know?—a cover forever unattributed as far as I can tell.

Recycled cover art, popular both early and late in TMF's history, has not been noted.

Cover artists: Karl Cerasoli 3/3; Lari Davidson 8/3, 8/4, 8/5; Doerrer 2/6; Brad W. Foster 6/6, 7/1, 7/2, 7/3, 7/4, 7/5, 7/6, 8/1, 8/2; Al Frick 2/1; Mary Ann Grochowski 3/2; Frank Hamilton 2/2, 2/5; Ron Harris 1/2; August Mead 3/4; Robert S. Napier 4/1, 4/3; Stu Shippman 1/3, 1/5, 1/6.; Guy Townsend 1/1

# A

"A" IS FOR ALIBI (Grafton) (R) 7/6/50
A.E. Martin's Pel Pelham: Spruiker
  Detective (Deeck)        9/5/3-6*
A.S.F. THE STORY OF A GREAT
  CONSPIRACY (Rhode) (IAC) 3/2/21
*A Suitable Job for a Woman* (letter-
  zine) (MS)               9/1/6
*Aarons, Edward S.* Also see Ronns,
  Edward
  ASSIGNMENT AFGHAN DRAGON
    (M*F)                  1/5/32
    (SSC)                  5/5/15*
Abandoned Queens and Some Notes on
  Unintentional Plagiarism
  (Strøm)                  9/1/10-16
  L: Deeck 9/2/47; Lachman 9/2/47
*Abbey, Edward*
  Obituary (Lachman)       11/3/52
*Abbot, Anthony*
  ABOUT THE MURDER OF A
  MAN AFRAID OF WOMEN
    (IAC)                  13/2/53-4
    (IAC)                  13/2/52-4
  THE SHUDDERS (R)         9/5/38
ABOUT THE MURDER OF A MAN
  AFRAID OF WOMEN (Abbot)
    (IAC)                  13/2/53-4
*Academe*
  Bleeding the Fun Out (Isaac) 7/5/3-6
  Bloody Balaclava (Bakerman)
                           7/1/23-9
  Pseudonymous Professors
    (Barbato)              1/4/3-6
  L: Adey 5/4/44; Albert 5/4/43; Asdell
  7/2/42; Crider 5/1/36; Doerrer
  5/1/36; Fisher 4/6/46; Isaac 7/2/43,
  7/4/39; Loeser 5/1/47; Masser
  5/2/40; Restaino 7/3/48; Toole
  5/1/43; Wooster 5/5/46
Academy Chicago (IAC)      8/1/19
ACCORDING TO ST. JOHN (Babula)
  (TAR)                    12/2/55
Acheson, Edward
  THE GRAMMARIAN'S FUNERAL
    (R)                    9/2/39
ACT OF LOVE (Lansdale) (R)  5/3/36
ACTS OF MERCY (Pronzini/Malzberg)
  (R)                      2/5/37
Adams, Cleve F.
  THE BLACK DOOR (M*F)     P/30

Adams, Clifton
  DEATH'S SWEET SONG
    (M*F)                  2/2/35
Adams, Harold
  THE MAN WHO MET THE TRAIN
    (TAR)                  11/2/63
  THE MAN WHO MISSED THE
    PARTY (TAR)            11/4/73
  MURDER (M*F)             6/1/37
*Adams, Harriet*
  Obituary (Lachman)       6/4/33
Adams, Herbert
  THE GOLDEN APE (IAC)     6/3/22
  VICTORY SONG (TBR)       13/3/61-2
Adams, Tom. See AGATHA
  CHRISTIE: THE ART OF HER
  CRIMES
Adamson, Lydia
  A CAT IN THE MANGER
    (TAR)                  13/1/47
*Adcock, Thomas*
  SEA OF GREEN (TAR)       12/2/53
  L: Shibuk 12/4/102
Addams, Charles
  THE WORLD OF CHAS ADDAMS
    (IAC)                  13/4/84
*Adey, Robert C.S.*
  DEATH LOCKED IN (w/Greene,
    ed.) (IAC)             9/5/23
  L: 1/3/51; 2/3/73; 2/4/57; 3/1/59;
  3/3/60; 3/5/46; 4/3/48; 5/1/31;
  5/3/43; 5/4/44; 5/5/47; 5/6/53;
  6/1/47; 6/2/49; 6/3/49; 7/1/49;
  7/2/43; 7/4/43; 7/5/2; 8/1/43;
  8/3/47; 9/1/46; 13/1/78-9;
  13/3/102-3
  Reviews:
    BONEGRINDER (Lutz)     6/4/22
    BRIGHTLIGHT (Bernard)  4/3/42
    COCAINE AND BLUE EYES
      (Zackel)             7/5/40
    CROSS THAT PALM WHEN I
      COME TO IT (Southcott) 5/2/38
    DEATH DROP (Gill)      5/4/34
    DEATH IN A SLEEPING CITY
      (Wainwright)         7/4/34
    DEATH OF A FAVORITE GIRL
      (Gilbert)            7/1/42
    EXTRA COVER (Smith)    7/2/39
    GAMES (Pronzini)       6/1/45
    GOODNIGHT AND GOOD–BYE
      (Harris)             7/1/42

Adey, Robert C.S., continued
Reviews continued
GREEN FOR DANGER (Brand)
8/2/40
THE HANDS OF HEALING
MURDER (D'Amato) 6/4/18
HERO BY PROXY (Teilhet)
5/3/40
HIS MASTER'S VOICE (Low)
5/3/40
JOHN CREASEY'S CRIME
COLLECTION 1981 (Harris,
ed.) 6/2/46
THE JUDGE AND HIS HANG-
MAN (Durrenmatt) 7/2/39
KILL 3 (Shulman) 7/4/34
LOOKING FOR RACHEL
WALLACE (Parker) 5/5/36
A MAN CALLED SCAVENER
(Greenaway) 5/4/33
THE MAN RESPONSIBLE
(Robinett) 7/5/39
MURDER AT WILLOW RUN
(Collins) 7/5/40
MURDER '97 (Gruber) 7/4/34
THE MYSTERY GUILD
ANTHOLOGY 5/2/38
NEVER CROSS A VAMPIRE
(Kaminsky) 6/4/18
THE PENNY MURDERS (Black)
5/5/37
PRACTISE TO DECEIVE
(Bradshaw) 7/1/42
PRISONER OF THE DEVIL
(Hardwick) 6/4/36
PUBLIC EYE: MARKER CALLS
THE TUNE (Marriott) 7/4/33
THE SECOND DEADLY SIN
(Sanders) 5/4/33
SERGEANT VERITY AND THE
BLOOD ROYAL (Selwyn)
3/6/48
SERGEANT VERITY AND THE
SWELL MOB (Selwyn) 6/4/29
SOME DIE HARD (Brett) 7/5/39
SPENCE IN PETAL PARK
(Allen) 7/5/40
THE TURN-UP (Sewart) 5/2/38
UNBECOMING HABITS (Heald)
6/5/50
WHO IS TEDDY VILLANOVA?
(Berger) 5/5/36

Adey, Robert C.S., continued
Reviews continued
WINTER'S CRIMES 12 (Watson,
ed.) 6/2/46
YOU NICE BASTARD (Newman)
2/2/37
Two from the Telly 5/6/19-20,32
L: Reineke 6/4/49
Adkins, Jan
COOKIE (TAR) 11/1/50
DEADLINE FOR FINAL ART (MS)
(TAR) 12/3/8-9; 13/1/47-8
Adler, Bill, and Thomas Chastain
THE PICTURE PERFECT
MURDERS (R) 12/4/91-4
ADVANTAGE MISS SEETON
(Charles) (TAR) 13/1/52-3
ADVENT OF DYING (O'Marie) (R)
9/1/41
ADVENTURES OF CARDIGAN, THE
(Nebel) (R) 4/101
ADVENTURES OF HERLOCK
SHOLMES, THE (Todd) (R) 2/5/41
ADVENTURES OF JULES DE
GRANDIN, THE (Quinn) (R) 1/2/42
ADVENTURES OF MAX LATIN, THE
(Davis) (TNSPE) 10/2/49
Sorry, John D., But... (Apostolou)
11/3/15-8
ADVENTURES OF SANDY WEST,
PRIVATE EYE (Wright) (IAC)
9/2/29
ADVENTURES OF SATAN HALL,
THE (Daly) (TNSPE) 10/2/49
AELIAN FRAGMENT, THE
(Bartram) (M*F) 2/5/31
AFFAIR AT ROYALTIES, THE
(Baxt) (R) 7/4/29
AFFAIR OF THE BLOOD-STAINED
EGG COSY, THE (Anderson) (R)
1/5/42
AFFAIR OF THE CORPSE ESCORT,
THE (Knight) (M*F) 3/6/35
AFFAIR OF THE FAINTING BUT-
LER, THE (Knight) (TBR) 10/3/54
AFFAIR, THE (Snow) (R) 4/6/34
AFFAIRS OF O'MALLEY, THE
(MacHarg) (TBR) 11/3/60
William MacHarg's O'Malley (Dove)
8/6/14-8
AFRAID IN THE DARK (Derby) (R)
6/2/40

*Africa*
Black and White and Dead (Isaac)
6/4/12-8
Crime Fiction in Kenya (Tolley)
10/2/25-8
AFRICAN MILLIONAIRE, AN (Allen)
(IAC)                          5/1/17
Rogues for the New Century
(Dueren)              5/3/11-14
AFTER MIDNIGHT (Nielsen) (M*F)
3/2/28
AFTER THE FIRST DEATH (Cormier)
(R)                           3/6/42
AGAINST THE WIND (Household)
(R)                           3/2/49
AGATHA (Tynan) (IAC)     4/1/13
AGATHA CHRISTIE COMPANION,
THE (Fitzgibbon) (IAC)     4/6/31
AGATHA CHRISTIE COMPANION,
THE: THE COMPLETE GUIDE TO
AGATHA CHRISTIE'S LIFE AND
WORK (Sanders/Lovallo) (IAC)
8/2/21 & 32
AGATHA CHRISTIE CROSSWORD
PUZZLE BOOK, THE (IAC)  6/1/28
AGATHA CHRISTIE: FIRST LADY
OF CRIME (Keating, ed.) (R) (IAC)
2/1/32; 2/4/16
Agatha Christie Is Still Alive and Well
(Kabatchnik)           2/6/9-10
AGATHA CHRISTIE MYSTERY, THE
(Murdoch) (R)              1/2/4
AGATHA CHRISTIE: THE ART OF
HER CRIMES (M*F) (IAC)
6/2/33; 6/3/24
AGATHA CHRISTIE WHO'S WHO,
THE (Toye) (IAC)           4/6/31
AGREEMENT TO KILL (Rabe) (M*F)
1/2/24
Aickman, Robert
COLD HAND IN MINE (M*F)2/6/31
Aird, Catherine
HARM'S WAY (R)           9/6/35
A LATE PHOENIX (IAC) (R)
5/2/11; 5/5/35
PASSING STRANGE (M*F)  5/4/21
Alan, Marjorie
DARK PROPHECY (TBR)   11/4/62
ALBATROSS MURDERS, THE
(Jones) (R)              9/5/44
Albert, Walter
L: 1/1/42; 2/2/54; 2/3/64; 4/1/40;
6/6/43

*Albert, Walter,* continued
The Line-Up                4/5/9-12
Murder by Mail: A Dealer Checklist
3/5/7-10,16*
MYSTERY AND DETECTIVE
FICTION: AN INTERNA-
TIONAL BIBLIOGRAPHY OF
SECONDARY SOURCES (IAC)
(MS)              8/4/30; 8/5/5
Reel Murders (Movie Reviews)
6/2/21-6; 6/3/27-9; 6/4/34-6;
6/6/23-5; 7/1/36-8; 7/2/27-30;
7/3/29-31; 7/4/24-6; 7/5/31-4;
8/1/23-5; 8/2/26-8; 8/3/30-2;
8/4/34-6; 8/5/32-3;9/1/37-8;
9/2/31-2; 9/3/36-8;9/5/29-31;
10/3/47-51; 12/2/75-9
Reviews:
ANOTHER WEEPING WOMAN
(Zochert)              6/4/41
A CRACKING OF SPINES
(Lewis)                6/3/43
KRIMINALITERATURE PA
SVENSKA 1749-1985 [CRIME
FICTION IN SWEDEN 1749-
1985] (Hedman)         9/5/37
NOLAN #5: HARD CASH
(Collins)              6/4/40
SCI FI (Marshall)        6/3/43
WHAT WILL HAVE HAP-
PENED (Champigny)      5/4/28
The Skene Melvin Bibliography of
Critical Writing          5/3/5-10
Alderson, Martha
Ann Morice: The Deadly Serious
Business of Not Being Serious
(w/Chouteau)           6/6/5-8*
Deadly Edges of the Gay Blade
7/3/23-8*
L:                          7/4/37
Light and Sound by Joseph Hansen
8/3/12-7
Reviews:
ADVENT OF DYING (O'Marie)
9/1/41
BACKTRACK (Hansen)    8/1/31
CORRIDORS OF DEATH
(Edwards)              8/2/29
DEAD ON CUE (Morice)   8/6/45
DOUBLE NEGATIVE (Carakeet)
8/2/31
HOLLOW VENGEANCE
(Morice)               6/3/40

Alderson, Martha, continued
  Reviews continued
    THE MISSING MADONNA
      (O'Marie)            11/1/78
    MURDER BY PROXY (Morice)
                          8/1/36
    MURDER IN THE TITLE (Brett)
                          7/6/41
    MURDER POST-DATED
      (Morice)            8/1/36
    NIGHTWORK (Hansen)    8/1/32
    PUBLISH AND BE KILLED
      (Morice)            8/6/46
    SLEEP OF DEATH (Morice)
                          7/2/34
    SLEEP WHILE I SING (Wright)
                          10/1/74
    THE TARTAN SELL (Gash)
                          8/6/45
    A THIEF OF TIME (Hillerman)
                          10/3/65
    THE VEIL OF IGNORANCE
      (Quill)             11/1/78
Aldington, The Rev. Claire. See Holland,
  Isabelle
Aldyne, Nathan
    COBALT (R)            7/2/32
    Deadly Edges of the Gay Blade
      (Alderson)          7/3/23-8*
Alexander, David
    DIE, LITTLE GOOSE (M*F)   2/1/30
Alexander, Gary
    UNFUNNY MONEY (TAR)
                          12/2/53-4
Alexander, Patrick
    DEATH OF A THIN-SKINNED
      ANIMAL (M*F) (R) 2/4/36; 2/5/35
Alexandersson, Jan, and Iwan Hedman
    Leslie Charteris and the Saint: Five
      Decades of Partnership   4/4/21-7
ALFRED HITCHCOCK ANTHOLOGY
  #27: MURDER AND OTHER MIS-
  HAPS (Jordan, ed.) (IAC)  12/2/64-5
Alfred Hitchcock's Mystery Magazine
  (IAC)                   3/3/49
ALIBI TOO SOON, AN (Ormerod)
  (TAR)                   10/4/45
ALICIA'S TRUMP (Mathewson) (M*F)
                          5/2/15
Alington, C.A.
    GOLD AND GAITERS (TBR)
                          13/2/71

ALL EXITS BARRED (Portway) (R)
                          2/3/52
ALL FALL DOWN (Strong) (TCITC)
                          3/4/18
ALL THE GLITTERS (Powers) (IAC)
                          12/4/43-4
Allan, Stella
    AN INSIDE JOB (M*F)   6/3/37
Allbeury, Ted
    DEEP PURPLE (TAR)     13/1/48
    THE JUDAS FACTOR (TAR) 11/2/63
Allegretto, Michael
    BLOOD STONE (TAR)     11/1/50
    THE DEAD OF WINTER (TAR)
                          12/2/54
Allen, Francis
    DEATH IN GENTLE GROVE (M*F)
                          P/29
    FIRST COME, FIRST KILL (TBR)
                          11/3/58
Allen, Grant
    AN AFRICAN MILLIONAIRE
      (IAC)               5/1/17
    Rogues for the New Century
      (Dueren)            5/3/11-14
Allen, H. Warner, and E.C. Bentley
    TRENT'S OWN CASE (IAC) 10/1/62
Allen, Henry Wilson
    Obituary (Lachman)    13/4/88
Allen, Leslie
    MURDER IN THE ROUGH
      (TBR)               12/3/71-2
Allen, Michael
    SPENCE AND THE HOLIDAY
      MURDERS (M*F)       3/3/34
    SPENCE AT THE BLUE BAZAAR
      (M*F)               3/6/37
    SPENCE IN PETAL PARK (R)
                          7/5/40
Allen, Steve
    THE TALK SHOW MURDERS
      (M*F)               6/3/30
Allen, Woody
    SIDE EFFECTS (IAC)    6/3/23
ALIAS FOR DEATH (Reynolds) (TBR)
                          13/3/53-4
ALLIGATOR (Katz) (R)     1/3/45
Allingham, Margery. Also see Margery
    Allingham Society
    CAMPION'S CAREER: A STUDY
      OF THE NOVELS OF
      MARGERY ALLINGHAM
      (Pike) (R) (MS) (IAC)
        9/2/2; 10/1/67; 10/2/55

Allingham, Margery, continued
THE CASE OF THE LATE PIG (R)
  (IAC)            10/1/75; 12/1/23
DANCERS IN MOURNING (IAC)
                        8/3/25
FLOWERS FOR THE JUDGE
  (IAC)                 8/3/25
INK IN HER BLOOD (Martin) (R)
                        11/2/98
MR. CAMPION AND OTHERS (R)
                  10/1/75; 13/4/51
MR. CAMPION: CRIMINOLOGIST
  (R)                   10/1/75
THE RETURN OF MR. CAMPION
  (TAR) (R)       13/1/48 & 58-60
L: Cleary 10/4/60; Lachman 10/2/84
ALTER EGO (Arrighi) (IAC)    12/4/46
Alter, Robert Edmond
  CARNY KILL (TBR)       10/3/58
Alner, James Z.
  THE CAPITAL MURDER (TBR)
                        13/1/45-6
Altrocchi, Rudolph
  SLEUTHING IN THE STACKS
  (TCITC)                3/2/12
Altshuler, Harry
  Obituary (Lachman)     12/4/48-9
ALUMNI MURDERS, THE (Ruse)
  (M*F)                  5/2/23
ALVAREZ JOURNAL, THE (Burns)
  (M*F)                   P/28
Alverson, Charles
  NOT SLEEPING, JUST DEAD
  (M*F)                  2/2/34
ALWAYS ASK A POLICEMAN
  (Truss) (TBR)          11/2/90
AMADEUS (Shaffer) (IAC)   8/4/33
AMAZING ADVENTURES OF
  LESTER LEITH, THE (Gardner)
  (IAC)                  5/1/17
Amazing Grace (Sampson)   6/4/23-9
AMBER EFFECT, THE (Prather) (R)
                        8/6/42
Ambler, Eric
  A COFFIN FOR DIMITRIOS (R)
                        2/4/39
  THE DARK FRONTIER (TAR)
                        13/1/48-9
AMBUSHERS, THE (Hamilton) (R)
                        1/2/38

Ames, Delano
  FOR OLD CRIME'S SAKE (R)
                        7/5/44
  MURDER, MAESTRO, PLEASE
  (R)                    7/5/43
Amis, Kingsley
  THE CRIME OF THE CENTURY
  (TAR)                 12/2/54-5
  THE RIVERSIDE VILLAS
  MURDER (R)             3/3/41
AMOK (Fox) (R)           3/5/43
Amor, Paul Fusey
  THE PEOPLE'S REPUBLIC
  (TAR)                  12/2/55
AMPERSAND PAPERS, THE (Innes)
  (M*F)                  3/5/39
AMPURIAS EXCHANGE, THE
  (Ross) (M*F)           2/1/2
ANAGRAM DETECTIVES, THE
  (Schier) (R)      3/2/44; 4/1/32
ANARCHAOS (Clark) (R)     4/3/42
Anderson, Carol
  L:                     2/6/60
Anderson, Dame Judith
  Obituary (Lachman)     13/4/92
Anderson, Frederick Irving
  Science and Technology in the
    Writings of Frederick Irving
    Anderson (Fisher)   13/4/12-32
Anderson, James
  THE AFFAIR OF THE BLOOD-
    STAINED EGG COSY (R)  1/5/42
  ASSAULT AND MATRIMONY
  (M*F)                  6/2/32
Anderson, John R.L.
  DEATH IN THE CHANNEL (M*F)
                        3/2/36
  FESTIVAL (M*F)          4/2/37
  (SSC)                   4/2/11
Andress, Lesley
  CAPER (M*F)             4/4/34
Andrews, Mark
  BODY RUB (R)            1/5/41
Andreyev, Leonid
  Leonid Andreyev and Jim Thompson
  (Fellows)              11/2/59-61
ANDROMACHE OR THE INADVER-
  TENT MURDER (Monteilhet) (R)
                        13/2/76-7
ANGEL (Brewer) (R)        5/6/47
ANGEL ESQUIRE (Wallace) (IAC)
                        11/3/48

ANGEL EYES (Estleman) (M*F) 6/2/34
ANGEL EYES (Hunt) (R) 1/4/51
Angus, Sylvia
DEAD TO RITES (IAC) 4/3/32
Ann Morice: The Deadly Serious
Business of Not Being Serious
(Chouteau/Alderson) 6/6/5-8*
Annesley, Michael
(SSC) 5/5/15*
Anonymous [Philip Wylie and Bernard
Bergman]
THE SMILING CORPSE (R) 6/2/41
Another Chapter from Death of a .300
Hitter (Avallone) 1/1/3-5; 1/2/11-14
L: Scott 1/3/58
ANOTHER MAN'S POISON (Holman)
(TBR) 11/1/47
ANOTHER MORGUE HEARD FROM
(Davis) (TBR) 13/3/52-3
ANOTHER WEEPING WOMAN
(Zochert) (M*F) (R) 4/5/30; 6/4/41
Anthony, David
THE ORGANIZATION (R) 3/4/47
STUD GAME (R) (M*F)
2/6/42; 3/3/35
L: Broset 2/5/56
Anthony, Evelyn
THE LEGEND (M*F) 1/1/32
THE RENDEZVOUS (R) 2/1/39
THE SILVER FALCON (R) 2/6/42
Apocryphalization of Holmes, The
(Bleiler) 4/5/3-5
L: Bleiler 5/1/36; Nieminski 4/6/40
Apostolou, John L.
L: 6/6/49; 10/4/59; 12/2/83-4
Reviews:
THE LADY KILLER (Togawa)
10/1/71
THE THIRD LADY (Natsuki)
11/2/103
Sorry, John D., But... 11/3/15-8
Appel, William
WATCHER WITHIN (IAC) 7/5/28
APPLEBY TALKING (Innes) (IAC)
10/1/64
APRIL SHROUD, AN (Hill) (R)
13/1/71-2
ARCHANGEL (Seymour) (R) 9/2/37
Archer, Jeffrey
SHALL WE TELL THE
PRESIDENT? (R) 2/6/36
Archer, Lew. See Macdonald, Ross

ARIADNE CLUE, THE (Clemeau)
(MS) 6/1/1
ARMAGEDDON GAME, THE
(Washburn) (M*F) 1/5/33
ARMCHAIR DETECTIVE INDEX,
THE (VOLUMES 1–10, 1967–1977)
(Stilwell) (MS) 4/3/1
Armchair Detective, The (magazine)
The Curmudgeon in the Corner
(Loeser) 3/2/3-12,20
Armchair Reviewer, The (column)
(Hubin)
10/4/43-8; 11/1/50-69; 11/2/63-81;
11/3/71-83; 11/4/73-82;
12/2/53-62; 12/3/81-8; 12/4/51-9;
13/1/47-54; 13/2/43-51; 13/3/75-82
L: Shibuk 11/3/86
Armstrong, Anthony
THE TRAIL OF FEAR (R) 1/4/53
Armstrong, Charlotte
A LITTLE LESS THAN KIND (IAC)
11/4/48
SEVEN SEATS TO THE MOON
(R) 3/1/39
Armstrong, Margaret
THE BLUE SANTO MURDER
MYSTERY (TBR) 11/3/68
THE MAN WITH NO FACE (TBR)
11/3/68
Arnold, Armin, and Joseph Schmidt
RECLAMS KRIMINAL-
ROMANFUHRER (R) 7/2/36
Arrighi, Mel
ALTER EGO (IAC) 12/4/46
Obituary (Lachman) 8/6/36
TURKISH WHITE (M*F) 2/1/23
ARROW POINTING NOWHERE
(Daly) (R) P/34
Art
L: Brener 6/2/49; Goode 6/2/48;
Hamilton 2/2/44; Wenstrup 6/1/50
Article I Couldn't Publish, The
(Townsend) 1/1/18-20
L: Nevins 1/2/47-8
AS HER WHIMSEY TOOK HER:
CRITICAL ESSAYS ON DOROTHY
L. SAYERS (Hannay, ed.) (R) 3/5/45
ASCENT OF D–13, THE (Garve)
(IAC) 8/4/31
Asdell, Philip T.
L: 4/1/40; 7/2/42

Ashby, Ruth, and Robert J. Randisi,
   eds.
THE BLACK MOON (R)   12/4/81-2
ASHENDEN (Maugham) (IAC)   2/6/28
Ashford, F.U.
   A PACKET OF TROUBLE (M*F)
                           5/4/25
Ashford, Jeffrey
   A CONFLICT OF INTEREST (TAR)
                           13/1/49
   HOSTAGE TO DEATH (M*F)
                           2/5/26
   SLOW DOWN THE WORLD
   (M*F)                   2/1/28
*Ashton-Kirk*
   A Few Kind Words for Ashton-Kirk
   (Sampson)               7/6/3-12
Asimov, Isaac
   ASIMOV'S MYSTERIES (R)   1/6/47
   ASIMOV'S SHERLOCKIAN
   LIMERICKS (R)           2/4/42
   BANQUETS OF THE BLACK
   WIDOWERS (R)            8/3/37
   THE BIG APPLE MYSTERIES
   (IAC) (w/Greenberg/Waugh, ed.)
                           6/4/32
   IN JOY STILL FELT (IAC)   6/1/27
   IN MEMORY YET GREEN (IAC)
                           6/1/27
   MURDER AT THE ABA (R)   1/2/39
   TANTALIZING LOCKED ROOM
   STORIES (w/Waugh/Greenberg,
   ed.) (R)                7/2/33
   "Ten"                   8/4/29
   THE THIRTEEN CRIMES OF
   SCIENCE FICTION (w/Waugh/
   Greenberg, ed.) (R)     4/3/45
   THE 13 HORRORS OF
   HALLOWEEN (w/Waugh/
   Greenberg, ed.) (IAC)   8/1/17
   TWELVE CRIMES OF
   CHRISTMAS (w/Greenberg/
   Waugh, ed.) (IAC)       6/3/22
   WHO DONE IT? (w/Laurance, ed.)
   (R)                     4/4/48
ASIMOV'S MYSTERIES (Asimov) (R)
                           1/6/47
ASIMOV'S SHERLOCKIAN
   LIMERICKS (Asimov) (R)   2/4/42
Asinov, Eliot
   SAY IT AIN'T SO (M*F)   2/3/45
ASK FOR ME TOMORROW (Millar)
   (M*F)                   1/4/37

ASSAULT AND MATRIMONY
   (Anderson) (M*F)        6/2/32
ASSAULT ON A QUEEN (Finney)
   (MS)                    12/3/12
ASSIGNMENT AFGHAN DRAGON
   (Aarons) (M*F)          1/5/32
AT DEATH'S DOOR (TAR) (Barnard)
                           11/2/63
AT ONE FELL SWOOP (Mills) (TBR)
                           11/3/59
ATHABASCA (MacLean) (R)   4/5/40
Atkey, Bertram
   MR. DASS: A NOVEL OF PUR-
   SUIT AND PUNISHMENT
   (R)                     2/5/37
ATLANTIS FIRE (Goshgarian) (R)
                           6/6/37
Atlee, Philip
   THE MAKASSAR STRAIT
   CONTRACT (M*F)          1/3/40
ATTENDING PHYSICIAN, THE
   (Dominic) (M*F)         4/2/39
ATTIC REVIVALS (Drew, ed.) (MS)
                           7/3/4
Aucott, Robert
   L:          1/1/43; 5/1/45; 5/2/47
AUDITION FOR MURDER (Carlson)
   (R)                     10/3/70
*Audley, David.* See Price, Anthony
Auster, Paul
   CITY OF GLASS (R)       9/6/38
Austin, Hugh
   THE MILKMAID'S MILLIONS (R)
                           9/5/39
*Australia*
   An Australian Bibliomystery (Tolley)
                           10/3/37-8
   Australian Bibliomystery, An: Ligny's
   Lake (Tolley)           10/3/37-8
AUTHOR BITES THE DUST, AN
   (Upfield) (R) (TCITC)   P/32; 3/2/12
AUTOBIOGRAPHY (Milne) (IAC)
                           8/5/31
AUTOBIOGRAPHY, AN (Christie)
   (IAC)                   4/1/13
AUTOPSY (Feegel) (M*F)    3/2/27
*Avallone, Michael*
   Another Chapter from Death of a
   .300 Hitter   1/1/3-5; 1/2/11-14
   THE BIG STIFFS (R)      2/5/39
   THE CASE OF THE BOUNCING
   BETTY (R)               1/2/46

*Avallone, Michael,* continued
THE CASE OF THE VIOLENT
   VIRGIN (R)       1/2/46
THE DOCTOR'S WIFE (R)   3/1/43
THE FLOWER-COVERED
   CORPSE (IAC)       6/1/28
LITTLE MISS MURDER (IAC)
                   12/1/ 24
(SSC)            5/5/16*
Two Short Chapters from Death of a
   .300 Hitter        P/11-12
Avon Classic Crime Collection, The
   (Meyerson)     1/5/19-20*
   L: Briney 1/6/56; Meyerson 1/6/57
AXE TO GRIND, AN (Wallace) (TAR)
                  13/2/50
Axelrod, Nancy
   L:              4/6/48
Axton, David
   PRISON OF ICE (R)     1/6/46
AZOR! (Henaghan) (M*F)   2/3/45

# B

"B" IS FOR BURGLAR (Grafton)
   (IAC)            8/5/30
Babson, Marian
   DEATH IN FASHION (IAC)  9/5/27
   MURDER, MURDER, LITTLE
      STAR (M*F)      4/3/34
Babula, William
   ACCORDING TO ST. JOHN
      (TAR)        12/2/55
BABY BLUE RIP-OFF, THE (Collins)
   (R)             7/1/39
BACH FESTIVAL MURDERS, THE
   (Bloch) (R)       9/5/40
BACKLASH (Philips) (M*F)   P/31
BACKTRACK (Hansen) (R)   8/1/31
Backward Reviewer, The (column)
   (Deeck)
      10/2/61-70; 10/3/53-64;
      11/1/38-49; 11/2/83-95;
      11/3/57-70; 11/4/57-72;
      12/2/41-52; 12/3/70-80;
      12/4/61-72; 13/1/35-46;
      13/2/59-75; 13/3/50-64; 13/4/66-82
   L: Masser 13/1/81-2; Penchenat
     11/3/94; Shibuk 11/3/87
*Bacon, Peggy*
   Obituary (Lachman)   9/3/34
BAD COMPANY (Cody) (R)  8/3/39
BAD FOR BUSINESS (Stout)
   (TBR)        12/2/48-9

Baddock, James
   THE FAUST CONSPIRACY
      (TAR)        12/2/56
Badgley, Anne V.
   THE REMBRANDT DECISIONS
      (IAC)        3/2/24
BAG MAN, THE (McAuliffe) (R)
                   5/5/40
Bagby, George
   COUNTRY AND FATAL (M*F)
                   4/4/41
   GUARANTEED TO FADE (M*F)
                   3/4/38
   I COULD HAVE DIED (M*F)
                   3/5/39
   MUGGER'S DAY (M*F)   3/6/39
   THE ORIGINAL CARCASE (M*F)
                   2/4/34
   THE SITTING DUCK (M*F) 6/1/35
   THE TOUGH GET GOING (M*F)
                   2/6/33
   TWO IN THE BUSH (M*F)   P/25
*Bagley, Desmond*
   THE ENEMY (R)       3/6/43
   Interview (Bakerman)  7/2/13-18,26
   WINDFALL (R) 8/3/39
   L: Bakerman 7/3/46; Denton 7/3/43;
     Goode 7/3/47; Nevins 7/4/45
Bailey, F. Lee
   SECRETS (M*F)       3/3/33
Bailey, Frankie Y.
   OUT OF THE WOODPILE: BLACK
      CHARACTERS IN CRIME AND
      DETECTIVE FICTION (R)
                  13/2/91-3
Bailey, H.C.
   BLACK LAND, WHITE LAND (R)
                   P/38
   THE GARSTON MURDER CASE
      (IAC)        11/1/26
   THE RED CASTLE MYSTERY
      (M*F)        1/5/35
BAIT MONEY (Collins) (R)   1/6/50
Baker, Asa. Also see Halliday, Brett
   MUM'S THE WORD FOR
      MURDER (TBR)   13/2/64-5
Baker, Russell
   SO THIS IS DEPRAVITY (IAC)
                   6/3/23
*Baker, W. Howard*
   (SSC)           6/1/7*
   L: Van Tilburg 6/2/50

Bakerman, Jane S.
Bloody Balaclava: Charlotte Mac-
  Leod's Campus Comedy Mysteries
                              7/1/23-9
Bowlers, Beer, Bravado, and Brains:
  Anthony Gilbert's Arthur Crook
                              2/4/5-13
C.B. Greenfield: The Metaphor Is
  the Man               7/6/24-9
Gene Stratton–Porter: Mistress of the
  Mini-Mystery          3/1/3-9
Humor, Horror, and Intellect: Giles
  Mont of Ruth Rendell's A
  JUDGEMENT IN STONE 5/4/5-10
Hunter and Hunted: Comparison and
  Contrast in Tony Hillerman's
  PEOPLE OF DARKNESS 5/1/3-10
An Interview with Desmond Bagley
                              7/2/13-18,26
Let the Public Decide: An Interview
  with Nicolas Freeling      8/6/19-24
L:      2/2/42; 2/3/71; 4/1/40; 7/3/46
Murder on the Sunshine Coast: L.R.
  Wright's Experiments with Theme
  and Form              11/4/3-10
One in Two: Some Personality
  Studies by Ruth Rendell
                              5/6/21-8,32
Piercing the Closed Circle: The
  Technique of Point of View in
  Works by P.D. James    1/5/3-16
Reviews:
  "A" IS FOR ALIBI (Grafton)
                              7/6/50
  AFRAID IN THE DARK (Derby)
                              6/2/40
  AFTER THE FIRST DEATH
    (Cormier)            3/6/42
  BAD COMPANY (Cody)    8/3/39
  BANKER (Francis)       7/3/33
  THE BLANK WALL (Holding)
                              1/5/46
  THE BLOOD OF AN ENG-
    LISHMAN (McClure)   5/2/37
  "C" IS FOR CORPSE (Grafton)
                              8/5/35
  A CASE OF LOYALTIES
    (Wallace)            10/2/72
  CASTANG'S CITY (Freeling)
                              4/5/40
  CAUGHT DEAD IN PHILA-
    DELPHIA (Roberts)    10/4/55
  CEREMONY (Parker)     6/3/38

Bakerman, Jane S., continued
Reviews continued
  THE CHIEF INSPECTOR'S
    DAUGHTER (Radley)    5/4/34
  THE CHILDREN'S ZOO
    (O'Donnell)          6/2/39
  THE COST OF SILENCE
    (Yorke)              4/5/41
  A COUNTRY KIND OF DEATH
    (McMullen)           4/2/46
  THE DANGER (Francis)  8/2/37
  DANGEROUS FUNERAL
    (McMullen)           4/2/45
  THE DARK WIND (Hillerman)
                              6/4/43
  DAYS OF MISFORTUNE (Stein)
                              1/6/52
  DEADFALL (Cory)       3/4/46
  DEADLOCK (Paretsky)   8/2/36
  DEATH IN THE MORNING
    (Radley)             5/2/31
  DEATH IN THE ROUND
    (Morice)             5/5/36
  DEATH OF A THIN–SKINNED
    ANIMAL (Alexander)  2/5/35
  DEATH OF AN EXPERT
    WITNESS (James)     2/2/36
  DEATH ON ACCOUNT (Yorke)
                              6/1/42
  DEVIL'S WORK (Yorke)
                              7/5/49; 7/6/50
  DUPE (Cody)           7/4/27
  THE ENEMY (Bagley)    3/6/43
  EVERY SECOND THURSDAY
    (Page)               8/4/39
  FALSE WITNESS (Uhnak) 6/1/41
  FATE WORSE THAN DEATH
    (Radley)             8/5/36
  FINAL NOTICE (Valin)  7/4/28
  THE FOURTH WALL (Paul)
                              7/4/27
  GOING FOR THE GOLD
    (Lathen)             5/3/34
  GREEN GROW THE DOLLARS
    (Lathen)             6/4/44
  THE HAND OF DEATH (Yorke)
                              7/5/42
  HEADCASE (Cody)       8/4/41
  I AM THE CHEESE (Cormier)
                              3/6/42
  THE INVESTIGATION (Uhnak)
                              2/1/41
  A LATE PHOENIX (Aird)  5/5/35

- 9 -

Bakerman, Jane S., continued
  Reviews continued
    LETTER FROM THE DEAD
      (Clarke)                6/2/38
    THE LONG SHORT CUT
      (Garve)                 2/5/35
    THE LOVE TALKERS (Peters)
                              5/5/33
    THE LUCK RUNS OUT
      (MacLeod)               4/2/49
    THE LUXEMBOURG RUN
      (Ellin)                 2/5/36
    MAJOR INQUIRY (Henderson)
                              8/4/40
    THE MARK TWAIN MURDERS
      (Skom)                  11/2/102
    MASTER OF THE MOOR
      (Rendell)               6/4/42
    THE MEMORIAL HALL
      MURDER (Langton)        5/2/35
    THE MENACE WITHIN
      (Curtiss)               3/5/42
    THE MINUTEMAN MURDER
      (Langton)               5/2/36
    THE MURDER OF MIRANDA
      (Millar)                3/4/46
    NATURAL ENEMY (Langton)
                              7/5/41
    THE NIGHT LORDS (Freeling)
                              4/2/42
    THE NIGHT SHE DIED
      (Simpson)               5/5/34
    NO WORD FROM WINIFRED
      (Cross)                 8/5/37
    NOT THAT KIND OF PLACE
      (Fyfield)               13/3/84-6
    THE POINT OF MURDER
      (Yorke)                 5/2/33
    REST YOU MERRY (MacLeod)
                              4/2/48
    THE ROSARY MURDERS
      (Kienzle)               4/2/41
    THE SCENT OF FEAR (Yorke)
                              5/3/35
    THE SHADOW KNOWS
      (Johnson)               7/5/42
    SIX FEET UNDER (Simpson)
                              7/5/48
    THE SKULL BENEATH THE
      SKIN (James)            7/3/33
    A SLEEPING LIFE (Rendell)
                              3/2/45

Bakerman, Jane S., continued
  Reviews continued
    THE SPINSTER'S SECRET
      (Gilbert)               5/2/33
    STILL MISSING (Gutcheon)
                              7/5/48
    STING OF THE BEE (Worrell)
                              7/5/40
    THE SUSPECT (Wright)     9/5/32
    SWEET DEATH, KIND DEATH
      (Cross)                 8/2/37
    A TALENT FOR DESTRUC-
      TION (Radley)           6/4/42
    THE TENTH VIRGIN (Stewart)
                              8/3/38
    THIS DOWNHILL PATH
      (Clarke)                5/5/33
    TWICE SHY (Francis)      6/3/39
    UNTIL DEATH DO US PART
      (McMullen)              8/3/38
    THE VIRGIN IN THE ICE
      (Peters)                6/6/33
    THE WIDOW (Freeling)     6/1/42
    WINDFALL (Bagley)        8/3/39
    THE WITHDRAWING ROOM
      (MacLeod)               4/6/38
    WOLFNIGHT (Freeling)     6/4/46
  Tension and Duality: Daphne du
    Maurier's "Don't Look Now"
                              3/4/8-10
  The Writer's Probe: Ruth Rendell as
    Social Critic            3/5/3-6
  L: Floyd 4/1/37
Balaclava Agricultural College
  Bloody Balaclava (Bakerman)
                              7/1/23-9
Ball, Brian
  DEATH OF A LOW-HANDICAP
    MAN (M*F)                 3/2/36
Ball, John
  THE EYES OF BUDDHA (M*F)
    (R)            1/3/40; 1/5/45
  L:                          1/3/51
  THE MYSTERY STORY (ed.) (R)
                           1/2/29 & 32
  Obituary (Lachman)         11/1/36
  THEN CAME VIOLENCE (M*F)
    (R)             4/3/39; 4/5/37
  TROUBLE FOR TALLON (R)
                              5/5/31
  THE VAN (TAR)              11/4/73
Ballantine Espionage/Intelligence
  Library (IAC)              6/1/30

**Ballard, W. Todhunter**
MURDER CAN'T STOP (R)    3/4/42
Obituary (Lachman)    8/1/21
SAY YES TO MURDER (R)    2/3/53
THE SEVEN SISTERS (R)    2/5/39
Ballinger, Bill S.
HEIST ME HIGHER (R)    1/4/52
THE TOOTH AND THE NAIL
   (TBR)    13/4/82
Ballinger, John
   L:    4/1/44
Balopole, Donna
   Review: UNCLE SILAS: A TALE
   OF BARTRAM-HAUGH (Le
   Fanu)    2/1/45
*Bandy, Franklin.* Also see Franklin,
   Eugene
THE BLACKSTOCK AFFAIR
   (M*F)    4/4/33
DECEIT AND DEADLY LIES
   (M*F)    3/3/33
Obituary (Lachman)    9/3/34
L: McCahery 3/4/53
BANKER (Francis) (R)    7/3/33
*Bankier, William*
The Cream of Queen (Floyd)    9/3/26
Banks, Jeff
Favorite Magazine Issues: Manhunt
   (3:6), June 1955    4/6/7-8
I Remember...B–Movies    4/5/13-7
I Remember...Pulp Mysteries–
   Mystery Pulps    3/4/19-22
I Remember...Radio Mysteries
   3/5/17-9
Immoderate Homage to Modesty
   4/2/8-10*
The Joe Gall Series (w/Kelley)
   3/2/26-35*
Le Carré's Spy Novels (w/Dawson)
   2/5/22-5*
L: 1/2/51; 1/3/56; 1/4/55; 2/1/52;
   2/2/41; 2/3/59; 2/5/51; 2/6/43;
   3/1/52; 4/1/43; 5/1/42; 5/4/41;
   6/4/46; 7/3/49; 7/4/41; 8/1/47;
   8/4/48; 8/6/49; 9/2/48; 9/3/48;
   9/4/4-49; 9/6/49; 10/1/96;
   10/2/83; 12/2/84-7
The Len Deighton Series (w/Dawson)
   3/1/11-3*
The Matt Helm Series (w/Townsend)
   2/2/3-11*
Mickey Spillane's Mike Hammer:
   The Great Cover-Up    8/4/17-20

*Banks, Jeff,* continued
Mystery Mosts:
   (Movie) Actress & Roles    10/1/66
   All Alliteration    11/2/16
   Alliteration—The Finishing
     Stroke    12/2/16
   A Best-Selling Title Pattern
     10/2/77
   Bulldogs    11/3/83-4
   Comic Book Heroes    9/5/31
   Comic Book Heroes Again 10/3/76
   Crime and Rhyme, Another
     Time    12/2/35-6
   Double Alliteration    11/2/35
   The Eternal Question    11/3/103-4
   EQ by the Numbers    12/2/32
   EQ's Device    12/4/104
   Extreme Alliteration    11/4/45-6
   Fanzine Article Writers    10/2/52
   Favorite Titles    11/2/56-7
   Fu Manchus    11/3/18
   Hero Roles    9/6/34
   Invoking Poe    11/2/96-7
   Kemelman's Rabbi Title Pattern
     11/3/44
   L.O.C.s    10/2/47
   Long Careers    9/2/8
   Longest Titles    9/5/22
   Longest Media Series Titles
     12/3/64; 12/4/28
   Magazines    9/2/6
   Most Continuing Mystery Roles,
     Radio & TV Combined    12/4/20
   Most Performances (Movie, TV,
     radio)    9/2/7-8
   Most Reviewed Authors    11/2/96
   Most Revived Character on
     Radio    12/2/80
   Most Revived Mystery Series on
     TV    12/2/40
   Movie Sidekicks    11/2/98
   Mr. Private Eye    12/3/44-6
   Mystery by the Yard    11/2/61-2
   Mystery/Crime TV Aimed at Kids
     11/2/7-8
   Participation in Most Continuing
     Casts of Radio Mystery Series
     12/4/50
   Philip Marlowe's Crime
     Statistics    12/2/104
   Philo Vance    11/4/81-2
   Plays    9/3/35
   Poe's Key Word    9/4/39

Banks, Jeff, continued
  Mystery Mosts continued
    Poe's Other Word (a.k.a. Our
      Generic Label)     10/2/24
    Police Procedurals    11/2/95-6
    Pop Films       11/4/71-2
    Pop Movies on TV    11/4/28
    Pop Movie Rentals    12/2/10
    Prolificity       9/3/38
    Radio Sidekicks    11/2/97-8
    Repetitious Titles  9/4/45; 10/3/52
    Repetitious Titles One Final Time
                11/2/46
    Saintly Statistics    12/2/27-8
    Secretaries      11/2/62
    Serials        10/1/54
    Serials Revisited    10/2/84
    Series Episodes    10/1/104
    Sherlockian Stats    11/2/81-2
    TCOT Title Pattern    9/3/49
    Team Players    11/2/35-6
    Van Dine's Pattern    11/3/55-6
    What Rhymes! with Crimes
                11/3/13-4
  The Quiller Report (w/Dawson)
                4/1/8-11*
  Reviews:
    THE AFFAIR AT ROYALTIES
      (Baxt)       7/4/29
    ARCHANGEL (Seymour)  9/2/37
    ATLANTIS FIRE (Goshgarian)
                6/6/37
    THE BEAVER PAPERS (Jacobs/
      Jones)      8/1/34
    THE BLACK MOON (Randisi/
      Ashby, eds.)    12/4/81-2
    BURGLARS CAN'T BE
      CHOOSERS (Block)    8/2/40
    THE BUTCHER'S BOY (Perry)
                8/3/43
    CITY OF GLASS (Auster) 9/6/38
    DANCING BEAR (Crumley)
                8/1/34
    FADE (Cormier)    12/4/82-3
    FERNANDA (Miller)    1/2/44
    HAZZARD (Brown)    9/6/38
    IN THE HEAT OF THE
      SUMMER (Katzenbach) 8/3/42
    THE KILLING MAN
      (Spillane) (audio) 12/3/92
    THE KING IS DEAD (Queen)
                7/3/34

Banks, Jeff, continued
  Reviews continued
    LABYRINTH (Land)    9/6/40
    THE MAN WITH BOGART'S
      FACE (Fenady)    1/3/44
    THE MORDIDA MAN (Thomas)
                8/2/31
    MURDER AT HOBCAW
      BARONY (Roosevelt) 10/2/71
    OUT (Rey)       9/2/38
    THE RIVERSIDE VILLAS
      MURDER (Amis)    3/3/41
    SEVEN SILENT MEN (Behn)
                9/1/43
    SHARP PRACTICE (Farris) 8/3/42
    SHOTGUN SATURDAY NIGHT
      (Crider)      10/2/72
    THE SLEEPERS OF ERIN
      (Gash)      9/6/39
    SLOB (Miller)      9/6/40
    THE TAINTED JADE (Blaine)
               13/1/55-6
    THE TENTH COMMANDMENT
      (Sanders)     9/2/39
    THROUGH THE EYES OF
      EVIL (Blair)    8/3/43
    TIME TO MURDER AND
      CREATE (Block)    8/3/41
    TIMOTHY'S GAME (Sanders)
               13/1/56-7
    TOUCH OF DEATH
      (Sadler)     12/4/80-1
    WHEN IN GREECE (Lathen)
                7/1/41
    THE WIDENING GYRE (Parker)
                8/2/30
  Spade Trumps Unplayed  8/6/3-6
  The Tiger Mann Series  2/3/32-3*
  When Is This Stiff Dead? Detective
    Stories and Definitions of Death
    (w/Thompson)    2/6/11-16
  L: Kimura 13/2/96; Nehr 2/6/43
Banks, Oliver
  THE REMBRANDT PANEL (R)
                4/6/37
Bannister, Jo
  THE GOING DOWN OF THE SUN
    (R)       13/4/96-7
  SHARDS (TAR)    13/1/49-50
Bannon, Barbara A.
  Obituary (Lachman)    13/3/69
BANQUETS OF THE BLACK
  WIDOWERS (Asimov) (R)  8/3/37

*Bantam Books* (IAC)        4/4/20
BAPTISM FOR THE DEAD (Irvine)
  (TAR)      11/1/61; 11/2/73
Barak, Michael
  THE ENIGMA (M*F) (R)
           3/1/36; 3/6/44
Barbato, Joseph
  The Mysteries of the Pseudonymous
    Professors      1/4/3-6
Barbero, Kevin
  L:       7/4/50
*Bardin, John Franklin*
  Obituary (Lachman)    5/6/31-2
BARETTA (Patrick) (R)    2/1/40
*Bargainnier, Earl*
  British Murder and British Detective
    Fiction     6/4/19-22
  COMIC CRIME (ed.) (IAC)  10/2/56
  The Dr. Davie Novels of V.C.
    Clinton-Baddeley    8/1/8-13
  Joe Orton's and Tom Stoppard's
    Burlesques of the Detective
    Genre    7/1/18-22
  Lady Molly of Scotland Yard
        7/4/15-9
  Obituary (MS)    9/1/2-3
  The Old Man in the Corner  7/6/21-3
*Bark, Conrad Voss*
  (SSC)     4/2/11
Barlay, Stephen
  BLOCKBUSTERS (M*F)    2/1/21
BARLOW EXPOSED (Jones) (M*F)
        2/3/42
Barnard, Robert
  AT DEATH'S DOOR (TAR) 11/2/63
  THE CASE OF THE MISSING
    BRONTË (R)    8/1/26
  A CITY OF STRANGERS (TAR)
        13/1/50
  DEATH AND THE CHASTE
    APPRENTICE (TAR)  13/1/50-1
  DEATH OF A PERFEFCT
    MOTHER (M*F)    5/6/38
  DEATH OF A SALESPERSON
    AND OTHER UNTIMELY
    EXITS (TAR) (IAC) 12/2/56 & 68
  FÊTE FATALE (R)    8/5/34
  A LITTLE LOCAL MURDER
    (IAC)    8/3/26; 9/3/30
  SCHOOL FOR MURDER (R)
        8/3/44
  THE SKELETON IN THE GRASS
    (TAR)    11/1/51

*Barnard, Robert*, continued
  A TALENT TO DECEIVE (IAC)
        4/6/31; 10/2/57
Barns, Glenn M.
  MURDER IS A GAMBLE (M*F)
    (R)    1/1/28; 9/4/44
Barroll, Clare
  A STRANGE PLACE FOR
    MURDER (M*F)    3/6/34
*Barry, Mike* [Barry N. Malzberg, q.v.]
  Fear and Loathing with the Lone
    Wolf (Kelley)    1/5/17-8*
Barry, Nora
  SHERBOURNE'S FOLLY (M*F)
        3/3/39
Barth, Richard
  DEADLY CLIMATE (TAR)  11/2/64
Barton, Billy
  Mae West: Mistress of Mystery?
    Almost...    6/6/2,18
  PAST MURDER IMPERFECT
    (M*F)    6/1/35
  Review: MURDER IN THE WHITE
    HOUSE (Truman)    5/5/31
  Speaking with Myself    5/4/13-7
Bartram, George
  THE AELIAN FRAGMENT (M*F)
        2/5/31
Barzun, Jacques, and Wendell Hertig
  Taylor
  A CATALOGUE OF CRIME (R)
        11/4/83
Bass, Milton
  THE BELFAST CONNECTION
    (TAR)    11/4/74
Bates, David
  L:     1/1/47
*Batman*
  L: Banks 12/84-5; Lansdale 2/6/47
BATTLING PROPHET, THE (Upfield)
  (R)    11/4/87
*Baxt, George*
  THE AFFAIR AT ROYALTIES (R)
        7/4/29
  Little Old Ladies (Nehr)    3/4/3-7
  THE NEON GRAVEYARD (M*F)
        4/2/31
  A PARADE OF COCKEYED
    CREATURES (R)    3/4/42
BAXTER TRUST, THE (Hailey) (TAR)
        11/1/60; 11/2/71
Bayer, Oliver Weld
  PAPER CHASE (TBR)    13/2/67-8

Bayne, Harry M.
  L:                                    13/2/95
  A Neglected Detective Novel:
    Bellamann's THE GRAY MAN
    WALKS (w/Fisher)       12/4/3-19
BEADED BANANA, THE (Scherf)
  (M*F)                             3/1/31
BEAK! (Nithologist) (R)         1/3/47
BEAMS FALLING: THE ART OF
  DASHIELL HAMMETT (Wolfe)
  (IAC)                             6/4/32
BEASTLY TALES (Paretsky, ed.)
  (IAC)                         12/2/66-7
Beaton, M. C.
  DEATH OF A GOSSIP (R) 13/1/72-4
  DEATH OF A PERFECT WIFE (R)
                                  13/1/72-4
  DEATH OF AN OUTSIDER (R)
                                  13/1/72-4
Beaty, David
  CONE OF SILENCE (R)        7/2/35
BEAUTIFUL MRS. DAVENANT,
  THE (Tweedale) (TBR)       12/3/79
BEAUTY–MASK MURDER, THE
  (Shore) (TBR)                11/4/70
BEAUTY QUEEN KILLER, THE
  (Creasey) (IAC)             10/3/42
BEAVER PAPERS, THE (Jacobs/Jones)
  (R)                              8/1/34
Becklund, Jack
  GOLDEN FLEECE (TAR)       13/3/75
BED OF NAILS (Puckett) (TAR)
                                   12/4/53
Bede, The Rev. Simon. See Byfield,
  Barbara Ninde
BEDSIDE, BATHTUB & ARMCHAIR
  COMPANION TO AGATHA
  CHRISTIE, THE (Riley/McAllister)
  (R) (IAC)            4/1/43; 4/3/31
BEDSIDE COMPANION TO CRIME,
  THE (Keating) (R)        12/3/100-1
Beechcroft, William
  SECRET KILLS (TAR)       11/2/64-5
Beeding, Francis
  DEATH WALKS IN EASTREPPS
    (IAC)                          5/5/17
    (SSC)                       4/2/11-2
BEETHOVEN CONSPIRACY, THE
  (Hauser) (R)                    9/2/44
Behind the Scenes at Bouchercon 9, Or
  It Was Murder at the Bismarck!
  (Grochowski)              2/6/3-6,8

Behn, Noel
  SEVEN SILENT MEN (R)      9/1/43
BELFAST CONNECTION, THE (Bass)
  (TAR)                           11/4/74
Bell, Josephine
  Let's Hear It for Josephine Bell
    (Gottschalk)         11/2/47-56*
Bell, Vicars
  DEATH AND THE NIGHT
    WATCHES (TCITC)          3/4/17
Bellairs, George
  CORPSE AT THE CARNIVAL
    (TBR)                        11/1/39
Bellamann, Henry
  A Neglected Detective Novel
    (Bayne/Fisher)           12/4/3-19
Bellamy, Ralph
  Obituary (Lachman)         13/4/92-3
Bellem, Robert Leslie
  DAN TURNER, HOLLYWOOD
    DETECTIVE (R)              8/2/35
BELLRINGER STREET (Richardson)
  (R)                            13/3/87-8
BELLS AT OLD BAILEY, THE
  (Bowers) (TBR)             12/4/62-3
Belsky, Dick
  SOUTH STREET (R)          12/1/42
Bennett, Margot
  THE MAN WHO DIDN'T FLY (R)
                                   5/4/30
BENSON MURDER CASE, THE (Van
  Dine) (TCITC) (IAC)   3/2/10; 8/3/27
Bentley, E.C., and H. Warner Allen
  TRENT'S OWN CASE (IAC) 10/1/62
Benton, Kenneth
  CRAIG AND THE MIDAS TOUCH
    (M*F)                           P/29
    (SSC)                          4/2/12
Berckman, Evelyn
  A CASE IN NULLITY (IAC)  5/2/11
  DO YOU KNOW THIS VOICE?
    (IAC)                          7/5/26
Berg, Barry
  HIDE AND SEEK (TAR)      11/4/74
Berger, Thomas
  WHO IS TEDDY VILLANOVA?
    (R)                     1/4/46; 5/5/36
Bergman, Andrew
  THE BIG KISS-OFF OF 1944
    (M*F) (R)          1/3/38; 8/2/34
  HOLLYWOOD AND LEVINE (R)
                                   8/2/34

Bergman, Bernard. See SMILING
CORPSE, THE
Berkeley, Anthony
THE POISONED CHOCOLATES
MYSTERY (IAC)          6/6/20
TOP STORY MURDER (M*F)
1/1/32
TRIAL AND ERROR (IAC) (R)
6/6/20; 8/6/43
Bernard, Trevor
BRIGHTLIGHT (R) (M*F) (R)
2/1/31 & 37; 2/4/32; 4/3/42
BERNHARDT'S EDGE (Wilcox)
(TAR)                  10/4/47
BEST DETECTIVE STORIES OF
THE YEAR—1977 (Hoch, ed.)
(M*F)                   2/1/21
BEST MARTIN HEWITT DETEC-
TIVE STORIES (Morrison) (R)
1/5/38
BEST SELLER: A NOSTALGIC CEL-
EBRATION OF THE LESS-THAN-
GREAT BOOKS YOU HAVE AL-
WAYS BEEN AFRAID TO ADMIT
YOU LOVED (Bocca) (R)      6/6/35
Best Short Stories of 1986, The
(Lachman)               9/3/32
Best Short Stories of 1987 (Lachman)
10/3/43-4
Best Short Stories of 1989, The
(Lachman)              12/2/72-4
Betcherman, Barbara
SUSPICIONS (M*F)          4/4/38
Betteridge, Don [Bernard Newman, q.v.]
(SSC)                    6/1/7*
BEWARE YOUNG LOVERS
(Pentecost) (M*F)         4/3/40
BEYOND THE PRIZE (Denning) (R)
3/3/43
Bibliography. Also see Secondary
Sources
THE BIBLIOGRAPHY OF CRIME
FICTION 1749–1975 (Hubin)
(IAC) (R)          3/3/17 & 48
CLOAK–AND–DAGGER BIBLI-
OGRAPHY: AN ANNOTATED
GUIDE TO SPY FICTION (Smith)
(R)                     1/4/50
CRIME, DETECTIVE, ESPI-
ONAGE, MYSTERY, AND
THRILLER FICTION & FILM: A
COMPREHENSIVE BIB-
LIOGRAPHY OF CRITICAL
WRITING THROUGH 1979
(Skene Melvin) (R)        5/2/30

CRIME FICTION, 1749–1980: A
COMPREHENSIVE BIBLIOG-
RAPHY (Hubin) (IAC) (R)
8/2/21; 9/3/40
HEROINES: A BIBLIOGRAPHY OF
WOMEN SERIES CHAR-
ACTERS IN MYSTERY, ES-
PIONAGE, ACTION, SCIENCE
FICTION, FANTASY, HORROR,
WESTERN, ROMANCE AND
JUVENILE NOVELS (Drew) (MS)
11/4/2
MYSTERY AND DETECTIVE
FICTION: AN INTERNA-
TIONAL BIBLIOGRAPHY OF
SECONDARY SOURCES (Albert)
(IAC)                   8/4/30
REX STOUT: AN ANNOTATED
PRIMARY AND SECONDARY
BIBLIOGRAPHY (Townsend/
McAleer/Sapp/Schemer) (R) 5/2/29
BIBLIOGRAPHY OF CRIME FICTION
1749–1975, THE (Hubin) (IAC)
(R)                3/3/17 & 48
L: Lyles 3/4/58
Bickham, Jack
DAY SEVEN (TAR)          11/1/51
Biederman, Marcia
POST NO BONDS (TAR)     11/1/51
BIG APPLE MYSTERIES, THE (Asi-
mov/Greenberg/Waugh, eds.)
(IAC)                   6/4/32
BIG BANG (Goulart) (R)      7/3/37
BIG CHILL, THE (Copper) (R)  4/6/36
BIG KISS-OFF OF 1944, THE
(Bergman) (M*F) (R)  1/3/38; 8/2/34
Big-Nose Charlie. See Tyler, Charles W.
BIG SLEEP, THE (movie)
L: Lansdale 2/4/58
BIG STIFFS, THE (Avallone) (R) 2/5/39
BIG TRENCHCOAT IN THE SKY,
THE (Lovell) (TAR)       10/4/43
BIGGER THEY COME, THE (Fair)
(R)                    12/1/ 37
Biggers, Earl Derr
KEEPER OF THE KEYS (IAC)
10/3/39
Bigwood, James; Stephen Youngkin,
and Raymond Cabana, Jr.
THE FILMS OF PETER LORRE
(R)                    10/3/71
Bill Pronzini Revisited (Kelley) 2/5/5-6
L: Breen 2/6/43

BILLIARD ROOM MYSTERY, THE
(Flynn) (TBR)     13/3/51-2
BILLINGSGATE SHOAL (Boyer) (R)
6/3/39
BILLION DOLLAR BRAIN, THE
(Deighton) (R)     2/1/38
Bingham, John
MINISTRY OF DEATH (M*F)
2/5/26
Binyon, T.J.
'MURDER WILL OUT': THE DE-
TECTIVE IN FICTION (R)
12/1/31-3
Bird, Al
MURDER SO REAL (M*F)   3/1/35
BIRD IN THE NET (Parrish) (TAR)
10/4/45
*Birkett, Sam.* See Payne, Laurence
Birkley, Dolan [D.B. Olsen, q.v.]
THE BLUE GERANIUM
(TBR)     12/2/42-3
BISHOP AS PAWN (McInerny) (M*F)
3/5/35
*Bishop, Jim*
Twice-Told Tale of Murder (Floyd)
6/1/21-6
*Bishop, Paul*
CITADEL RUN (TNSPE) (MS)
10/2/49; 12/3/7
(MS)     7/3/5
BITTER WATER (Clark) (TAR)
13/1/53-4
BLACK ABDUCTOR (James)
Crystal-Ball Stories (Strøm)
12/3/47-52
BLACK ALIBI (Woolrich) (IAC)
7/1/34
Black and White and Dead: James
McClure's South Africa (Isaac)
6/4/12-8
L: Goode 6/6/42
BLACK ANGEL, THE (Woolrich)
(IAC)     7/1/34
BLACK AS HE'S PAINTED (Marsh)
(IAC)     10/4/49
BLACK AURA (Sladek) (R) (M*F)
3/4/48; 4/2/37
BLACK BAT'S INVISIBLE ENEMY,
THE (Jones) (R)     11/4/98
BLACK CABINET, THE (Lovesey,
ed.) (IAC)     12/2/67
Black, Cary Joseph
L:     1/1/43

BLACK CASTLE, THE (Daniels) (R)
2/4/46
*Black Characters in Mysteries*
OUT OF THE WOODPILE: BLACK
CHARACTERS IN CRIME AND
DETECTIVE FICTION (Bailey)
(R)     13/2/91-3
BLACK CHRONICLE (Hayes) (TBR)
13/1/36-7
BLACK DAHLIA (Ellroy) (TNSPE)
10/2/48
The New Rippers (Tolley)12/3/57-63
BLACK DOOR, THE (Adams) (M*F)
P/30
BLACK HEARTS AND SLOW
DANCING (TAR) (Emerson) 11/2/68
Black, Ian Stuart
JOURNEY TO A SAFE PLACE
(M*F)     4/2/39
THE MAN ON THE BRIDGE
(M*F)     2/1/27
BLACK LAND, WHITE LAND
(Bailey) (R)     P/38
Black, Lionel
THE PENNY MURDERS (M*F)
(R)     5/1/23; 5/5/37
*Black Mask.* Also see Pulps
THE BLACK MASK BOYS (Nolan)
(IAC)     9/5/24
Captain Joseph T. Shaw's Black
Mask Scrapbook (Hagemann)
7/1/2-6
COMPREHENSIVE INDEX TO
BLACK MASK, 1920–1951
(Hagemann) (IAC)     7/2/22
Some Very Tough People (Sampson)
8/5/7-17*
BLACK MOON, THE (Randisi/Ashby,
eds.) (R)     12/4/81-2
*Black Mystery Writers*
L: Deeck 11/3/96
BLACK ORCHIDS (Stout) (IAC) 6/3/25
BLACK PATH OF FEAR, THE
(Woolrich) (IAC)     7/1/35
BLACK ROSE MURDER, THE
(McGuire) (TBR)     13/1/44-5
BLACK SEVEN (Kendall) (TBR)
13/3/63-4
BLACK SHROUDS, THE (Little)
(TBR)     10/3/55
BLACK VALENTINE (Sargent) (IAC)
11/1/27

BLACK WIDOWER (Moyes) (R)
(M*F)                    1/6/47; 2/4/35
*Blackburn, John*
(SSC)                              4/2/12
BLACKHEATH POISONINGS, THE
(Symons) (M*F)                     3/5/37
Blackmon, Anita
MURDER À LA RICHELIEU
(TBR)                             12/4/64
BLACKSTOCK AFFAIR, THE
(Bandy) (M*F)                      4/4/33
Blades, Joe, et al.
GUIDE TO MOVIES ON VIDEO
CASSETTE (IAC)                    11/4/55
Blain, W. Edward
PASSION PLAY (TAR)           12/2/56-7
Blaine, Richard
THE TAINTED JADE (R)          13/1/55-6
Blair, Alpha
THROUGH THE EYES OF EVIL
(R)                                8/3/43
Blair, Lucinda
THE PLACE OF THE DEVILS (R)
2/1/37
*Blair, Peter.* See Anderson, J.R.L.
*Blaise, Modesty.* See O'Donnell, Peter
*Blake, Andy and Arabella.* See Powell,
Richard
Blake, Nicholas
THE DREADFUL HOLLOW (R)
5/4/33
MALICE IN WONDERLAND (R)
9/1/40
MURDER WITH MALICE (IAC)
9/3/31
Blame Stephen Sondheim (Bleiler)
5/1/15-6
L: Briney 5/2/42
BLAND BEGINNING (Symons) (IAC)
9/4/37
BLANK WALL, THE (Holding) (R)
(IAC)             1/5/46; 13/4/85-6
*Blankfort, Michael*
Obituary (Lachman)               7/4/23
BLATCHINGTON TANGLE, THE
(Cole) (TBR)                      11/3/64
Bleeck, Oliver [Ross Thomas, q.v.]
NO QUESTIONS ASKED (R) 1/2/14
Bleeding the Fun Out (Isaac)     7/5/3-6
L: Lachman 8/1/43

Bleiler, E.F.
The Apocryphalization of Holmes
4/5/3-5
Blame Stephen Sondheim    5/1/15-6
Chance and Illogic and THE
BLACK BOX MURDER            2/1/8
A Chinese Detective in San
Francisco                    5/3/2-4
The Dilemma of Datchery     4/4/7-15
His Own Desert              3/4/11,15
L: 2/1/60; 2/5/46; 3/5/50; 5/1/36;
5/3/44; 6/3/48; 6/4/47; 6/6/45;
7/2/44; 7/4/40; 8/1/39; 8/2/42;
8/5/42
The Policeman: A Victorian Novel
6/2/7-10
Reviews:
ANDROMACHE OR THE
INADVERTENT MURDER
(Monteilhet)            13/2/76-7
AN APRIL SHROUD (Hill)
13/1/71-2
DEAD MR. NIXON (White/Scott)
3/2/43
DEATH OF A GOSSIP (Beaton)
13/1/72-4
DEATH OF A PERFECT WIFE
(Beaton)                13/1/72-4
DEATH OF AN OUTSIDER
(Beaton)                13/1/72-4
THE DOORBELL RANG (Stout)
13/2/77-8
FELLOW PASSENGER
(Household)             13/1/74-5
HALLOWE'EN PARTY (Christie)
13/1/75-6
KRIMINALLITTERATURENS
KAVALKADE: KRIMINAL-
OG DETEKTIVHISTORIEN I
BILLEDER OG TEKST (La
Cour/Mogensen)             7/6/35
THE LAST HOUSEPARTY
(Dickinson)                8/2/39
ROAD BLOCK (Waugh)
13/2/79-80
THE RUSSIA HOUSE (Le
Carré)                  12/4/76-7
THERE ARE NO GHOSTS IN
THE SOVIET UNION (Hill)
13/2/80-1
VALLEY OF SMUGGLERS
(Upfield)               13/2/78-9

Bleiler, E.F., continued
Some Thoughts on Peacock Feet
6/3/14-21,13
Sweden's Commitment to Mystery
Fiction          2/5/7-8
To Be and Not To Be     6/6/3-4,18
TREASURY OF VICTORIAN
GHOST STORIES (ed.) (MS) 6/1/1
Vincent Starrett vs. Arthur Machen:
or, How Not To Communicate
over Eight Years of Corres-
pondence          3/6/11-4
BLESSING WAY, THE (Hillerman)
(IAC)          11/1/23
BLIND PIG, THE (Jackson) (M*F)
3/6/27
BLIND SEARCH, THE (Egan) (R)
(M*F)          1/4/47; 1/5/31
Bloch, Blanche
THE BACH FESTIVAL MURDERS
(R)          9/5/40
Bloch, Robert
THE KING OF TERRORS: TALES
OF MADNESS AND DEATH
(R)          1/6/43
L:          1/1/40
SUCH STUFF AS SCREAMS ARE
MADE OF (R)          3/3/44
Blochman, Lawrence G.
SEE YOU AT THE MORGUE (R)
10/1/76
Block, Lawrence. Also see Harrison,
Chip
THE BURGLAR IN THE CLOSET
(M*F)          3/3/38
THE BURGLAR WHO LIKED TO
QUOTE KIPLING (M*F)   3/6/40
BURGLARS CAN'T BE CHOOS-
ERS (M*F) (R)     2/4/36; 8/2/40
DEADLY HONEYMOON (IAC)
8/4/30
Here Comes the Judge (Crider)   3/6/8
INTRODUCING CHIP HARRISON
(IAC)          8/5/30
MONA (M*F)          3/2/38
THE SINS OF THE FATHERS (R)
(M*F)          1/2/22; 2/4/30
A STAB IN THE DARK (R)   7/4/33
TIME TO MURDER AND
CREATE (R)          8/3/41
WHEN THE SACRED GINMILL
CLOSES (R)          8/4/42

BLOCKBUSTERS (Barlay) (M*F)
2/1/21
Blom, K. Arne
The Crime Story in Sweden 7/5/16-25
The Detective Hero in the Comics
6/1/8-15
Donald Goines: An Appreciation
9/4/17-24
L:          6/6/41; 12/2/93-4
THE MOMENT OF TRUTH (R)
1/4/45
A Report from Scandinavia
8/2/19-20; 8/3/19-20
Scandinavian Mystery Scene 8/4/24-6
Spillane's Hammer     12/3/35-43
BLOOD AND JUDGMENT (Gilbert)
(IAC)          11/3/47
BLOOD BROTHER, BLOOD
BROTHER (Peebles) (M*F)   4/2/37
BLOOD IN YOUR EYE (Wilmot)
(M*F)          2/1/30
BLOOD MONEY (Collins) (R)   1/6/50
BLOOD OF AN ENGLISHMAN, THE
(McClure) (R)          5/2/37
BLOOD ON HER SHOE (Field) (TBR)
13/3/54
BLOOD ORANGE (Llewellyn) (TAR)
11/3/74
BLOOD-RED DREAMS, THE
(Collins) (M*F)          2/1/27
BLOOD SHOT (Paretsky) (TAR)
11/1/65; 11/2/77
BLOOD STONE (Allegretto) (TAR)
11/1/50
BLOOD TEST (Kellerman) (IAC) 9/5/27
BLOODIED IVY, THE (Goldsborough)
(TAR) (R) 11/1/58; 11/2/69; 12/3/95-6
BLOODLIST (Elrod) (TAR)   12/3/93-5
Bloody Balaclava: Charlotte MacLeod's
Campus Comedy Mysteries
(Bakerman)          7/1/23-9
BLOODY INSTRUCTIONS (Woods)
(IAC)          10/1/63
Blow and Manciple: The Dottering
Detectives (Deeck)     10/1/55-60*
Blow, William. See Hopkins, Kenneth
BLOWBACK (Pronzini) (M*F)   1/5/32
BLUE FLAME (Gilmore) (IAC)   7/5/27
BLUE GERANIUM, THE (Birkley)
(TBR)          12/2/42-3
BLUE HAMMER, THE (Macdonald)
(R)          1/2/38
Blue Jean Billy. See Tyler, Charles W.

BLUE LEADER (Wager) (R)     5/5/40
BLUE MASCARA TEARS (McKim-
    mey) (R)                7/5/45
BLUE SANTO MURDER MYSTERY,
    THE (Armstrong) (TBR)   11/3/68
BLUNT INSTRUMENT, A (Heyer)
    (R)                     10/1/85
Boardinghouse Novels: A Preliminary
    Checklist (Deeck)    11/3/3-13*
    L: Adey 13/1/78-9; Cleary 12/2/87-8;
    Hay 12/2/98; Hazen 12/2/100-1
*Bocca, Geoffrey*
    BEST SELLER: A NOSTALGIC
    CELEBRATION OF THE LESS-
    THAN-GREAT BOOKS YOU
    HAVE ALWAYS BEEN AFRAID
    TO ADMIT YOU LOVED (R)
                            6/6/35
    Obituary (Lachman)      7/5/30
BODY AND SOIL (McInerny) (R)
                            11/4/85
Body in the Library, The: Twentieth-
    Century Crime and Mystery
    Writers and the Mystery World in
    Our Time (Wooster)    5/1/11-4
    L: Aucott 5/2/47; Crider 5/2/41;
    Dueren 5/3/44
BODY IN THE ROAD, THE (Dalton)
    (TBR)                   11/4/64
BODY OF A GIRL, THE (Gilbert) (R)
                            3/4/48
BODY RUB (Andrews) (R)      1/5/41
BODY SCISSORS (Doolittle) (TAR)
                            13/3/77-8
BODY THAT WASN'T UNCLE, THE
    (Yates) (M*F)           3/5/39
BOGMAIL (McGinley) (M*F) (R)
                            5/5/21 & 29
*Bognor, Simon.* See Heald, Tim
BOHANNON'S WAY (Hansen) (IAC)
                        11/1/31; 12/67-8
*Bond, Christopher.* See Martyn,
    Wyndham
*Bond, James.* See Fleming, Ian
*Bond, Raleigh Verne*
    Obituary (Lachman)      11/4/55
BONE (Chesbro) (TAR)        11/4/75
BONEGRINDER (Lutz) (M*F) (R)
                        2/4/36; 6/4/22
BONEPILE (Dold) (IAC)       11/1/24
Bonett, John and Emery
    DEAD LION (IAC)         6/4/30

*Bonfiglioli, Kyril*
    The Honorable Charlie Mortdecai
    (Deeck)                 9/3/22-6
*Boniface, Marjorie*
    Little Old Ladies (Nehr)  3/4/3-7
Bonn, Thomas L.
    UNDER COVER (IAC)       6/6/21
BONNET MAN, THE (Weill) (M*F)
                            3/5/36
Bonney, Joseph L.
    MURDER WITHOUT CLUES (TBR)
                            11/2/84
*Book Clubs*
    MURDER BY MAIL: THE
    HISTORY OF THE MYSTERY
    BOOK CLUBS WITH COM-
    PLETE CHECKLIST (Cook) (MS)
                            3/2/1
BOOK FOR BANNING, A (Easton)
    (M*F)                   5/4/26
BOOK OF THE DEAD, THE (Richard-
    son) (TAR) (R)     12/4/55; 13/3/88-9
Books of Geoffrey Homes, The
    (Dukeshire)          3/3/19-21*
Books of Nicholas Luard, The
    (Dukeshire)             4/1/12
*Bookstores*
    (TCITC)              3/2/3-12,20
    Maps of Xiccarph (Sampson)
                            6/6/9-18
    L: Briney 3/2/55; Meyerson 2/4/54,
    2/5/54
Booth, Charles G.
    MURDER AT HIGH TIDE (M*F)
                            3/4/40
*Borden, Lizzie*
    Great T-Shirt Media Event and
    Mystery Quiz (Nevins)   5/6/7-9
    L: Briney 6/1/49
*Borgo Press*
    Townsend comments       13/1/88
BORN VICTIM (Waugh) (IAC)  3/3/18
Bornemark, Kjell-Olof
    THE HENCHMAN (TAR)     13/1/51
"Borrowed Jewels Well Display'd":
    Literary Allusions in the Writings of
    Sara Woods (Sarjeant)  12/2/17-27
Borthwick, J.S.
    THE CASE OF THE HOOK-
    BILLED KITES (R)       7/3/35
*Boston Blackie*
    Old Time Radio Lives (Larsen)
                            5/6/3-6,9

Boucher, Anthony
  A Consummation Devoutly to Be
    Wished (Christopher)    9/2/9-19
  EXEUNT MURDERERS, THE
    BEST MYSTERY STORIES OF
    ANTHONY BOUCHER (R) 8/2/35
  THE SEVEN OF CALVARY (R)
                          5/5/40
Bouchercon
  Behind the Scenes at Bouchercon 9
    (Grochowski)       2/6/3-6,8
  Bouchercon, 1978: IX and Counting
    (Yates)            3/1/15-20
  Bouchercon Scrapbook (Townsend/
    Nieminski)         4/6/19-30
  Bouchercon VIII (Grochowski)
                       2/2/15-8,14
  Bouchercon X: Two Views (Lach-
    man/Grochowski)      3/5/11-3
  Bouchercon XXII (MS)    12/1/ 3
  (MS)                    10/3/2
  On Fans and Bouchercon (Town-
    send)                5/5/11-3
  Pow-Wow on the Potomac: Boucher-
    con XI (Nieminski)   4/6/12-8
  A Report on Bouchercon 7 (Scott)
                         P/18-21
  L: Adey 5/1/31; Briney 1/1/45;
    Moffatt 1/1/43; Scott 6/4/47;
    Stilwell 11/1/81; Thompson 1/2/47
  Bouchercon, 1978: IX and Counting
    (Yates)            3/1/15-20
  L: Briney 3/2/55; Nieminski 3/2/50
  Bouchercon Scrapbook (Townsend/
    Nieminski)         4/6/19-30
  Bouchercon VIII: "Murder at the
    Waldorf" (Grochowski) 2/2/15-8,14
  L: Lansdale 2/3/61
  Bouchercon X: Two Views (Lachman/
    Grochowski)          3/5/11-3
  Bouchercon XXII (MS)    12/1/ 3
Bourgeau, Art
  A LONELY WAY TO DIE (M*F)
                          4/5/29
Bova, Ben
  THE MULTIPLE MAN (R)    2/1/35
Bowen, Robert Sidney
  MAKE MINE MURDER (TBR)
                         13/4/72
Bowers, Dorothy
  THE BELLS AT OLD BAILEY
    (TBR)               12/4/62-3

Bowlers, Beer, Bravado, and Brains:
    Anthony Gilbert's Arthur Crook
    (Bakerman)           2/4/5-13
  L: Nieminski 2/5/46
Bowling Green University Popular
    Press (MS)            9/2/1-2
Box, Edgar [Gore Vidal, q.v.]
  THREE BY BOX (R)        3/1/44
Boyd, Edward, and Bill Knox
  THE VIEW FROM DANIEL PIKE
    (R)                   3/1/40
Boyer, Rick
  BILLINGSGATE SHOAL (R)  6/3/39
  THE DAISY DUCKS (R)     9/1/43
  THE PENNY FERRY (R)     8/3/37
  THE WHALE'S FOOTPRINTS
    (TAR)                11/1/51
Boylan, Eleanor
  WORKING MURDER (R)     11/4/86
Boyle, Andrew
  Obituary (Lachman)      13/3/69
Brabazon, James
  DOROTHY L. SAYERS (R)   6/1/39
Bradley, Geoff
  L:    7/4/41; 12/1/58-60; 13/3/96-7
  Reviews:
    THE BIGGER THEY COME
      (Fair)              12/1/37
    THE CASE OF THE INVISIBLE
      THIEF (Haughey)    12/1/36-7
Bradshaw, George
  PRACTISE TO DECEIVE (R) 7/1/42
BRAGG'S HUNCH (Lynch) (M*F)
                          6/5/41
Brahams, Caryl
  Obituary (Lachman)      7/2/25
Braine, John
  FINGER OF FIRE (R)      3/6/45
  THE PIOUS AGENT         2/3/52
BRAIN–WAVES AND DEATH (Rich)
  (TBR)                 13/1/35-6
Brand, Christiana
  BUFFET FOR UNWELCOME
    GUESTS: THE BEST MYSTERY
    SHORT STORIES OF CHRISTI-
    ANA BRAND (Nevins/Greenberg,
    eds.) (IAC) (R)      8/2/22 & 35
  DEATH IN HIGH HEELS (R)10/1/77
  GREEN FOR DANGER (R) (IAC)
      2/6/38; 6/4/30; 8/2/40; 11/3/50
  Obituary (Lachman)      10/3/44-5

Brand, Max
Young Detective Kildare (Herzog)
7/2/2-10
BRANDENBURG HOTEL, THE
(Winslow) (M*F) (R)    1/1/31; 1/2/42
Brandstetter, Dave. See Hansen, David
Brandt, Carl E.
Obituary (Lachman)    13/3/72
Branson, H.C.
THE LEADEN BUBBLE (R) 10/1/78
Branston, Frank
SERGEANT RITCHIE'S CON-
SCIENCE (M*F)    3/5/35
AN UP AND COMING STAR
(M*F)    2/1/25
BRASS RING, THE (Padgett) (TBR)
11/3/62
Braun, Lilian Jackson
THE CAT WHO PLAYED
BRAHMS (R)    9/6/35
THE CAT WHO PLAYED POST
OFFICE (R)    9/6/36
THE CAT WHO TALKED TO
GHOSTS (R)    13/1/66-7
Little Old Men (Nehr)    4/4/2-6
BRAZILIAN SLEIGH RIDE (Fish)
(IAC)    11/1/28
BREAK IN (Francis) (R)    9/2/36
BREAKDOWN (Pronzini) (TAR)
13/2/47
Brean, Herbert
THE CLOCK STRIKES THIRTEEN
(M*F)    3/4/41
THE TRACES OF BRILLHART
(IAC)    13/3/65
Breen, Jon L.
THE GATHERING PLACE (R)
(IAC)    8/2/38; 8/3/26; 9/2/28
HAIR OF THE SLEUTHHOUND
(IAC)    6/3/24
The Journal of Ratiocinative
Research    1/5/16; 5/5/14
L: 2/1/54; 2/3/66; 2/5/45; 2/6/43;
3/1/47; 3/2/54; 3/3/52; 3/4/53;
4/2/58; 5/1/34; 5/2/46; 5/3/43;
7/3/50; 8/3/49; 8/5/46; 13/3/103-4
LISTEN FOR THE CLICK (R)
7/3/32; 8/1/16
NOVEL VERDICTS: A GUIDE TO
COURTROOM FICTION (IAC)
8/4/30

Breen, Jon L., continued
Reviews:
THE AFFAIR (Snow)    4/6/34
THE BIG CHILL (Copper)    4/6/36
THE BIG KISS–OFF OF 1944
(Bergman)    8/2/34
BUFFET FOR UNWELCOME
GUESTS (Nevins/Greenberg,
eds.)    8/2/35
THE CASE OF THE BURIED
CLOCK (Gardner)    7/6/37
DAN TURNER, HOLLYWOOD
DETECTIVE (Bellem)    8/2/35
DEAD IN THE WATER (Wood)
8/1/37
EXEUNT MURDERERS (Nevins/
Greenberg, eds.)    8/2/35
THE GLASS HIGHWAY
(Estleman)    7/6/38
HOLLYWOOD AND LEVINE
(Bergman)    8/2/34
HOW TO WRITE BEST SELL-
ING FICTION (Koontz)    5/6/43
THE LIE DIRECT (Woods)    7/6/37
LIZZIE (Hunter)    8/3/44
MURDER AT THE SMITH-
SONIAN (Truman)    7/6/36
MURDER ISN'T ENOUGH
(Flynn)    8/1/37
MURDER ON CUE (Dentinger)
7/6/40
MURDER ON LOCATION
(Kennedy)    7/6/36
THE MYSTERY HALL OF
FAME (Pronzini/Greenberg/
Waugh, eds.)    8/2/33
A PARTY TO MURDER
(Underwood)    8/1/31
SCHOOL FOR MURDER
(Barnard)    8/3/44
TOP CRIME (Pachter, ed.)    8/2/33
TRUE DETECTIVE (Collins)
8/2/34
THE WAYS OF THE HOUR
(Cooper)    8/1/30
WHAT ABOUT MURDER? (IAC)
(R)    5/4/18 & 28
Brener, Carol
L:    6/2/49
Bresler, Fenton
THE MYSTERY OF GEORGES
SIMENON (IAC)    8/2/23

Breslin, Jimmy, and Dick Schapp
  .44 (R)                             3/5/43
Bretnor, Reginald
  A KILLING IN SWORDS (M*F)
                                      2/6/31
Brett, John
  WHO'D HIRE BRETT? (M*F) 5/5/23
Brett, Simon
  CAST, IN ORDER OF DISAP-
    PEARANCE (M*F)          1/1/29
  THE DEAD SIDE OF THE MIKE
    (R)                     5/2/28
  MRS, PRESUMED DEAD (R)
                    11/4/93; 13/1/60-1
  MURDER IN THE TITLE (R) 7/6/41
  A NICE CLASS OF CORPSE (R)
                            11/4/93
  NOT DEAD, ONLY RESTING (R)
                             9/3/40
  SITUATION TRAGEDY (M*F)
                             6/3/35
  SO MUCH BLOOD (R)         1/5/37
  STAR TRAP (M*F)           2/5/27
Brett, Stephen [Stephen Mertz, q.v.]
  SOME DIE HARD (R)         7/5/39
Brewer, Gay
  Raymond Chandler Without His
    Knight: Contracting Worlds in
    THE BLUE DAHLIA and
    PLAYBACK              13/3/37-49
Brewer, Gil
  ANGEL (R)                 5/6/47
Brickhill, Paul
  Obituary (Lachman)        13/3/69
BRIDE WORE BLACK, THE
    (Woolrich) (IAC)        9/3/30
  L: Shibuk 9/4/49
BRIDESMAID, THE (Rendell)
    (TAR)                   12/4/54
Bridge, Ann
    (SSC)                   5/3/20*
BRIGHT ORANGE FOR THE
    SHROUD (MacDonald) (R)  6/2/44
BRIGHTLIGHT (Bernard) (R) (M*F)
    (R)     2/1/31 & 37; 2/4/32; 4/3/42
  L: Lansdale 2/5/47
Briney, Bob
  L: 1/1/45; 1/3/52; 1/5/56; 1/6/56;
    2/1/55; 2/2/45; 2/3/70; 2/4/52;
    2/6/53; 3/1/46; 6/1/49; 12/2/102-3;
    13/1/83-5
  The Line-Up                 P/22

Briney, Bob, continued
  Reviews:
    THE DANCING MEN (Hubbard)
                             5/5/38
    DEADFALL (Laumer)        5/5/43
    LIGNY'S LAKE (Courtier)  5/5/42
    THE LUCK RUNS OUT
      (MacLeod)              5/5/37
    MURDER TRAPP (Franklin)
                             5/5/42
    MY FOE OUTSTRETCH'D BE-
      NEATH THE TREE (Clinton-
      Baddeley)              5/5/37
    ROAST EGGS (Clark)       5/4/36
    SHORT CIRCUIT (Oriol)    5/5/39
    TELL YOU WHAT I'LL DO
      (Cecil)                5/5/38
    THE THREE WORLDS OF
      JOHNNY HANDSOME
      (Godey)                5/5/43
  The (Very Temporary) Return of
    Skull-Face               2/2/21-4
Brisco, Patty
  Encore! (McSherry)         12/1/9-22
British Murder and British Detective
  Fiction (Bargainnier)      6/4/19-22
Brock, Lynn
  THE KINK (R)               12/1/44
Broecker, Jay
  L:                         2/3/57
BROKEN CONSORT (Gollin) (R)
                             12/1/39
BROKEN PENNY, THE (Symons)
    (IAC)                    10/3/41
BROKEN VASE, THE (Stout) (IAC)
                             6/3/25
BROKER, THE (Collins) (R)    1/6/50
BROKER'S WIFE, THE (Collins) (R)
                             1/6/50
Bronte, Louisa
  MOONLIGHT AT GREYSTONES
    (M*F)                    1/1/31
Broset, Myrtis
  L: 1/2/48; 1/6/58; 2/1/59; 2/2/42,59;
    2/3/72; 2/5/56; 4/6/47; 5/1/45;
    6/4/48; 7/4/46
  Reviews:
    BARETTA (Patrick)        2/1/40
    THE BILLION DOLLAR BRAIN
      (Deighton)             2/1/38
    THE BLIND SEARCH (Egan)
                             1/4/47

*Broset, Myrtis,* continued
*Reviews* continued
THE BRANDENBURG HOTEL
(Winslow)    1/2/42
BRIGHTLIGHT (Bernard)  2/1/37
BY HOOK OR CROOK (Lathen)
    1/6/42
CIRCLE OF FIRE (Sadler)  1/4/47
DEATH IN ECSTASY (Marsh)
    2/1/37
ENTER A MURDERER (Marsh)
    2/3/54
EVEN THE WICKED (McBain)
    1/5/40
FAT CHANCE (Laumer)    2/3/55
FELICIA (Effinger)    3/3/46
FROM LONDON FAR (Innes)
    1/4/48
GENTLE ALBATROSS (Foote-
Smith)    1/2/42
THE HANGED MEN (Harper)
    2/3/54
HELL'S FULL (Harrison)  2/6/42
HORSE UNDER WATER
(Deighton)    2/5/44
THE HUNTED (Leonard)  2/1/35
IN THE LAMB WHITE DAYS
(Hall)    2/1/36
THE JAPANESE CORPSE (van
de Wetering)    2/6/41
JUSTICE ENDS AT HOME,
AND OTHER STORIES
(Stout) (McAleer, ed.)  3/5/43
THE KILLERS OF STARFISH
(Gillis)    1/6/43
THE LAW'S DELAY (Woods)
    1/4/48
THE MINUTEMAN MURDERS
(Langton)    1/2/41
THE MULTIPLE MAN (Bova)
    2/1/35
MURDER FOR CHARITY
(Ponder)    2/3/55
MUSIC TO MURDER BY
(Hinkle)    2/5/44
THE PATCHWORK MAN
(Harper)    2/5/44
THE PERFECT CORPSE
(Wright)    1/4/47
THE PLACE OF THE DEVILS
(Blair)    2/1/37
THE PRETTY PINK SHROUD
(Ferrars)    2/6/41

*Broset, Myrtis,* continued
*Reviews* continued:
THE QUESTION OF MAX
(Cross)    2/5/44
THE RHEINGOLD ROUTE
(Maling)    3/5/42
SCALES OF JUSTICE (Marsh)
    2/1/38
THE SILVER FALCON
(Anthony)    2/6/42
A SIMPLE ACT OF KINDNESS
(Estes)    2/3/56
STUD GAME (Anthony)  2/6/42
TEN PLUS ONE (McBain)  1/4/47
THE TERMINAL CONNECTION
(Moore)    1/5/41
THEY FOUND HIM DEAD
(Heyer)    1/6/42
TUMBLEWEED (van de
Wetering)    1/2/42
WHERE THERE'S SMOKE
(McBain) ·    1/5/40
THE Z PAPERS (Simmons) 1/6/42
Brown, Carter
THE DEADLY KITTEN (R)  3/2/47
DONAVAN'S DELIGHT (R)  3/6/47
THE INVISIBLE FLAMINI (M*F)
    3/5/38
NEGATIVE IN BLUE (R)  1/4/48
THE SPANKING GIRLS (R) 11/4/92
THE STRAWBERRY–BLONDE
JUNGLE (M*F)    3/6/35
THE STRIPPER (M*F)  1/5/34
THE WANTON (M*F)    P/26
*Brown, Father.* See Chesterton, G.K.
*Brown, Fredric*
FABULOUS CLIPJOINT (MS)  9/1/7
(IAC)    11/1/31
THE LENIENT BEAST (IAC)11/3/46
NIGHT OF THE JABBERWOCK
(M*F)    3/6/40
THE SCREAMING MIMI (IAC)
    11/3/46
WE ALL KILLED GRANDMA
(M*F)    1/2/24
L: Schubert 12/1/65
Brown, Hosanna
I SPY, YOU DIE (R)    10/1/79
*Brown, R.D.*
HAZZARD (R)    9/6/38
Obituary (Lachman)    13/1/30

Brown, Zenith Jones. Also see Ford,
  Leslie
  Obituary (Lachman)           8/1/21
Browne, Coral
  Obituary (Lachman)           13/3/72
Browne, Howard. Also see Evans, John
  HALO IN BRASS (IAC)          10/4/51
  PORK CITY (TNSPE)            10/2/50
Browne, Pat
  DIMENSIONS OF DETECTIVE
    FICTION (w/Ray Browne/
    Landrum, ed.) (R)          1/4/50
  HEROES AND HUMANITIES: DE-
    TECTIVE FICTION AND CUL-
    TURE (w/Ray Browne) (MS)   9/2/1
Browne, Ray B.
  DIMENSIONS OF DETECTIVE
    FICTION (w/Pat Browne/Landrum,
    ed.) (R)                   1/4/50
  HEROES AND HUMANITIES: DE-
    TECTIVE FICTION AND CUL-
    TURE (w/Pat Browne) (MS)   9/2/1
Browning, Tod (RM)             6/6/24
BROWN'S REQUIEM (Ellroy) (M*F)
                               6/3/36
Brownstone Books
  (MS)           5/5/1-2; 8/5/22,28,33
  L: Masliah 13/1/88; Townsend reply
    13/1/88
BROWNSTONE HOUSE OF NERO
  WOLFE, THE (Darby) (R)       7/6/32
Bruccoli, Matthew J.
  A MATTER OF CRIME(w/Layman,
    ed.) (IAC)                 11/1/33
  RAYMOND CHANDLER: A DE-
    SCRIPTIVE BIBLIOGRAPHY (R)
                               3/6/49
  ROSS MACDONALD (R)           8/1/35
  L: Townsend 8/2/46
Bruce, Jean
  (SSC)                        4/2/13
Bruce, Leo
  CASE WITH FOUR CLOWNS (R)
                               10/1/82
  CASE WITH NO CONCLUSION
    (R)                        10/1/81
  COLD BLOOD (R)               1/1/34
  DEATH IN ALBERT PARK (M*F)
                               4/2/35
  FURIOUS OLD WOMEN (R)        8/3/36
Brussel, James A.
  Obituary (Lachman)           6/6/49

Brust, Toby
  L:                           4/5/45
Buchan, John
  THE THIRTY-NINE STEPS (R)
                               2/6/37
  THE THREE HOSTAGES (R)       6/2/43
Buchanan, Patrick
  A MURDER OF CROWS (M*F)
                               1/1/28
BUCK PASSES FLYNN, THE
  (Mcdonald) (R) (IAC)  6/1/40; 6/4/32
Buckley, William F.
  L: Grand 2/6/45
Budd, Lanning (Lanny) Prescot
  (SSC)                        7/1/30*
BUFFET FOR UNWELCOME
  GUESTS: THE BEST MYSTERY
  SHORT STORIES OF CHRISTI-
  ANA BRAND (Nevins/Greenberg,
  eds.) (IAC) (R)          8/2/22 & 35
BUGLES BLOWING, THE (Freeling)
  (R)                          1/5/44
BUILD MY GALLOWS HIGH
  (Homes) (R)                  3/4/49
BULLET FOR A STAR (Kaminsky)
  (M*F) (R)              2/1/25 & 44
Bunn, Thomas
  CLOSET BONES (M*F)           2/3/46
  CLOSING COSTS (MS)           12/3/10
Burack, A.S.
  WRITING SUSPENSE AND MYS-
    TERY FICTION (ed.) (R)     2/2/39
BURGLAR IN THE CLOSET, THE
  (Block) (M*F)                3/3/38
BURGLAR WHO LIKED TO QUOTE
  KIPLING, THE (Block) (M*F)
                               3/6/40
BURGLARS CAN'T BE CHOOSERS
  (Block) (M*F) (R)     2/4/36; 8/2/40
Burke, J.F.
  THE KAMA SUTRA TANGO
    (M*F)                      2/1/22
Burke, James Lee
  HEAVEN'S PRISONERS (R) 10/3/73
  A MORNING FOR FLAMINGOS
    (TAR)                      13/1/51
  NEON RAIN (R)                10/3/73
Burke, Richard
  MURDER ON HIGH HEELS (TBR)
                               13/4/76-7
Burkholz, Herbert
  STRANGE BEDFELLOWS (TAR)
                               11/1/52

Burley, W.J.
  THREE-TOED PUSSY (R)   1/6/52
  WYCLIFFE AND THE SCAPE-
    GOAT (M*F)         3/6/38
  WYCLIFFE AND THE SCHOOL-
    GIRLS (M*F)         P/29
BURN THIS (McCloy) (M*F)  4/4/42
*Burnett, W.R.*
  GOODBYE, CHICAGO (R)  5/3/38
  Obituary (Lachman)     6/4/33
BURNED WOMAN, THE (Mathis)
  (TAR)             11/3/78
BURNING COURT, THE (Carr) (IAC)
                11/4/54
BURNING OF BILLY TOOBER, THE
  (Ross) (M*F)        P/28
*Burns, Rex*
  THE ALVAREZ JOURNAL (M*F)
                P/28
  THE FARNSWORTH SCORE
    (M*F)           1/5/29
    (IAC)           5/5/17
  THE KILLING ZONE (TAR) 11/1/52
  SPEAK FOR THE DEAD (M*F)
                3/1/34
Burton, Miles
  THE MAN WITH THE TAT-
    TOOED FACE (M*F)   4/4/41
Busch, Niven
  THE TITAN GAME (TAR)  12/2/57
Bush, Christopher
  THE CASE OF THE COUNTER-
    FEIT COLONEL (M*F)  1/4/39
  THE CASE OF THE PLATINUM
    BLONDE (R)      12/1/46
  DEAD MAN'S MUSIC (TBR)11/2/85
  THE KITCHEN CAKE MURDER
    (TBR)         13/1/42-3
Business Before Everything: The Hard-
  Boiled World of Matt Helm (Skinner)
            10/1/39-53*
BUSTILLO (Royce) (M*F)  1/3/38
BUT DEATH RUNS FASTER
  (McGivern) (R)     10/1/89
BUTCHER'S BOY, THE (Perry) (IAC)
  (R)       8/1/16; 8/3/43
BUTCHER'S THEATER, THE
  (Kellerman) (TAR)  11/1/62; 11/2/73
Butler, Gwendoline
  COFFIN IN FASHION (TAR)
            13/1/51-2
  THE DULL DEAD (TBR)  13/1/46

Butler, Ragan
  CAPTAIN NASH AND THE
    HONOUR OF ENGLAND (M*F)
                2/2/34
  CAPTAIN NASH AND THE
    WROTH INHERITANCE (M*F)
                2/3/46
Butler, Richard C.
  Dell "Map Back" Checklist, 1–300
            1/2/17-22*
  L:             1/2/47
  Popular Library Paperback Checklist,
    1–200         1/3/5-8*
BUTTERFLY HUNTER, THE (van de
  Wetering) (R)      7/3/42
Butterworth, Michael. Also see Kemp,
  Sara
  REMAINS TO BE SEEN (M*F)
                2/4/35
  X MARKS THE SPOT (M*F) 3/1/35
BUYER BEWARE (Lutz) (R) (M*F)
           1/3/43; 1/4/37
BUZZARDS PICK THE BONES
  (Thomas) (TBR)    13/1/43
BY ANY ILLEGAL MEANS (Mac-
  kenzie) (TAR)     12/3/86
BY FREQUENT ANGUISH (Dean)
  (R)            7/5/45
BY HOOK OR CROOK (Lathen) (R)
                1/6/42
*Byfield, Barbara Ninde*
  Clergy-Detectives (Cleary)  9/3/3-21
  FOREVER WILT THOU DIE
    (M*F)          2/5/32
  A PARCEL OF THEIR FORTUNES
    (M*F)          4/2/38
*Byrd, David (artist)*
  L: Brener 6/2/49; Goode 6/2/48;
    Wenstrup 6/1/50
Byrd, Max
  CALIFORNIA THRILLER (M*F)
    (IAC)     5/5/22; 6/3/23
  TARGET OF OPPORTUNITY
    (TAR)        11/2/65

# C

"C" IS FOR CORPSE (Grafton)
  (IAC)      9/1/35; 9/3/32
C.B. GREENFIELD: NO LADY IN
  THE HOUSE (Kallen) (R)  6/5/49
C.B. GREENFIELD: PIANO BIRD
  (Kallen) (R)      8/2/29

C.B. Greenfield: The Metaphor Is the
Man (Bakerman) 7/6/24-9
C.B. GREENFIELD: THE TAN-
GLEWOOD MURDERS (Kallen)
(M*F) (R) 5/1/21; 5/5/41
Cabana, Raymond, Jr.; Stephen
Youngkin, and James Bigwood
THE FILMS OF PETER LORRE
(R) 10/3/71
Cadell, Elizabeth
THE CORNER SHOP (TBR) 10/2/65
CAESAR CODE, THE (Simmel)
(M*F) 1/1/29
CAIN (Hoopes) (IAC) 7/2/24
Cain, James M.
CAIN (Hoopes) (IAC) 7/2/24
Cain, Jenny. See Pickard, Nancy
Cairns, Alison
NEW YEAR RESOLUTION (R)
9/2/25
Cake, Patrick
THE PRO–AM MURDERS (IAC)
3/3/49
CALIFORNIA THRILLER (Byrd)
(M*F) (IAC) 5/5/22; 6/3/23
Callaghan, Richard S., Jr.
L: 7/4/36; 8/1/44
Callan. See Mitchell, James
Callen, James R.
L: 7/4/46
Callendar, Newgate
L: Meyerson 1/2/48
Calvin & Hobbes
L: Banks 12/2/84-5
CAMBRIDGE THEOREM, THE (Cape)
(TAR) 13/3/75-6
CAMERA CLUE, THE (Coxe) (M*F)
6/6/30
Cameron, Lou
FILE ON A MISSING REDHEAD
(R) 3/1/40
Camp, John
THE FOOL'S RUN (TAR) 11/4/78
Campbell, Alice
THEY HUNTED A FOX (TBR)
11/4/60
Campbell, Harriette
CRIME IN CRYSTAL (TBR) 10/2/70
Campbell, Keith
GOODBYE GORGEOUS (M*F)
5/2/18
Campbell, Ramsey
THE INFLUENCE (TAR) 11/1/52

Campion, Albert. See Allingham,
Margery
CAMPION'S CAREER: A STUDY OF
THE NOVELS OF MARGERY
ALLINGHAM (Pike) (R) (MS) (IAC)
9/2/2; 10/1/67; 10/2/55
L: Deeck 9/4/47
Can We Reach Agreement?
(Christopher) 8/1/14-5
L: Christopher 8/2/43
CAN A MERMAID KILL? (Dewey)
(M*F) 6/5/42
CAN OF WORMS, A (Chase) (R)
3/6/44
Cannell, Dorothy
MUM'S THE WORD (TAR) 13/1/52
CANNIBAL WHO OVERATE, THE
(Pentecost) (IAC) 12/4/45
Cape, Tony
THE CAMBRIDGE THEOREM
(TAR) 13/3/75-6
CAPER (Andress) (M*F) 4/4/34
Caper Novels of Tony Kenrick, The
(Kelley) 2/4/3-4
CAPITAL MURDER, THE (Alner)
(TBR) 13/1/45-6
CAPITOL CRIME, A (Meyer) (IAC)
3/2/22
CAPTAIN CUT–THROAT (Carr)
(TCITC) 3/4/17
Captain Easy
The Detective Hero in the Comics
(Blom) 6/1/8-15
Captain Joseph T. Shaw's Black Mask
Scrapbook (Hagemann) 7/1/2-6
CAPTAIN NASH AND THE
HONOUR OF ENGLAND (Butler)
(M*F) 2/2/34
CAPTAIN NASH AND THE WROTH
INHERITANCE (Butler) (M*F)
2/3/46
Caputo, Rudolph R.
Obituary (Lachman) 13/4/88-9
Carakeet, David
DOUBLE NEGATIVE (R)
6/5/48; 8/2/31 & 32
Cardwell, Ann
CRAZY TO KILL (TBR) 11/4/65
Carey, Bernice
Obituary (Lachman) 12/2/70-1
CARLOS CONTRACT, THE (Phillips)
(R) 4/2/50

Carlson, P.M.
AUDITION FOR MURDER (R)
10/3/70
MURDER IN THE DOG DAYS (R)
13/2/83-4
MURDER MISREAD (R)  13/3/83-4
MURDER UNRENOVATED (R)
10/3/70
CARNAGE AT CHRISTHAVEN
(Chrysostom Society) (TAR)  12/2/58
Carnell, Jennifer
MURDER, MYSTERY AND MAY-
HEM (R) (TAR)  12/1/39; 12/2/57
CARNY KILL (Alter) (TBR)  10/3/58
CAROL IN THE DARK, A (Jordan) (R)
11/4/90
Carr, Glyn
L: Adey 3/3/60
Carr, Jess
Obituary (Lachman)  12/4/47
Carr, John Dickson. Also see Dickson,
Carter
THE BURNING COURT (IAC)
11/4/54
CAPTAIN CUT-THROAT (TCITC)
3/4/17
THE CASE OF THE CONSTANT
SUICIDES (IAC)  11/4/53
THE CROOKED HINGE (R)  1/4/41
DARK OF THE MOON (IAC) 9/3/31
THE DEAD SLEEP LIGHTLY
(Greene, ed.) (R) (IAC)
7/6/49; 8/1/26; 8/3/28; 10/2/74
THE DEMONIACS (IAC)  11/4/52
THE DOOR TO DOOM AND
OTHER DETECTIONS (Greene,
ed.) (M*F)  4/5/35
THE EMPEROR'S SNUFF-BOX
(IAC)  8/4/30
THE FOUR FALSE WEAPONS
(IAC)  11/4/52
HAG'S NOOK (R)  P/35
IN SPITE OF THUNDER (IAC)
9/1/35
(IAC)  3/2/21; 4/4/19
John Dickson Carr (1906–1977)
(Carr)  1/3/3-4
The Life and Times of Gideon Fell
(Lachman)  2/3/3-18
THE LIFE OF SIR ARTHUR
CONAN DOYLE (IAC)  10/2/59
THE LOST GALLOWS (IAC) 9/1/36

Carr, John Dickson, continued
THE MAD HATTER MYSTERY
(IAC)  11/4/52
THE MAD HATTER MYSTERY and
the Tower of London: Some
Thoughts on the Tower and a
Suggestion for the Dates (Keirans)
13/3/23-30
The Mysterious John Dickson Carr
(French)  1/6/13-4
(MS)  1/2/1
PANIC IN BOX C (IAC)  9/2/28
SCANDAL AT HIGH CHIMNEYS
(R)  5/4/32
THE SLEEPING SPHINX (M*F)
2/5/34
The Social World in Dr. Gideon
Fell's Shorter Cases (Christopher)
13/3/3-22
Some Thoughts on Peacock Feet
(Bleiler)  6/3/14-21
TO WAKE THE DEAD (IAC)
11/4/52
L: Briney 1/1/45, 1/5/56, 2/1/55;
French 1/6/58, 2/1/50, 2/2/48;
Greene 8/2/47, 10/3/77; Lachman
1/1/42; Nevins 1/4/57, 5/3/46
Carr, John "Dixon"
L: Briney 2/1/55; McSherry 2/1/52
Carr, Wooda Nicholas II
John Dickson Carr (1906–1977)
1/3/3-4
Carrel, Mark
THE EMERALD (M*F)  4/4/36
Carson, Robert
Obituary (Lachman)  7/4/23
Carter, Nick
THE COYOTE CONNECTION
(M*F)  6/1/38
SUICIDE SEAT (M*F)  4/5/32
L: Crider 6/3/47
Carter, Steven R.
Freedom and Mystery in John
Fowles' THE ENIGMA  3/5/14-6
Carvic, Heron
Little Old Ladies (Nehr)  3/4/3-7
PICTURE MISS SEETON (M*F)
1/4/38
The Singular Miss Seeton (Chouteau)
8/6/7-10
CASE IN NULLITY, A (Berckman)
(IAC)  5/2/11

Case in Point: Gorky Park (Dove)
6/4/9-11,18
CASE OF LOYALTIES, A (Wallace)
(R)                                    10/2/72
CASE OF NEED, A (Hudson) (IAC)
5/2/10
CASE OF SONIA WAYWARD, THE
(Innes) (M*F) (IAC)  2/6/35; 11/4/47
CASE OF SPIRITS, A (Lovesey) (R)
1/6/48
CASE OF THE ABSENT-MINDED
PROFESSOR, THE (Stein) (TBR)
13/3/54-5
CASE OF THE AMOROUS AUNT,
THE (Gardner) (R)              1/3/49
CASE OF THE BEAUTIFUL BEG-
GAR, THE (Gardner) (R)     1/4/54
CASE OF THE BIGAMOUS SPOUSE,
THE (Gardner) (R)             1/1/37
CASE OF THE BLONDE BONANZA,
THE (Gardner) (R)             1/2/10
CASE OF THE BOUNCING BETTY,
THE (Avallone) (R)            1/2/46
CASE OF THE BURIED CLOCK,
THE (Gardner) (R)             7/6/37
CASE OF THE CARELESS CUPID,
THE (Gardner) (R)             1/5/50
CASE OF THE CONSTANT GOD,
THE (King) (TBR)       13/2/69-70
CASE OF THE COPY-HOOK KILL-
ING, THE (Howes) (M*F)     4/4/33
CASE OF THE CONSTANT SUI-
CIDES, THE (Carr) (IAC)     11/4/53
CASE OF THE COUNTERFEIT COL-
ONEL, THE (Bush) (M*F)     1/4/39
CASE OF THE DARING DIVORCÉE,
THE (Gardner) (R)             1/3/49
CASE OF THE DOWAGER'S
ETCHINGS, THE (King) (TBR)
13/2/69-70
CASE OF THE DUBIOUS BRIDE-
GROOM, THE (Gardner) (IAC)
7/4/20
CASE OF THE FABULOUS FAKE,
THE (Gardner) (R)             1/5/51
CASE OF THE GRINNING
GORILLA, THE (Gardner) (IAC)
6/3/25
CASE OF THE HOOK-BILLED
KITES, THE (Borthwick) (R)  7/3/35
CASE OF THE HORRIFIED HEIRS,
THE (Gardner) (R)             1/3/50

CASE OF THE ICE–COLD HANDS,
THE (Gardner) (R)             1/2/45
CASE OF THE INVISIBLE THIEF,
THE (Haughey) (TBR) (R)
10/3/54; 12/1/36-7
CASE OF THE KIDNAPPED ANGEL,
THE (Cunningham) (R)       7/4/32
CASE OF THE LAME CANARY,
THE (Gardner) (IAC)          8/3/25
CASE OF THE LATE PIG, THE
(Allingham) (R) (IAC)
10/1/75; 12/1/23
CASE OF THE LAZY LOVER, THE
(Gardner) (M*F)               5/3/33
CASE OF THE LONELY HEIRESS,
THE (Gardner) (IAC)          7/4/20
CASE OF THE LUCKY LEGS, THE
(Gardner) (IAC)               13/1/29
CASE OF THE MEXICAN KNIFE,
THE (Homes) (R)               3/4/49
CASE OF THE MISCHIEVOUS
DOLL, THE (Gardner) (R)     1/2/45
CASE OF THE MISSING BRONTÊ,
THE (Barnard) (R)             8/1/26
CASE OF THE PERJURED PARROT,
THE (Gardner) (M*F)         6/6/26
CASE OF THE PHANTOM FINGER-
PRINTS, THE (Crossen) (TBR)
12/3/75-6
CASE OF THE PHANTOM FOR-
TUNE, THE (Gardner) (R)    1/3/50
CASE OF THE PLATINUM BLONDE,
THE (Bush) (R)              12/1/ 46
CASE OF THE QUEENLY CONTES-
TANT, THE (Gardner) (R)     1/5/50
CASE OF THE RELUCTANT
MODEL, THE (Gardner) (R)  1/1/37
CASE OF THE SHAPELY SHADOW,
THE (Gardner) (R)             1/1/36
CASE OF THE SLIDING POOL, THE
(Cunningham) (M*F)          5/6/35
CASE OF THE SPURIOUS SPIN-
STER, THE (Gardner) (R)     1/1/36
CASE OF THE STEPDAUGHTER'S
SECRET, THE (Gardner) (R)  1/2/45
CASE OF THE TROUBLED TRUS-
TEE, THE (Gardner) (R)     1/4/54
CASE OF THE UNCONQUERED
SISTERS, THE (Downing) (M*F)
3/4/40
CASE OF THE VAGABOND VIRGIN,
THE (Gardner) (IAC)          6/3/25

CASE OF THE VIOLENT VIRGIN,
THE (Avallone) (R)          1/2/46
CASE OF THE WORRIED WAIT-
RESS, THE (Gardner) (R)     1/4/54
CASE OF TOO MANY MURDERS,
THE (Chastain) (TAR)    12/2/59-60
CASE WITH FOUR CLOWNS (Bruce)
(R)                         10/1/82
CASE WITH NO CONCLUSION
(Bruce) (R)                 10/1/81
*Caspary, Vera*
Obituary (Lachman)          9/4/38
CASSIS...RESORT TO VENGEANCE
(Walker) (M*F)              3/6/35
Casson, Stanley
MURDER BY BURIAL (TBR)
                            10/3/62
CAST, IN ORDER OF DISAP-
PEARANCE (Brett) (M*F)      1/1/29
CASTANG'S CITY (Freeling) (R)
                            4/5/40
CASTLES BURNING (Lyons) (M*F)
                            5/1/27
CASUAL AFFAIRS (O'Donnell) (R)
                            8/6/41
CAT AND MOUSE (Gault) (TAR)
                   11/1/58; 11/2/70
CAT IN THE MANGER, A (Adamson)
(TAR)                       13/1/47
CAT WHO PLAYED BRAHMS, THE
(Braun) (R)                 9/6/35
CAT WHO PLAYED POST OFFICE,
THE (Braun) (R)             9/6/36
CAT WHO TALKED TO GHOSTS,
THE (Braun) (R)           13/1/66-7
CATALOGUE OF CRIME, A (Barzun/
Taylor) (R)                 11/4/83
Catalyst Club, The (Deeck)  11/1/7-12*
CATCH A FALLING CLOWN
(Kaminsky) (R)              7/1/40
CATCH ME: KILL ME (Hallahan)
(IAC)                       3/2/23
CATS DON'T SMILE (Olsen) (TBR)
(R)                11/2/93; 12/1/51-2
Caudwell, Sarah
THE SIRENS SANG OF MURDER
(TAR)                       12/2/58
CAUGHT DEAD IN PHILADELPHIA
(Roberts) (R)               10/4/55
CAVALIER IN WHITE, THE (Muller)
(R)                         8/4/39
CAVANOUGH QUEST, THE
(Gifford) (M*F) (R)    1/3/39 & 44

CEASE UPON THE MIDNIGHT (Troy)
(TBR)                     13/1/38-9
Cecil, Henry
TELL YOU WHAT I'LL DO (R)
                            5/5/38
CEMETERIES ARE FOR DYING
(Story) (R)                 7/5/47
*Censorship*
(MS)              8/4/3-8; 8/6/1-2
L: Breen 8/5/46; Deeck 8/5/44;
Dillon 9/1/47; Gault 8/6/49;
Lachman 8/5/43; Napier 8/5/50,
8/6/47; Traylor 8/5/43; Townsend
comments 8/5/44
CEREMONY (Parker) (M*F) (R)
                        6/3/36 & 38
Chaber, M.E. [Ken Crossen, q.v.]
ONCE UPON A CRIME (M*F) P/23
CHAIN OF CHANCE, THE (Lem)
(M*F)                       3/5/35
CHAIN REACTION (Guild) (IAC)
                            8/4/31
*Challis, Mary*
CRIMES PAST (M*F)           5/2/24
L: Breen 5/3/43; Young 5/3/44
Chamberlain, Anne
THE TALL DARK MAN (IAC)
                            8/4/31
Chambers, Dana
SOME DAY I'LL KILL YOU (R)
                            4/6/34
Chambers, Robert
THE NEON PREACHER (M*F)
                            2/3/45
Chambers, Whitman
DEAD MEN LEAVE NO FINGER-
PRINTS (TBR)                10/3/60
*Chambrun, Pierre.* See Pentecost, Hugh
Champigny, Robert
WHAT WILL HAVE HAPPENED:
A PHILOSOPHICAL AND
TECHNICAL ESSAY ON
MYSTERY STORIES (R)   5/4/28
Chance and Illogic and THE BLACK
BOX MURDER (Bleiler)        2/1/8
L: Adey 2/3/73; McCahery 2/5/55;
Wooster 2/4/55, 2/5/53
*Chandler, Raymond*
CHANDLERTOWN: THE LOS
ANGELES OF PHILIP
MARLOWE (Thorpe) (R)   8/3/33
The "I" in the Private Eye (Saylor)
                          9/1/23-7

*Chandler, Raymond,* continued
THE LADY IN THE LAKE
  (R)                    3/2/46
THE LIFE OF RAYMOND
  CHANDLER (MacShane)
  (IAC)               2/4/15
The Medical Practitioner in the
  Writings of Raymond Chandler
  (Skinner)         11/2/37-46
PHILIP MARLOWE: A CEN-
  TENNIAL CELEBRATION
  (Preiss, ed.) (TAR)     11/4/75
POODLE SPRINGS (w/Parker)
  (IAC)             11/4/49
RAYMOND CHANDLER: A
  DESCRIPTIVE BIBLIOGRAPHY
  (Bruccoli) (R)       3/6/49
RAYMOND CHANDLER AND
  FILM (Luhr) (IAC) (RM)
                7/2/24 & 30
Raymond Chandler on Film (Pross)
     1/6/3-10*; 2/3/27-31,40
Raymond Chandler on Film:
  Addendum (Shibuk)   2/4/14
RAYMOND CHANDLER
  SPEAKING (R)      1/6/45
Raymond Chandler Without His
  Knight: Contracting Worlds in
  THE BLUE DAHLIA and
  PLAYBACK (Brewer) 13/3/37-49
SELECTED LETTERS OF RAY-
  MOND CHANDLER (MacShane,
  ed.) (M*F) (IAC)  6/1/32; 10/2/58
UNKNOWN THRILLER: THE
  SCREENPLAY OF PLAYBACK
  (IAC)             9/4/35
CHANDLERTOWN: THE LOS
  ANGELES OF PHILIP MARLOWE
  (Thorpe) (R)        8/3/33
CHANGELING CONSPIRACY, THE
  (McCloy) (M*F)     1/6/38
CHARITY ENDS AT HOME (Watson)
  (M*F)            2/6/34
Charles, Hampton [James Melville, q.v.]
  ADVANTAGE MISS SEETON
  (TAR)          13/1/52-3
  MISS SEETON AT THE HELM
  (TAR)           13/1/53
*Charles, Robert*
  A CLASH OF HAWKS (M*F) P/23
  (SSC)           6/1/15*
*Charles Scribner's Crime Novel Award*
  (MS)            5/3/1

CHARLIE M (Freemantle) (M*F) (R)
         2/3/41; 4/2/50
CHARLIE'S ANGELS (Franklin)
  (M*F)           1/4/39
CHARM OF FINCHES, A (Thielen)
  (TBR)          12/3/78
CHARMING MURDER, THE (Shay)
  (R)             9/6/45
*Charter Books* (IAC)     4/4/19
*Charteris, Leslie*
  Leslie Charteris (Alexandersson/
    Hedman)       4/4/21-7
  THE SAINT AND THE TEMPLAR
    TREASURE (M*F)  3/6/31
  THE SAINT IN NEW YORK
    (R)            1/5/46
CHARTERIS MYSTERY, THE
  (Fielding) (TBR)    12/2/51
*Charyn, Jerome*
  ELSINORE (TAR)    13/3/76
*Chase, James Hadley*
  A CAN OF WORMS (R)  3/6/44
  CONSIDER YOURSELF DEAD
    (R)            2/6/40
  MY LAUGH COMES LAST
    (R)            2/3/51
  YOU MUST BE KIDDING
    (R)            3/6/44
*Chastain, Thomas*
  THE CASE OF TOO MANY
    MURDERS (TAR)  12/2/59-60
  The New Police Procedural
    (French)        2/4/17-8
  THE PICTURE PERFECT MUR-
    DERS (w/Adler) (R)  12/4/91-4
  VITAL STATISTICS (M*F)  2/3/44
*Chavasse, Paul.* See Fallon, Martin
*Chesbro, George*
  BONE (TAR)       11/4/75
  CITY OF WHISPERING STONE
    (M*F)          3/1/33
  THE COLD SPELL OF SACRED
    STONE (TAR)    11/1/53
  (IAC)             4/4/20
  JUNGLE OF STEEL AND STONE
    (TNSPE)       10/2/51
  SECOND HORSEMAN OUT OF
    EDEN (TAR)     11/4/76
  SHADOW OF A BROKEN MAN
    (R)            2/1/42
*Chesney, Kellow*
  THE VICTORIAN UNDER-
    GROUND (R)       P/34

CHESS MYSTERIES OF SHERLOCK
HOLMES, THE (Smullyan) (IAC)
4/4/18
*Chester, George Randolph*
Rogues for the New Century
(Dueren)           5/3/11-14
*Chesterton, Gilbert K.*
The Exit of Father Brown (Strøm)
13/4/42-4
THE FATHER BROWN OMNIBUS
(IAC)               7/5/26
Father Brown's Final Adventure
(Christopher)      13/4/33-41
Cheyney, Peter
DARK INTERLUDE (M*F)      P/27
URGENT HANGMAN (R)12/4/100-1
YOU CAN'T KEEP THE CHANGE
(R)                2/4/44
CHICAGO GIRL, THE (Kenrick)
(M*F)              1/2/24
CHIEF INSPECTOR'S DAUGHTER,
THE (Radley) (M*F) (R)
5/2/22; 5/4/34
Childerness, George
MURDER IN FALSE FACE (TBR)
10/3/63
Childers, Erskine
THE RIDDLE OF THE SANDS (R)
1/6/49
CHILDREN'S ZOO, THE (O'Donnell)
(R)                6/2/39
Childress, Mark
V FOR VICTOR (TAR)       11/4/76
Childs, Timothy
COLD TURKEY (M*F)        3/6/30
CHILL RAIN IN JANUARY, A
(Wright) (TAR)     12/4/59
CHILL, THE (Macdonald) (IAC) 7/4/21
*Chillingworth, Judge Curtiss Eugene*
Twice-Told Tale of Murder (Floyd)
6/1/21-6
CHINA EXPERT, THE (Delving)
(M*F)              2/1/24
CHINESE CONSORTIUM, THE
(Rilla) (M*F)      4/5/34
Chinese Detective in San Francisco, A
(Bleiler)          5/3/2-4
L: Goode 6/1/48, 6/2/48
CHINESE DOLL, THE (Tucker) (TBR)
13/4/74-5
CHINESE FIRE DRILL, THE (Wolfe)
(R)                1/2/40

Chiu, Tony
PORT ARTHUR CHICKEN (M*F)
4/2/36
CHOICE OF CRIMES, A (Egan)
(M*F)              5/2/15
Chouteau, Neysa
Ann Morice: The Deadly Serious
Business of Not Being Serious (w/
Alderson)          6/6/5-8*
The Singular Miss Seeton  8/6/7-10
CHRISTMAS STALKINGS (MacLeod,
ed.) (R)           13/4/49-50
*Christie, Agatha*
AGATHA (Tynan) (IAC)     4/1/13
THE AGATHA CHRISTIE COM-
PANION (Fitzgibbon) (IAC) 4/6/31
THE AGATHA CHRISTIE COM-
PANION: THE COMPLETE
GUIDE TO AGATHA
CHRISTIE'S LIFE AND
WORK (Sanders/Lovallo) (IAC)
8/2/21 & 32
THE AGATHA CHRISTIE CROSS-
WORD PUZZLE BOOK (IAC)
6/1/28
AGATHA CHRISTIE: FIRST LADY
OF CRIME (Keating, ed.) (R)
(IAC)              2/1/32; 2/4/16
Agatha Christie Is Still Alive and
Well (Kabatchnik)        2/6/9-10
THE AGATHA CHRISTIE MYS-
TERY (Murdoch) (R)      1/2/4
AGATHA CHRISTIE: THE ART OF
HER CRIMES (M*F) (IAC)
6/2/33; 6/3/24
THE AGATHA CHRISTIE WHO'S
WHO (Toye) (IAC)        4/6/31
AN AUTOBIOGRAPHY (IAC)4/1/13
THE BEDSIDE, BATHTUB &
ARMCHAIR COMPANION TO
AGATHA CHRISTIE (Riley/
McAllister) (R) (IAC)
4/1/43; 4/3/31
CURTAIN (R)             9/5/33
EASY TO KILL (IAC)      6/3/25
HALLOWE'EN PARTY (R)13/1/75-6
THE LIFE AND TIMES OF MISS
JANE MARPLE (Hart) (IAC)
10/2/58
THE MAN IN THE BROWN SUIT
(TBR)              13/2/63-4
THE MOUSETRAP AND OTHER
PLAYS (IAC)        3/3/18

Christie, Agatha, continued
  MURDER UNDER THE SUN
    (IAC)                          6/3/25
  THE SECRET ADVERSARY (IAC)
                                   9/2/29
  THE SEVEN DIALS MYSTERY
    (R)                            6/2/44
  SLEEPING MURDERS (R)    9/5/33
  The Solving Sixth (Sampson)  5/5/3-6
  L: Grand 2/6/45
Christie, Gene
  L:                               7/4/49
Christopher, J.R.
  Can We Reach Agreement?  8/1/14-5
  The Complexity of The Nine
    Tailors                    7/4/3-9*
  A Consummation Devoutly to Be
    Wished: Four More Collections of
    Anthony Boucher's Mysteries
                               9/2/9-19
  Ellery Queen, Sports Fan   10/3/3-24
  Father Brown's Final Adventure
                               13/4/33-41
  L: 7/2/47; 7/4/35; 8/2/43; 9/3/45;
    11/1/83; 13/2/103; 13/3/99
  The Social World in Dr. Gideon
    Fell's Shorter Cases      13/3/3-22
  Three "Unknown" Stories—Two of
    Them Unpublished—by Dorothy
    L. Sayers                 11/1/15-21
  Who Really Wrote THE G-STRING
    MURDERS?                  8/3/18, 20
  Why Isn't There a Volume of
    Dorothy L. Sayers' Letters?
                               12/4/29-33
CHRONICLES OF MARTIN HEWITT
  (Morrison) (TCITC)             3/4/17
Churchill, Jill
  GRIME AND PUNISHMENT (R)
                               13/4/95-6
Chrysostom Society
  CARNAGE AT CHRISTHAVEN
    (TAR)                        12/2/58
Chubin, Barry
  THE 13TH DIRECTORATE (TAR)
                                 11/2/65
CINDERELLA AFTER MIDNIGHT
  (Zackel) (M*F)                 5/1/23
Cinecon (RM)                   12/2/75-6
Cinevent
  1984 (RM) 8/3/30; 1985 & 1986
    (RM) 8/4/34; 1987 (RM) 9/3/36-8;
    Cinevent 20 (RM) 10/3/47; (RM)
    12/2/75-6

CINNAMON MURDER, THE (Crane)
  (M*F)                          1/5/35
CINNAMON SKIN (MacDonald)
  (M*F)                          6/6/27
CIRCLE OF FIRE (Sadler) (R)
                          1/3/47; 1/4/47
CIRCULAR STAIRCASE, THE
  (Rinehart) (R)                 1/5/38
  L: Briney 1/6/56
Cirni, Jim
  THE COME ON (TAR)       12/2/58-9
CITADEL RUN (Bishop) (TNSPE)
  (MS)              10/2/49; 12/3/7
CITY OF GLASS (Auster) (R)   9/6/38
CITY OF STRANGERS, A (Barnard)
  (TAR)                         13/1/50
CITY OF WHISPERING STONE
  (Chesbro) (M*F)                3/1/33
CITY SLEUTHS AND TOUGH GUYS
  (McCullough, ed.) (IAC)    12/2/66
Clark, Curt
  ANARCHAOS (R)                  4/3/42
Clark, Douglas
  BITTER WATER (TAR)      13/1/53-4
  DEADLY PATTERN (R)        3/3/46
  GOLDEN RAIN (R)            7/5/46
  ROAST EGGS (R) (M*F)
                          5/4/36; 5/6/36
Clark, Gail
  DULCIE BLIGH (M*F)         2/5/27
Clark, Jim
  L:                             1/2/50
Clark, Mary Higgins
  LOVES MUSIC, LOVES TO
    DANCE (TAR)              13/3/76
  MURDER ON THE AISLE (IAC)
                                 9/5/23
Clarke, Anna
  THE LADY IN BLACK (M*F) 2/5/30
  LETTER FROM THE DEAD (M*F)
    (R)                5/5/21; 6/2/38
  THIS DOWNHILL PATH (R) 5/5/33
Clarke, T(homas) E(rnest) B(ennett)
  Obituary (Lachman)        11/3/52
CLASH OF HAWKS, A (Charles)
  (M*F)                           P/23
Clason, Clyde B.
  MURDER GONE MINOAN (R)
                                 3/3/46
CLASSIC ENGLISH CRIME, A (Heald,
  ed.) (R)                    13/4/49
Cleary, Jon
  MURDER SONG (TAR)      13/1/54

- 32 -

Cleary, Maryell
Contemporary Clergy-Detectives
9/3/3-21
The Greatest Misogynist of Them All
13/4/61-5
John D. MacDonald and the Real
Murders 11/3/19-22
L: 8/4/49; 9/3/44; 9/4/47; 10/4/60;
11/3/95; 12/2/87-90; 13/2/103-4;
13/3/98
Reviews:
AUDITION FOR MURDER
(Carlson) 10/3/70
THE BATTLING PROPHET
(Upfield) 11/4/87
THE BLOODIED IVY (Golds-
borough) 12/3/95-6
BODY AND SOIL (McInerny)
11/4/85
A CAROL IN THE DARK
(Jordan) 11/4/90
THE CAT WHO PLAYED
BRAHMS (Braun) 9/6/35
THE CAT WHO PLAYED POST
OFFICE (Braun) 9/6/36
THE CAT WHO TALKED TO
GHOSTS (Braun) 13/1/66-7
THE COLLECTED SHORT
FICTION OF NGAIO
MARSH (Greene, ed.) 11/4/85
COLLOQUIUM ON CRIME
(Winks, ed.) 11/4/89
COOL REPENTANCE (Fraser)
8/1/33
THE DARK WIND (Hillerman)
10/3/66
DEAD AND DOGGONE (Conant)
13/2/88-9
DEAD BY MORNING (Simpson)
13/1/57-8
DEADLINE FOR A CRITIC
(Kienzle) 10/3/68
DEATH AND THE PREGNANT
VIRGIN (Haymon) 8/1/32
A DEATH FOR A DOCTOR
(Giroux) 11/4/90
THE DEEDS OF THE
DISTURBER (Peters) 11/4/87
DESIGN FOR MURDER (Hart)
10/3/68
A DINNER TO DIE FOR
(Dunlap) 13/1/61-2

*Cleary, Maryell,* continued
*Reviews* continued
DOUBLE NEGATIVE (Carakeet)
8/2/32
THE FALSE INSPECTOR DEW
(Lovesey) 10/3/69
A FATAL ADVENT (Holland)
13/2/89-90
THE FORTIETH BIRTHDAY
BODY (Wolzien) 13/2/86-7
A GATHERING OF SAINTS
(Lindsey) 13/2/90-1
GRIME AND PUNISHMENT
(Churchill) 13/4/95-6
HARM'S WAY (Aird) 9/6/35
HEREWITH THE CLUES
(Wheatley) 8/3/40
INK IN HER BLOOD (Martin)
11/2/98
INTO THE VALLEY OF DEATH
(Hervey) 11/4/91
THE LAST COINCIDENCE
(Goldsborough) 12/3/95
MALICE IN WONDERLAND
(Blake) 9/1/40
THE MANTRAP GARDEN
(Sherwood) 9/6/36
THE MORMON MURDERS
(Naifeh/Smith) 13/2/90-1
MRS. MEEKER'S MONEY
(Disney) 9/6/37
MRS, PRESUMED DEAD (Brett)
13/1/60-1
THE MURDER AT THE MUR-
DER AT THE MIMOSA INN
(Hess) 10/3/69
MURDER AT THE NEW YORK
WORLD'S FAIR (Dana) 9/6/37
MURDER AT THE PTA
LUNCHEON (Wolzien)
13/2/85-6
MURDER IN THE DOG DAYS
(Carlson) 13/2/83-4
MURDER MISREAD (Carlson)
13/3/83-4
MURDER UNRENOVATED
(Carlson) 10/3/70
MYSTERIUM AND MYSTERY:
THE CLERICAL CRIME
NOVEL (Spencer) 13/1/62-6
A NEW LEASH ON DEATH
(Conant) 13/2/87-8

Cleary, Maryell, continued
  Reviews continued
    POISON FOR ONE (Rhode)9/3/39
    PRECIOUS BLOOD (Haddam)
      (R)                13/4/103-4
    A QUESTION OF GUILT
      (Fyfield)            13/2/84-5
    THE RED HOUSE MYSTERY
      (Milne)                  8/5/38
    THE RETURN OF MR.
      CAMPION (Allingham)
                            13/1/58-60
    THE SANCTUARY SPARROW
      (Peters)                 8/1/33
    SATAN IN ST. MARY'S
      (Doherty)               11/4/88
    SAVARIN'S SHADOW (Goyne)
                              13/2/82-3
    SKINWALKERS (Hillerman)
                              10/3/66
    TRIAL AND ERROR (Berkeley)
                               8/6/43
    THE VEILED ONE (Rendell)
                              12/4/86-7
    A VERY PARTICULAR MUR-
      DER (Haymon)     12/4/85-6
    WARRANT FOR X (MacDonald)
                               8/4/46
    WORKING MURDER (Boylan)
                              11/4/86
    THE YELLOW ROOM
      (Rinehart)              9/4/40
Cleeve, Brian
  DARK BLOOD, DARK TERROR
    (IAC)                    3/2/23
  VICE ISN'T PERFECT (IAC) 3/2/23
Clemeau, Carol
  THE ARIADNE CLUE (MS)  6/1/1
Clergy as Detectives
  Contemporary Clergy Detectives
    (Cleary)               9/3/3-21
  MYSTERIUM AND MYSTERY:
    THE CLERICAL CRIME NOVEL
    (Spencer) (R)       12/1/33-5
  L: Cleary 11/3/95
CLIENT PRIVILEGE (Tapply)
  (TAR)                    12/4/57
Cliffhanger Press (MS)
            9/1/6; 9/2/2; 10/3/2
Clifford, Charles L.
  WHILE THE BELLS RANG (M*F)
                            5/3/30

Clinton-Baddeley, V.C.
  The Dr. Davie Novels (Bargainnier)
                             8/1/8-13
  MY FOE OUTSTRETCH'D BE-
    NEATH THE TREE (R) (M*F)
    (R)          P/39; 3/1/37; 5/5/37
  L: Adey 1/3/51; Hubin 1/3/56
CLOAK–AND–DAGGER BIBLI-
  OGRAPHY: AN ANNOTATED
  GUIDE TO SPY FICTION (Smith)
  (R)                        1/4/50
CLOCK STRIKES THIRTEEN, THE
  (Brean) (M*F)              3/4/41
CLOSE TO DEATH (Crowe) (M*F)
                             3/6/33
CLOSET BONES (Bunn) (M*F) 2/3/46
CLOSING COSTS (Bunn) (MS) 12/3/10
Closing the Gap: A Critique
  (Nieminski)          7/3/6-15,31
  L: Cook 6/3/49, 7/4/34; Goode
    7/4/49
Clouzot, Henri-Georges (RM)  6/6/24-5
Clubfoot (Dr. Adolf Grundt). See
  Williams, Valentine
CLUE IN THE MIRROR, THE
  (Morland) (TBR)         12/2/51-2
CLUE OF THE EYELASH, THE
  (Wells) (R)             12/1/56-7
CLUE OF THE JUDAS TREE, THE
  (Ford) (M*F)               6/3/31
Cluster, Dick
  RETURN TO SENDER (TAR)11/2/66
CLUTCH OF VIPERS, A (Scott)
  (M*F)                      3/6/38
COBALT (Aldyne) (R)          7/2/32
Cobb, Belton
  MURDER: MEN ONLY (TBR)
                            13/3/62-3
Cobb, Jeff
  The Detective Hero in the Comics
    (Blom)                 6/1/8-15
COCAINE AND BLUE EYES (Zackel)
  (R)                        7/5/40
Cody, Liza
  BAD COMPANY (R)            8/3/39
  DUPE (R)                   7/4/27
  HEADCASE (R)               8/4/41
Coe, Tucker [Donald E. Westlake, q.v.]
  WAX APPLE (R)                P/20
COFFIN & CO. (Simon) (TNSPE)
                            10/2/49
COFFIN COUNTRY (Stein) (M*F)
                             1/6/39

COFFIN FOR DIMITRIOS, A
(Ambler) (R)              2/4/39
COFFIN IN FASHION (Butler) (TAR)
                          13/1/51-2
Coggin, Joan
WHO KILLED THE CURATE?
(TBR)                 13/2/66-7
Cohen, Octavus Roy
THE CORPSE THAT WALKED
(R) (IAC)        1/6/54; 3/2/22
Cohen, Stephen Paul
ISLAND OF STEEL (TAR)  11/2/66
Cohn, Jan
IMPROBABLE FICTION: THE
LIFE OF MARY ROBERTS
RINEHART (IAC)        8/2/23
COIGN OF VANTAGE (McAleer)
(TAR)                 11/3/75
COLD BLOOD (Bruce) (R)    1/1/34
COLD HAND IN MINE (Aickman)
(M*F)                 2/6/31
COLD SPELL OF SACRED STONE,
THE (Chesbro) (TAR)   11/1/53
COLD TURKEY (Childs) (M*F) 3/6/30
COLD WAR FILE, THE (East) (IAC)
                          8/2/21
COLD WAR SWAP, THE (Thomas)
(IAC)                 10/3/39
Cole, Don
L:              1/5/59; 3/1/48
Cole, G.D.H. and Margaret
THE BLATCHINGTON TANGLE
(TBR)                 11/3/64
*Coles, Manning*
Crime Novelists as Writers of Chil-
dren's Fiction (Sarjeant)  12/1/5-8
(SSC)                 4/3/23*
COLLECTED SHORT FICTION OF
NGAIO MARSH, THE (Greene, ed.)
(R) (IAC) (TAR)
        11/4/85; 12/2/69; 12/3/87
*Collections*
L: Bleiler 6/4/47
*Collectors*
L: Briney 2/3/70; Broset 1/6/58;
Doerrer 2/2/51; Hedman 2/5/57;
Meyerson 1/6/57; Nehr 2/4/60;
Waterhouse 2/1/51
Collee, John
KINGSLEY'S TOUCH (IAC)  9/3/32
Collier, John
FANCIES AND GOODNIGHTS
(IAC)                 8/3/27

Collins, Anna Ashwood
DEADLY RESOLUTIONS (R)
                          12/1/38
Collins, Max Allan
THE BABY BLUE RIP-OFF (R)
                          7/1/39
BAIT MONEY (R)            1/6/50
BLOOD MONEY (R)           1/6/50
THE BROKER (R)            1/6/50
THE BROKER'S WIFE (R)     1/6/50
THE DEALER (R)            1/6/50
DYING IN THE POST-WAR
WORLD (R)             13/4/50
HARD CASH (R)      6/1/44; 6/4/40
HUSH MONEY (R)            5/6/45
KILL YOUR DARLINGS (IAC)
                          11/1/28
L:                        6/1/47
NEON MIRAGE (TAR)        11/2/66
NICE WEEKEND FOR A MURDER
(R)                   10/1/72
SCRATCH FEVER (R)         6/3/41
THE SLASHER (R)           2/1/42
TRUE DETECTIVE (R)        8/2/34
Collins, Michael
THE BLOOD-RED DREAMS (M*F)
                          2/1/27
MURDER AT WILLOW RUN (R)
                          7/5/40
THE NIGHTRUNNERS (M*F)
                          2/6/33
*Collins, Wilkie*
In the Footsteps of Wilkie Collins
(Hazen)               11/1/13-14
THE MOONSTONE (IAC)    6/6/21
COLLOQUIUM ON CRIME (Winks,
ed.) (R)              11/4/89
COMA (Cook) (R)           3/6/45
COME MORNING (Gores) (IAC) 9/4/37
COME ON, THE (Cirni) (TAR)
                          12/2/58-9
COME-ON, THE (Yorke) (M*F) 3/6/28
COMEDY OF TERRORS, A (Innes)
(IAC)                 9/4/36
COMIC CRIME (Bargainnier, ed.)
(IAC)                 10/2/56
*Comics*
The Detective Hero in the Comics
(Blom)                6/1/8-15
(MS)                  11/1/2
L: Goode 6/2/48; Goodrich 6/3/46
COMPLETE GUIDE TO SHERLOCK
HOLMES, THE (Hardwick) (IAC)
                          10/2/56

Complexity of The Nine Tailors, The
(Christopher) 7/4/3-9*
L: Christopher 8/2/43; Tolley
8/1/45, 8/2/43
COMPREHENSIVE INDEX TO
BLACK MASK, 1920–1951
(Hagemann) (IAC) 7/2/22
COMPROMISING POSITIONS
(Isaacs) (R) 3/4/43
Compton, Guy
DISGUISE FOR A DEAD
GENTLEMAN (TBR) 13/2/70-1
*Computers*
L: Hazen 10/4/59; Reynolds 7/6/46;
Townsend comments 7/3/44
CONAN DOYLE, PORTRAIT OF AN
ARTIST (Symons) (IAC) 10/2/56
Conant, Susan
DEAD AND DOGGONE (R)
13/2/88-9
A NEW LEASH ON DEATH (R)
13/2/87-8
Conaway, J.C.
THE DEADLY SPRING (R) 1/5/41
CONE OF SILENCE (Beaty) (R) 7/2/35
CONFESS, FLETCH (Mcdonald) (R)
1/5/37
CONFLICT OF INTEREST, A
(Ashford) (TAR) 13/1/49
CONJURER'S COFFIN (Cullingford)
(R) 12/1/45
Connington, J.J.
DEATH AT SWAYTHLING COURT
(TBR) 13/2/64
CONSIDER YOURSELF DEAD
(Chase) (R) 2/6/40
Constantine, K.C.
JOEY'S CASE (TNSPE) (TAR)
10/2/52; 11/2/67
ROCKSBURG RAILROAD
MURDERS (IAC) 10/1/60
Consummation Devoutly to Be Wished,
A: Four More Collections of
Anthony Boucher's Mysteries
(Christopher) 9/2/9-19
L: Christopher 9/3/45
Contemporary Clergy Detectives
(Cleary) 9/3/3-21
L: Deeck 9/4/47; West 9/4/49
*Continental Op.* See Hammett, Dashiell
*Contributors to TMF*
L: Cook 11/3/97; Kaiser 11/3/90;
Townsend comments 11/3/90

Cook, Charles K.
An Index to TMF Volumes I–V
6/5/1-40
L: 11/3/97; 13/3/94
Reviews:
BELLRINGER STREET
(Richardson) 13/3/87-8
DEAD WINTER (Tapply) 11/4/95
THE KILLING MAN
(Spillane) 12/3/91-2
THE LATIMER MERCY
(Richardson) 13/3/86-7
MISS MELVILLE REGRETS
(Smith) 12/4/78-9
MISS MELVILLE RETURNS
(Smith) 12/4/77
MRS., PRESUMED DEAD (Brett)
11/4/93
MURDER AT THE OLD
VICARAGE (McGown) 12/1/36
MURDER IN THE ENGLISH
DEPARTMENT (Minor)
11/4/94
A NICE CLASS OF CORPSE
(Brett) 11/4/93
THE SPANKING GIRLS (Brown)
11/4/92
SPY HOOK (Deighton) 12/3/89-90
SPY LINE (Deighton) 12/3/90-1
*Cook, Michael*
Closing the Gap: A Critique
(Nieminski) 7/3/6-15,31
L: 2/6/60; 3/1/54; 4/1/47; 5/2/48;
5/4/46; 6/3/49; 7/4/35
MONTHLY MURDERS: A
CHECKLIST AND CHRON-
OLOGICAL LISTING OF FIC-
TION IN THE DIGEST–SIZE
MYSTERY MAGAZINES IN THE
UNITED STATES AND
ENGLAND (MS) (M*F)
6/2/5; 6/4/37
(MS) 4/1/2
MYSTERY, DETECTIVE, AND
ESPIONAGE FICTION: A
CHECKLIST OF FICTION IN
U.S. PULP MAGAZINES, 1915–
1974 (w/Miller) (R) 11/1/75
Review: CRIME, DETECTIVE, ES-
PIONAGE, MYSTERY, AND
THRILLER FICTION & FILM
(Skene Melvin) 5/2/30

Cook, Robin
  COMA (R)           3/6/45
  SPHINX (R)         3/6/46
Cook, Thomas H.
  FLESH AND BLOOD (TAR) 11/4/77
  SACRIFICIAL GROUND (TAR)
                11/2/67
  STREETS OF FIRE (TAR)   12/2/60
COOKIE (Adkins) (TAR)   11/1/50
COOKING SCHOOL MURDERS,
  THE (Rich) (R)       7/2/38
COOL REPENTANCE (Fraser)
  (R)              8/1/33
Cooper-Clark, Diana
  DESIGNS OF DARKNESS: IN-
  TERVIEWS WITH DETECTIVE
  NOVELISTS (R)      7/5/35
  L: Huang 8/2/44
Cooper, James Fenimore
  THE WAYS OF THE HOUR
  (R)              8/1/30
Copper, Basil
  THE BIG CHILL (R)     4/6/36
  THE CURSE OF THE FLEERS (R)
  (M*F)       2/1/35; 2/3/46
  THE WEREWOLF (R)     2/4/46
COPPERFIELD CHECKLIST OF
  MYSTERY AUTHORS, THE
  (Granovetter/McCullum) (IAC)
                10/2/57
COPS AND CONSTABLES: AMER-
  ICAN AND BRITISH FICTIONAL
  POLICEMEN (MS)     9/1/7
Copyright Dates
  L: Briney 5/5/45
Corbett, James
  GALLOWS WAIT (R)   10/1/83
  MURDER WHILE YOU WAIT
  (TBR)         13/4/66-8
Cord, Talos. See MacLeod, Robert
Corey, Herbert
  CRIME AT COBB'S HOUSE
  (TBR)          13/1/38
Cork, Barry
  DEAD BALL (TAR)   11/4/77
Corley, Edward
  Obituary (Lachman)   6/3/25
Cormier, Robert
  AFTER THE FIRST DEATH
  (R)             3/6/42
  FADE (R)       12/4/82-3
  I AM THE CHEESE (R)   3/6/42
  L: Crider 4/1/43

Cornell Woolrich: The Last Years
  (Nevins) - Part I 8/5/23-8; Part II
  8/6/11-14,18; Part III 9/1/17-22; Part
  IV 9/3/25-31; Conclusion 9/6/5-30
CORNER OF PARADISE, A (Holton)
  (M*F)          2/1/22
CORNER SHOP, THE (Cadell)
  (TBR)          10/2/65
Cornwell, Bernard
  WILDTRACK (MS)     12/1/4
CORONER (Noguchi) (IAC)   8/2/24
CORPSE AT THE CARNIVAL
  (Bellairs) (TBR)     11/1/39
CORPSE DIED TWICE, THE (Frost)
  (TBR)         13/3/55
CORPSE FOR A CANDIDATE, A
  (Geller) (M*F)     4/3/39
CORPSE FOR CHRISTMAS, A (TBR)
  (Kane)         11/2/94
CORPSE ON THE DIKE, THE (van
  de Wetering) (M*F)    1/1/30
CORPSE ON THE TOWN (Roeburt)
  (TBR)        13/3/55-6
CORPSE THAT CAME BACK, THE
  (Piper) (TBR)     11/3/57
CORPSE THAT WALKED, THE
  (Cohen) (R)    (IAC) 1/6/54; 3/2/22
CORPSE WITH THE DIRTY FACE,
  THE (Walling) (M*F)   3/6/33
CORPUS CHRISTMAS (Maron)
  (TAR)         12/3/86
CORPUS DELECTABLE (Powell)
  (TBR)         11/1/46
CORRIDORS OF DEATH (Edwards)
  (R)            8/2/29
CORRIDORS OF POWER: THE
  WORLD OF JOHN LE CARRÉ
  (Wolfe) (IAC)     10/2/55
Corrigan, Mark
  (SSC)          7/4/12*
CORRUPT AND ENSNARE (Nevins)
  (M*F) (IAC)   3/1/31; 4/1/14
Cory, Desmond
  DEADFALL (R)     3/4/46
  (SSC)        4/3/23-4*
COST OF SILENCE, THE (Yorke)
  (R)            4/5/41
COTTAGE SINISTER (Patrick) (TBR)
  (R)      11/1/44; 12/1/52-3
COTTON COMES TO HARLEM
  (Himes) (R)     13/1/68-70
Cotton, Gunston. See Grayson, Rupert

COUNTRY AND FATAL (Bagby)
(M*F)                                4/4/41
COUNTRY-HOUSE BURGLAR, THE
(Gilbert) (IAC)                 11/1/23
COUNTRY KIND OF DEATH, A
(McMullen) (R)                  4/2/46
COUNTRY OF THE HEART (Smith)
(TAR)                               10/4/46
Coupe, Stuart
L:                                    13/3/97-8
COURTESY OF DEATH, THE
(Household) (R)                 4/3/45
Courtier, S.H.
An Australian Bibliomystery
(Tolley)                         10/3/37-8
LIGNY'S LAKE (R)            5/5/42
Courtine, Robert J. (compiler)
MADAME MAIGRET'S RECIPES
(IAC)                             10/4/52
COVER HER FACE (James) (TCITC)
(IAC)               3/4/16; 9/1/34
COWLED MENACE, THE (Hawkins)
(M*F)                                2/4/35
Cox, Randy
L:                         3/1/54; 3/2/52
Cox, Richard
SAM 7 (R)                       2/3/50
Cox, William R.
DEATH ON LOCATION (M*F)
                                       3/2/38
Obituary (Lachman)        11/1/36
Coxe, George Harmon
THE CAMERA CLUE (M*F)
                                       6/6/30
THE GLASS TRIANGLE (M*F)
                                       1/5/36
Obituary (Lachman)          8/2/25
WOMAN AT BAY (M*F)       1/2/26
Coyne, John
HOBGOBLIN (R)               6/6/39
COYOTE CONNECTION, THE (Carter)
(M*F)                                6/1/38
L: Crider 5/1/36
CRACK IN THE TEACUP, THE
(Gilbert) (IAC)                 11/1/23
CRACKING OF SPINES, A (Lewis)
(R) (M*F)       4/5/38; 6/3/43; 6/5/45
Craig, Alisa. (Charlotte MacLeod, q.v.)
A PINT OF MURDER (M*F)
                                       4/4/42
CRAIG AND THE MIDAS TOUCH
(Benton) (M*F)                  P/29

Craig, Mary Shura
Obituary (Lachman)         13/1/31
Craig, Peter. See Benton, Kenneth
Craigie, Gordon
(SSC)                          4/3/24-5*
Crais, Robert
STALKING THE ANGEL
(R)                               12/1/44
Cramer, Susan
L:                                    2/1/55
Crane, Caroline
THE PEOPLE NEXT DOOR (TAR)
                                       11/2/67
Crane, Frances
THE CINNAMON MURDER (M*F)
                                       1/5/35
CRAZY MURDER SHOW (Scott)
(TBR)                             11/4/69
CRAZY TO KILL (Cardwell) (TBR)
                                       11/4/65
Cream of Queen, The (Floyd): (June,
August 1986) 8/4/27-8; (Oct. 1986)
8/6/31-2; (Nov.–Dec., Jan.-Feb.)
9/1/31-2; (March–April) 9/2/20;
(May–June) 9/3/27-8
Creasey, John. Also see Deane,
Norman; Marric, J.J.
THE BEAUTY QUEEN KILLER
(IAC)                             10/3/42
Crime Novelists as Writers of
Children's Fiction (Sarjeant)
                                       13/2/36-42
DEATH OF A POSTMAN (IAC)
                                       10/3/42
THE EXTORTIONERS (R)    5/6/47
THE GELIGNITE GANG (IAC)
                                       10/3/42
(SSC)          4/2/12-3*; 4/3/24-5*
THE TOFF AMONG THE
MILLIONS (M*F)            3/2/36
WAIT FOR DEATH (IAC)     8/5/30
CREATIVE KIND OF KILLER, A
(Early) (IAC)                    8/6/34
Creed, Will
DEATH COMES GRINNING (TBR)
                                       10/3/60
CREEP, THE (Dodson) (IAC)    4/6/33
Crews, Gary
Reviews:
A SLEEPING LIFE (Rendell)
                                       3/2/46
THE UNSPEAKABLE (Ransome)
                                       3/3/45

Crider, Bill
CURSED TO DEATH (TNSPE)
  (IAC)          10/2/50; 10/4/53
DEAD ON THE ISLAND (TAR)
                    13/3/77
DEATH ON THE MOVE (TAR)
                    11/4/78
DYING VOICES (TAR)      12/2/59
Here Comes the Judge: The "Nero"
  Award             3/6/8
L: 2/4/58; 2/5/56; 2/6/44; 3/1/55;
  3/2/50; 3/3/52; 3/4/57; 4/1/43;
  4/3/50; 5/1/36; 5/2/41; 5/4/39;
  5/5/44; 5/6/53; 6/3/47
ONE DEAD DEAN (TAR)    11/2/68
Reviews:
  ACT OF LOVE (Lansdale)  5/3/36
  ANARCHAOS (Clark)      4/3/42
  ANGEL (Brewer)         5/6/47
  ATHABASCA (MacLean)    4/5/40
  THE BAG MAN (McAuliffe)
                         5/5/40
  BEST SELLER (Bocca)    6/6/35
  BEYOND THE PRIZE (Denning)
                         3/3/43
  BLOODLIST (Elrod)    12/3/93-5
  BLUE LEADER (Wager)    5/5/40
  THE HOG MURDERS
    (DeAndrea)           3/6/47
  KICK START (Rutherford) 3/3/43
  KIKI (Gill)            3/6/48
  KILMAN'S LANDING (Judson)
                         2/5/40
  A MADNESS OF THE HEART
    (Neely)              3/3/42
  MIKE DIME (Fantoni)    6/1/43
  MY BROTHER, THE DRUG-
    GIST (Kaye)          3/6/48
  THE ORGANIZATION
    (Anthony)            3/4/47
  PAGODA (Phillips)      3/1/39
  THE TENTH COMMANDMENT
    (Sanders)            4/5/39
  TEXAS WIND (Reasoner)  4/6/38
  TWOSPOT (Pronzini/Wilcox)
                         2/6/36
  WILSON'S GOLD (Tippette)
                         4/3/42
SHOTGUN SATURDAY NIGHT
  (IAC) (R)        10/1/63; 10/2/72
TOO LATE TO DIE (IAC) (R)
                    8/5/29; 8/6/39

CRIME AND MYSTERY: THE 100
  BEST BOOKS (Keating) (IAC) (R)
                    10/2/52; 11/1/71
CRIME AND PUZZLEMENT (Treat)
  (R)             6/5/50; 7/4/33
CRIME AT COBB'S HOUSE (Corey)
  (TBR)               13/1/38
CRIME CONDUCTOR, THE
  (MacDonald) (TBR)   13/3/56-7
CRIME, DETECTIVE, ESPIONAGE,
  MYSTERY, AND THRILLER
  FICTION & FILM: A COMPRE-
  HENSIVE BIBLIOGRAPHY OF
  CRITICAL WRITING THROUGH
  1979 (Skene Melvin) (R)    5/2/30
  The Skene Melvin Bibliography
    (Albert)            5/3/5-10
  L: Breen 5/2/46
Crime Fiction in Kenya (Tolley)
                      10/2/25-8
CRIME FICTION, 1749-1980: A
  COMPREHENSIVE BIBLIOG-
  RAPHY (Hubin) (IAC) (R)
                    8/2/21; 9/3/40
  L: Hubin 5/1/39
CRIME IN CRYSTAL (Campbell)
  (TBR)               10/2/70
Crime Novelists as Writers of Children's
  Fiction (Sarjeant)
  Manning Coles         12/1/ 5-8
  John Creasey          13/2/36-42
  Freeman Wills Crofts  12/3/67-9
  Cyril Hare            12/4/39-42
  Laurence Meynell      13/1/23-6
  Dorothy L. Sayers     13/4/53-60
  Sir Basil Thomson     13/3/31-6
  Clifford Witting      12/2/37-9
  L: Adey 13/3/102-3
Crime Novels of Harold R. Daniels,
  The (Kelley)          3/4/13-5
CRIME OF ONE'S OWN, A
  (Grierson) (TCITC)     3/4/16
CRIME OF THE CENTURY, THE
  (Amis) (TAR)         12/2/54-5
CRIME ON THE CUFF (Weiner)
  (TBR)               11/3/62
Crime Story in Sweden, The (Blom)
                      7/5/16-25
Crime Writers Congress
  A Report on The Third (Hedman)
                      5/6/10-2
CRIMES PAST (Challis) (M*F)  5/2/24

CRIMSON JOY (Parker) (TAR)
11/1/65; 11/2/77
Crisp, N.J.
THE LONDON DEAL (R)    3/4/47
THE ODD JOB MAN (R)    4/1/30
Crispin, Edmund
THE GLIMPSES OF THE MOON
(R) (M*F)    3/2/47; 5/1/20
THE MOVING TOYSHOP (R) 2/1/43
CROC' (James) (R)    1/3/45
Crofts, Freeman Wills
INSPECTOR FRENCH'S
GREATEST CASE (IAC)    9/1/35
SIR JOHN MAGILL'S LAST
JOURNEY (R)    P/10
Cronin, George
DEATH OF A DELEGATE (M*F)
3/6/38
Crook, Arthur. See Gilbert, Anthony
CROOKED HINGE, THE (Carr)
(R)    1/4/41
CROOKED WOOD (Underwood)
(M*F)    3/3/36
Cropper, Michael
L:    3/4/57
Reviews:
DEATH OF A LAKE (Upfield)
3/4/50
MAN OF TWO TRIBES
(Upfield)    3/4/51
THE MOUNTAINS HAVE A
SECRET (Upfield)    3/4/51
MURDER MUST WAIT
(Upfield)    3/4/51
THE SALAMANDER (West)
3/5/44
WINGS ABOVE THE DIA-
MANTINA (Upfield)    3/4/51
Crosby, John
Obituary (Lachman)    13/3/69
Crosby, Lee
TOO MANY DOORS (TBR) 13/3/62
Cross, Amanda
THE JAMES JOYCE MURDER
(IAC)    13/1/27-8
NO WORD FROM WINIFRED (R)
8/5/37
THE QUESTION OF MAX (R)
2/5/44
SWEET DEATH, KIND DEATH
(R)    8/2/37
CROSS PURPOSES (Thomas) (R)
2/6/41

CROSS THAT PALM WHEN I
COME TO IT (Southcott) (R)    5/2/38
Crossen, Ken. Also see Chaber, M.E.
THE CASE OF THE PHANTOM
FINGERPRINTS (TBR)    12/3/75-6
Will the Real Ken Crossen Please
Stand Up (Thorpe)    1/2/5-10*
L: Crider 2/6/44
CROSSWORD MYSTERY, THE
(Gillespie) (M*F)    5/5/21
Crowe, John
CLOSE TO DEATH (M*F)    3/6/33
WHEN THEY KILL YOUR WIFE
(M*F)    1/6/38
CROWING HEN, THE (Davis)
(M*F)    3/2/40
CROWN COURT (Follett) (M*F) 2/6/32
Crozier, John
MURDER IN PUBLIC (TBR) 11/4/68
Crumley, James
DANCING BEAR (R)   7/6/41; 8/1/34
THE LAST GOOD KISS (M*F)
3/3/31
Crystal-Ball Stories (Strøm)   12/3/47-52
CRYSTAL BLUE PERSUASION,
THE (Philbrick) (TNSPE)    10/2/49
CRYSTAL CLEAR CASE, THE
(Head) (M*F)    2/3/43
CUBAN INFERNO (Victor) (IAC)
6/3/22
Cuddy, John Francis. See Healy,
Jeremiah
Cullingford, Guy
CONJURER'S COFFIN (R)    12/1/45
CUMBERLAND DECISION, THE
(Silverman) (M*F)    2/3/47
Cumberland, Marten
THE KNIFE WILL FALL (M*F)
5/2/16
Cunningham, A.B.
The Greatest Misogynist of Them All
(Cleary)    13/4/61-5
MURDER WITHOUT WEAPONS
(M*F)    3/2/40
Cunningham, E.V.
THE CASE OF THE KIDNAPPED
ANGEL (R)    7/4/32
THE CASE OF THE SLIDING
POOL (M*F)    5/6/35
Cunningham, Major "Brains." See
Thorne, E.P.
CUP OF DEATH, A (Thomson)
(TAR)    10/4/46

CUPID (Reid) (TAR)          13/2/48
CURIOSITY OF MR. TREADGOLD,
  THE (Williams) (TBR)       11/4/61
Curmudgeon in the Corner, The
  (Loeser)       3/2/3-12,20; 3/4/16-8
CURSE OF THE FLEERS, THE
  (Copper) (R) (M*F)    2/1/35; 2/3/46
CURSED TO DEATH (Crider)
  (TNSPE) (IAC)     10/2/50; 10/4/53
CURTAIN (Christie) (R)         9/5/33
CURTAIN FALL (Dewhurst) (R) 7/4/31
CURSES! (Elkins) (TAR)       11/4/79
Curtis, Mike
  THE SAVAGE WOMEN (R)   1/5/41
Curtiss, Elizabeth
  NINE DOCTORS AND A
    MADMAN (TBR)        12/4/65-6
Curtiss, Ursula
  THE MENACE WITHIN (IAC) (R)
                    3/2/24; 3/5/42
Cushing, Louise E.
  MURDER WITHOUT REGRET
    (TBR)               11/2/85
Cushman, Dan
  OPIUM FLOWER (M*F)       P/25
Cussler, Clive
  NIGHT PROBE (M*F)        6/5/44
  RAISE THE TITANIC! (R)   1/4/44
CUTTER AND BONE (Thornburg)
  (R)                    1/4/43
CYPHER, THE (Gordon) (M*F) 2/4/32

# D

DAFFODIL AFFAIR, THE (Innes)
  (IAC)                  8/4/31
Dahl, Roald
  Obituary (Lachman)      13/1/31
DAISY DUCKS, THE (Boyer) (R)
                         9/1/43
Dale, Alzina Stone
  THE OUTLINE OF SANITY
    (IAC)                7/2/25
Dalton, Moray
  THE BODY IN THE ROAD
    (TBR)                11/4/64
Daly, Carroll John
  THE ADVENTURES OF SATAN
    HALL (TNSPE)         10/2/49
  In Defense of Carroll John Daly
    (Mertz)             2/3/19-22*
  MURDER FROM THE EAST
    (R)                  2/6/40
  L: Meyerson 2/6/48

Daly, Elizabeth
  ARROW POINTING NOWHERE
    (R)                   P/34
  DEADLY NIGHTSHADE (R)   P/33
  DEATH AND LETTERS (M*F)
                          5/5/25
D'Amato, Barbara
  THE HANDS OF HEALING MUR-
    DER (IAC) (M*F) (R)
                5/1/17; 5/2/21; 6/4/18
DAN TURNER, HOLLYWOOD
  DETECTIVE (Bellem) (R)   8/2/35
Dana, Freeman [Phoebe Atwood
    Taylor, q.v.]
  MURDER AT THE NEW YORK
    WORLD'S FAIR (R)       9/6/37
DANCE CARD, THE (Feegel)
  (R)                     6/5/48
DANCE HALL OF THE DEAD
  (Hillerman) (IAC)       11/1/23
DANCER'S DEBT (Lutz) (R)  10/4/57
DANCERS IN MOURNING
  (Allingham) (IAC)        8/3/25
DANCING BEAR (Crumley) (R)
                  7/6/41; 8/1/34
DANCING MEN, THE (Hubbard)
  (R)                     5/5/38
DANGER BY MY SIDE (MacKinnon)
  (R)                     3/4/49
DANGER IN PARADISE (Fleischman)
  (M*F)                   5/4/25
DANGER, THE (Francis) (R)  8/2/37
DANGER WITHIN, THE (Gilbert)
  (IAC)                  11/3/47
DANGEROUS CONCEITS (Moore)
  (TAR)                  11/3/81
DANGEROUS DAVIES, THE LAST
  DETECTIVE (Thomas) (IAC) 6/6/20
DANGEROUS FUNERAL (McMullen)
  (R)                     4/2/45
DANGEROUS HORIZONS (Sampson)
  (MS)                   13/1/2
Daniels, Harold R.
  The Crime Novels of Harold R.
    Daniels (Kelley)      3/4/13-5
Daniels, Les
  THE BLACK CASTLE (R)    2/4/46
Dannay, Frederic. Also see Queen,
    Ellery
  Obituary (Lachman)       6/6/49
Darby, Ken
  THE BROWNSTONE HOUSE OF
    NERO WOLFE (R)        7/6/32
  L: Samoian 8/2/48; Scott 8/3/48;
    Shine 8/1/42; White 8/1/42

DARK BLOOD, DARK TERROR
(Cleeve) (IAC)                3/2/23
DARK CRIMES, GREAT *NOIR*
FICTION (Gorman, ed.) (R) 13/4/48-9
DARK FRONTIER, THE (Ambler)
(TAR)                        13/1/48-9
DARK INTERLUDE (Cheyney)
(M*F)                          P/27
DARK OF THE MOON (Carr)
(IAC)                         9/3/31
DARK PROPHECY (Alan) (TBR)
                             11/4/62
DARK SIDE OF GENIUS, THE: THE
LIFE OF ALFRED HITCHCOCK
(Spoto) (R) (IAC)       7/2/31; 7/5/27
DARK WIND, THE (Hillerman) (R)
(IAC)        6/4/43; 10/3/66; 12/1/24
DARKNESS AT PEMBERLEY
(White) (IAC)                 2/5/3
DARKNESS FALLS (Schneider)
(IAC)                        11/3/49
DAS PHANOMEN SIMMEL: ZUR
REZEPTION EINES BEST SELLER-
AUTHORS UNTER SCHULEM
UND IM LITER-ATURUNTER-
RICHT (Weber) (R)            7/5/44
DASHIELL HAMMETT: A DE-
SCRIPTIVE BIBLIOGRAPHY
(Layman) (R)                 3/6/49
DASHIELL HAMMETT TOUR, THE
(Herren) (IAC)        7/2/25; 13/4/86
*Dast* (Swedish magazine) (MS)     5/3/1
The History and Activities of Mystery
Fans in Sweden (and Scandinavia)
(Hedman)                 3/4/12,15
L: Seeger 2/6/50, 3/2/57
Datesh, John Nicholas
THE JANUS MURDER (M*F) 3/5/40
DAUGHTER OF TIME, THE (Tey)
(IAC)                         8/6/35
Davenport, John, and Dylan Thomas
THE DEATH OF THE KING'S
CANARY (TBR)            12/2/44-5
*David, Thayer*
L: Harwood 3/4/60
DAVIDSON CASE, THE (Rhode)
(IAC)                         8/5/29
*Davidson, Muriel*
Obituary (Lachman)            8/1/21
*Davie, Dr. R.V.* See Clinton-Baddeley,
V.C.
Davis, Dorothy Salisbury
SCARLET NIGHT (M*F)      4/4/39

Davis, Frederick C. Also see Ransome,
Stephen
ANOTHER MORGUE HEARD
FROM (TBR)              13/3/52-3
THE DEADLY MISS ASHLEY
(M*F)                         1/1/28
Davis, Gordon. See Hunt, E. Howard
Davis, Hank
Mr. and Mrs. North, and Mr. and
Mrs. Lockridge          1/1/21-6
Davis, Kenn
DEAD TO RIGHTS (R)           5/6/44
Davis, Lindsey
SHADOWS IN BRONZE (R)
                            13/4/101-2
SILVER PIGS (R)
                    12/1/40-1; 12/4/83-4
Davis, Means
MURDER WITHOUT WEAPON
(TBR)                        10/2/66
Davis, Mildred
THREE MINUTES TO MIDNIGHT
(R)                           4/1/29
*Davis, Norbert*
THE ADVENTURES OF MAX
LATIN (TNSPE)               10/2/49
Sorry, John D., But... (Apostolou)
                            11/3/15-8
Davis, Reginald
THE CROWING HEN (M*F) 3/2/40
Davis, Tech
TERROR AT COMPASS LAKE
(TBR)                       12/4/66-7
*Davison, Gilderoy*
(SSC)                       5/3/20-1*
*Dawson, Harry D.*
The Fathers and Sons of John Le
Carré                       5/3/15-7
Le Carré's Spy Novels  (w/Banks)
                            2/5/22-5*
L: Banks 2/5/51
DAY OF WRATH (Valin) (R)    7/4/32
DAY SEVEN (Bickham) (TAR) 11/1/51
*Dayland, Dr. Nancy*
Doctor Wonderful (Sampson)
                            5/6/13-8*
DAYS OF MISFORTUNE (Stein) (R)
                              1/6/52
*de la Bath, Hubert Bonisseur.* See
Bruce, Jean
*de la Torre-Bueno, Theodore*
Obituary (Lachman)          13/4/89

*de la Torre, Lillian*
  DETECTIONS OF DR. SAM:
    JOHNSON (IAC)            8/3/27
  "Dr. Sam: Johnson and Monboddo's
    Ape Boy" (IAC)          8/4/33
  DR. SAM: JOHNSON, DETECTOR
    (IAC)                   8/3/27
*De Noux, O'Neill*
  GRIM REAPER (R)          10/3/75
  "Tell It Like It Was": An Interview
    with O'Neill De Noux (Skinner)
                           13/2/5-17*
DEAD AND DOGGONE (Conant)
  (R)                      13/2/88-9
DEAD AND NOT BURIED (Prescott)
  (R)                      9/5/46
DEAD ARE DISCREET, THE (Lyons)
  (M*F)                    P/29
DEAD BALL (Cork) (TAR)    11/4/77
DEAD BY MORNING (Simpson)
  (R)                      13/1/57-8
DEAD EASY FOR DOVER (Porter)
  (R)                      4/1/31
DEAD IN THE MORNING (Yorke)
  (M*F)                    4/2/40
DEAD IN THE WATER (Wood)
  (R)              7/6/31; 8/1/37
DEAD IS THE DOOR-NAIL (Haggard)
  (TBR)                    11/2/94
DEAD LETTER (Valin) (R) (M*F)
                     5/6/46; 6/6/26
DEAD LION (Bonett) (IAC)   6/4/30
DEAD LOW TIDE (MacDonald)
  (M*F)                    1/3/40
DEAD MAN CONTROL (Reilly) (TBR)
  (R)             11/3/64; 12/1/543-4
DEAD MAN'S HANDLE (O'Donnell)
  (R)                      8/6/41
DEAD MAN'S MUSIC (Bush)
  (TBR)                    11/2/85
DEAD MATTER (Frimmer) (M*F)
                           6/5/44
DEAD MEN LEAVE NO FINGER-
  PRINTS (Chambers) (TBR)  10/3/60
DEAD MR. NIXON (White/Scott)
  (R)                      3/2/43
DEAD OF THE NIGHT (Rhode)
  (R)                      9/6/43
DEAD OF WINTER, THE (Allegretto)
  (TAR)                    12/2/54
DEAD ON CUE (Morice) (R)   8/6/45
DEAD ON THE ISLAND (Crider)
  (TAR)                    13/3/77

DEAD ON TIME (Keating) (TAR) (R)
                   12/3/83; 13/3/89-91
DEAD PIGEON ON BEETHOVEN
  STREET (Fuller) (M*F)    P/25
DEAD RECKONING (Llewellyn)
  (TAR)                    11/1/57
DEAD RUN (Foxx) (M*F)      2/4/34
DEAD RUN (Lockridge) (R)
                     P/36; 1/1/28
DEAD SEED, THE (Gault) (IAC) 9/5/28
DEAD SIDE OF THE MIKE, THE
  (Brett) (R)              5/2/28
DEAD SLEEP LIGHTLY, THE (Carr)
  (Greene, ed.) (R) (IAC)
            7/6/49; 8/1/26; 8/3/28; 10/2/74
DEAD TO RIGHTS (Davis) (R)  5/6/44
DEAD TO RITES (Angus) (IAC) 4/3/32
DEAD UPON THE STICK (Upton)
  (R)                      8/5/34
DEAD WINTER (Tapply) (R)   11/4/95
DEADFALL (Cory) (R)        3/4/46
DEADFALL (Laumer) (R)      5/5/43
DEADFALL (Pronzini) (R)    8/5/39
DEADLIGHT (Roy) (R)        2/5/42
DEADLINE FOR A CRITIC (Kienzle)
  (R)                      10/3/68
DEADLINE FOR DESTRUCTION
  (Leonard) (TBR)          11/4/62
DEADLINE FOR FINAL ART (Adkins)
  (MS) (TAR)       12/3/8-9; 13/1/47-8
DEADLOCK (Paretsky) (R)    8/2/36
DEADLY CLIMATE (Barth)
  (TAR)                    11/2/64
DEADLY DAMES, THE (Douglas)
  (M*F)                    1/3/42
Deadly Edges of the Gay Blade
  (Alderson)               7/3/23-8*
  L: White 7/4/47
DEADLY EXCITEMENTS:
  SHADOWS AND PHANTOMS
  (Sampson) (MS)           11/3/2
DEADLY HONEYMOON (Block)
  (IAC)                    8/4/30
DEADLY KITTEN, THE (Brown)
  (R)                      3/2/47
DEADLY MISS ASHLEY, THE
  (Davis) (M*F)            1/1/28
DEADLY NIGHTSHADE (Daly)
  (R)                      P/33
DEADLY PATTERN (Clark)
  (R)                      3/3/46
DEADLY PETARD (Jeffries)
  (R)                      7/6/42

DEADLY RESOLUTIONS (Collins)
(R)                              12/1/38
DEADLY SPRING, THE (Conaway)
(R)                               1/5/41
DEAD-NETTLE (Hilton) (M*F)  2/5/26
DEAL OF THE CENTURY, THE
(Martin) (M*F)                1/5/33
DEALER, THE (Collins) (R)    1/6/50
Dean, Amber
SNIPE HUNT (M*F)            3/4/40
Dean, Gregory
MURDER ON STILTS (R)       9/5/41
*Dean, Robert George*
Obituary (Lachman)          11/4/55
ON ICE (R)                  10/1/83
Dean, S.F.X.
BY FREQUENT ANGUISH
(R)                           7/5/45
Dean, Spencer
PRICE TAG FOR MURDER
(R)                           9/6/43
DeAndrea, William L.
THE HOG MURDERS (R) (IAC)
                    3/6/47; 11/3/48
KILLED IN THE RATINGS (IAC)
(TAR)       5/6/30; 9/1/33; 11/2/68
THE LUNATIC FRINGE (M*F)
                              5/1/24
*Deane, Norman* [John Creasey, q.v.]
(SSC)           6/1/15*; 7/4/12-3*
DEATH AFTER BREAKFAST
(Pentecost) (M*F)            5/2/20
DEATH AMONG THE ANGELS
(Putre) (TAR)             13/2/47-8
DEATH & CHICANERY (MacDonald)
(R)                           3/4/50
DEATH AND LETTERS (Daly)
(M*F)                         5/5/25
DEATH AND THE CHASTE AP-
PRENTICE (Barnard) (TAR)
                          13/1/50-1
DEATH AND THE GOOD LIFE
(Hugo) (R) (M*F)     5/2/27; 5/3/31
DEATH AND THE NIGHT
WATCHES (Bell) (TCITC)       3/4/17
DEATH AND THE PREGNANT
VIRGIN (Haymon) (R)          8/1/32
DEATH AT CHARITY'S POINT
(Tapply) (R)                  8/3/36
DEATH AT CRANE'S COURT
(Dillon) (TBR)            13/3/57-8
DEATH AT SWAYTHLING COURT
(Connington) (TBR)         13/2/64

DEATH AT THE BAR (Marsh) (R)
(IAC)              2/1/40; 4/4/20
DEATH AT THE CUT (Kiker)
(TAR)                        11/3/71
DEATH AT THE OPERA (Mitchell)
(R)                           2/5/42
DEATH AT YEW CORNER, THE
(Forrest) (M*F)               5/2/24
DEATH BED (Greenleaf) (M*F) 6/6/28
DEATH BEFORE DYING, A (Wilcox)
(TAR)                        12/4/59
DEATH BY WATER (Innes) (R)   P/31
DEATH CAP (Thompson) (M*F) 3/1/37
DEATH CATCHES UP WITH MR.
KLUCK (Xantippe) (TBR)    11/2/92
DEATH COMES GRINNING (Creed)
(TBR)                        10/3/60
*Death, Definitions of*
When Is This Stiff Dead?
(Thompson/Banks)      2/6/11-16
L: Nevins 3/2/59
DEATH DEMANDS AN AUDIENCE
(Reilly) (TBR) (R)    12/1/55; 11/4/68
DEATH DISTURBS MR. JEFFERSON
(Hocking) (TCITC)             3/2/11
DEATH DROP (Gill) (R)         5/4/34
DEATH FOR A DOCTOR, A (Giroux)
(R)                          11/4/90
DEATH GOES ON SKIS (Spain)
(M*F)                         1/6/40
DEATH GOES SKIING (Schier)
(IAC)                         4/3/32
DEATH HAS DEEP ROOTS (Gilbert)
(IAC)                        11/3/47
DEATH IN A MILLION LIVING
ROOMS (McGerr) (TBR)      11/4/58
DEATH IN A SLEEPING CITY
(Wainwright) (R)              7/4/34
DEATH IN A SMALL SOUTHERN
TOWN (McKinney) (MS)         9/5/2
DEATH IN ALBERT PARK (Bruce)
(M*F)                         4/2/35
DEATH IN CHINA, A (Hiaasen/
Montalbano) (IAC)         11/4/47
DEATH IN CONNECTICUT (Linzee)
(M*F)                         1/5/33
DEATH IN DONEGAL BAY (Gault)
(R)                           8/3/46
DEATH IN ECSTASY (Marsh)
(R)                           2/1/37
DEATH IN FASHION (Babson)
(IAC)                         9/5/27

DEATH IN GENTLE GROVE (Allen)
(M*F)                                    P/29
DEATH IN HIGH HEELS (Brand)
(R)                                      10/1/77
DEATH IN THE BLACKOUT
(Gilbert) (R)                            9/5/42
DEATH IN THE CHANNEL
(Anderson) (M*F)                         3/2/36
DEATH IN THE MORNING (Radley)
(R)                                      5/2/31
DEATH IN THE RAIN (Parrish)
(IAC)                                    11/3/49
DEATH IN THE ROUND (Morice)
(R)                                      5/5/36
DEATH IS A FRIEND (MacKenzie)
(M*F)                                    1/5/34
DEATH IS LIKE THAT (Spain)
(R)                                      2/4/44
DEATH LOCKED IN (Adey/Greene,
eds.) (IAC)                              9/5/23
DEATH MEETS 400 RABBITS (Stein)
(M*F)                                    5/1/27
DEATH, MY DARLING DAUGH-
TERS (Stagge) (M*F)                      2/4/32
DEATH NOTES (Rendell) (M*F) 5/6/38
DEATH OF A BANKER (Wynne)
(TCITC)                                  3/2/11
DEATH OF A DELEGATE (Cronin)
(M*F)                                    3/6/38
DEATH OF A DISSENTER (Lamb)
(TBR)                                    13/4/81-2
DEATH OF A DOLL (Lawrence)
(TBR)                                    11/2/84
DEATH OF A DON (Shaw)
(M*F)                                    6/1/38
DEATH OF A FAVORITE GIRL
(Gilbert) (R)                            7/1/42
DEATH OF A GOSSIP (Beaton)
(R)                                      13/1/72-4
DEATH OF A HOLLOW MAN
(Graham) (TAR) (R)
                              12/3/81; 13/2/81-2
DEATH OF A LAKE (Upfield)
(R)                                      3/4/50
DEATH OF A LOW-HANDICAP
MAN (Ball) (M*F)                         3/2/36
Death of a Movie Detective (Obituary)
(Lachman)                                8/3/29-30
Death of a Mystery Writer (Obituaries)
(Lachman)
6/1/29-30; 6/3/25-6; 6/4/33; 6/6/49;
7/1/35; 7/2/25-6; 7/4/23; 7/5/29-30;
9/3/33-5; 9/4/38-9; 9/5/28; 11/1/36-7;
11/3/52-5; 11/4/55-6; 12/1/28-9;
12/2/70-2; 12/4/47-9; 13/1/30-4;
13/2/58; 13/3/69-73; 13/4/88-94

Death of a Mystery Writer's Friend
(Obituary) (Lachman)                     8/3/29
DEATH OF A NURSE (McBain)
(R)                                      1/4/44
DEATH OF A PERFEFCT MOTHER
(Barnard) (M*F)                          5/6/38
DEATH OF A PERFECT WIFE
(Beaton) (R)                             13/1/72-4
DEATH OF A POSTMAN (Creasey)
(IAC)                                    10/3/42
DEATH OF A SALESPERSON AND
OTHER UNTIMELY EXITS
(Barnard) (TAR) (IAC)  12/2/56 & 68
DEATH OF A SPINSTER (Duncombe)
(R)                                      9/4/43
DEATH OF A THIN-SKINNED
ANIMAL (Alexander) (M*F) (R)
                              2/4/36; 2/5/35
DEATH OF AN AD MAN (Eichler)
(R)                                      9/5/40
DEATH OF AN AIRMAN (Sprigg)
(TBR)                                    12/3/79-80
DEATH OF AN EXPERT WITNESS
(James) (R) (M*F)            2/2/36; 2/3/47
DEATH OF AN OLD GIRL
(Lemarchand) (IAC)                       4/4/19
DEATH OF AN OUTSIDER (Beaton)
(R)                                      13/1/72-4
DEATH OF MR. DODSLEY (Ferguson)
(TBR)                                    13/2/74-5
DEATH OF THE KING'S CANARY,
THE (Thomas/Davenport) (TBR)
                              12/2/44-5
DEATH ON A QUIET DAY (Innes)
(IAC)                                    13/4/83-4
DEATH ON ACCOUNT (Yorke)
(R)                                      6/1/42
DEATH ON DEMAND (Hart)
(IAC)                                    12/4/46
DEATH ON LOCATION (Cox)
(M*F)                                    3/2/38
DEATH ON THE ENO (Mackay)
(M*F)                                    6/1/36
DEATH ON THE LIMITED (Denbie)
(R)                                      P/38
DEATH OUT OF THIN AIR (Towne)
(TCITC)                                  3/4/17
DEATH PAINTS THE PICTURE
(Lariar) (TBR)                           11/1/43
DEATH PLAYS SOLITAIRE
(Goldman) (TBR)                          11/1/43
DEATH ROLE (Llewellyn) (MS)
                                         12/1/2

- 45 -

DEATH SCENE (Suyker) (R)    6/5/50
DEATH STALK (Langley) (M*F)
                                3/6/27
DEATH TAKES A DIVE (Heath)
  (TBR)                    11/3/63
DEATH THUMBS A RIDE (Lilly)
  (TBR)                    13/4/78-9
DEATH TO DRUMBEAT (Lane)
  (TBR)                    13/3/50-1
DEATH TRAPS (Strahan) (TBR)
                           13/1/37-8
DEATH TRICK (Stevenson) (IAC)
                                9/1/33
DEATH UNDER PAR (Law) (M*F)
  (R)                      5/3/32 & 39
DEATH UNDER SAIL (Snow)
  (IAC)                         3/3/49
DEATH WALKS IN EASTREPPS
  (Beeding) (IAC)          5/5/17
DEATH WEARS A RED HAT
  (Kienzle) (R)            4/2/41
DEATH WEARS A WHITE
  GARDENIA (Popkin) (R)    12/1/55-6
DEATH WISH (Garfield) (IAC) 11/4/51
DEATH'S SWEET SONG (Adams)
  (M*F)                         2/2/35
DEATHBITE (Maryk/Monahan)
  (R)                      4/2/43
DECEIT AND DEADLY LIES
  (Bandy) (M*F)            3/3/33
DECKARE OCH THRILLERS PA
  SVENSKA, 1864–1973
  Sweden's Commitment to Mystery
  Fiction (Bleiler)        2/5/7-8
DECOYS (Hoyt) (M*F)        5/2/14
Deduction in Duplicate (Mosier)
                           7/2/19-21,30
Deeck, William F.
  A.E. Martin's Pel Pelham: Spruiker
    Detective             9/5/3-6*
  The Backward Reviewer (column)
    10/2/61-70; 10/3/53-64;
    11/1/38-49; 11/2/83-95;
    11/3/57-70; 11/4/57-71;
    12/2/41-52; 12/3/70-80;
    12/4/61-72; 13/1/35-46;
    13/2/59-75; 13/3/50-64; 13/4/66-82
  Blow and Manciple: The Dottering
    Detectives            10/1/55-60*
  Boardinghouse Novels: A Preliminary
    Checklist             11/3/3-13*
  The Catalyst Club       11/1/7-12*

Deeck, William F., continued
  Five Star Mysteries: A Tentative
    Checklist             11/2/17-23*
  Further Gems from the Literature
    8/6/27-30; 9/1/28-30,27; 9/2/21-3;
    9/4/32-4; 9/6/31-4; 10/3/32-36;
    11/4/29-34; 13/2/29-35
  The Honorable Charlie Mortdecai: An
    Oxymoron              9/3/22-6
  Index to The Mystery Fancier
    Volume 6: 10/4/61-84; Volume 7:
    10/4/85-104; Volume 8: 10/3/81-
    104; Volume 9: 10/2/85-104;
    Volume 10: 11/1/85-104; Volume
    11: 12/1/69-104; Volume 12:
    13/1/89-104
  L: 7/4/42; 7/6/43; 8/1/38; 8/5/44;
    9/1/45; 9/2/46; 9/4/47; 9/5/48;
    10/1/98; 10/2/78; 10/3/80; 11/3/96;
    12/2/81-2; 13/1/87-8; 13/3/93-4
  Miss Julia Tyler: Detective Manqué
                           13/1/7-22*
  (MS)                     10/2/1
  Reviews:
    THE ALBATROSS MURDERS
      (Jones)              9/5/44
    THE BACH FESTIVAL
      MURDERS (Bloch)      9/5/40
    THE BEDSIDE COMPANION TO
      CRIME (Keating)      12/3/100-1
    A BLUNT INSTRUMENT
      (Heyer)              10/1/85
    BUT DEATH RUNS FASTER
      (McGivern)           10/1/89
    THE CASE OF THE LATE PIG
      (Allingham)          10/1/75
    THE CASE OF THE PLATINUM
      BLONDE (Bush)        12/1/46
    CASE WITH FOUR CLOWNS
      (Bruce)              10/1/82
    CASE WITH NO CONCLUSION
      (Bruce)              10/1/81
    A CATALOGUE OF CRIME
      (Barzun/Taylor) (R)  11/4/83
    CATS DON'T SMILE (Olsen)
                           12/1/51-2
    THE CHARMING MURDER
      (Shay)               9/6/45
    THE CLUE OF THE EYELASH
      (Wells)              12/1/56-7
    CONJURER'S COFFIN (Culling-
      ford)                12/1/45

*Deeck, William F.*, continued
*Reviews* continued

COTTAGE SINISTER (Patrick)
12/1/52-3
DEAD AND NOT BURIED
(Prescott)          9/5/46
DEAD MAN CONTROL
(Reilly)          12/1/53-4
DEAD OF THE NIGHT (Rhode)
9/6/43
DEATH DEMANDS AN
AUDIENCE (Reilly)    12/1/55
DEATH IN HIGH HEELS
(Brand)          10/1/77
DEATH IN THE BLACKOUT
(Gilbert)          9/5/42
DEATH OF A SPINSTER
(Duncombe)          9/4/43
DEATH OF AN AD MAN
(Eichler)          9/5/40
DEATH WEARS A WHITE
GARDENIA (Popkin) 12/1/55-6
THE ELEVEN OF DIAMONDS
(Kendrick)          12/1/48
F.O.B. MURDER (Hitchens)
10/1/86
FORTY WHACKS (Homes)
10/1/87
GALLOWS WAIT (Corbett)
10/1/83
THE GRAMMARIAN'S
FUNERAL (Acheson)    9/2/39
I COULD MURDER HER
(Lorac)          9/3/43
I SPY, YOU DIE (Brown)   10/1/79
THE KINK (Brock)      12/1/44
THE LADY IN THE MORGUE
(Latimer)          9/4/42
THE LEADEN BUBBLE
(Branson)          10/1/78
THE MASTER MYSTERY
(Small)          9/6/44-5
THE MILKMAID'S MILLIONS
(Austin)          9/5/39
MOTTO FOR MURDER
(Mace)          12/1/49-50
MR. CAMPION AND OTHERS
(Allingham)          10/1/75
MR. CAMPION: CRIMINOL-
OGIST (Allingham)    10/1/75
MURDER BY THE CLOCK
(King)          12/1/48-9

*Deeck, William F.*, continued
*Reviews* continued

MURDER IN CHURCH (Hughes)
9/5/43
MURDER IS A GAMBLE
(Barns)          9/4/44
MURDER LOVES COMPANY
(Mersereau)          9/4/41
MURDER OF A NYMPH
(Neville)          12/1/50-1
MURDER OF A SUICIDE
(Ferrars)          9/5/41
MURDER ON EVERY FLOOR
(Demarest)          12/1/46-7
MURDER ON STILTS (Dean)
9/5/41
'MURDER WILL OUT'
(Binyon)          12/1/31-3
MUSEUM PIECE NO. 13
(King)          9/5/44
MYSTERIES (Library of
Congress)          12/1/35
MYSTERIUM AND MYSTERY
(Spencer)          12/1/33-5
MYSTERY AT FRIAR'S
PARDON (MacDonald) 9/5/37
MYSTERY INDEX (Olderr) 9/6/41
ON ICE (Dean)          10/1/83
ONE ANGEL LESS (Roden)
12/1/54-5
THE ONE THAT GOT AWAY
(McCloy)          9/5/45
OUT OF THE WOODPILE
(Bailey)          13/2/91-3
PERSONS UNKNOWN
(MacDonald)          9/5/38
PICK YOUR VICTIM (McGerr)
10/1/89
PRICE TAG FOR MURDER
(Dean)          9/6/43
THE PROFESSOR KNITS A
SHROUD (Van Arsdale) 9/6/47
PUZZLE IN PORCELAIN
(Gresham)          10/1/84
THE PUZZLE OF THE SILVER
PERSIAN (Palmer)    9/4/43
THE SCREAMING KNIFE
(Vardeman)          12/4/73-6
SEE YOU AT THE MORGUE
(Blochman)          10/1/76
THE SHUDDERS (Abbot)  9/5/38
SKULDOGGERY (Flora)  9/4/42

*Deeck, William F.,* continued
  *Reviews* continued
    SOMETHING TO HIDE
      (MacDonald)      10/1/88
    A VARIETY OF WEAPONS
      (King)      12/1/47-8
    WALKING SHADOW
      (Offord)      12/1/51
    WHERE THERE'S SMOKE
      (Sterling)      9/2/40
    Thomas Polsky's Curtains Trilogy
      12/4/21-33*
    Vulcan Publications: An Annotated
      Checklist      12/3/53-6*
    L: Lachman 10/1/98; Phillips 10/3/78;
      Samoian 10/1/97
DEEDS OF THE DISTURBER, THE
  (Peters) (R)      11/4/87
DEEP DIVE (Hornig) (TNSPE)
      10/2/51; 11/1/55
DEEP PURPLE (Allbeury) (TAR)
      13/1/48
Degeneration of Donald Hamilton, The
  (Kelley)      1/6/11-12
*Deighton, Len*
  THE BILLION DOLLAR BRAIN
    (R)      2/1/38
  HORSE UNDER WATER (R) 2/5/44
  The Len Deighton Series (Banks/
    Dawson)      3/1/11-3*
  The Quiller Report (Banks/Dawson)
      4/1/8-11*
  SPY HOOK (TAR) (R)
      11/4/78; 12/3/89-90
  SPY LINE (TAR) (R)
      12/2/60-1; 12/3/90-1
  SPY SINKER (TAR)      13/3/77
  (SSC)      4/3/24*
  SS-GB (R)      3/4/50
  XPD (M*F)      5/4/27
*Delacorte, George T.*
  Obituary (Lachman)      13/3/72
Delahaye, Michael
  STALKING-HORSE (TAR)  11/1/53
Dell "Map Back" Checklist, 1–300
  (Butler)      1/2/17-22*
  L: Williams 1/5/57
*Dell, Mary*
  (SSC)      6/1/15*; 7/4/12-3*
Delman, David
  THE NICE MURDERERS (M*F)
      2/1/22

DELORME IN DEEP WATER (Lister)
  (TBR)      13/2/72-3
Delving, Michael
  THE CHINA EXPERT (M*F) 2/1/24
  THE DEVIL FINDS WORK (R)
      1/6/50
  DIE LIKE A MAN (R)  P/37; 1/6/50
  SMILING, THE BOY FELL DEAD
    (R)      1/6/50
Demarest, Ann
  MURDER ON EVERY FLOOR
    (TBR) (R)    11/1/45; 12/1/46-7
DeMarr, Mary Jean
  Reviews:
    COMPROMISING POSITIONS
      (Isaacs)      3/4/43
    THE EXPENDABLE MAN
      (Hughes)      5/2/31
    IT NEVER RAINS IN LOS
      ANGELES (Flowers)    4/1/30
    A PARADE OF COCKEYED
      CREATURES (Baxt)    3/4/42
    THREE MINUTES TO
      MIDNIGHT (Davis)    4/1/29
*Deming, Richard.* Also see Franklin,
  Max
  Obituary (Lachman)      8/2/25
  SHE'LL HATE ME TOMORROW
    (M*F)      P/28
DEMON IN MY VIEW, A (Rendell)
  (M*F)      1/3/37
DEMONIACS, THE (Carr) (IAC)
      11/4/52
Demouzon
  MOUCHE (M*F)      5/2/21
*Dempsey and Makepeace*
  A Gun-Toting Yankee (Skinner)
      8/6/25-6,30
*Dempsey, Sister Mary Teresa.* See
  O'Marie, Sister Carol Ann
*Denbie, Roger*
  DEATH ON THE LIMITED (R) P/38
  L: Shibuk 2/2/55
Denning, Mark
  BEYOND THE PRIZE (R)    3/3/43
*Dennis, Robert C.*
  Obituary (Lachman)      8/1/21
Dentinger, Jane
  MURDER ON CUE (R)    7/6/40
Denton, Frank
  L:      7/3/43
DEPART THIS LIFE (Ferrars) (R)
      8/1/17

DER KRIMINALROMAN [THE DE-
TECTIVE NOVEL] (Nusser) (R)
7/3/40
Derby, Mark
AFRAID IN THE DARK (R)  6/2/40
Derrick, Lionel
DIVINE DEATH (M*F)  2/1/26
DESIGN FOR MURDER (Hart)
(R)  10/3/68
DESIGN FOR MURDER (Kummer)
(TBR)  12/2/50-1
DESIGN IN EVIL (King) (TBR) 10/3/64
DESIGNS OF DARKNESS: INTER-
VIEWS WITH DETECTIVE NOV-
ELISTS (Cooper-Clark) (R)  7/5/35
DESTROYER #31, THE: THE HEAD
MEN (Sapir/Murphy) (M*F)  2/4/33
DESTROYER 37, THE: BOTTOM
LINE (Sapir/Murphy) (M*F)  3/6/31
Detection by Other Means (Sampson)
7/1/7-17*
DETECTIONARY (IAC)  4/6/33
DETECTIONS OF DR. SAM: JOHN-
SON (de la Torre) (IAC)  8/3/27
Detective Hero in the Comics, The
(Blom)  6/1/8-15
Detective Stories Vs. Thrillers
L: Cleary 11/3/95
DETECTIVE IN HOLLYWOOD, THE
(Tuska) (R)  2/4/38
L: Albert 2/3/64
Detective Story Magazine
(IAC)  11/1/30
The Murder Cases of Pinklin West
(Sampson)  8/1/3-7
Peterman from the Old School
(Sampson)  5/4/2-4
Pirates in Candyland (Sampson)
6/3/7-13*
The Solving Sixth (Sampson) 5/5/3-6
DETECTIVE WORE SILK DRAW-
ERS, THE (Lovesey) (R)  6/2/42
DETOUR AT NIGHT (Endore)
(TBR)  10/2/69
Deverell, William
NEEDLES (R)  6/1/45
DEVIANT BEHAVIOR (Emerson)
(TAR)  11/1/57; 11/2/69
DEVICES AND DESIRES (James)
(TAR)  12/3/82-3
DEVIL FINDS WORK, THE (Delving)
(R)  1/6/50

DEVIL IN A BLUE DRESS (Mosley)
(MS)  12/1/3-4
DEVIL IN THE BELFRY, THE
(Thorndike) (TBR)  13/2/73-4
DEVIL'S WORK (Yorke) (R)
7/5/49-7/6/50
Devine, Dominic
SUNK WITHOUT A TRACE
(M*F)  4/2/31
Dewey, Thomas B.
CAN A MERMAID KILL?
(M*F)  6/5/42
THE TAURUS TRAP (M*F)  P/24
Dewhurst, Eileen
CURTAIN FALL (R)  7/4/31
Dexter, Colin
SERVICE OF ALL THE DEAD
(M*F)  4/3/35
THE SILENT WORLD OF NICH-
OLAS QUINN (M*F)  2/2/34
Diamond, I.A.L.
Obituary (Lachman)  10/3/45
DIAMOND STUD (Singer) (M*F)
1/2/28
DIAMONDS IN THE DUMPLINGS
(Shane) (M*F)  3/4/39
Dibdin, Michael
THE TRYST (TAR)  12/2/61
Dick, Philip K.
Obituary (Lachman)  6/3/26
Dickens, Charles
The Dilemma of Datchery
(Bleiler)  4/4/7-15
Edwin's Mystery and Its History
(Fisher)  4/5/6-8
THE MYSTERY OF EDWIN
DROOD and Harvard Magazine
L: Bleiler 7/4/40
(MS)  7/3/1
Sunshine and Shadow (Fisher)
11/4/11-28
To Be and Not To Be (Bleiler)
6/6/3-4
L: Bleiler 4/6/42, 7/4/40; Fisher
5/1/48; Nieminski 4/6/40
Dickenson, Fred
KILL 'EM WITH KINDNESS
(TBR)  12/4/63
Obituary (Lachman)  9/3/34
Dickinson, Peter
THE LAST HOUSEPARTY (R)
8/2/39
WALKING DEAD (M*F)  2/5/27

Dickson, Carter [John Dickson Carr, q.v.]
  FATAL DESCENT (w/Rhode)
    (IAC)                          9/5/26
  THE GILDED MAN (IAC)    11/4/53
  A GRAVEYARD TO LET (IAC)
                                13/1/29-30
  HE WOULDN'T KILL PATIENCE
    (IAC)                        11/4/53
  THE READER IS WARNED (IAC)
                                  11/4/53
  THE WHITE PRIORY MURDERS
    (IAC)                          6/4/31
DICTIONARY OF CONTEMPORARY
  SLANG, THE (Thorne) (IAC)
                                13/4/84-5
DIE AFTER DARK (Pentecost)
    (M*F)                          1/3/38
DIE LIKE A MAN (Delving) (R)
                            P/37; 1/6/50
DIE, LITTLE GOOSE (Alexander)
    (M*F)                          2/1/30
DIEHARD, THE (Jackson) (M*F) 2/1/25
Dietrich, Robert. See Hunt, E. Howard
Dilemma of Datchery, The (Bleiler)
                                  4/4/7-15
  L: Saxon 4/5/45; Toole 4/5/46
Dillon, Eilís
  DEATH AT CRANE'S COURT
    (TBR)                       13/3/57-8
Dillon, Perry
  L:           2/6/51; 3/2/60; 9/1/47
  Review: THE GLIMPSES OF THE
    MOON (Crispin)               3/2/47
DiMarco, Jefferson. See Disney, Doris
  Miles
DIMENSIONS OF DETECTIVE
  FICTION (Landrum/Browne/Browne,
  eds.) (R)                       1/4/50
DIMINISHING RETURNS (Withers)
    (TBR)                       12/2/45-6
Dinelli, Mel
  Obituary (Lachman)            13/4/89
DINNER TO DIE FOR, A (Dunlap)
    (R)                         13/1/61-2
"Diplomat"
  MURDER IN THE STATE
    DEPARTMENT (TBR) 12/2/49-50
    (SSC)                        4/3/25*
DIRTY LAUNDRY (Hamil) (M*F)
                                  3/5/37
DIRTY TRICKS (Way) (M*F)     2/4/31

DISAPPEARANCE OF ROGER TRE-
  MAYNE, THE (Graeme) (R)    1/2/41
DISCRETION (Linzee) (R)        3/3/47
DISGUISE FOR A DEAD GENTLE-
  MAN (Compton) (TBR)    13/2/70-1
DISTANT DANGER (van de Wetering,
  ed.) (IAC)                    11/1/32
Disney, Doris Miles
  MRS. MEEKER'S MONEY (R)
                                  9/6/37
  Three Gentle Men (DeMarr) 3/3/5-14
  WINIFRED (IAC)              10/4/51
DIVINE DEATH (Derrick) (M*F) 2/1/26
DO YOU KNOW THIS VOICE?
  (Berckman) (IAC)             7/5/26
DOCTOR, LAWYER... (Wilcox)
  (M*F)                         2/1/23
Doctor Wonderful (Sampson) 5/6/13-8*
  L: Schultheis 6/2/48
DOCTOR'S WIFE, THE (Avallone)
  (R)                           3/1/43
Documents in the Case, The (Letters)
  1/1/39-47; 1/2/47-54; 1/3/51-8;
  1/4/55-60; 1/5/53-60; 1/6/55-60;
  2/1/50-60; 2/2/41-61; 2/3/57-76;
  2/4/49-61; 2/5/45-60; 2/6/43-60;
  3/1/46-62; 3/2/50-62; 3/3/50-62;
  3/4/53-62; 3/5/46-50,16; 4/1/37-48;
  4/2/54-62; 4/3/47-40; 4/4/49-50;
  4/5/44-9; 4/6/40-50; 5/1/30-50;
  5/2/39-50; 5/3/41-6; 5/4/38-46;
  5/5/44-8; 5/6/49-53; 6/1/46-50;
  6/2/48-50; 6/3/44-50; 6/4/45-9;
  6/6/40-9; 7/1/43-5; 7/2/40-50;
  7/3/43-50; 7/4/35-50; 7/6/43-9;
  8/1/38-46; 8/2/42-9; 8/3/47-50,24;
  8/4/48-50; 8/5/40-50; 8/6/47-50;
  9/1/45-50; 9/2/45-9; 9/3/44-9;
  9/4/46-49; 9/5/47-9; 9/6/49;
  10/1/91-103; 10/2/78-84; 10/3/77-80;
  10/4/58-60; 11/3/85-103; 12/1/58-68;
  12/2/81-103; 12/4/102-4; 13/1/79-88;
  13/2/94-104; 13/3/93-104
  L: Doerrer 2/6/54
Dodson, Daniel
  Obituary (Lachman)            13/1/31
Dodson, Susan
  THE CREEP (IAC)              4/6/33
Doerrer, David H.
  Index of Books Reviewed in TMF:
    Volume Two - 3/2/26-9; Volume
    Three 4/2/3-7; Volume Four
    5/2/3-5; Volume Five 6/1/2-7

*Doerrer, David H.,* continued
  Lachman's Reviews in TMF Volumes
    Two Through Four        5/2/6-9
    L: 2/2/51, 56; 2/3/63; 2/4/49; 2/6/54;
    3/1/50; 3/3/55; 3/4/62; 4/1/44;
    4/2/54*; 4/5/47; 5/1/37; 6/1/46;
    7/1/46
  Miss Marple She Isn't      2/6/7-8
  Reviews:
    THE BIBLIOGRAPHY OF
      CRIME FICTION 1749–1975
      (Hubin)              3/3/48
    THE PARROT MAN (Middle-
      miss)                2/2/39
    L: Doerrer 4/5/47; LaPorte 4/3/47
DOGTOWN (IAC) (Lambert) 13/3/66-7
Doherty, P. C.
  SATAN IN ST. MARY'S (R) 11/4/88
Dold, Gaylord
  BONEPILE (IAC)          11/1/24
*Dolson, Hildegarde*
  Little Old Ladies (Nehr)   3/4/3-7
Dominic, R.B. [Emma Lathen, q.v.]
  THE ATTENDING PHYSICIAN
    (M*F)                   4/2/39
Donahue, Jack
  THE LADY LOVED TOO WELL
    (M*F)                   2/5/28
Donald Goines: An Appreciation
  (Blom)                  9/4/17-24
DONAVAN'S DELIGHT (Brown)
  (R)                     3/6/47
DON'T CRY FOR ME (Gault) (IAC)
                          5/4/19
Doolittle, Jerome
  BODY SCISSORS (TAR)  13/3/77-8
Doom with a View (Film and TV
    reviews) (Lachman)
  10/1/64-6; 11/4/54-5; 12/1/25-28;
  12/2/69-70; 13/3/73-4; 13/4/86-8
  L: Fellows 13/1/80-1
Doon, Greg
  Review: THE ANAGRAM DETEC-
    TIVES (Schier)        3/2/44
DOOR TO DOOM AND OTHER
  DETECTIONS, THE (Carr) (Greene,
  ed.) (M*F)              4/5/35
DOORBELL RANG, THE (Stout)
  (R)                    13/2/77-8
Doran, Michael
  L: 2/2/43; 2/4/56; 2/5/48; 2/6/46;
  3/1/50; 3/2/62; 3/4/54

DOROTHY AND AGATHA (Larsen)
  (R)                    13/4/102
DOROTHY L. SAYERS (Brabazon)
  (R)                    6/1/39
DOROTHY L. SAYERS: A LITERARY
  BIOGRAPHY (Hone) (R)   3/5/45
DOROTHY SAYERS: A REFERENCE
  GUIDE (Hall) (IAC)     7/2/23
DOROTHY L. SAYERS: NINE
  LITERARY STUDIES (Hall)
  (IAC)                  6/3/23
*Dossier, The* (MS)        6/2/5
DOUBLE NEGATIVE (Carakeet)
  (R)             6/5/48; 8/2/31
DOUBLE OR QUITS (Fair) (M*F)
                          1/2/23
Douglas, Malcolm
  THE DEADLY DAMES (M*F)
                          1/3/42
  PURE SWEET HELL (M*F)   P/29
Dove, George N.
  Case in Point: Gorky Park
                       6/4/9-11,18
  THE POLICE PROCEDURAL
    (IAC)                 7/2/23
  Reviews:
    THE BUTTERFLY HUNTER
      (van de Wetering)   7/3/42
    CASUAL AFFAIRS (O'Donnell)
                          8/6/41
    END-GAME (Gilbert)    6/6/36
    LIGHTNING (McBain)    8/3/45
    THE MAINE MASSACRE (van
      de Wetering)        3/2/49
    TANTALIZING LOCKED ROOM
      STORIES (Asimov/Waugh/
      Greenberg, eds.)    7/2/33
  The Rural Policeman in American
    Mystery Fiction       8/4/21-3
  The Weevil in Bencurd, Or, The
    Cop Abroad         2/6/17-19,16
  William MacHarg's O'Malley:
    Transitional Cop      8/6/14-8
Dove, George N. and Helenhill
  Review: THE CASE OF THE
    ·HOOK-BILLED KITES
    (Borthwick)           7/3/35
DOVER AND THE CLARET
  TAPPERS (Porter) (TAR)  12/4/52
*Dover Publications* (MS) (IAC)
                       2/2/2,62; 5/4/19
  L: Bleiler 2/1/60; Portser 2/3/72

*Dowling, Father Roger.* See McInerny,
Ralph
DOWN IN THE VALLEY (Pierce)
(TAR)                          12/4/51-2
Downing, Todd
THE CASE OF THE UNCON-
QUERED SISTERS (M*F)  3/4/40
Downing, Warwick
THE GAMBLER, THE MINSTREL,
AND THE DANCE HALL
QUEEN (M*F)               1/1/30
*Doyle, Arthur Conan.* Also see
Holmes, Sherlock
CONAN DOYLE, PORTRAIT OF
AN ARTIST (Symons) (IAC)
10/2/56
Encore! (McSherry)       12/1/9-22
THE LIFE OF SIR ARTHUR
CONAN DOYLE (Carr)
(IAC)                       10/2/59
THE RETURN OF SHERLOCK
HOLMES (IAC)           9/2/29
THE VALLEY OF FEAR (IAC)
3/2/21
Dr. Davie Novels of V.C. Clinton-
Baddeley, The (Bargainnier) 8/1/8-13
DR. JEKYLL AND MR. HOLMES
(Estleman) (M*F)          4/2/34
DR. JOE BELL: MODEL FOR
SHERLOCK HOLMES (Liebow)
(MS) (IAC)           6/1/1; 7/2/23
DR. SAM: JOHNSON, DETECTOR
(de la Torre) (IAC)          8/3/27
*Drachman, Theodore S., M.D.*
Obituary (Lachman)       11/1/37
DRAGON HUNT (Garrity) (M*F)
4/2/38
Drake, Jake
ROGUE AGENT (TAR)      13/3/78
*Drake, Kerry*
The Detective Hero in the Comics
(Blom)                   6/1/8-15
DREADFUL HOLLOW, THE (Blake)
(R)                         5/4/33
DREAM DETECTIVE, THE (Rohmer)
L: Briney 2/2/45
DREAM OF DANGER (Nolder)
Encore! (McSherry)       12/1/9-22
Drew, Bernard A.
ATTIC REVIVALS (MS)      7/3/4
*Drood, Edwin.* See Dickens, Charles
DROWNED HOPES (Westlake)
(TAR)                      12/4/58

*Drummond, Bulldog*
(SSC)                       4/5/22*
Drummond, Ivor
THE NECKLACE OF SKULLS
(M*F)                      1/6/39
Drummond, John Keith
MASS MURDER (TAR)     13/3/78-9
Drummond, June
JUNTA (TAR)               12/2/62
SLOWLY THE POISON (M*F)
2/1/29
DuBois, Theodora
THE LISTENER (IAC)        3/2/24
Dueren, Fred
The Great Merlini        4/4/28-32
L:           4/3/49; 5/3/44; 7/3/50
Reviews:
THE AGATHA CHRISTIE
COMPANION (Sanders/
Lovallo)                 8/2/32
THE BUCK PASSES FLYNN
(Mcdonald)               6/1/40
THE BUTTERFLY HUNTER
(van de Wetering)       7/3/42
THE CASE OF THE MISSING
BRONTË (Barnard)        8/1/26
C.B. GREENFIELD: THE
TANGLEWOOD MURDERS
(Kallen)                  5/5/41
COBALT (Aldyne)          7/2/32
DEAD TO RIGHTS (Davis) 5/6/44
DEADLY PETARD (Jeffries)
7/6/42
FÊTE FATALE (Barnard)    8/5/34
FLETCH AND THE WIDOW
BRADLEY (Mcdonald)    6/1/40
FOR OLD CRIME'S SAKE
(Ames)                   7/5/44
THE GRAIL TREE (Gash)   8/3/35
THE GREAT BRITISH DETEC-
TIVES (Goulart, ed.)     7/4/30
THE HAMBURG SWITCH
(Ross)                    4/4/46
INTRODUCING C.B. GREEN-
FIELD (Kallen)            5/5/41
THE LURE (Picano)        4/4/46
MOTOR CITY BLUES (Estleman)
4/4/46
MURDER, MAESTRO, PLEASE
(Ames)                   7/5/43
MURDER POST-DATED
(Morice)                 8/2/40
THE OLD DICK (Morse)    6/1/40

Dueren, Fred, continued
  Reviews continued
    THE OLD DIE YOUNG
      (Lockridge)                5/3/39
    THE RIGHT TO SING THE
      BLUES (Lutz)               8/4/44
    THE SEVEN OF CALVARY
      (Boucher)                  5/5/40
    UBER SIMENON [ON
      SIMENON] (Schmolders/Strich,
      eds.)                      7/4/30
    UNHAPPY RETURNS
      (Lemarchand)               7/5/44
    WATSON'S CHOICE (Mitchell)
                                 5/3/39
  Rogues for the New Century
                                 5/3/11-14
Düerrenmatt, Friedrich
  THE JUDGE AND HIS
    HANGMAN (R)                  7/2/39
  Obituary (Lachman)             13/1/31-2
  L: Goode 7/3/47
Duff, Howard
  Obituary (Lachman)             12/4/49
Dukeshire, Theodore P.
  The Books of Geoffrey Homes
                                 3/3/19-21*
  The Books of Nicholas Luard    4/1/12
  Kim Philby, Master Spy in Fact and
    Fiction                      3/6/14
  Reviews:
    AGAINST THE WIND
      (Household)                3/2/49
    ALL EXITS BARRED (Portway)
                                 2/3/52
    BLACK AURA (Sladek)          3/4/48
    BUILD MY GALLOWS HIGH
      (Homes)                    3/4/49
    A CAN OF WORMS (Chase)
                                 3/6/44
    THE CARLOS CONTRACT
      (Phillips)                 4/2/50
    CHARLIE M (Freemantle)       4/2/50
    CONSIDER YOURSELF DEAD
      (Chase)                    2/6/40
    CROSS PURPOSES (Thomas)
                                 2/6/41
    DANGER BY MY SIDE
      (MacKinnon)                3/4/49
    DEADLIGHT (Roy)              2/5/42
    DEATH & CHICANERY
      (MacDonald)                3/4/50
    THE ENIGMA (Barak)           3/6/44

Dukeshire, Theodore P., continued
  Reviews continued
    ESCAPE (MacDonald)           3/4/50
    FINGER OF FIRE (Braine)      3/6/45
    GOODNIGHT AND GOOD-BYE
      (Harris)                   4/2/50
    HERE COMES CHARLIE M
      (Freemantle)               4/2/50
    THE HUMMING BOX
      (Whittington)              3/4/49
    A KILLING IN ROME
      (Rostand)                  2/3/51
    KYD FOR HIRE (Harris)        2/3/52
    THE LAST KILL (Wells)        4/1/30
    THE LUCKY STIFF (Rice)       2/5/43
    THE MAN WHO MURDERED
      GOLIATH (Homes)            2/5/43
    THE MAN WHO MURDERED
      HIMSELF (Homes)            2/5/42
    THE MIRABILIS DIAMOND
      (Odlum)                    2/5/43
    MURDER AT CAMBRIDGE
      (Patrick)                  2/5/43
    MURDER FROM THE EAST
      (Daly)                     2/6/40
    MY LAUGH COMES LAST
      (Chase)                    2/3/51
    THE ODD JOB MAN (Crisp)
                                 4/1/30
    OUT OF CONTROL (Liddy)
                                 3/6/44
    THE PIOUS AGENT (Braine)
                                 2/3/52
    THE STIFF UPPER LIP (Israel)
                                 3/2/49
    SS-GB (Deighton)             3/4/50
    THE SUNDAY PIGEON
      MURDERS (Rice)             2/5/43
    TO RUN A LITTLE FASTER
      (Gardner)                  2/6/41
    WOLFSBANE (Thomas)           3/4/49
    YOU MUST BE KIDDING
      (Chase)                    3/6/44
  Robert Rostand and Mike
    Locken                       2/4/4,14
  Vladimir Gull                  4/3/22
DULCIE BLIGH (Clark) (M*F)       2/5/27
DULL DEAD, THE (Butler)
  (TBR)                          13/1/46
Du Maurier, Daphne
  Obituary (Lachman)             11/3/52
  Tension and Duality (Bakerman)
                                 3/4/8-10

Dumbfounded in Keelerland (Scott)
1/1/12-17
DUMMY MURDER CASE, THE
(Ozaki) (TBR)                    10/3/57
Duncan, W. Glenn
POOR DEAD CRICKET (IAC)
11/1/24
Duncombe, Frances
DEATH OF A SPINSTER (R) 9/4/43
Dunlap, Susan
A DINNER TO DIE FOR (R)
13/1/61-2
PIOUS DECEPTION (R)  12/1/41-2
*Dunnett, Dorothy*
(SSC)                    7/4/13*
Dunning, John
Looking for Rachel Wallace
(Kelley)                4/3/29-30
DUPE (Cody) (R)              7/4/27
*Durell, Sam*
(SSC)                    5/5/15*
L: Stilwell 5/4/44
*Duvall, Richard and Grace*
Amazing Grace (Sampson)  6/4/23-9
DUVEEN LETTER, THE (Leather)
(M*F)                    4/5/33
DYING DAY (Mitchell) (TAR) 11/3/81
DYING FALL, A (Wade) (IAC)  5/6/30
Dying Gasps (Townsend)       1/2/54
DYING IN THE POST-WAR WORLD
(Collins) (R)            13/4/50
DYING SPACE (Murphy) (M*F) 6/3/35
DYING VOICES (Crider) (TAR) 12/2/59

# E

*Eagle, Major Tom.* See Elston, Allan
Vaughn
EAGLES FLY (Flannery) (IAC)  4/6/31
EAR IN THE WALL, THE (Reeve)
(IAC)                    13/2/54-5
EARLY AUTUMN (Parker) (M*F)
(IAC)                5/2/25; 9/5/25
Early, Jack
A CREATIVE KIND OF KILLER
(IAC)                    8/6/34
East, Andy
THE COLD WAR FILE (IAC) 8/2/21
East, Roger
MURDER REHEARSAL (TBR)
12/3/77-8
Easton, Nat
A BOOK FOR BANNING (M*F)
5/4/26

EASY TO KILL (Christie) (IAC)  6/3/25
Ebersohn, Wessel
A LONELY PLACE TO DIE
(R)                      4/1/35
*Echoes* (Johnson, ed.) (MS)  6/4/2; 7/3/5
Eddenden, A.E.
A GOOD YEAR FOR MURDER
(TAR)                    11/1/53
*Eden, Dorothy*
Obituary (Lachman)           6/3/26
*Edgar Awards*
THE EDGAR WINNERS (Pronzini,
ed.) (IAC)              4/4/18
L: Breen 5/2/46; Hubin 5/1/39
EDGAR WINNERS, THE (Pronzini,
ed.) (IAC)              4/4/18
EDGE, THE (Francis) (TAR)  11/4/80
Edmonds, Andy
HOT TODDY (IAC)        12/1/25-8
Edwards, Ruth Dudley
CORRIDORS OF DEATH (R) 8/2/29
Edwards, Samuel
THE VIDOCQ DOSSIER (R)  5/3/36
EDWIN OF THE IRON SHOES
(Muller) (M*F) (IAC)  2/3/48; 3/2/23
*Edwin's Mystery and Its History*
(Fisher)                 4/5/6-8
L: Bleiler 4/6/42, 5/1/46
Effinger, George Alec
FELICIA (M*F) (R)   1/2/24; 3/3/46
SHADOW MONEY (TAR)    11/1/53
Egan, Leslie [Elizabeth Linington, q.v.]
THE BLIND SEARCH (R) (M*F)
1/4/47; 1/5/31
A CHOICE OF CRIMES (M*F)
5/2/15
LOOK BACK ON DEATH (M*F)
3/3/36
MOTIVE IN SHADOW (M*F) 4/2/40
RANDOM DEATH (M*F)     6/3/32
Eichler, Alfred
DEATH OF AN AD MAN (R) 9/5/40
EIGHT FACES AT THREE (Rice)
(IAC)                    11/4/48
EIGHTY DOLLARS TO STAMFORD
(Fletcher) (M*F)             P/25
11 DEADLY SINS (Sullivan, ed.)
(IAC)                    12/2/64
ELEVEN OF DIAMONDS, THE
(Kendrick) (TBR) (R)11/4/64; 12/1/48
Elkins, Aaron
CURSES! (TAR)              11/4/79

Ellery Queen, Sports Fan (Christopher)
10/3/3-24
L: Christopher 11/1/83
ELLERY QUEEN'S ANTHOLOGY –
VOL. 41 (Queen, ed.) (R)      6/2/43
ELLERY QUEEN'S BAD SCENES
(IAC)                          12/2/65
ELLERY QUEEN'S INTERNATIONAL
CASE BOOK (Queen) (TCITC)
3/4/17
*Ellery Queen's Mystery Magazine.* See
Cream of Queen; IAC 3/3/49,
7/4/21-22, 8/1/19
ELLERY QUEEN'S 1961 ANTHOL-
OGY (Queen, ed.) (R)         6/2/42
Ellin, Stanley
KINDLY DIG YOUR GRAVE AND
OTHER WICKED STORIES
(R)                        1/1/35
THE LUXEMBOURG RUN (M*F)
(R)              2/3/44; 2/5/36
THE SPECIALTY OF THE HOUSE
AND OTHER STORIES (R) 4/5/42
STAR LIGHT, STAR BRIGHT
(M*F)                      4/3/38
Ellington, James
SHOOT THE WORKS (R)      7/6/31
Ellroy, James
BLACK DAHLIA (TNSPE)   10/2/48
BROWN'S REQUIEM (M*F)  6/3/36
SUICIDE HILL (R)          9/2/42
Elrod, P. N.
BLOODLIST (TAR)       12/3/93-5
ELSINORE (Charyn) (TAR)     13/3/76
*Elston, Allan Vaughan*
Tracking with Major Eagle (Lybeck)
11/2/3-16*
L: Lybeck 11/1/82
*Elston, Robert*
Obituary (Lachman)         10/1/66
EMERALD, THE (Carrel) (M*F) 4/4/36
Emerson, Earl W.
BLACK HEARTS AND SLOW
DANCING (TAR)       11/2/68
DEVIANT BEHAVIOR (TAR)
11/1/57; 11/2/69
YELLOW DOG PARTY (TAR)
13/3/80
EMMA CHIZZIT AND THE QUEEN
ANNE KILLER (Hall) (TAR)
12/3/81-2
EMPEROR'S SHIELD, THE (Sanders)
(TAR)                   13/2/49

EMPEROR'S SNUFF-BOX, THE
(Carr) (IAC)               8/4/30
EMPTY COPPER SEA, THE
(MacDonald) (M*F)          3/6/38
EMPTY HOUSE, THE (Gilbert)
(M*F)                      3/6/31
*Emshwiller, Ed*
Obituary (Lachman)         12/4/49
Encore! (McSherry)        12/1/9-22
ENCYCLOPEDIA BROWN AND
THE CASE OF THE MIDNIGHT
VISITORS (Sobol) (IAC)     4/5/24
ENCYCLOPEDIA OF FRONTIER
AND WESTERN FICTION (Tuska/
Piekarski, eds.) (IAC) (R)8/1/18 & 29
ENCYCLOPEDIA OF MYSTERY AND
DETECTION, THE (Steinbrunner/
Penzler, eds.) (R)          P/13
L: Groff 1/2/51; Kelley 1/1/39
ENCYCLOPEDIA SHERLOCKIANA,
THE (Tracey) (IAC)         4/1/15
END OF THE LINE (OCork) (M*F)
6/3/34
*Endore, Guy*
DETOUR AT NIGHT (TBR) 10/2/69
END-GAME (Gilbert) (R)     6/6/36
ENDPLAY (Toepfer) (M*F)    2/1/29
ENEMY, THE (Bagley) (R)    3/6/43
ENIGMA, THE (Barak) (M*F) (R)
3/1/36; 3/6/44
ENORMOUS SHADOW, THE
(Harling) (IAC)            5/6/31
ENTER A MURDERER (Marsh)
(R)                        2/3/54
ENTHUSIAST, THE (Hill) (M*F)3/6/28
*Epstein, Jon*
Obituary (Lachman)         13/1/33
EQMM Cover Murders, The (fiction)
(Lachman)                1/1/6-11
L: Groff 1/2/51; Lachman 1/2/51;
Scott 1/2/53
EQMM Cover Story, The (fiction)
(Thompson)                1/2/3-4
ERLE STANLEY GARDNER: THE
CASE OF THE REAL PERRY
MASON (Hughes) (R)         2/4/37
ESCAPE (MacDonald) (R)     3/4/50
Eshleman, John M.
THE LONG CHASE (TBR)
13/4/68-70
THE LONG WINDOW (TBR)
13/4/68-70

ESPRIT DE CORPSE (Kane) (TBR)
                                    10/3/53
Estes, Winston M.
  A SIMPLE ACT OF KINDNESS
    (R)                         2/3/56
Estleman, Loren D.
  ANGEL EYES (M*F)             6/2/34
  DR. JEKYLL AND MR. HOLMES
    (M*F)                       4/2/34
  GENERAL MURDERS (TAR)
                                11/4/79
  THE GLASS HIGHWAY (R)  7/6/38
  MOTOR CITY BLUE (R) (M*F)
                      4/4/46; 5/3/27
  PEEPER (R)             12/4/99-100
  SILENT THUNDER (TAR)    11/4/79
  WHISKEY (TAR)           13/3/79
Estow, Daniel
  THE MOMENT OF FICTION
    (M*F)                       3/6/39
*Europe*
  British Murder and Detective Fiction
    (Bargainnier)        6/4/19-22
  German Secondary Literature
    (Goode)               7/5/7-15
  Recent European Works (Bleiler)
                          2/3/23-6
  Scandinavian Mystery Scene
    (Blom)                8/4/24-6
  Sweden's Commitment to Mystery
    Fiction (Bleiler)      2/5/7-8
Eustis, Helen
  THE HORIZONTAL MAN
    (IAC)                       7/1/33
Evans, Fallon
  PISTOLS AND PEDAGOGUES
    (TBR)                     11/1/48
*Evans, Homer.* See Paul, Elliot
Evans, John [Howard Browne, q.v.]
  HALO FOR SATAN (M*F)    4/3/41
Evans, Kenneth
  A RICH WAY TO DIE (M*F) 3/6/40
EVEN THE WICKED (McBain) (R)
                      1/4/44; 1/5/40
Evening with Martha Grimes, An
    (Gottschalk)          12/3/65-6
Evermay, March
  THEY TALKED OF POISON
    (TBR)                     11/1/42
Everson, William
  MORE CLASSICS OF THE HOR-
    ROR FILM (RM)             9/5/30

EVERY INCH A LADY (Fleming)
  (M*F)                         2/6/32
EVERY SECOND THURSDAY (Page)
  (R)                           8/4/39
EVIDENCE (Weisman) (M*F)   5/6/39
EVIL GNOME, THE (Robeson)
  (M*F)                          P/24
EVIL MEN DO, THE (Fitzsimmons)
  (TBR)                        11/1/42
EVIL OF THE DAY (Sterling)
  (IAC)                         5/6/30
EXCELLENT NIGHT FOR A MUR-
  DER, AN (Rath) (M*F)       3/6/36
EXEUNT MURDERERS, THE BEST
  MYSTERY STORIES OF AN-
  THONY BOUCHER (Nevins/
  Greenberg, eds.) (IAC)      8/2/22
The Exit of Father Brown (Strøm)
                             13/4/42-4
EXIT SHERLOCK HOLMES (Hall)
  (M*F) (R)      1/5/31 & 51; 3/5/44
EXPENDABLE MAN, THE (Hughes)
  (R) (IAC)          5/2/31; 9/5/26
Explosive Novels of Richard L.
  Graves, The (Kelley)     3/6/9-10
EXTORTIONERS, THE (Creasey)
  (R)                           5/6/47
EXTRA COVER (Smith) (R)    7/2/39
EYE FOR JUSTICE, AN (Randisi, ed.)
  (IAC)                        11/1/34
EYE OF OSIRIS, THE (Freeman)
  (IAC)                        11/3/51
EYES OF BUDDHA, THE (Ball)
  (M*F) (R)          1/3/40; 1/5/45
EYES OF PREY (Sandford) (TAR)
                             13/2/49-50

# F

F.O.B. MURDER (Hitchens) (R) 10/1/86
FABULOUS CLIPJOINT (Brown)
  (MS)                          9/1/7
FACE OF A STRANGER, THE (Perry)
  (R)                         13/1/76-7
FADE (Cormier) (R)          12/4/82-3
FADEAWAY (Rosen) (R) (IAC)
                      9/2/43; 12/4/45
FAGO (Roueché) (M*F)         2/3/43
Fair, A.A. [Erle Stanley Gardner, q.v.]
  THE BIGGER THEY COME
    (R)                       12/1/37
  DOUBLE OR QUITS (M*F)    1/2/23
Fairlie, Gerard
  THE MUSTER OF THE
    VULTURES (IAC)          3/2/22

FALLBACK (Nieswand) (R)      6/6/38
FALLEN CURTAIN, THE (Rendell)
   (R)                      3/4/45
FALLING STAR (Moyes) (IAC) 10/3/41
*Fallon, Martin* [Harry Patterson, q.v.]
   (SSC)                   4/3/28*
FALSE INSPECTOR DEW, THE
   (Lovesey) (R)          10/3/69
FALSE WITNESS (Uhnak) (R)   6/1/41
FAMILY REUNION (Harrington)
   (M*F)                   6/5/42
FANCIES AND GOODNIGHTS
   (Collier) (IAC)         8/3/27
FANDANGO INVOLVEMENT, THE
   (Mahon) (M*F)           6/2/33
FANGS OF THE HOODED DEMON,
   THE (Marsh) (TAR)      11/3/76
*Fans*
   On Fans and Bouchercon
   (Townsend)             5/5/11-3
Fantoni, Barry
   MIKE DIME (M*F) (R)
                         5/4/26; 6/1/43
*Fanzines*
   The Line-Up: (Briney) P/22; (Rall)
   1/1/38; 2/1/20; (Albert) 4/5/9-12
FAREWELL GESTURE (Ormerod)
   (TAR)                  13/2/46
FARNSWORTH SCORE, THE (Burns)
   (M*F)                   1/5/29
Farris, John
   SHARP PRACTICE (R)      8/3/42
*Farrow, Marcus.* See Ross, Angus
FASCINATOR, THE (York) (M*F)
                           1/5/35
FAT CHANCE (Laumer) (R)
                         1/5/43; 2/3/55
FATA MORGANA (Kotzwinkle)
   (R)                     1/4/46
FATAL ADVENT, A (Holland)
   (R)            12/1/40; 13/2/89-90
FATAL ATTRACTION (movie)
   (IAC)                  11/4/54
FATAL DESCENT (Rhode/Dickson)
   (IAC)                   9/5/26
FATAL REUNION (Saperstein)
   (IAC)                   9/5/25
FATE WORSE THAN DEATH
   (Radley) (R)            8/5/36
FATHER BROWN OMNIBUS, THE
   (Chesterton) (IAC)      7/5/26
Father Brown's Final Adventure
   (Christopher)         13/4/33-41

Fathers and Sons of John Le Carré,
   The (Dawson)           5/3/15-7
   L: Wooster 5/5/47
Fattest Man in the Medical Profession,
   The (Sampson)         7/3/16-22*
FAULT LINES (White) (TAR)
                    11/1/69; 11/2/80
FAUST CONSPIRACY, THE (Baddock)
   (TAR)                  12/2/56
*Faust, Frederick.* See Brand, Max
*Faust, Ron*
   Running Hot and Cold with Ron
   Faust (Kelley)         5/4/11-2
FAVOR (Hall) (TAR)   11/1/60; 11/2/72
*Favorite Books*
   L: Callaghan 7/4/36, 8/1/44; Deeck
   7/6/44; Floyd 4/6/44; Reynolds
   7/6/46
Favorite Magazine Issues: Manhunt
   (3:6), June 1955 (Banks)   4/6/7-8
Fear and Loathing with the Lone Wolf
   (Kelley)               1/5/17-8*
FEAR TO TREAD (Gilbert) (IAC)
                          11/3/47
FEARFUL SYMMETRY (Waltch)
   (TAR)             11/1/68; 11/2/80
Feder, Sue
   Reviews:
   BROKEN CONSORT (Gollin)
                          12/1/39
   DEADLY RESOLUTIONS
   (Collins)              12/1/38
   A FATAL ADVENT (Holland)
                          12/1/40
   FULL CLEVELAND (Roberts)
                          12/1/38
   THE GRANDFATHER
   MEDICINE (Hager)       12/1/43
   HAL'S OWN MURDER CASE
   (Martin)               12/1/38
   A LITTLE CLASS ON MURDER
   (Hart)                 12/1/42
   THE MOTHER SHADOW
   (Howe)                 12/1/43
   MURDER, MYSTERY AND
   MAYHEM (Carnell)       12/1/39
   PIOUS DECEPTION (Dunlap)
                          12/1/41-2
   A RARE BENEDICTINE
   (Peters)               12/1/39
   THE SHAPE OF DREAD (Muller)
                          12/1/40

Feder, Sue, continued
    Reviews continued
        SILENT PARTNER (Kellerman)
            12/1/43
        SILVER PIGS (Davis)    12/1/40-1
        SOUTH STREET (Belsky) 12/1/42
        STALKING THE ANGEL
            (Crais)    12/1/44
        UNORTHODOX PRACTICES
            (Piesman)    12/1/41
        YESTERDAY'S NEWS
            (Healy)    12/1/41
Fedora, Johnny. See Cory, Desmond
Feegel, John R.
    AUTOPSY (M*F)    3/2/27
    THE DANCE CARD (R)    6/5/48
FELICIA (Effinger) (M*F) (R)
            1/2/24; 3/3/46
Fell, Gideon. See Carr, John Dickson
FELLOW PASSENGER (Household)
    (R)    13/1/74-5
Fellows, J.O.C.
    Leonid Andreyev and Jim Thompson:
        A Comparison    11/2/59-61
    L: 10/2/81; 12/2/90-1 & 101;
        13/1/80-1
    Some Reminiscences of a Mystery
        Fancier    12/2/11-16
    The Value of Gould    13/1/3-6
Fenady, Andrew J.
    THE MAN WITH BOGART'S
        FACE (M*F) (R)    1/3/39 & 44
Fenster, Bob
    THE LAST PAGE (IAC)    11/4/49
Fenton, Lawrie. See Annesley, Michael
Ferguson, John
    DEATH OF MR. DODSLEY
        (TBR)    13/2/74-5
Fernald, Chester Bailey
    A Chinese Detective in San
        Francisco (Bleiler)    5/3/2-4
    L: Goode 6/1/48
FERNANDA (Miller) (R)    1/2/44
Ferrars, E.X.
    DEPART THIS LIFE (R)    8/1/17
    FROG IN THE THROAT (M*F)
            5/2/23
    MURDER OF A SUICIDE (R) 9/5/41
    THE PRETTY PINK SHROUD
        (R)    2/6/41
Ferrer, Jose
    Obituary (Lachman)    13/4/93

Ferris, Paul
    HIGH PLACES (M*F)    1/5/30
    FESTIVAL (Anderson) (M*F)    4/2/37
    FÊTE FATALE (Barnard) (R)    8/5/34
    Few Kind Words for Ashton-Kirk, A
        (Sampson)    7/6/3-12
Fiction
    The EQMM Cover Murders
        (Lachman)    1/1/6-11
    The EQMM Cover Story
        (Thompson)    1/2/3-4
Field, Evan
    WHAT NIGEL KNEW (M*F) 6/1/34
Field, Medora
    BLOOD ON HER SHOE (TBR)
            13/3/54
Fielding, A.
    THE CHARTERIS MYSTERY
        (TBR)    12/2/51
FIELDS OF EDEN, THE (Hinkemeyer)
        (M*F)    3/1/33
Fiene, Judith
    L:    2/3/73
FIFTH GRAVE, THE (Latimer) (TBR)
            10/2/61; 11/1/49
    L: Deeck 10/3/80; Hay 10/4/58
FIFTH PASSENGER, THE (Young)
        (IAC)    6/1/29
FILE ON A MISSING REDHEAD
        (Cameron) (R)    3/1/40
Films. See Movies
FILMS OF HOPALONG CASSIDY,
    THE (Nevins) (IAC)    13/4/87-8
FILMS OF PETER LORRE, THE
    (Youngkin/Bigwood/Cabana)
        (R)    10/3/71
FILMS OF SHERLOCK HOLMES,
    THE (Steinbrunner/Michaels)
        (R)    3/3/43
FINAL NOTICE (Valin) (R) (M*F) (R)
            5/2/29; 6/2/34; 7/4/28
FIND A CROOKED SIXPENCE
    (Thompson) (M*F)    2/5/26
FIND SHERRI! (Swan) (M*F)    4/3/36
FIND THIS WOMAN (Prather)
        (R)    2/1/47
FINGER OF FIRE (Braine) (R)    3/6/45
FINGERS OF DEATH (Grant)
        (M*F)    2/1/26
FINISHING STROKE, THE (Queen)
        (IAC)    10/4/49
Finnegan, Robert
    THE LYING LADIES (TBR) 13/1/41

Finney, Jack
ASSAULT ON A QUEEN (MS)
12/3/12
THE NIGHT PEOPLE (M*F)   2/3/41
TIME AND AGAIN (IAC)     2/6/28
FIRST COME, FIRST KILL (Allan)
(TBR)                 11/3/58
Fischer, Bruno
THE FLESH WAS COLD (M*F)
1/1/27
THE GIRL BETWEEN (M*F)  3/2/38
HOUSE OF FLESH (M*F)    3/6/32
QUOTH THE RAVEN (M*F)   1/2/25
*Fish, Mame*
Obituary (Lachman)        13/4/93
*Fish, Robert L.*
BRAZILIAN SLEIGH RIDE
(IAC)                 11/1/28
THE GOLD OF TROY (M*F)  5/1/25
KEK HUUYGENS, SMUGGLER
(R)                    2/5/41
Obituary (MS) (IAC)     5/2/1 & 12
L: Nevins 5/2/50
Fisher, Benjamin Franklin IV
Edwin's Mystery and Its History
4/5/6-8
L: 4/6/46; 5/1/48; 7/4/46; 10/3/77;
11/1/84; 13/3/99-100
A Neglected Detective Novel:
Bellamann's THE GRAY MAN
WALKS (w/Bayne)      12/4/3-19
Science and Technology in the
Writings of Frederick Irving
Anderson              13/4/12-32
Sunshine and Shadow in THE
MYSTERY OF EDWIN
DROOD               11/4/11-28
Fisher, Carla J.
L:                        3/1/57
Fisher, David E.
VARIATION ON A THEME
(M*F)                  5/6/38
Fisher, Steve
I WAKE UP SCREAMING
(IAC)                 10/4/50
Fitt, Mary
MIZMAZE (M*F) (TBR)
5/3/28; 11/1/41
Fitzgibbon, Russell H.
THE AGATHA CHRISTIE
COMPANION (IAC)      4/6/31

Fitzsimmons, Cortland
THE EVIL MEN DO (TBR)   11/1/42
THE GIRL IN THE CAGE (w/
Mulholland) (TBR)       11/4/57
FIVE ROADS TO DEATH (Philips)
(M*F)                  2/5/31
Five Star Mysteries: A Tentative
Checklist (Deeck)     11/2/17-23*
L: Greene 12/2/97-8
*Flagg, Webster.* See Johns, Veronica
Parker
Flannery, Sean
EAGLES FLY (IAC)         4/6/31
HOLLOW MEN (IAC)        6/6/21
*Flashgun Casey*
Old Time Radio Lives (Larsen)
4/6/9-11
Fleischman, A.S.
DANGER IN PARADISE
(M*F)                  5/4/25
SHANGHAI FLAME (M*F)   2/4/30
Fleissner, Robert F.
The Onomastics of Sherlock 8/3/21-4
*Fleming, Ian*
The Article I Couldn't Publish
(Townsend)           1/1/18-20
The Real Originality of Ian Fleming
(McSherry)           11/4/35-45
(SSC)                  4/3/26*
L: Van Tilburg 5/3/41, 5/5/48
Fleming, Joan
EVERY INCH A LADY (M*F)
2/6/32
TO MAKE AN UNDERWORLD
(M*F)                  1/1/33
*Fleming, Roger.* See Harvester, Simon
FLESH AND BLOOD (Cook)
(TAR)                 11/4/77
FLESH WAS COLD, THE (Fischer)
(M*F)                  1/1/27
FLETCH (Mcdonald) (M*F) (R)
1/3/37; 1/5/37
FLETCH AND THE WIDOW BRAD-
LEY (Mcdonald) (M*F) (R)
6/1/36 & 40
Fletcher, Lucille
EIGHTY DOLLARS TO
STAMFORD (M*F)        P/25
FLEUR-DE-LIS AFFAIR, THE (Ross)
(M*F)                  1/1/30
Flinn, Denny Martin
SAN FRANCISCO KILLS (TAR)
13/3/80

FLOATING ADMIRAL, THE (Various
  authors) (IAC)    4/3/33
Flora, Fletcher
  SKULDOGGERY (R)    9/4/42
FLORENTINE WIN, THE (La Barre)
  (TAR)    11/3/73
FLOWER-COVERED CORPSE, THE
  (Avallone) (IAC)    6/1/28
FLOWERED BOX, THE (Green)
  (M*F)    5/2/20
Flowers, Charles
  IT NEVER RAINS IN LOS
    ANGELES (R)    4/1/30
FLOWERS FOR THE JUDGE
  (Allingham) (IAC)    8/3/25
Floyd, Frank
  The Cream of Queen: (June, August
    1986) 8/4/27-8; (October 1986)
    8/6/31-2; (November–December,
    January–February) 9/1/31-2;
    (March–April) 9/2/20; (May–June)
    9/3/27-8
  L: 3/4/60; 3/5/47; 4/1/37; 4/6/44;
    5/4/43; 5/6/49; 7/3/49; 7/4/42;
    8/4/50; 8/5/40; 9/1/48; 9/3/46
  Reviews:
    BREAK IN (Francis)    9/2/36
    BRIGHT ORANGE FOR THE
      SHROUD (MacDonald)  6/2/44
    "Lizzie Borden in the P.M."
      (Henson)    9/1/31
    THE LONELY SILVER RAIN
      (MacDonald)    8/4/45
    MURDER IN E MINOR
      (Goldsborough)    8/6/37
    "Oil and Water" (Bankier)  9/3/27
    THE QUICK RED FOX
      (MacDonald)    6/2/44
    "Rumpole and the Sporting Life"
      (Mortimer)    9/1/31
    "Rumpole and the Younger Gen-
      eration" (Mortimer)    9/3/28
    SEND ANOTHER HEARSE
      (Masur)    8/4/45
    SWING LOW, SWING DEAD
      (Gruber)    6/2/46
    TO PROVE A VILLAIN
      (Townsend)    9/1/39
  Twice-Told Tale of Murder  6/1/21-6
FLY ON THE WALL, THE (Hillerman)
  (IAC)    11/1/23; 12/2/63

Flynn, Brian
  THE BILLIARD ROOM MYSTERY
    (TBR)    13/3/51-2
Flynn, Don
  MURDER ISN'T ENOUGH (R)
        8/1/37
FOG (Williams/Sims) (TBR)  11/3/69
Follett, James
  CROWN COURT (M*F)    2/6/32
FOLLOW THIS FAIR CORPSE (Smith)
  (TBR)    13/2/61-2
FOOL'S RUN, THE (Camp) (TAR)
    11/4/78
Foote-Smith, Elizabeth
  GENTLE ALBATROSS (R)  1/2/42
  NEVER SAY DIE (M*F)    2/1/24
FOOTSTEPS OF DEATH (Gunn)
  (MS)    12/3/10-11
FOR OLD CRIME'S SAKE (Ames)
  (R)    7/5/44
Forbes, Stanton
  THE WILL AND LAST
    TESTAMENT OF CONSTANCE
    COBBLE (M*F)    4/3/37
Ford, George
  'GATOR (R)    1/3/45
Ford, John M.
  THE SCHOLARS OF NIGHT
    (TAR)    11/1/54
Ford, Leslie
  THE CLUE OF THE JUDAS TREE
    (M*F)    6/3/31
  MURDER IN THE O.P.M.
    (TBR)    13/4/79-80
FOREVER WILT THOU DIE (Byfield)
  (M*F)    2/5/32
Forrest, Richard. Also see Woods,
  Stockton
  THE DEATH AT YEW CORNER
    (M*F)    5/2/24
  THE WIZARD OF DEATH
    (M*F)    1/5/29
Forsyte, Charles
  To Be and Not To Be (Bleiler)6/6/3-4
FORTIETH BIRTHDAY BODY, THE
  (Wolzien) (R)    13/2/86-7
.44 (Breslin/Schapp) (R)    3/5/43
FORTY WHACKS (Homes) (R) 10/1/87
Foster, Brad W.
  L:    7/2/47
  Foul Play Press (MS)  3/5/2; 5/2/1
  FOUR FALSE WEAPONS, THE (Carr)
    (IAC)    11/4/52

Four Gees (Sampson)          12/3/13-34
  L: Briney 13/1/83-5
FOUR JUST MEN (Wallace) (IAC)
                             9/1/36
FOURTH CODEX, THE (Houston)
  (TAR)                      11/1/56
FOURTH WALL, THE (Paul)
  (R)                        7/4/27
Fowles, John
  Freedom and Mystery (Carter)
                             3/5/14-6
Fox, George
  AMOK (R)                   3/5/43
Fox, James M.
  Obituary (Lachman)         11/3/53
Foxx, Jack [Bill Pronzini, q.v.]
  DEAD RUN (M*F)             2/4/34
  FREEBOOTY (M*F)            1/2/23
  WILDFIRE (M*F)             3/3/38
  L: Frazier 2/6/53; Nevins 3/1/55
Francis, Dick
  BANKER (R)                 7/3/33
  BREAK IN (R)               9/2/36
  THE DANGER (R)             8/2/37
  THE EDGE (TAR)             11/4/80
  HIGH STAKES (IAC)          6/1/28
  KNOCKDOWN (M*F)            1/3/40
  RISK (R)                   8/1/17
  SMOKESCREEN (IAC)          2/6/28
  STRAIGHT (MS)              12/1/4
  TRIAL RUN (M*F)            3/6/30
  TWICE SHY (R) (M*F)
                             6/3/39; 6/4/43
  WHIP HAND (M*F) (IAC)
                             4/4/37; 5/2/11
  L: Adey 8/1/43; Reynolds 6/6/42*
Franciscus, James
  Obituary (Lachman)         13/3/72
Franklin, Eugene [Franklin Bandy, q.v.]
  MURDER TRAPP (R)           5/5/42
Franklin, Max
  CHARLIE'S ANGELS (M*F)     1/4/39
Fraser, Antonia
  COOL REPENTANCE (R)        8/1/33
  (IAC)                      5/5/19
Frauenglas, Robert A.
  Law, Lawyers and Justice in the
    Novels of Joe L. Hensley   4/1/3-7
Frazier, Gerie
  Introducing Alexandra Roudybush
                             3/3/2-4
  L: 1/6/55; 2/1/59; 2/4/59; 2/6/53;
    3/1/58

Frazier, Gerie, continued
  Reviews:
    THE FALLEN CURTAIN
      (Rendell)              3/4/45
    A GUILTY THING SURPRISED
      (Rendell)              3/4/44
    A JUDGEMENT IN STONE
      (Rendell)              3/4/44
    SHAKE HANDS FOREVER
      (Rendell)              3/4/45
    SOME LIE AND SOME DIE
      (Rendell)              3/4/44
    TO FEAR A PAINTED DEVIL
      (Rendell)              3/4/45
    WOLF TO THE SLAUGHTER
      (Rendell)              3/4/45
Fredericks, Arnold
  Amazing Grace (Sampson)    6/4/23-9
Fredman, Mike
  KISSES LEAVE NO FINGER-
    PRINTS (M*F)             4/5/32
  YOU CAN ALWAYS BLAME THE
    RAIN (M*F)               4/4/36
FREE FALL IN CRIMSON
  (MacDonald) (M*F) (R) (IAC)
                             5/4/23 & 31; 12/4/44
FREEBOOTY (Foxx) (M*F)       1/2/23
Freeborn, Brian
  GOOD LUCK, MISTER CAIN
    (M*F)                    1/4/37
  TEN DAYS, MISTER CAIN?
    (M*F)                    2/6/32
Freedom and Mystery in John Fowles'
  THE ENIGMA (Carter)        3/5/14-6
FREELANCE DEATH (Taylor)
  (TAR)                      11/1/67; 11/2/79
Freeling, Nicholas
  THE BUGLES BLOWING (R) 1/5/44
  CASTANG'S CITY (R)         4/5/40
  Interview (Bakerman)       8/6/19-24
  THE NIGHT LORDS (R)        4/2/42
  NOT AS FAR AS VELMA
    (R)                      12/3/103-4
  SABINE (M*F)               3/2/36
  THE WIDOW (R)              6/1/42
  WOLFNIGHT (R)              6/4/46
Freeman, Lucy, ed.
  THE MURDER MYSTIQUE
    (IAC)                    7/2/24
Freeman, R. Austin
  THE EYE OF OSIRIS (IAC) 11/3/51
  THE RED THUMB MARK
    (IAC)                    9/1/34

Freemantle, Brian
CHARLIE M (M*F) (R)
    2/3/41; 4/2/50
HERE COMES CHARLIE M (M*F)
  (R)    3/4/38; 4/2/50
THE RUN AROUND (TAR) 11/4/80
  (SSC)    7/4/13*
L: Deeck 7/6/43; Van Tilburg 8/1/44
Fremlin, Celia
THE SPIDER-ORCHID (M*F) 2/6/30
French, Larry L.
L:    1/6/59; 2/1/50; 2/2/47; 2/4/57
The Mysterious John Dickson
  Carr    1/6/13-4
Obituary (Cover)    3/1
Professor Without a Pseudonym
    2/2/12-14
The Professorial Sleuth of Roy
  Winsor    2/1/3-4
Review: MORTAL STAKES
  (Parker)    2/1/32
Thomas Chastain and the New Police
  Procedural    2/4/17-8
L: Nevins 3/1/55
FRENCH KEY MYSTERY, THE
(Gruber) (R)    1/5/47
FRIDAY HARBOR MURDERS, THE
(Weeks) (TAR)  11/1/68; 11/2/80
Friedman, Kinky
WHEN THE CAT'S AWAY (TAR)
    11/1/58; 11/2/69
Friedman, Mickey
MAGIC MIRROR (TAR)  11/1/54
PAPER PHOENIX (R)  8/4/38
FRIEND IN DEED, A (Jagoda)
(M*F)    2/4/33
FRIENDS OF EDDIE COYLE, THE
(Higgins) (IAC)  10/4/52
FRIGOR MORTIS (McInerny)
(TAR)    12/3/85-6
Frimmer, Steven
DEAD MATTER (M*F)  6/5/44
FROG IN THE THROAT (Ferrars)
(M*F)    5/2/23
FROM LONDON FAR (Innes) (R)
(IAC)    1/4/48; 5/4/18
Frost, Barbara
THE CORPSE DIED TWICE
  (TBR)    13/3/55
FROZEN ASSETS (Leasor)
(TAR)    12/3/84-5
Fu Manchus (Mystery Mosts)
L: Briney 12/2/102-3

Fugate, Francis L. and Roberta B.
SECRETS OF THE WORLD'S
  BEST-SELLING WRITER
  (M*F)    5/2/13
FULL CLEVELAND (Roberts)
  (R) (TAR)  12/1/38; 12/4/56
Fuller, Roy
Obituary (Lachman)  13/4/89-90
THE SECOND CURTAIN
  (IAC)    13/4/83
Fuller, Samuel
DEAD PIGEON ON BEETHOVEN
  STREET (M*F)  P/25
Funct, David E.
The Tod Hunter Question  6/4/3-8
L: Apostolou 6/6/48; Bleiler 6/6/47;
  Lewis 6/6/49; Strong 6/6/47
FUNERAL SITES (Mann) (M*F) 6/6/29
FURIOUS OLD WOMEN (Bruce)
  (R)    8/3/36
Furst, Alan
YOUR DAY IN THE BARREL
  (M*F)    P/28
Further Excursions into the Wacky
  World of Harry Stephen Keeler
  (Scott)    1/4/13-24
Further Gems from the Literature
  (Deeck)
  8/6/27-30; 9/1/28-30,27; 9/2/21-3,
  9/4/32-4; 9/6/31-4; 10/3/32-6;
  11/4/29-34; 13/2/29-35
Fyfield, Frances
NOT THAT KIND OF PLACE
  (R)    13/3/84-6
A QUESTION OF GUILT (R)
    13/2/84-5; 13/3/84-5
SHADOWS ON THE MIRROR
  (TAR)    13/3/80-1

# G

"G.B.": A STORY OF THE GREAT
  WAR (Morris) (TBR)  11/3/64
G-STRING MURDERS, THE (Lee)
  (TBR)    10/2/63
Who Really Wrote (Christopher)
    8/3/18,20
Gage, Edwin
PHOENIX NO MORE (M*F) 3/1/36
Gagnon, Louise
L:    5/2/49; 6/1/50; 7/6/43
Gaines, Mary Kay
Review: ROBAK'S RUN (Hensley)
    12/4/79-80

Gall, Joe
  The Joe Gall Series (Kelley/
    Banks)            3/2/26-35*
Gallant, Gladys S.
  LIVING IMAGE (M*F)        3/1/35
Gallison, Kate
  UNBALANCED ACCOUNTS (IAC)
    (R)            8/4/31; 8/6/40
Galloway, David
  LAMAAR RANSOM—PRIVATE
    EYE (TBR)            10/2/64
GALLOWS WAIT (Corbett) (R) 10/1/83
Galwey, G.V.
  THE LIFT AND THE DROP
    (TBR)            13/4/75-6
GAMBLER, THE MINSTREL, AND
  THE DANCE HALL QUEEN, THE
  (Downing) (M*F)        1/1/30
GAME WITHOUT RULES (Gilbert)
  (IAC) 11/1/22
GAMEKEEPER'S GALLOWS (Hilton)
  (M*F)            1/6/38
GAMES (Pronzini) (R) (IAC) (R)
            1/2/25; 3/2/22; 6/1/45
Gann, Ernest K.
  Obituary (Lachman)        13/4/90
Gardiner, Dorothy
  Little Old Men (Nehr)        4/4/2-6
  THE SEVENTH MOURNER
    (TBR)            13/4/71-2
  THE TRANS-ATLANTIC GHOST
    (M*F)            3/5/41
Gardner, Erle Stanley. Also see Fair,
  A.A.
  THE AMAZING ADVENTURES
    OF LESTER LEITH (IAC) 5/1/17
  THE CASE OF THE AMOROUS
    AUNT (R)            1/3/49
  THE CASE OF THE BEAUTIFUL
    BEGGAR (R)            1/4/54
  THE CASE OF THE BIGAMOUS
    SPOUSE (R)            1/1/37
  THE CASE OF THE BLONDE
    BONANZA (R)            1/2/10
  THE CASE OF THE BURIED
    CLOCK (R)            7/6/37
  THE CASE OF THE CARELESS
    CUPID (R)            1/5/50
  THE CASE OF THE DARING
    DIVORCÉE (R)            1/3/49
  THE CASE OF THE DUBIOUS
    BRIDEGROOM (IAC)        7/4/20
  THE CASE OF THE FABULOUS
    FAKE (R)            1/5/51

Gardner, Erle Stanley, continued
  THE CASE OF THE GRINNING
    GORILLA (IAC)            6/3/25
  THE CASE OF THE HORRIFIED
    HEIRS (R)            1/3/50
  THE CASE OF THE ICE-COLD
    HANDS (R)            1/2/45
  THE CASE OF THE LAME
    CANARY (IAC)            8/3/25
  THE CASE OF THE LAZY
    LOVER (M*F)            5/3/33
  THE CASE OF THE LONELY
    HEIRESS (IAC)            7/4/20
  THE CASE OF THE LUCKY LEGS
    (IAC)            13/1/29
  THE CASE OF THE MIS-
    CHIEVOUS DOLL (R)        1/2/45
  THE CASE OF THE PERJURED
    PARROT (M*F)            6/6/26
  THE CASE OF THE PHANTOM
    FORTUNE (R)            1/3/50
  THE CASE OF THE QUEENLY
    CONTESTANT (R)            1/5/50
  THE CASE OF THE RELUCTANT
    MODEL (R)            1/1/37
  THE CASE OF THE SHAPELY
    SHADOW (R)            1/1/36
  THE CASE OF THE SPURIOUS
    SPINSTER (R)            1/1/36
  THE CASE OF THE STEPDAUGH-
    TER'S SECRET (R)        1/2/45
  THE CASE OF THE TROUBLED
    TRUSTEE (R)            1/4/54
  THE CASE OF THE VAGABOND
    VIRGIN (IAC)            6/3/25
  THE CASE OF THE WORRIED
    WAITRESS (R)            1/4/54
  ERLE STANLEY GARDNER: THE
    CASE OF THE REAL PERRY
    MASON (Hughes) (R)        2/4/37
  THE HUMAN ZERO: THE SCI-
    ENCE FICTION STORIES OF
    ERLE STANLEY GARDNER
    (Greenberg/Waugh, eds.)
    (M*F)            5/2/13
    (IAC)            5/4/20
  Rings of Death (Sampson)        10/1/3
  L: Floyd 9/3/46
Gardner, John
  ICEBREAKER (R)            7/3/39
  TO RUN A LITTLE FASTER
    (R)            2/6/41
    (SSC)            4/3/25*
  L: Breen 7/3/50; Denton 7/3/44

*Garfield*
L: Banks 12/2/84-5
*Garfield, Brian*
  DEATH WISH (IAC) 11/4/51
  I, WITNESS (ed.) (IAC) 2/6/29
  RECOIL (M*F) 1/5/34
  The Vengeance Novels of Brian
    Garfield (Kelley) 2/1/5-6
  WHAT OF TERRY CONISTON?
    (M*F) 1/2/25-6
  L: Banks 2/2/41; Gorman 2/2/48;
    Lansdale 2/3/62
GARSTON MURDER CASE, THE
  (Bailey) (IAC) 11/1/26
*Garland Publishing* (MS) 8/5/5-6
*Garrett, Randall*
  Obituary (Lachman) 10/3/45
  Some Recent Hybrids (Kelley)
    6/2/16-8
Garrity [David James Garrity]
  DRAGON HUNT (M*F) 4/2/38
  KISS OFF THE DEAD (M*F) 6/2/35
Garve, Andrew
  THE ASCENT OF D-13 (IAC) 8/4/31
  THE LESTER AFFAIR (IAC) 5/2/10
  THE LONG SHORT CUT (R) 2/5/35
  TWO IF BY SEA (IAC) 8/4/31
Gash, Jonathan
  THE GRAIL TREE (M*F) (R)
    4/5/34; 8/3/35
  THE JUDAS PAIR (M*F) 2/3/47
  THE SLEEPERS OF ERIN
    (R) 9/6/39
  THE TARTAN SELL (R) 8/6/45
*Gat, Dimitri*
  NEVSKY'S RETURN (IAC) 7/4/21
  L: Deeck 7/6/44
GATHERING OF SAINTS, A (Lindsey)
  (R) 13/2/90-1
GATHERING PLACE, THE (Breen) (R)
  (IAC) 8/2/38; 8/3/26; 9/2/28
  L: Breen 8/3/49; Townsend 8/2/46,
    8/3/50
'GATOR (Ford) (R) 1/3/45
GAUDY NIGHT (Sayers) (IAC) 8/5/31
Gault, William Campbell
  CAT AND MOUSE (TAR)
    11/1/58; 11/2/70
  THE DEAD SEED (IAC) 9/5/28
  DEATH IN DONEGAL BAY
    (R) 8/3/46
  DON'T CRY FOR ME (IAC) 5/4/19
  L: 8/6/49

Geherin, David
  JOHN D. MacDONALD (IAC) 7/2/23
  SONS OF SAM SPADE (IAC) 4/3/32
GELIGNITE GANG, THE (Creasey)
  (IAC) 10/3/42
Geller, Michael
  A CORPSE FOR A CANDIDATE
    (M*F) 4/3/39
GEMINI CONTENDERS, THE
  (Ludlum) (R) 3/1/42
GEMINI TRIP (Law) (M*F) 2/1/26
Gene Stratton-Porter: Mistress of the
  Mini-Mystery (Bakerman) 3/1/3-9
  L: Floyd 3/4/60; Loeser 3/2/58
GENERAL MURDERS (Estleman)
  (TAR) 11/4/79
GENTLE ALBATROSS (Foote-Smith)
  (R) 1/2/42
George, Elizabeth
  A SUITABLE VENGEANCE
    (TAR) 13/3/81
*Gerard, Francis*
  (SSC) 5/3/21*
German Secondary Literature
  (Goode) 7/5/7-15
GET-RICH-QUICK WALLINGFORD
  Rogues for the New Century
    (Dueren) 5/3/11-14
GHOST IT WAS, THE (Hull)
  (TBR) 11/3/61
GHOST OF A CHANCE (Roos)
  (TBR) 11/3/58
GHOST OF THE HARDY BOYS: AN
  AUTOBIOGRAPHY (McFarlane)
  (R) 7/3/36
GIANT KILLER (Hyman) (IAC) 6/6/21
Gibson, Walter B. Also see Grant,
  Maxwell
  THE SHADOW SCRAPBOOK
    (IAC) (R) 4/1/13; 4/2/51
*Gide, Andre*
  Gide's "Vatican Cellars" (Horn)
    6/2/11-5
  Gide's "Vatican Cellars": The Popular
    Detective Novel Parodied (Horn)
    6/2/11-5
GIDEON'S DRIVE (Marric) (M*F)
    2/1/28
*Giesy, J.B.*
  Detection by Other Means
    (Sampson) 7/1/7-17

Gifford, Thomas
THE CAVANOUGH QUEST (M*F)
(R) 1/3/39 & 44
THE GLENDOWER LEGACY
(M*F) 3/3/34
*Gilbert, Anthony*
Bowlers, Beer, Bravado, and Brains
(Bakerman) 2/4/5-13
DEATH IN THE BLACKOUT
(R) 9/5/42
THE SPINSTER'S SECRET
(R) 5/2/33
*Gilbert, Elliot L.*
Obituary (Lachman) 13/3/69
*Gilbert, Michael*
BLOOD AND JUDGMENT
(IAC) 11/3/47
THE BODY OF A GIRL (R) 3/4/48
THE COUNTRY-HOUSE
BURGLAR (IAC) 11/1/23
THE CRACK IN THE TEACUP
(IAC) 11/1/23
THE DANGER WITHIN
(IAC) 11/3/47
DEATH HAS DEEP ROOTS
(IAC) 11/3/47
DEATH OF A FAVORITE GIRL
(R) 7/1/42
THE EMPTY HOUSE (M*F) 3/6/31
END-GAME (R) 6/6/36
FEAR TO TREAD (IAC) 11/3/47
GAME WITHOUT RULES
(IAC) 11/1/22
HE DIDN'T MIND DANGER
(IAC) 11/3/47
THE KILLING OF KATIE
STEELSTOCK (M*F) 4/5/30
MR. CALDER AND MR. BEHRENS
(IAC) 6/4/31
OVERDRIVE (IAC) 11/1/23
SMALLBONE DECEASED
(IAC) 11/1/22
L: Wright 13/2/94-5
GILDED MAN, THE (Dickson)
(IAC) 11/4/53
Giles, Raymond
SHAMUS (R) 2/3/52
Gill, B.M.
DEATH DROP (R) 5/4/34
Gill, Bartholomew
McGARR AND THE SIENESE
CONSPIRACY (M*F) 3/1/32
McGARR ON THE CLIFFS OF
DOVER (M*F) 3/3/39

Gill, John
KIKI (R) 3/6/48
Gillespie, Robert B.
THE CROSSWORD MYSTERY
(M*F) 5/5/21
THE LAST OF THE HONEY-
WELLS (TAR) 11/1/59; 11/2/70
Gillis, Jackson
THE KILLERS OF STARFISH
(R) 1/6/43
*Gilman, Dorothy*
(SSC) 5/3/19*
Gilmore, Joseph
BLUE FLAME (IAC) 7/5/27
GIRL BETWEEN, THE (Fischer)
(M*F) 3/2/38
GIRL IN THE CAGE, THE (Fitzsim-
mons/Mulholland) (TBR) 11/4/57
GIRL'S HEAD, THE (Jepson)
(R) 1/3/43
Giroux, E. X.
A DEATH FOR A DOCTOR
(R) 11/4/90
*Giroux, Leo*
Obituary (Lachman) 12/2/71
Glantz, Dorothy
L: 2/1/54
GLASS HIGHWAY, THE (Estleman)
(R) 7/6/38
GLASS TRIANGLE, THE (Coxe)
(M*F) 1/5/36
GLENDOWER LEGACY, THE
(Gifford) (M*F) 3/3/34
GLIMPSES OF THE MOON, THE
(Crispin) (R) (M*F) 3/2/47; 5/1/20
L: Breen 3/3/52
GLITTER DOME, THE (Wambaugh)
(R) 5/5/28
GLORY GAME, THE (Williamson)
(M*F) 2/4/30
GO WEST, INSPECTOR GHOTE
(Keating) (M*F) 5/6/33
GOD SAVE THE CHILD (Parker) (R)
(M*F) 1/1/26; 3/4/39
Godey, John
THE THREE WORLDS OF
JOHNNY HANDSOME (R) 5/5/43
Godfrey, Thomas, ed.
MURDER FOR CHRISTMAS
(IAC) 9/5/24
*Goines, Donald*
Donald Goines: An Appreciation
(Blom) 9/4/17-24

GOING DOWN OF THE SUN, THE
(Bannister) (R)                    13/4/96-7
GOING FOR THE GOLD (Lathen)
(M*F) (R)                        5/3/32 & 34
GOLD AND GAITERS (Alington)
(TBR)                                13/2/71
Gold Medal Boys, The (Tuttle)
                                    10/3/25-31
GOLD OF TROY, THE (Fish)
(M*F)                                 5/1/25
GOLD SOLUTION, THE (Resnicow)
   L: Resnicow 9/1/49; Townsend
      comment 9/1/48
GOLDEN APE, THE (Adams)
(IAC)                                 6/3/22
GOLDEN DRESS, THE (Montgomery)
(TBR)                                13/2/72
GOLDEN FLEECE (Becklund)
(TAR)                                13/3/75
GOLDEN RAIN (Clark) (R)       7/5/46
GOLDFISH BOWL, THE (Gough)
(TAR)            11/1/59; 11/2/70-1
Goldman, Amy E.
   L:                                 2/4/56
Goldman, Lawrence
   TIGER BY THE TAIL (M*F)   3/5/37
Goldman, R.L.
   DEATH PLAYS SOLITAIRE
   (TBR)                              11/1/43
Goldsborough, Robert
   THE BLOODIED IVY (TAR)
          11/1/58; 11/2/69; 12/3/95-6
   THE LAST COINCIDENCE
   (R)                                12/3/95
   MURDER IN E MINOR (R)     8/6/37
Goldsmsith, Ilse
   L:         1/1/44; 2/1/58; 4/2/59
Goldstein, Arthur D.
   A PERSON SHOULDN'T DIE LIKE
      THAT (TBR)                 13/3/59-60
Goldstone, Adrian Homer
   L:                                 1/1/46
Gollin, James
   BROKEN CONSORT (R)      12/1/39
GONE MAN, THE (Solomon)
(M*F)                                 2/2/35
GONE, NO FORWARDING (Gores)
(M*F) (R)                 2/5/28; 4/2/51
GOOD BEHAVIOR (Westlake)
(R)                                    9/1/42
GOOD LUCK, MISTER CAIN
(Freeborn) (M*F)                     1/4/37

GOOD NEIGHBOR MURDER, THE
(Pierson) (TBR)                      13/2/74
GOOD NIGHT, SHERIFF (Steeves)
(TBR)                                11/1/46
GOOD NIGHT TO KILL, A
(O'Donnell) (TAR)                    11/3/82
GOOD OLD STUFF, THE
(MacDonald) (R)                       8/1/18
GOOD YEAR FOR MURDER, A
(Eddenden) (TAR)                     11/1/53
GOODBYE, CHICAGO (Burnett)
(R)                                    5/3/38
GOODBYE, GORGEOUS (Campbell)
(M*F)                                 5/2/18
GOODBYE, L.A. (Sinclair) (TAR)
                          11/1/67; 11/2/79
Goodchild, George
   JACK O'LANTERN (IAC)       4/6/33
Goode, Greg
   German Secondary Literature 7/5/7-15
   L: 5/6/51; 6/1/48; 6/2/48; 6/3/46;
      6/6/41; 7/2/47; 7/3/47; 7/4/49
   Reviews:
   CONE OF SILENCE (Beaty)
                                       7/2/35
   THE DANCE CARD (Feegel)
                                       6/5/48
   DAS PHANOMEN SIMMEL:
      ZUR REZEPTION EINES
      BESTSELLER-AUTHORS
      UNTER SCHULEMUND IM
      LITERATURUNTERRICHT
      (Weber)                         7/5/44
   DER KRIMINALROMAN [THE
      DETECTIVE NOVEL]
      (Nusser)                        7/3/40
   DOUBLE NEGATIVE (Carakeet)
                                       6/5/48
   MISSION M.I.A. (Pollock)   6/4/47
   NEEDLES (Deverell)          6/1/45
   NO HIGHWAY (Shute)          7/2/35
   RECLAMS KRIMINAL-
      ROMANFUHRER (Arnold/
      Schmidt)                        7/2/36
   THE SMILING CORPSE
      (Anonymous)                     6/2/41
   A SORT OF SAMURAI
      (Melville)                      6/6/34
   SUMMER FIRES (Reiss)        6/3/42
   UBER ERIC AMBLER            7/3/41
   THE VIOLENT MAN (Van
      Vogt)                           8/4/41
   THE WAGES OF ZEN
      (Melville)                      5/6/45

GOODNIGHT AND GOOD-BYE
(Harris) (R) (M*F) (R)
4/2/50; 5/3/31; 7/1/42
Goodrich, Jim
L: 1/2/49; 2/1/56; 4/2/59; 4/4/49;
5/1/41; 6/3/46; 6/6/43; 11/3/97;
12/2/93-3
Gordon, Alex
THE CYPHER (M*F)          2/4/32
Gordon, Alison
SAFE AT HOME (TAR)      13/3/81-2
*Gordon, Milton A.*
Obituary (Lachman)        12/4/49
Gores, Joe
COME MORNING (IAC)        9/4/37
GONE, NO FORWARDING (M*F)
(R)                2/5/28; 4/2/51
Gorman, Dave
L:                        2/2/48
Gorman, Ed, ed.
DARK CRIMES, GREAT *NOIR*
FICTION (R)          13/4/48-9
THE SECOND BLACK LIZARD
ANTHOLOGY OF CRIME
FICTION (IAC)        11/1/32
Goshgarian, Gary
ATLANTIS FIRE (R)          6/6/37
GOSPEL LAMB, THE (Scott)
(M*F)                    5/3/29
Gottschalk, Jane
An Evening with Martha
Grimes              12/ 3/65-6
Let's Hear It for Josephine Bell
11/2/47-56*
L: 3/1/58; 3/3/59; 4/1/39; 5/1/42;
12/2/94-6; 13/1/86-7; 13/3/95-6
Nancy Pickard: Arrived      13/2/23-8
A Query and a Note: Stewart's
THORNYHOLD          12/4/35-8
Reviews:
DOROTHY AND AGATHA
(Larsen)            13/4/102
THE FACE OF A STRANGER
(Perry)            13/1/76-7
THE OLD CONTEMPTIBLES
(Grimes)            13/1/77-8
THE OLD SILENT (Grimes)
12/3/96-7
SHADOWS IN BRONZE
(Davis)            13/4/101-2
SILVER PIGS (Davis)    12/4/83-4
Gough, Lawrence
THE GOLDFISH BOWL (TAR)
11/1/59; 11/2/70

Goulart, Ron
BIG BANG (R)              7/3/37
THE GREAT BRITISH
DETECTIVES (ed.) (R)     7/4/30
THE HARDBOILED DICKS: AN
ANTHOLOGY AND STUDY OF
PULP DETECTIVE FICTION
(ed.) (R)            1/2/37
SKYROCKET STEELS (IAC) 4/6/33
Gould, Heywood
ONE DEAD DEBUTANTE
(M*F)                1/2/23
*Gould, Nat*
The Value of Gould (Fellows)
13/1/3-6
GOULDEN FLEECE, THE (Obstfeld)
(M*F)                3/6/34
Goyne, Richard
THE LIPSTICK CLUE
(TBR)              12/3/76-7
SAVARIN'S SHADOW (R)13/2/82-3
Graeme, Bruce
THE DISAPPEARANCE OF
ROGER TREMAYNE (R)    1/2/41
Grafton, Sue
"A" IS FOR ALIBI (R)        7/6/50
"B" IS FOR BURGLAR (IAC) 8/5/30
"C" IS FOR CORPSE (IAC) (R)
8/4/38; 8/5/35; 9/1/35; 9/3/32
Graham, Caroline
DEATH OF A HOLLOW MAN
(TAR) (R)      12/3/81; 13/2/81-2
*Graham, Richard.* See Welcome, John
GRAIL TREE, THE (Gash) (M*F)
(R)              4/5/34; 8/3/35
GRAMMARIAN'S FUNERAL, THE
(Acheson) (R)            9/2/39
*Granby, Col. Alistair.* See Beeding,
Francis
Grand, Mitchell
L:                2/6/45; 3/1/48
GRAND MODENA MURDER, THE
(Gribble) (M*F)          3/4/39
GRANDFATHER MEDICINE, THE
(Hager) (R)            12/1/43
Granger, Bill
PUBLIC MURDERS (M*F)    4/3/35
Granovetter, Pamela, and Karen
Thomas McCullum
THE COPPERFIELD CHECKLIST
OF MYSTERY AUTHORS (IAC)
10/2/57
A SHOPPING LIST OF MYSTERY
CLASSICS (IAC)        10/2/56

Grant, Charles L.
  THE HOUR OF THE OXRUN
    DEAD (M*F)      2/3/41
  THE SOUND OF MIDNIGHT
    (M*F)      3/3/37
*Grant, Colonel Duncan. See Seton,*
*Graham*
*Grant, Dr. David. See Mair, George B.*
Grant, Maxwell [Walter Gibson, q.v.]
  FINGERS OF DEATH (M*F) 2/1/26
  GREEN EYES (M*F)    1/3/42
Grant-Adamson, Lesley
  GUILTY KNOWLEDGE (TAR)
      11/1/59; 11/2/71
GRAVE ERROR (Greenleaf)
  (M*F)      5/4/23
GRAVE MISTAKE (Marsh)
  (IAC)      4/3/32
GRAVEDIGGER (Hansen)
  (M*F)      6/4/41
*Graves, Richard L.*
  The Explosive Novels of Richard L.
    Graves (Kelley)    3/6/9-10
*Gravesend Books (MS)*    4/3/2; 6/3/2
GRAVEYARD TO LET, A (Dickson)
  (IAC)      13/1/29-30
GRAY FLANNEL SHROUD (Slesar)
  (IAC)      5/6/29
*Grayson, Rupert*
  (SSC)      6/2/19*
GREAT BLACK KANBA (Little)
  (TBR)      13/4/77
GREAT BRITISH DETECTIVES
  (Greenberg/Hoch, eds.) (IAC) 11/1/34
GREAT BRITISH DETECTIVES,
  THE (Goulart, ed.) (R)    7/4/30
GREAT DETECTIVES (Penzler, ed.)
  (IAC)      2/4/15
GREAT DETECTIVES (Symons)
  (R)      6/3/41
GREAT DYING, THE (Hsu)
  (TNSPE)      10/2/50
GREAT IMPERSONATION, THE
  (Oppenheim) (R)      2/3/49
GREAT INSURANCE MURDERS,
  THE (Propper) (TBR)    10/3/59
Great Lizzie Borden T-Shirt Media
  Event and Mystery Quiz
  (Nevins)      5/6/7-9
Great Merlini, The (Dueren)  4/4/28-32
Greatest Misogynist of Them All, The
  (Cleary)      13/4/61-5

*Greeley, Father Andrew*
  Clergy-Detectives (Cleary)   9/3/3-21
Green, Alan
  WHAT A BODY! (IAC)    5/6/29
*Green, Anna Katherine*
  THE LEAVENWORTH CASE
    (IAC)      6/6/21
  L: McFarland 1/1/40
GREEN ARCHER, THE (Wallace)
  (R)      9/6/47
GREEN EYES (Grant) (M*F)   1/3/42
GREEN FOR DANGER (Brand) (R)
  (IAC) (R)  (IAC)
    2/6/38; 6/4/30; 8/2/40; 11/3/50
*Green, Gregory George Gordon. See*
*Mann, Jack*
GREEN GROW THE DOLLARS
  (Lathen) (R)      6/4/44
Green, Thomas J.
  THE FLOWERED BOX (M*F) 5/2/20
Greenberg, Martin H., ed.
  THE BIG APPLE MYSTERIES
    (w/Asimov/Waugh) (IAC)  6/4/32
  BUFFET FOR UNWELCOME
    GUESTS: THE BEST MYSTERY
    SHORT STORIES OF
    CHRISTIANA BRAND (w/
    Nevins) (IAC)      8/2/22
  EXEUNT MURDERERS, THE
    BEST MYSTERY STORIES OF
    ANTHONY BOUCHER (w/
    Nevins) (IAC)      8/2/22
  GREAT BRITISH DETECTIVES (w/
    Hoch) (IAC)      11/1/34
  THE HUMAN ZERO: THE SCI-
    ENCE FICTION STORIES OF
    ERLE STANLEY GARDNER (w/
    Waugh) (Gardner) (M*F)  5/2/13
  LOCKED ROOM PUZZLES (w/
    Pronzini) (IAC)    11/1/33
  THE MAMMOTH BOOK OF
    PRIVATE EYE STORIES (w/
    Pronzini) (IAC)    11/1/33
  MR. PRESIDENT, PRIVATE EYE
    (w/Nevins) (IAC)    11/1/34
  THE MYSTERY HALL OF FAME
    (w/Pronzini/Waugh) (R)  8/2/33
  TANTALIZING LOCKED ROOM
    STORIES (w/Asimov/Waugh)
    (R)      7/2/33
  THE THIRTEEN CRIMES OF
    SCIENCE FICTION (w/Asimov/
    Waugh) (R)      4/3/45

*Greenberg, Martin H., ed.,* continued
  THE 13 HORRORS OF HALLO-
    WEEN (w/Asimov/Waugh)
    (IAC)                    8/1/17
  TWELVE CRIMES OF CHRIST-
    MAS (w/Asimov/Waugh)
    (IAC)                    6/3/22
Greenburg, Dan
  LOVE KILLS (M*F) (R) 3/1/31 & 42
*Greene, Douglas G.*
  THE COLLECTED SHORT
    FICTION OF NGAIO MARSH
    (ed.) (IAC) (TAR)
          11/4/85; 12/2/69; 12/3/87
  THE DEAD SLEEP LIGHTLY
    (Carr) (ed.) (R) (IAC)
      7/6/49; 8/1/26; 8/3/28; 10/2/74
  DEATH LOCKED IN (w/Adey, ed.)
    (IAC)                    9/5/23
  THE DOOR TO DOOM AND
    OTHER DETECTIONS (Carr)
    (ed.) (M*F)              4/5/35
  L: 8/2/47; 8/3/49; 10/1/92; 10/3/77;
    12/2/97-8
  The Social World in Dr. Gideon
    Fell's Shorter Cases (Christopher)
                            13/3/3-22
*Greene, Graham*
  Obituary (Lachman)       13/3/69-70
Greene, Paulette
  L:                        7/4/39
*Greenfield, C.B.* See Kallen, Lucille
*Greenhill Crime Classics* (MS)  9/1/5-6
Greenleaf, Stephen
  DEATH BED (M*F)           6/6/28
  GRAVE ERROR (M*F)         5/4/23
  STATE'S EVIDENCE (M*F)    6/6/30
*Greenstreet, Sidney*
  MASTERS OF MENACE:
    GREENSTREET AND LORRE
    (Sennett) (R)           7/2/37
Greenwood, John [John Buxton Hilton,
    q.v.]
  MISTS OVER MOSLEY (IAC)
                            10/3/40
  MOSLEY BY MOONLIGHT
    (IAC)                   10/3/40
*Gregg Press* (MS)          3/5/34
Gresham, Elizabeth
  PUZZLE IN PORCELAIN (R)10/1/84
Gribble, Leonard R.
  THE GRAND MODENA MURDER
    (M*F)                   3/4/39

Grierson, Edward
  A CRIME OF ONE'S OWN
    (TCITC)                 3/4/16
Grierson, Francis D.
  THE SMILING DEATH (TBR)
                            13/2/60-1
*Griffin, John*
  (SSC)                    6/2/19-20*
GRIM REAPER (De Noux) (R)  10/3/75
GRIME AND PUNISHMENT
    (Churchill) (R)         13/4/95-6
*Grimes, Martha*
  An Evening with Martha Grimes
    (Gottschalk)            12/3/65-6
  THE OLD CONTEMPTIBLES
    (R)                     13/1/77-8
  THE OLD SILENT (R)        12/3/96-7
Grise Notes (Townsend)      8/1/46
Grochowski, Mary Ann
  Behind the Scenes at Bouchercon 9,
    Or It was Murder at the Bismarck!
                            2/6/3-6,8
  Bouchercon VIII: "Murder at the
    Waldorf"                2/2/15-8,14
  Bouchercon X: Two Views (w/
    Lachman)                3/5/11-3
  L:                  2/3/66; 4/2/56
  Reviews:
    DEATH AT THE OPERA
      (Mitchell)            2/5/42
    THE MISADVENTURES OF
      SHERLOCK HOLMES
      (Queen, ed.)          3/3/40
    THE RED RIGHT HAND
      (Rogers)              2/5/42
Groff, Mary
  L:                        1/2/51
Grothe, David
  Review: ROSS MACDONALD
    (Bruccoli)              8/1/35
Grove, Marjorie J.
  YOU'LL DIE TONIGHT (IAC)4/5/26
Gruber, Frank
  THE FRENCH KEY MYSTERY
    (R)                     1/5/47
  MURDER '97 (R)            7/4/34
  SWING LOW, SWING DEAD
    (R)                     6/2/46
*Grundt, Dr. Adolf (Clubfoot).* See
  Williams, Valentine
GUARANTEED TO FADE (Bagby)
    (M*F)                   3/4/38

Guest, Judith, and Rebecca Hill
KILLING TIME IN ST. CLOUD
(TAR)          11/1/59; 11/2/71
GUIDE TO MOVIES ON VIDEO
CASSETTE (Blades et al.)
(IAC)                    11/4/55
Guild, Nicholas
CHAIN REACTION (IAC)     8/4/31
GUILTY, BUT— (Kyle) (IAC)  8/4/32
GUILTY BYSTANDER (Miller)
(R)                      1/5/49
GUILTY KNOWLEDGE (Grant-
Adamson) (TAR)   11/1/59; 11/2/71
GUILTY THING SURPRISED, A
(Rendell) (R)            3/4/44
*Gull, Vladimir*
Vladimir Gull (Dukeshire)  4/3/22
GUN IN CHEEK (Pronzini) (IAC)7/2/23
Gunn, Victor
FOOTSTEPS OF DEATH
(MS)               12/3/10-11
Gun-Toting Yankee in King Arthur's
Court, A: The Violent World of
Dempsey and Makepeace
(Skinner)             8/6/25-6,30
Gutcheon, Beth
STILL MISSING (R)        7/5/48
*Guthrie, A.B.*
NO SECOND WIND (M*F)     4/3/36
Obituary (Lachman)       13/3/70
*Gutteridge, Lindsay* (TBR)   11/1/49

# H

Haddad, C.A.
THE MOROCCAN (M*F)       3/3/33
OPERATION APRICOT (R)    2/4/45
Haddam, Jane
PRECIOUS BLOOD (R)   13/4/103-4
*Hadden, Richard.* See MacIsaac, Fred
Hagemann, E.R.
Captain Joseph T. Shaw's Black
Mask Scrapbook        7/1/2-6
COMPREHENSIVE INDEX TO
BLACK MASK, 1920–1951
(IAC)                    7/2/22
Hager, Jean
THE GRANDFATHER MEDICINE
(R)                     12/1/43
Haggard, Paul
DEAD IS THE DOOR-NAIL
(TBR)                   11/2/94

*Haggard, William*
(SSC)                    4/3/27*
YESTERDAY'S ENEMY (M*F)
1/4/37
HAG'S NOOK (Carr) (R)     P/35-6
*Hailey, Dr. Eustace.* See Wynne,
Anthony
Hailey, J.P.
THE BAXTER TRUST (TAR)
11/1/60; 11/2/71
HAIR OF THE SLEUTHHOUND
(Breen) (IAC)            6/3/24
*Hale, Christopher*
Little Old Ladies (Nehr)   3/4/3-7
MURDER ON DISPLAY (M*F)
4/3/40
*Halfaday Creek Stories*
The Saint of the North (Harwood)
3/6/3-7*
*Hall, Adam* [Elleston Trevor, q.v.]
The Quiller Report (Banks/
Dawson)               4/1/8-11*
(SSC)                    4/3/26-7*
L: Doerrer 4/5/47
Hall, F.H.
IN THE LAMB WHITE DAYS
(M*F) (R)           P/30; 2/1/36
Hall, Mary Bowen
EMMA CHIZZIT AND THE
QUEEN ANNE KILLER
(TAR)                 12/3/81-2
Hall, Parnell
FAVOR (TAR)       11/1/60; 11/2/72
Hall, Robert Lee
EXIT SHERLOCK HOLMES (M*F)
(R)          1/5/31 & 51; 3/5/44
THE KING EDWARD PLOT
(R)                      4/2/46
MURDER AT SAN SIMEON
(TNSPE) 10/2/50
Hall, Tanis
DOROTHY SAYERS: A REFER-
ENCE GUIDE (IAC)        7/2/23
Hall, Trevor L.
DOROTHY L. SAYERS: NINE
LITERARY STUDIES (IAC)6/3/23
Hallahan, William H.
CATCH ME: KILL ME (IAC)  3/2/23
*Halliday, Brett.* Also see Baker, Asa
MICHAEL SHAYNE'S LONG
CHANCE (M*F)          2/4/32
L: Nevins 7/4/45

HALLOWE'EN PARTY (Christie)
(R)                          13/1/75-6
HALO FOR SATAN (Evans)
(M*F)                            4/3/41
HALO IN BRASS (Browne)
(IAC)                           10/4/51
Halpern, Frank
L:                               1/1/40
HAL'S OWN MURDER CASE (Martin)
(R)                             12/1/38
*Hambledon, Thomas Elphinstone.* See
Coles, Manning
HAMBURG SWITCH, THE (Ross)
(R)                              4/4/46
Hamill, Pete
DIRTY LAUNDRY (M*F)         3/5/37
*Hamilton, Donald*
THE AMBUSHERS (R)          1/2/38
The Degeneration of Donald
Hamilton (Kelley)         1/6/11-12
The Hard-Boiled World of Matt
Helm (Skinner)        10/1/39-53*
THE INTRIGUERS (R)         4/3/46
LINK OF FIRE (MS)          12/3/7-8
The Matt Helm Series (Banks/
Townsend)              2/2/3-11*
MURDERERS' ROW (R)         1/5/50
THE RAVAGERS (R)           1/2/38
THE REMOVERS (R)           1/4/53
THE RETALIATORS (M*F)      1/1/30
THE TERRORIZERS (R)        1/6/48
L: Banks 2/1/52; Kelley 2/2/51
Hamilton, Frank
L:                               2/2/44
*Hammer, Mike.* See Spillane, Mickey
*Hammett, Dashiell*
BEAMS FALLING: THE ART OF
DASHIELL HAMMETT (Wolfe)
(IAC)                         6/4/32
DASHIELL HAMMETT: A DE-
SCRIPTIVE BIBLIOGRAPHY
(Layman) (R)                  3/6/49
THE DASHIELL HAMMETT TOUR
(Herren) (IAC)     7/2/25; 13/4/86
Hammett Revisited (Strøm)12/2/29-31
The "I" in the Private Eye
(Saylor)                    9/1/23-7
(IAC)                         8/1/19
THE MALTESE FALCON
(M*F)                         5/3/31
The Real Originality of Dashiell
Hammett (McSherry)    11/2/25-35

*Hamamett, Dashiell,* continued
SHADOW MAN: THE LIFE OF
DASHIELL HAMMETT (Layman)
(M*F)                         6/1/32
Spade Trumps Unplayed (Banks)
8/6/3-6
WOMAN IN THE DARK (R) 11/1/73
Hammett Revisited: Or, The Inscrutable
Investigator (Strøm)     12/2/29-31
HAMPTON HEAT (Weinman)
(TAR)                        10/4/47
Hancer, Kevin B.
THE PAPERBACK PRICE GUIDE
(IAC) (M*F)        4/6/32; 5/1/28
HAND OF DEATH, THE (Yorke)
(R)                           7/5/42
Handley, Alan
KISS YOUR ELBOW (M*F)   3/6/37
HANDS OF HEALING MURDER,
THE (D'Amato) (IAC) (M*F) (R)
5/1/17; 5/2/21; 6/4/18
HANGED MEN, THE (Harper) (M*F)
(R) (IAC)   1/2/28; 2/3/54; 2/5/3
L: Dillon 2/6/51
HANGING CAPTAIN, THE (Wade)
(IAC) (M*F)         6/1/29; 6/2/34
HANGMAN'S ROW (Stein)
(M*F)                         6/3/32
Hannay, Margaret P., ed.
AS HER WHIMSEY TOOK HER:
CRITICAL ESSAYS ON
DOROTHY L. SAYERS (R)3/5/45
*Hansen, Joseph*
BACKTRACK (R)               8/1/31
BOHANNON'S BOOK (IAC)
12/2/67-8
BOHANNON'S WAY (IAC) 11/1/31
Deadly Edges of the Gay Blade
(Alderson)                7/3/23-8*
GRAVEDIGGER (M*F)          6/5/41
(IAC)                         5/6/31
Light and Sound by Joseph Hansen
(Alderson)                  8/3/12-7
NIGHTWORK (R)               8/1/32
*Hansen, Robert P.* (TBR)      11/1/49
Hapgood, David, and Ben Weider
THE MURDER OF NAPOLEON
(IAC)                         8/1/16
HARD CASH (Collins) (R)      6/1/44
HARD TO KILL (Marcott) (M*F)  P/26
HARD TRADE (Lyons) (M*F)    5/4/24
HARDBALL (Sangster) (TAR)
11/1/66; 11/2/78

*Hardboiled* (magazine) (IAC)    11/1/31
HARDBOILED AMERICA: THE
   LURID YEARS OF PAPERBACKS
   (O'Brien) (R) (M*F)    5/6/42; 6/1/31
*Hard-Boiled Detective Fiction*
   The Crime Novels of Harold R.
      Daniels (Kelley)    3/4/13-5
   The Degeneration of Donald
      Hamilton (Kelley)    1/6/11-12
   Favorite Magazine Issues
      (Banks)    4/6/7-8
   Hammett Revisited: Or, The
      Inscrutable Investigator
      (Strøm)    12/2/29-31
   THE HARD-BOILED DETECTIVE:
      STORIES FROM BLACK MASK
      MAGAZINE (Ruhm, ed.) (R)
                   1/2/34 & 35
   THE HARDBOILED DICKS: AN
      ANTHOLOGY AND STUDY OF
      PULP DETECTIVE FICTION
      (Goulart, ed.) (R)    1/2/37
   The Hard-Boiled World of Matt
      Helm (Skinner)    10/1/39-53*
   The "I" in the Private Eye
      (Saylor)    9/1/23-7
   I Remember...Pulp Mysteries–
      Mystery Pulps (Banks)    3/4/19-22
   In Defense of Carroll John Daly
      (Mertz)    2/3/19-22*
   The Matt Helm Series (Banks/
      Townsend)    2/2/3-11*
   Move Over Spenser (Saylor)
                   10/2/43-7
   The Violent World of Mike Hammer
      (Traylor)    7/6/13-20
HARD-BOILED DETECTIVE, THE:
   STORIES FROM BLACK MASK
   MAGAZINE (Ruhm, ed.) (R)
                   1/2/34 & 35
   L: Meyerson 1/3/56
*Hard Boiled Dicks* (magazine)
   (MS)    6/3/3; 6/6/1
HARDBOILED DICKS, THE: AN
   ANTHOLOGY AND STUDY OF
   PULP DETECTIVE FICTION
   (Goulart, ed.) (R)    1/2/37
Hardinge, George, ed.
   WINTER'S CRIMES 9 (M*F) 3/1/32
Hardwick, Michael
   THE COMPLETE GUIDE TO
      SHERLOCK HOLMES (IAC)
                   10/2/56

*Hardwick, Michael,* continued
   PRISONER OF THE DEVIL
      (R)    6/4/36
   THE PRIVATE LIFE OF DOCTOR
      WATSON (R)    8/1/27
   SHERLOCK HOLMES: MY LIFE
      AND CRIMES (IAC)    8/4/30
*Hardy Boys*
   GHOST OF THE HARDY BOYS:
      AN AUTOBIOGRAPHY (Mc-
      Farlane) (R)    7/3/36
*Hare, Cyril*
   Crime Novelists as Writers of
      Children's Fiction (Sarjeant)
                   12/4/39-42
   TENANT FOR DEATH (IAC) 5/5/18
   THE WIND BLOWS DEATH
      (M*F)    6/6/31
Harling, Robert
   THE ENORMOUS SHADOW
      (IAC)    5/6/31
HARM'S WAY (Aird) (R)    9/6/35
Harper, David
   THE HANGED MEN (M*F) (R)
      (IAC)    1/2/28; 2/3/54; 2/5/3
   THE PATCHWORK MAN (R) 2/5/44
*Harper Perennial Library* (IAC)    5/4/19
*Harrigan and Hoeffler.* See Hood,
   James
Harrington, Joyce
   FAMILY REUNION (M*F)    6/5/42
   NO ONE KNOWS MY NAME
      (M*F)    6/2/36
Harris, Herbert, ed.
   JOHN CREASEY'S CRIME
      COLLECTION 1981 (R)    6/2/46
Harris, Timothy
   GOODNIGHT AND GOOD-BYE
      (R) (M*F) (R)
                   4/2/50; 5/3/31; 7/1/42
   KYD FOR HIRE (R)    2/3/52
Harrison, Chip [Lawrence Block, q.v.]
   MAKE OUT WITH MURDER
      (R)    1/2/45
   THE TOPLESS TULIP CAPER
      (R)    1/2/45
Harrison, William
   HELL'S FULL (R)    2/6/42
HARRY'S GAME (Seymour)
      (R)    2/1/44
Hart, Anne
   THE LIFE AND TIMES OF MISS
      JANE MARPLE (IAC)    10/2/58

Hart, Carolyn G.
 DEATH ON DEMAND (IAC) 12/4/46
 DESIGN FOR MURDER (R) 10/3/68
 A LITTLE CLASS ON MURDER
  (R)                          12/1/42
*Hart, Jeanne*
 Obituary (Lachman)           13/1/32
Hartshorne
 THE MEXICAN ASSASSIN
  (M*F)                        2/6/30
*Harvester, Simon*
 (SSC)              4/4/16*; 6/2/20*
Harwood, John
 L: 3/2/56; 3/3/53; 3/4/59; 3/5/49;
  4/1/41
 The Saint of the North: Black John
  Smith of Halfaday Creek  3/6/3-7*
Hatch, Robert
 L:                           10/1/94
HATCHETT (McGraw) (M*F)       1/2/26
Haughey, Thomas Bruce
 THE CASE OF THE INVISIBLE
  THIEF (TBR) (R)
          10/3/54; 12/1/36-7
HAUNTED BOOKSHOP, THE
 (Morley) (IAC)               7/5/27
Hauser, Thomas
 THE BEETHOVEN CONSPIRACY
  (R)                         9/2/44
Hawkins, Willard E.
 THE COWLED MENACE
  (M*F)                        2/4/35
Hay, Angie
 L:      10/4/58; 12/2/98; 13/2/96-7
*Hay, Sara Henderson*
 Obituary (Lachman)           9/4/38
*Haycraft, Howard*
 Obituary (Lachman)           13/4/90
Hayes, William Edward
 BLACK CHRONICLE (TBR)
          13/1/36-7
Haymon, S.T.
 DEATH AND THE PREGNANT
  VIRGIN (R)                  8/1/32
 RITUAL MURDER (R)            7/5/47
 A VERY PARTICULAR MURDER
  (R)                         12/4/85-6
*Hazeltine, Gillian. See Worts, George F.*
Hazen, Ruth
 In the Footsteps of Wilkie Collins
          11/1/13-14
 L:        10/4/59; 12/2/100-1
HAZZARD (Brown) (R)           9/6/38

HE DIDN'T MIND DANGER (Gilbert)
 (IAC)                        11/3/47
HE DIED OF MURDER! (Smith)
 (TBR)                        12/3/74
HE WOULDN'T KILL PATIENCE
 (Dickson) (IAC)              11/4/53
*Head, Lee*
 THE CRYSTAL CLEAR CASE
  (M*F)                        2/3/43
 Little Old Ladies (Nehr)     3/4/3-7
 Obituary (Lachman)           7/5/30
HEADCASE (Cody) (R)           8/4/41
HEADLESS VICTORY (Lifson)
 (M*F)                        3/3/38
*Heald, Max. See Hossent, Harry*
*Heald, Tim*
 A CLASSIC ENGLISH CRIME (ed.)
  (R)                         13/4/49
 (SSC)                        4/4/17*
 UNBECOMING HABITS (R)        6/5/50
*Healy, Jeremiah*
 Move Over Spenser (Saylor)
          10/2/43-7
 SWAN DIVE (R) (TAR)
          10/4/56; 11/1/54
 YESTERDAY'S NEWS (R) (TAR)
          12/1/41; 12/3/82
Heath, Eric
 DEATH TAKES A DIVE (TBR)
          11/3/63
 MURDER IN THE MUSEUM
  (TBR)                       11/3/63
 MURDER OF A MYSTERY
  WRITER (M*F)                3/2/39
HEAT'S ON, THE (Himes) (R)
          13/1/68-70
HEAVEN'S PRISONERS (Burke)
 (R)                          10/3/73
Hedman, Iwan
 DECKARE OCH THRILLERS PA
  SVENSKA, 1864–1973
  [DETECTIVE STORIES AND
  THRILLERS IN SWEDISH,
  1864–1973] (R)              2/5/7
 The History and Activities of
  Mystery Fans in Sweden (and
  Scandinavia)                3/4/12,15
 KRIMINALITERATURE PA
  SVENSKA 1749–1985 [CRIME
  FICTION IN SWEDEN 1749–
  1985] (R)                   9/5/37

*Hedman, Iwan*, continued
  Leslie Charteris and the Saint: Five
    Decades of Partnership (w/
    Alexandersson)      4/4/21-7
  L:      2/5/57; 4/2/60; 5/2/44; 5/5/47
  A Report on The Crime Writers Third
    International Congress      5/6/10-2
HEIST ME HIGHER (Ballinger)
  (R)                      1/4/52
*Helen, Sister Mary.* See O'Marie, Sister
  Carol Anne
HELL'S FULL (Harrison) (R)      2/6/42
*Hellman, Lillian*
  Obituary (Lachman)          8/3/29
*Helm, Matt.* See Hamilton, Donald
Hely, Elizabeth
  A MARK OF DISPLEASURE
    (TBR)                  11/3/67
Henaghan, Jim
  AZOR! (M*F)              2/3/45
HENCHMAN, THE (Bornemark)
  (TAR)                  13/1/51
Henderson, Laurence
  MAJOR INQUIRY (M*F) (R)
                        1/1/27; 8/4/40
HENDON'S FIRST CASE (Rhode)
  (R)                      4/4/44
Hendricks, Michael
  MONEY TO BURN (TAR)    12/3/82
*Hendryx, James B.*
  The Saint of the North (Harwood)
                        3/6/3-7*
*Hensley, Joe L.*
  Law, Lawyers and Justice
    (Frauenglas)          4/1/3-7
  L:      2/4/59; 2/6/49; 3/1/54; 5/4/38
  MINOR MURDERS (R) (M*F)
                        4/1/32; 4/2/36
  (MS)                    9/1/4-5
  OUTCASTS (R)              5/2/26
  ROBAK'S RUN (R)        12/4/79-80
Henson, Robert
  "Lizzie Borden in the P.M."
    (R)                    9/1/31
*Herbert, James*
  Some Recent Hybrids (Kelley)
                        6/2/16-8
HERE COMES CHARLIE M (Free-
  mantle) (M*F) (R)      3/4/38; 4/2/50
Here Comes the Judge: The "Nero"
  Award (Crider)          3/6/8

HEREWITH THE CLUES, THE
  FOURTH DENNIS WHEATLEY
  MURDER MYSTERY (Wheatley)
  (R)                      8/3/40
HERO BY PROXY (Teilhet) (R)  5/3/40
HEROES AND HUMANITIES:
  DETECTIVE FICTION AND
  CULTURE (Browne) (MS)      9/2/1
HEROINES: A BIBLIOGRAPHY OF
  WOMEN SERIES CHARACTERS
  IN MYSTERY, ESPIONAGE,
  ACTION, SCIENCE FICTION,
  FANTASY, HORROR, WESTERN,
  ROMANCE AND JUVENILE
  NOVELS (Drew) (MS)        11/4/2
Herren, Don
  THE DASHIELL HAMMETT TOUR
    (IAC)      7/2/25; 13/4/86
Hervey, Evelyn [H.R.F. Keating, q.v.]
  INTO THE VALLEY OF DEATH
    (R)                  11/4/91
Herzog, Evelyn
  L:                      7/4/43
  Young Detective Kildare    7/2/2-10
Hess, Joan
  MISCHIEF IN MAGGODY (TAR)
                        11/1/61; 11/2/72
  THE MURDER AT THE MURDER
    AT THE MIMOSA INN (R)
                        10/3/69
Heyer, Georgette
  A BLUNT INSTRUMENT (R)
                        10/1/85
  THEY FOUND HIM DEAD
    (R)                    1/6/42
Hiaasen, Carl, and William D.
  Montalbano
  A DEATH IN CHINA (IAC)  11/4/47
HIDDEN WAYS (Van de Water)
  (TBR)                  11/1/39
HIDE AND SEEK (Berg) (TAR) 11/4/74
Higgins, George V.
  THE FRIENDS OF EDDIE COYLE
    (IAC)                10/4/52
  KENNEDY FOR THE DEFENSE
    (R)                    4/5/43
  THE RAT ON FIRE (R)      5/2/26
Higgins, Jack [Harry Patterson, q.v.]
  STORM WARNING (R)        1/2/40
HIGH PLACES (Ferris) (M*F)    1/5/30
HIGH STAKES (Francis) (IAC)  6/1/28
HIGH, WIDE AND RANSOM (Tracy)
  (M*F)                  1/2/28

*Highsmith, Patricia* (IAC)  11/1/31
Hill, Alette L.
   L:  7/1/50
Hill, Headon
   THE NARROWING CIRCLE
     (R)  2/5/38
Hill, Peter
   THE ENTHUSIAST (M*F)  3/6/28
   THE HUNTERS (M*F)  1/3/37
Hill, Rebecca, and Judith Guest
   KILLING TIME IN ST. CLOUD
     (TAR)  11/1/59; 11/2/71
Hill, Reginald
   AN APRIL SHROUD (R)  13/1/71-2
   RULING PASSION (M*F)  2/3/42
   THERE ARE NO GHOSTS IN THE
     SOVIET UNION (IAC) (R)
       11/1/31; 12/2/68-9; 13/2/80-1
*Hillerman, Tony*
   THE BLESSING WAY (IAC) 11/1/23
   DANCE HALL OF THE DEAD
     (IAC)  11/1/23
   THE DARK WIND (R) (IAC)
       6/4/43; 10/3/66; 12/1/24
   THE FLY ON THE WALL (IAC)
       11/1/23; 12/2/63
   Hunter and Hunted (Bakerman)
       5/1/3-10
   (MS)  12/3/2-6
   SKINWALKERS (R) (IAC)
       10/3/66; 12/1/24-5
   A THIEF OF TIME (R)  10/3/65
Hilton, John Buxton. Also see Green-
   wood, John
   DEAD-NETTLE (M*F)  2/5/26
   GAMEKEEPER'S GALLOWS
     (M*F)  1/6/38
   SOME RUN CROOKED (M*F)
       3/1/34
Himes, Chester
   COTTON COMES TO HARLEM
     (R)  13/1/68-70
   THE HEAT'S ON (R)  13/1/68-70
   THE REAL COOL KILLERS
     (R)  13/1/68-70
Himmel, Randy
   L:  7/4/38
   Reviews:
     GHOST OF THE HARDY BOYS:
     AN AUTOBIOGRAPHY (Mc-
     Farlane)  7/3/36

*Himmel, Randy,* continued
   *Reviews* continued
     MASTERS OF MENACE:
     GREENSTREET AND LORRE
     (Sennett)  7/2/37
Himmell, Richard
   I HAVE GLORIA KIRBY (M*F)
       2/5/34
   THE TWENTY-THIRD WEB
     (R)  2/4/45
Hinkemeyer, Michael T.
   THE FIELDS OF EDEN (M*F)
       3/1/33
Hinkle, Vernon
   MUSIC TO MURDER BY (R) 2/5/44
HIS MASTER'S VOICE (Low)
   (R)  5/3/40
His Own Desert (Bleiler)  3/4/11,15
History and Activities of Mystery Fans
   in Sweden (and Scandinavia)
   (Hedman)  3/4/12,15
HITCH: THE LIFE AND TIMES OF
   ALFRED HITCHCOCK (Taylor)
   (R)  4/2/52
*Hitchcock, Alfred*
   ALFRED HITCHCOCK ANTHOL-
   OGY #27: MURDER AND
   OTHER MISHAPS (Jordan, ed.)
     (IAC)  12/2/64-5
   Alfred Hitchcock's Mystery Magazine
     (IAC)  3/3/49
   THE DARK SIDE OF GENIUS:
   THE LIFE OF ALFRED
   HITCHCOCK (Spoto) (R) (IAC)
       7/2/31; 7/5/27
   HITCH: THE LIFE AND TIMES OF
   ALFRED HITCHCOCK (Taylor)
     (R)  4/2/52
   MURDERERS' ROW (ed.) (M*F)
       1/1/33
Hitchens, Bert and Dolores
   F.O.B. MURDER (R)  10/1/86
   HOBGOBLIN (Coyne) (R)  6/6/39
*Hoch, Edward D.*
   BEST DETECTIVE STORIES OF
   THE YEAR–1977 (ed.) (M*F)
       2/1/21
   GREAT BRITISH DETECTIVES (w/
   Greenberg, ed.) (IAC)  11/1/34
   (IAC)  3/3/18,49
   THE NIGHT MY FRIEND (R)
       13/4/50-1

Hoch, Edward D., continued
THE THEFTS OF NICK VELVET
(R)                    2/6/39; 3/1/44
THE YEAR'S BEST MYSTERY
AND SUSPENSE STORIES, 1987
(ed.) (IAC)                9/5/24
THE YEAR'S BEST MYSTERY
AND SUSPENSE STORIES, 1988
(IAC)                     11/1/32
THE YEAR'S BEST MYSTERY
AND SUSPENSE STORIES, 1989
(IAC)                     12/2/65
THE YEAR'S BEST MYSTERY
AND SUSPENSE STORIES, 1991
(R)                       13/4/47
Hocking, Ann
DEATH DISTURBS MR.
JEFFERSON (TCITC)        3/2/11
HOG MURDERS, THE (DeAndrea)
(R) (IAC)         3/6/47; 11/3/48
Holding, Elisabeth Sanxay
THE BLANK WALL (R) (IAC)
1/5/46; 13/4/85-6
THE INNOCENT MRS. DUFF (IAC)
13/4/85-6
Holland, Isabelle
Clergy-Detectives (Cleary)   9/3/3-21
A FATAL ADVENT (R)
12/1/40; 13/89-90
HOLLOW MEN (Flannery) (IAC) 6/6/21
HOLLOW VENGEANCE (Morice)
(R)                        6/3/40
HOLLYWOOD AND LEVINE
(Bergman) (R)              8/2/34
HOLLYWOOD DETECTIVE:
GARRISON (Rovin) (R)       1/1/34
Holman, [Clarence] Hugh
ANOTHER MAN'S POISON
(TBR)                     11/1/47
Obituary (Lachman)         6/1/29
SLAY THE MURDERER (M*F)
(TBR)           P/24; 11/1/47
HOLMES-DRACULA FILE, THE
(Saberhagen) (R)           2/6/36
Holmes, Mr. See Bark, Conrad Voss
Holmes, Sherlock. Also see Doyle,
Arthur Conan
The Apocryphalization of Holmes
(Bleiler)                 4/5/3-5
ASIMOV'S SHERLOCKIAN
LIMERICKS (Asimov) (R)  2/4/42
Deduction in Duplicate (Mosier)
7/2/19-21,30

Holmes, Sherlock, continued
THE ENCYCLOPEDIA SHER-
LOCKIANA (Tracey) (IAC) 4/1/15
THE FILMS OF SHERLOCK
HOLMES (Steinbrunner/Michaels)
(R)                        3/3/43
(IAC)                      9/3/30
The Onomastics of Sherlock
(Fleissner)              8/3/21-4
THE PRIVATE LIFE OF DOCTOR
WATSON (Hardwick) (R)   8/1/27
L: Bradley 12/1/58-60; Harwood
3/5/49
Holt, Samuel
ONE OF US IS WRONG (IAC)
(R)                8/6/33; 8/6/40
Holton, Leonard
A CORNER OF PARADISE
(M*F)                      2/1/22
Homes, Geoffrey
The Books of Geoffrey Homes
(Dukeshire)              3/3/19-21*
BUILD MY GALLOWS HIGH
(R)                        3/4/49
THE CASE OF THE MEXICAN
KNIFE (R)                  3/4/49
FORTY WHACKS (R)          10/1/87
THE MAN WHO MURDERED
GOLIATH (R)                2/5/43
THE MAN WHO MURDERED
HIMSELF (R)                2/5/42
Homosexuality
Deadly Edges of the Gay Blade
(Alderson)               7/3/23-8*
Light and Sound by Joseph Hansen
(Alderson)               8/3/12-7
L: Fellows 10/2/82; Hatch 10/1/94;
Townsend comment 10/1/95
Hone, Ralph E.
DOROTHY L. SAYERS: A LIT-
ERARY BIOGRAPHY (R)  3/5/45
HONEYBATH'S HAVEN (Innes)
(M*F)                      2/5/29
Honorable Charlie Mortdecai, The: An
Oxymoron (Deeck)           9/3/22-6
Hood, James
(SSC)                      4/6/5*
HOODED VULTURE MURDERS,
THE (Koehler) (R)          3/3/47
HOODWINK (Pronzini) (M*F)   5/5/27
HOOK #1, THE: THE GILDED
CANARY (Latham) (M*F)      6/2/35

HOOKERS DON'T GO TO HEAVEN
(Roper) (M*F)                    1/2/26
Hoopes, Roy
   CAIN (IAC)                    7/2/24
*Hopkins, Kenneth*
   Blow and Manciple (Deeck)
                              10/1/55-60*
*Horan, James P.*
   Obituary (Lachman)            6/1/29
HORIZONTAL MAN, THE (Eustis)
   (IAC)                         7/1/33
Horn, Pierre L.
   Gide's "Vatican Cellars": The
   Popular Detective Novel
   Parodied                      6/2/11-5
*Horne, Charles.* See Tucker, Wilson
Hornig, Doug
   DEEP DIVE (TNSPE) (TAR)
                         10/2/51; 11/1/55
HORSE UNDER WATER (Deighton)
   (R)                           2/5/44
*Hossent, Harry*
   (SSC)                         5/3/19*
HOSTAGE: LONDON (Household)
   (R)                           2/3/50
HOSTAGE TO DEATH (Ashford)
   (M*F)                         2/5/26
HOT TODDY (Edmonds) (IAC)
                              12/1/25-8
   L: Nevins 12/2/91-2
HOUR OF THE OXRUN DEAD, THE
   (Grant) (M*F)                 2/3/41
HOUSE NEXT DOOR, THE
   (Stevenson) (TBR)            10/2/68
HOUSE OF FLESH (Fischer)
   (M*F)                         3/6/32
HOUSE THAT JACK BUILT, THE
   (McBain) (TAR)               11/3/76
*Household, Geoffrey*
   AGAINST THE WIND (R)          3/2/49
   THE COURTESY OF DEATH
   (R)                           4/3/45
   FELLOW PASSENGER (R)13/1/74-5
   HOSTAGE: LONDON (R)           2/3/50
   Obituary (Lachman)           11/1/37
   RED ANGER (R)                 2/2/40
   ROGUE MALE (R)                2/2/40
   WATCHER IN THE SHADOWS
   (R)                           2/2/40
Household in Kempenfeldt Square, The:
   Antony Maitland and the Writings of
   Sara Woods (Sarjeant)       10/4/3-40*

Houston, Robert
   THE FOURTH CODEX (TAR)
                                11/1/56
HOW TO WRITE BEST SELLING
   FICTION (Koontz) (R)          5/6/43
Howard, Clark
   "The Last One to Cry" (R)     8/4/27
   "The Wide Loop" (R)           8/6/31
HOWARD HUGHES AFFAIR, THE
   (Kaminsky) (M*F)              3/6/40
Howard, Robert E., and Richard A.
   Lupoff
   THE RETURN OF SKULL-FACE
   (R)                           2/2/21-4
*Howard, Vechel.* Also see LUCINDA
   MURDER WITH LOVE (M*F)5/6/37
   L: Shibuk 6/1/49
Howe, Melodie J.
   THE MOTHER SHADOW
   (R)                          12/1/43
Howes, Royce
   THE CASE OF THE COPY-HOOK
   KILLING (M*F)                 4/4/33
Howie, Edith
   NO FACE TO MURDER (TBR)
                                11/1/45
Hoyt, Richard
   DECOYS (M*F)                  5/2/14
   30 FOR A HARRY (M*F)          6/1/36
Hsu, Kenneth J.
   THE GREAT DYING (TNSPE)
                                10/2/50
Huang, Jim
   L:                            8/2/44
Hubbard, P.M.
   THE DANCING MEN (R)           5/5/38
   THE QUIET RIVER (M*F)         3/3/37
*Hubin, Allen J.*
   The Armchair Reviewer (column)
   10/4/43-8; 11/1/50-69; 11/2/63-81;
   11/3/71-83; 11/4/73-82;
   12/2/53-62; 12/3/81-8; 12/4/51-9;
   13/1/47-54; 13/2/43-51; 13/3/75-82
   THE BIBLIOGRAPHY OF CRIME
   FICTION 1749–1975 (IAC)
                             3/3/17 & 48
   CRIME FICTION, 1749–1980: A
   COMPREHENSIVE BIBLIOG-
   RAPHY (R)        8/2/21; 9/3/40-2
   L:    1/3/56; 5/1/39; 5/5/44; 13/2/96
   (MS)                         10/4/2
Hudson, Jeffrey
   A CASE OF NEED (IAC)          5/2/10

Huebner, Frederick D.
  JUDGMENT BY FIRE (IAC) 11/1/25
Hughes, Babette
  MURDER IN CHURCH (R)    9/5/43
Hughes, Dorothy B.
  ERLE STANLEY GARDNER: THE
    CASE OF THE REAL PERRY
    MASON (R)              2/4/37
  THE EXPENDABLE MAN (R)
    (IAC)          5/2/31; 9/5/26
  RIDE THE PINK HORSE (IAC)
                          10/3/40
Hughes, William
  SPLIT ON RED (M*F)      5/6/33
Hugo, Richard
  DEATH AND THE GOOD LIFE
    (R) (M*F)     5/2/27; 5/3/31
Hull, Richard
  A MATTER OF NERVES (R) 2/4/42
  THE GHOST IT WAS (TBR) 11/3/61
HUMAN ZERO, THE: THE SCIENCE
    FICTION STORIES OF ERLE
    STANLEY GARDNER (Gardner)
    (Greenberg/Waugh, eds.) (M*F)
                          5/2/13
Hume, Fergus
  That Pawn-Shop Gypsy
    (Sampson)             8/4/9-16
  L: Hay 10/4/58
HUMMING BOX, THE (Whittington)
    (R)                   3/4/49
Humor, Horror, and Intellect: Giles
    Mont of Ruth Rendell's A
    JUDGEMENT IN STONE
    (Bakerman)            5/4/5-10
Hunt, E. Howard
  ANGEL EYES (R)          1/4/51
  RETURN FROM VORKUTA
    (R)                   1/4/51
  WASHINGTON PAYOFF (R) 1/4/51
  WHERE MURDER WAITS
    (R)                   1/4/51
Hunt, Peter. Also see Yates, George
    Worthing
  MURDERS AT SCANDAL HOUSE
    (TBR)                 13/4/80-1
HUNTED, THE (Leonard) (R)   2/1/35
Hunter and Hunted: Comparison and
    Contrast in Tony Hillerman's
    PEOPLE OF DARKNESS (Baker-
    man)                  5/1/3-10
Hunter, Evan. Also see McBain, Ed
  LIZZIE (R)              8/3/44

Hunter, Harriet
  INCLINATION TO MURDER
    (M*F)                 3/6/33
HUNTER IN THE DARK (Thompson)
    (M*F)                 3/6/28
HUNTER OF THE BLOOD (Masterson)
    (M*F)                 1/5/30
Hunter, Tod
  The Tod Hunter Question (Funct)
                          6/4/3-8
HUNTERS, THE (Hill) (M*F)   1/3/37
Huntress: The Diana Rigg/Patrick
    Macnee Quarterly (MS)   5/6/2
Hurwood, Bernhardt
  Obituary (Lachman)      9/3/34
Husband-and-Wife Detectives
  Amazing Grace (Sampson)  6/4/23-9
  Looking Glass Detection (Isaac)
                          8/5/18-22
  Mr. and Mrs. North (Davis)  1/1/21-6
HUSH MONEY (Collins) (R)    5/6/45
Huston, Fran
  THE RICH GET IT ALL (M*F)
                          3/6/36
Huston, John
  Obituary (Lachman)      9/4/38
Hutter, Ernie
  Twice-Told Tale of Murder
    (Floyd)               6/1/21-6
Hutton, J.P.
  TOO GOOD TO BE TRUE (R) 2/1/47
Huxley, Elspeth
  MURDER AT GOVERNMENT
    HOUSE (IAC)           11/4/50
Hyams, Joe
  MURDER AT THE ACADEMY
    AWARDS (R)            8/1/33
Hyman, Tom
  GIANT KILLER (IAC)      6/6/21
HYTE MANEUVER, THE (Milton)
    (TAR)                 11/3/80

# I

I AM THE CAT (Kutak) (TBR) 11/1/38
I AM THE CHEESE (Cormier)
    (R)                   3/6/42
"I CAN'T DIE HERE" (Nolan)
    (TBR)                 11/4/66
I COULD HAVE DIED (Bagby)
    (M*F)                 3/5/39
I COULD MURDER HER (Lorac)
    (R)                   9/3/43

I HAVE GLORIA KIRBY (Himmell)
  (M*F)                    2/5/34
"I" in the Private Eye, The (Saylor)
                           9/1/23-7
I Remember...B–Movies (Banks)
                           4/5/13-7
  L: Nieminski 4/6/40; Shibuk 4/6/44
I Remember...Pulp Mysteries–Mystery
  Pulps (Banks)            3/4/19-22
  L: Harwood 3/5/49
I Remember...Radio Mysteries
  (Banks)                  3/5/17-9
  L: Harwood 4/1/41
I SPY, YOU DIE (Brown) (R)   10/1/79
I WAKE UP SCREAMING (Fisher)
  (IAC)                    10/4/50
I WAS MURDERED (Wilson)
  (TBR)                    12/4/68-9
I, WITNESS (Garfield, ed.) (IAC) 2/6/29
Iams, Jack
  Obituary (Lachman)       12/1/28
IBIZA SYNDICATE, THE (Reade)
  (M*F)                    2/1/29
ICARUS (Koepf) (TAR)       11/1/56
ICEBREAKER (Gardner) (R)    7/3/39
IF I DON'T TELL (Olson) (M*F)  P/27
IF I SHOULD MURDER (Laing)
  (TBR)                    12/2/47-8
IF YOU WANT A MURDER WELL
  DONE (Scherf) (M*F)        P/26
Immoderate Homage to Modesty
  (Banks)                  4/2/8-10*
  L: Crider 4/3/50; Doerrer 4/5/48;
  O'Donnell 4/4/49
IMPERSONAL ATTRACTIONS
  (Shankman) (IAC)         9/3/31
IMPOSSIBLE VIRGIN, THE
  (O'Donnell) (R)          1/6/54
IMPOSTER, THE (McCloy)
  (M*F)                    2/1/24
IMPROBABLE FICTION: THE LIFE
  OF MARY ROBERTS RINEHART
  (Cohn) (IAC)             8/2/23
In Defense of Carroll John Daly
  (Mertz)                  2/3/19-22*
  L: Crider 2/4/58; Mertz 2/4/59,
  2/5/49; Meyerson 2/4/54;
  Wooster 2/4/55
IN ENEMY HANDS (Sapir/Murphy)
  (M*F)                    1/2/28
IN HOLY TERROR (Sapir/Murphy)
  (R)                      1/3/49
IN JOY STILL FELT (Asimov)
  (IAC)                    6/1/27

In Memorium: John Nieminski
  (Liebow)                 9/2/3-6
IN MEMORY YET GREEN (Asimov)
  (IAC)                    6/1/27
IN SPITE OF THUNDER (Carr)
  (IAC)                    9/1/35
In the Footsteps of Wilkie Collins
  (Hazen)                  11/1/13-14
IN THE HEAT OF THE SUMMER
  (Katzenbach) (R)         8/3/42
IN THE LAKE OF THE MOON
  (Lindsey) (TAR)          11/1/56
IN THE LAMB WHITE DAYS (Hall)
  (M*F) (R)        P/30; 2/1/36
INCIDENT IN ICELAND, AN
  (Webster) (M*F)          4/2/32
INCLINATION TO MURDER
  (Hunter) (M*F)           3/6/33
Index of Books Reviewed in TMF
  (Doerrer): Volume Two
  3/1/26-9; Volume Three 4/2/3-7;
  Volume Four 5/2/3-5; Volume Five
  6/1/2-7
  L: Doerrer 3/1/50, 4/2/54
Index of Books Reviewed in TMF
  Volume I (Including the Preview
  Issue) (Meyerson)        2/1/9-14
Index to The Mystery Fancier (Deeck):
  Volume 6: 10/4/61-84; Volume 7:
  10/4/85-104; Volume 8: 10/3/81-104;
  Volume 9: 10/2/85-104; Volume 10:
  11/1/85-104; Volume 11:
  12/1/69-104; Volume 12: 13/1/89-104
Index to TMF Volumes I-V, An
  (Cook)                   6/5/1-40
  L: Doerrer 7/1/46; Stilwell 7/1/45
INFERNAL DEVICE, THE (Kurland)
  (R)                      3/3/45
INFILTRATOR, THE (York) (R)   P/16
INFLUENCE, THE (Campbell)
  (TAR)                    11/1/52
INFORMATION RECEIVED (Punshon)
  (TBR)                    11/3/65
INK IN HER BLOOD (Martin) (R)
  (IAC)          11/2/98; 12/1/23
Innes, Michael
  THE AMPERSAND PAPERS
    (M*F)                  3/5/39
  APPLEBY TALKING (IAC) 10/1/64
  THE CASE OF SONIA WAYWARD
    (M*F)          2/6/35; 11/4/47
  A COMEDY OF TERRORS
    (IAC)                  9/4/36

*Innes, Michael,* continued
THE DAFFODIL AFFAIR
(IAC) 8/4/31
DEATH BY WATER (R) P/31
DEATH ON A QUIET DAY
(IAC) 13/4/83-4
FROM LONDON FAR (R)
(IAC) 1/4/48; 5/4/18
HONEYBATH'S HAVEN
(M*F) 2/5/29
LORD MULLION'S SECRET
(M*F) 6/1/38
THE MAN FROM THE SEA
(IAC) 7/1/32
A NIGHT OF TERRORS (IAC)
11/3/50
ONE-MAN SHOW (IAC) 9/5/27
THE PAPER THUNDERBOLT
(IAC) 9/4/36
THE WEIGHT OF THE EVIDENCE
(IAC) 8/4/31
INNOCENT BLOOD (James)
(MS) 4/2/2
INNOCENT MRS. DUFF, THE
(Holding) (IAC) 13/4/85-6
INSIDE JOB, AN (Allan) (M*F) 6/3/37
INSPECTOR FRENCH'S GREATEST
CASE (Crofts) (IAC) 9/1/35
*International Polygonics* (MS) 3/5/2,34
Interview with Desmond Bagley, An
(Bakerman) 7/2/13-8,26
Interview with Ed McBain, An
(Skinner) 13/4/3-11
INTIMATE MEMOIRS (Simenon)
(R) 8/3/33
INTO THE VALLEY OF DEATH
(Hervey) (R) 11/4/91
INTRIGUERS, THE (Hamilton)
(R) 4/3/46
Introducing Alexandra Roudybush
(Frazier) 3/3/2-4
L: McCahery 3/4/53
INTRODUCING C.B. GREENFIELD
(Kallen) (R) (IAC) 5/5/41; 6/1/28
INTRODUCING CHIP HARRISON
(Block) (IAC) 8/5/30
INTRODUCTION TO THE
DETECTIVE STORY, AN (IAC)
(Panek) 10/2/54
INVESTIGATION, THE (Uhnak)
(R) 2/1/41
THE INVESTIGATION: Fiction and
Fact (Vicarel) 3/3/15-6
L: Bakerman 2/2/42

INVESTIGATION, THE: Fiction and
Fact (Vicarel) 3/3/15-6
L: Crider 3/4/57
*Invisibility*
A Study in Invisibility (McSherry)
11/3/23-43
INVISIBLE FLAMINI, THE (Brown)
(M*F) 3/5/38
Ireland, Donald
L: 7/3/50
Irvine, Robert P.
BAPTISM FOR THE DEAD (TAR)
11/1/61; 11/2/73
Irving, Clifford
TRIAL (MS) 12/3/11-12
Isaac, Fred
Bleeding the Fun Out 7/5/3-6
L: 7/2/43; 7/4/39; 7/6/44; 8/4/50
Looking Glass Detection: The Norths
and Bill Weigand Speak 8/5/18-22
Isaacs, Susan
COMPROMISING POSITIONS
(R) 3/4/43
Isely, Reymoure Keith
A STRANGE CODE OF JUSTICE
(IAC) 11/3/45
ISLAND OF STEEL (Cohen)
(TAR) 11/2/66
Israel, Peter
THE STIFF UPPER LIP (R)
(M*F) 3/2/49; 3/4/38
IT NEVER RAINS IN LOS ANGELES
(Flowers) (R) 4/1/30
It's About Crime (column) (Lachman)
2/4/15-6; 2/5/3-4; 2/6/27-9,16;
3/2/21-5; 3/3/17-18,49,14; 3/4/23-4;
4/1/13-6; 4/3/31-3; 4/4/18-20;
4/5/24-6; 4/6/31-3; 5/1/17-9;
5/2/10-12; 5/3/22-6; 5/4/18-20;
5/5/17-9; 5/6/29-32; 6/1/27-30;
6/3/22-6; 6/4/30-3; 6/6/19-22;
7/1/32-5; 7/2/22-6; 7/4/20-3;
7/5/26-30; 8/1/16-22; 8/2/21-8;
8/4/29-33; 9/1/33-6; 9/2/24-30;
9/3/29-35; 9/4/35-9; 9/5/23-8;
10/1/61-4; 10/2/53-60; 10/3/39-46;
10/4/49-54; 11/1/22-37; 11/3/45-55;
11/4/47-56; 12/1/23-30; 12/2/63-74;
12/4/43-50; 13/1/27-34; 13/2/52-8;
13/3/65-74; 13/4/83-94

# J

JACK O'LANTERN (Goodchild)
(IAC) 4/6/33

*Jack the Ripper Journal, The*
L: Nieminski 2/5/46
JACKPOT (Pronzini) (TAR)   12/4/52-3
Jackson, Jon A.
   THE BLIND PIG (M*F)   3/6/27
   THE DIEHARD (M*F)   2/1/25
Jacobs, Will, and Gerard Jones
   THE BEAVER PAPERS (R)   8/1/34
*Jacobson, Jerry*
   Encore! (McSherry)   12/1/9-22
Jaffery, Sheldon, ed.
   SELECTED TALES OF GRIM AND
    GRUE FROM THE HORROR
    PULPS (IAC)   11/1/35
Jagoda, Robert
   A FRIEND IN DEED (M*F)   2/4/33
Jahn, Mike
   THE QUARK MANEUVER
    (M*F)   1/5/31
James, David
   CROC' (R)   1/3/45
JAMES JOYCE MURDER, THE
   (Cross) (IAC)   13/1/27-8
*James, P.D.*
   COVER HER FACE (TCITC)
    (IAC)   3/4/16; 9/1/34
   DEATH OF AN EXPERT WIT-
    NESS (R) (M*F)   2/2/36; 2/3/47
   DEVICES AND DESIRES (TAR)
    (IAC)   12/3/82-3; 13/3/67
   A MIND TO MURDER (IAC) 9/2/24
   Piercing the Closed Circle
    (Bakerman)   1/5/3-16
   SHROUD FOR A NIGHTINGALE
    (M*F)   P/24
   THE SKULL BENEATH THE
    SKIN (R)   7/3/33
   AN UNSUITABLE JOB FOR A
    WOMAN (IAC)   7/1/32
JANUS MURDER, THE (Datesh)
   (M*F)   3/5/40
JAPANESE CORPSE, THE (van de
   Wetering) (M*F) (R)   2/5/28; 2/6/41
*Jaysnovitch, Andy*
   L:   6/1/47; 6/3/50; 7/4/48
   (MS)   10/2/2
   The Not So Private Eye   10/2/48-52
Jeffers, H. Paul
   RUBOUT AT THE ONYX
    (M*F)   5/6/37
Jeffries, Roderic
   DEADLY PETARD (R)   7/6/42
   MURDER BEGETS MURDER
    (M*F)   4/2/32

Jepson, Edgar
   THE GIRL'S HEAD (R)   1/3/43
   JERICHO MAN (Lutz) (R)   4/5/37
*Jessup, Richard*
   Obituary (Lachman)   6/6/49
*Jewish Detectives*
   L: Nieminski 4/6/41
Jobst, James
   L:   2/1/57
   Reviews:
    BULLET FOR A STAR
     (Kaminsky)   2/1/44
    HARRY'S GAME (Seymour)
      2/1/44
    LOOPHOLE: OR HOW TO ROB
     A BANK (Pollock)   2/1/44
    STEALING LILLIAN (Kenrick)
      2/1/45
Joe Gall Series, The (Kelley/
   Banks)   3/2/26-35*
Joe Orton's and Tom Stoppard's
   Burlesques of the Detective Genre
   (Bargainnier)   7/1/18-22
JOEY'S CASE (Constantine) (TNSPE)
   (TAR)   10/2/52; 11/2/67
JOHN CREASEY'S CRIME COLLEC-
   TION 1981 (R) (Harris, ed.)   6/2/46
JOHN D. MacDONALD (Geherin)
   (IAC)   7/2/23
John D. MacDonald and the Real
   Murders (Cleary)   11/3/19-22
   L: Cleary 12/2/88-9
John Dickson Carr (1906–1977)
   (Carr)   1/3/3-4
*JOHN DICKSON CARR MEMORIAL*
   *JOURNAL* (French, ed.)
   L: French 2/2/47; Lachman 2/2/53
*Johns, Berry*
   L: Sapp 3/5/50
*Johns, Veronica Parker*
   Little Old Men (Nehr)   4/4/2-6
   Obituary (Lachman)   10/3/45
Johnson, Diane
   THE SHADOW KNOWS (R)   7/5/42
*Johnson, Jean*
   Obituary (Lachman)   12/1/28
*Johnson, Johnson. See Dunnett, Dorothy*
*Johnson, Pamela Hansford*
   Obituary (Lachman)   5/5/18
Johnson, Tom, ed.
   Echoes (MS)   7/3/5
Johnson, William Oscar
   THE ZERO FACTOR (IAC)   4/3/33

Jones, Bradford
  (SSC)                  6/2/20*
Jones, Elwyn
  BARLOW EXPOSED (M*F)   2/3/42
Jones, G. Wayman
  THE BLACK BAT'S INVISIBLE
    ENEMY (R)           11/4/98
Jones, Gerard, and Will Jacobs
  THE BEAVER PAPERS (R)   8/1/34
Jones, Inigo
  THE ALBATROSS MURDERS
    (R)                   9/5/44
Jones, Robert Kenneth
  THE SHUDDER PULPS (IAC) 3/4/23
Jordan, Cathleen
  A CAROL IN THE DARK
    (R)               11/4/90
Jordan, Cathleen, ed.
  ALFRED HITCHCOCK ANTHOL-
    OGY #27: MURDER AND
    OTHER MISHAPS (IAC)
                  12/2/64-5
Journal of Ratiocinative Research, The
  (Breen)       1/5/16; 5/5/14
JOURNEY TO A SAFE PLACE
  (Black) (M*F)         4/2/39
JOURNEY TO THE HANGMAN
  (Upfield) (R)           P/32
*Judas*
  L: Fisher 11/1/84
JUDAS FACTOR, THE (Allbeury)
  (TAR)             11/2/63
JUDAS GOAT, THE (Parker) (M*F)
  (IAC)       3/3/37; 9/4/35
JUDAS PAIR, THE (Gash) (M*F) 2/3/47
JUDGE AND HIS HANGMAN, THE
  (Dürrenmatt) (R)       7/2/39
JUDGEMENT IN STONE, A (Rendell)
  (R)               3/4/44
  Humor, Horror, and Intellect
    (Bakerman)        5/4/5-10
  The Writer's Probe (Bakerman)
                  3/5/3-6
JUDGMENT BY FIRE (Huebner)
  (IAC)             11/1/25
Judgments (More Movie Reviews)
  (Traylor)        6/2/27-32
Judson, William
  KILMAN'S LANDING (R)   2/5/40
JUNGLE OF STEEL AND STONE
  (Chesbro) (TNSPE)    10/2/51
JUNTA (Drummond) (TAR)   12/2/62

Juri, Dorothy
  L:            1/5/53; 2/1/57
*Jury* (Swedish magazine)
  L: Seeger 2/6/50, 3/2/57
JUST A CORPSE AT TWILIGHT
  (Martin) (TBR)      12/2/41-2
JUSTICE (Simenon) (R)     8/4/43
JUSTICE ENDS AT HOME, AND
  OTHER STORIES (Stout) (McAleer,
  ed.) (R)            3/5/43
*Juvenile Mysteries.* See Crime Novelists
  as Writers of Children's Fiction
  L: Adey 13/3/102-3

# K

Kabatchnik, Amnon
  Agatha Christie Is Still Alive and
    Well            2/6/9-10
  Reviews:
    THE ADVENTURES OF
      CARDIGAN (Nebel)  11/4/101
    AGATHA CHRISTIE: FIRST
      LADY OF CRIME (Keating,
      ed.)             2/1/32
    ALLIGATOR (Katz)     1/3/45
    THE BLACK CASTLE
      (Daniels)          2/4/46
    THE BLUE HAMMER
      (Macdonald)       1/2/38
    BODY RUB (Andrews)   1/5/41
    CRIME AND MYSTERY: THE
      100 BEST BOOKS (Keating)
                  11/1/71
    CRIME FICTION, 1749–1980: A
      COMPREHENSIVE BIBLI-
      OGRAPHY (Hubin)   9/3/40
    CROC' (James)       1/3/45
    THE CURSE OF THE FLEERS
      (Copper)          2/1/35
    CURTAIN (Christie)    9/5/33
    THE DEAD SLEEP LIGHTLY
      (Carr) (Greene, ed.)  10/2/74
    THE DEADLY SPRING
      (Conaway)        1/5/41
    THE FILMS OF PETER LORRE
      (Youngkin/Bigwood/Cabana)
                  10/3/71
    'GATOR (Ford)       1/3/45
    LEW ARCHER, PRIVATE IN-
      VESTIGATOR (Macdonald)
                  2/4/47
    LOVE KILLS (Greenburg)  3/1/42

*Kabatchnik, Amnon,* continued
  *Reviews* continued
    MAIGRET AND THE HOTEL
      MAJESTIC (Simenon)    2/5/40
    THE MOMENT OF TRUTH
      (Blom)    1/4/45
    NAKED VILLAINY
      (Woods)    3/97-100
    NICE WEEKEND FOR A
      MURDER (Collins)    10/1/72
    OPERATION APRICOT
      (Haddad)    2/4/45
    THE PICTURE PERFECT MUR-
      DERS (Adler/Chastain)12/4/91-4
    POISON (McBain)    9/5/35
    RAISE THE TITANIC!
      (Cussler)    1/4/44
    THE SAVAGE WOMEN
      (Curtis)    1/5/41
    SINGLED OUT (Whitney)    3/1/42
    SLEEPING MURDERS
      (Christie)    9/5/33
    SNAKE (McClure)    1/1/35
    THE SOUND OF DETECTION
      (Nevins/Stanich)    10/2/74
    THE SUBJECT IS MURDER
      (Menendez)    12/4/87-91
    THE THETA SYNDROME
      (Trevor)    2/1/34
    THE TWENTY-THIRD WEB
      (Himmell)    2/4/45
    UNCOLLECTED CRIMES
      (Pronzini/Greenberg, eds.)
        11/1/70
    THE WEREWOLF (Copper) 2/4/46
    THE WHOLE SPY CATA-
      LOGUE (Knudson)    9/2/33
    WOMAN IN THE DARK
      (Hammett)    11/1/73
Kaiser, Harold D.
  L:    11/3/90
*Kallen, Lucille*
  C.B. Greenfield (Bakerman) 7/6/24-9
  C.B. GREENFIELD: NO LADY IN
    THE HOUSE (R)    6/5/49
  C.B. GREENFIELD: PIANO BIRD
    (R)    8/2/29
  C.B. GREENFIELD: THE TANGLE-
    WOOD MURDERS (M*F) (R)
      5/1/21; 5/5/41
  INTRODUCING C.B. GREEN-
    FIELD (R) (IAC)    5/5/41; 6/1/28

KAMA SUTRA TANGO, THE (Burke)
  (M*F)    2/1/22
Kaminsky, Stuart
  BULLET FOR A STAR (M*F)
    (R)    2/1/25 & 44
  CATCH A FALLING CLOWN
    (R)    7/1/40
  THE HOWARD HUGHES AFFAIR
    (M*F)    3/6/40
  MURDER ON THE YELLOW
    BRICK ROAD (M*F)    2/6/32
  NEVER CROSS A VAMPIRE (M*F)
    (R)    5/1/21; 6/4/18
  THINK FAST, MR. PETERS
    (TNSPE) (TAR)
      10/2/51; 11/1/61; 11/2/73
  YOU BET YOUR LIFE
    (M*F)    3/6/28
*Kane, Frank*
  ESPRIT DE CORPSE (TBR)  10/3/53
    (IAC)    3/2/24
Kane, Henry
  A CORPSE FOR CHRISTMAS
    (TBR)    11/2/94
*Kantor, Leonard*
  Obituary (Lachman)    8/3/28
Kaplan, Arthur
  A KILLING FOR CHARITY (M*F)
    (IAC)    P/27; 3/2/23
Karl, M.S.
  KILLER'S INK (TAR)
    11/1/61; 11/2/73
KATWALK (Kijewski) (TAR) 12/3/83-4
Katz, Shelley
  ALLIGATOR (R)    1/3/45
Katzenbach, John
  IN THE HEAT OF THE SUMMER
    (R)    8/3/42
*Kauffmann, Lane*
  Obituary (Lachman)    10/4/53
  THE PERFECTIONIST (TBR)11/2/91
  WALDO (TBR)    11/2/91
Kaye, Marvin
  MY BROTHER, THE DRUGGIST
    (R)    3/6/48
  THE SOAP OPERA SLAUGHTERS
    ·(R)    7/4/32
Kaye, William
  WRONG TARGET (M*F)    5/6/35
Keating, H.R.F. Also see Hervey,
  Evelyn
  AGATHA CHRISTIE: FIRST
    LADY OF CRIME (ed.) (R)
    (IAC)    2/1/32; 2/4/16

Keating, H.R.F., continued
THE BEDSIDE COMPANION TO
CRIME (R)              12/3/100-1
CRIME AND MYSTERY: THE 100
BEST BOOKS (IAC) (R)
10/2/52; 11/1/71
DEAD ON TIME (TAR) (R)
12/3/83; 13/3/89-91
GO WEST, INSPECTOR GHOTE
(M*F)                    5/6/33
THE MURDER OF THE MAHA-
RAJAH (M*F)             4/4/40
THE SHERIFF OF BOMBAY
(R)                      8/3/37
WHODUNIT? A GUIDE TO
CRIME, SUSPENSE AND SPY
FICTION (ed.) (R) (IAC)
7/1/40; 7/2/24
Keeler, Harry Stephen
Dumbfounded in Keelerland
(Scott)               1/1/12-17
Further Excursions (Scott)  1/4/13-24
L: Adey 1/3/51
Keene, Day
TAKE A STEP TO MURDER
(M*F)                    P/26
Keene, Oliver. See Walsh, J.M.
KEEPER OF THE KEYS (Biggers)
(IAC)                   10/3/39
Keirans, James E.
THE MAD HATTER MYSTERY and
the Tower of London: Some
Thoughts on the Tower and a Sug-
gestion for the Dates    13/3/23-30
Keith, Carlton
Obituary (Lachman)       13/3/70
KEK HUUYGENS, SMUGGLER
(Fish) (R)               2/5/41
Kellerman, Jonathan
BLOOD TEST (IAC)          9/5/27
THE BUTCHER'S THEATER
(TAR)            11/1/62; 11/2/73
SILENT PARTNER (R)       12/1/43
WHEN THE BOUGH BREAKS
(IAC)                    8/4/32
Kelley, George
Bill Pronzini Revisited   2/5/5-6
The Caper Novels of Tony
Kenrick                  2/4/3-4
The Crime Novels of Harold R.
Daniels                  3/4/13-5
The Degeneration of Donald
Hamilton                 1/6/11-12

Kelley, George, continued
The Explosive Novels of Richard L.
Graves                   3/6/9-10
Fear and Loathing with the Lone
Wolf                     1/5/17-8*
The Joe Gall Series (w/Banks)
3/2/26-35*
L: 1/1/39; 1/4/56; 1/5/57; 2/2/51;
4/1/48; 4/2/57
Looking for Rachel Wallace and
Ginger North             4/3/29-30
The Programmed Writing of Dean
R. Koontz                1/4/11-2
Reviews:
BAIT MONEY (Collins)     1/6/50
BLOOD MONEY (Collins)    1/6/50
THE BROKER (Collins)     1/6/50
THE BROKER'S WIFE
(Collins)                1/6/50
THE DEALER (Collins)     1/6/50
THE DEVIL FINDS WORK
(Delving)                1/6/50
DIE LIKE A MAN
(Delving)                1/6/50
DIMENSIONS OF DETECTIVE
FICTION (Landrum/Browne/
Browne, eds.)            1/4/50
FATA MORGANA (Kotz-
winkle)                  1/4/46
MATTERS OF FACT &
FICTION (Vidal)          1/5/39
MIDNIGHT SPECIALS
(Pronzini, ed.)          1/6/46
PRISON OF ICE (Axton)    1/6/46
THE RUNNING OF BEASTS
(Pronzini/Malzberg)      1/2/37
SHADOW OF A BROKEN MAN
(Chesbro)                2/1/42
THE SLASHER (Collins)    2/1/42
SMILING, THE BOY FELL
DEAD (Delving)           1/6/50
WHO IS TEDDY VILLANOVA?
(Berger)                 1/4/46
WRITING SUSPENSE AND
MYSTERY FICTION (Burack,
ed.)                     2/2/39
Running Hot and Cold with Ron
Faust                    5/4/11-2
Sinning with Lawrence Sanders
3/5/20-1
Some Recent Hybrids      6/2/16-8
The Suspense Novels of Bill
Pronzini                 1/2/15-16

*Kelley, George,* continued
  The Vengeance Novels of Brian
    Garfield                    2/1/5-6
Kelman, Judith
  PRIME EVIL (IAC)           8/6/33
  WHERE SHADOWS FALL
    (IAC)                    11/1/25
*Kemelman, Harry*
  Clergy-Detectives (Cleary)  9/3/3-21
  WEDNESDAY THE RABBI GOT
    WET (R)                   1/4/43
Kemp, Sarah (Michael Buterworth, q.v.)
  OVER THE EDGE (M*F)        3/6/37
Kendall, Carol
  THE BLACK SEVEN (TBR)
                             13/3/63-4
Kendrick, Baynard H.
  THE ELEVEN OF DIAMONDS
    (TBR) (R)      11/4/64; 12/1/48
Kennealy, Jerry
  POLO ANYONE? (TNSPE)   10/2/51
KENNEDY FOR THE DEFENSE
  (Higgins) (R)              4/5/43
Kennedy, George
  MURDER ON LOCATION
    (R)                      7/6/36
Kennedy, Milward
  POISON IN THE PARISH
    (TBR)                   11/4/63
*Kenrick, Tony*
  The Caper Novels of Tony Kenrick
    (Kelley)                 24/3-4
  THE CHICAGO GIRL (M*F)  1/2/24
  STEALING LILLIAN (R)     2/1/45
*Kenya.* Also see Africa
  Crime Fiction in Kenya
    (Tolley)               10/2/25-8
Kenyon, Michael
  MAY YOU DIE IN IRELAND
    (IAC)                    2/6/29
Kerr, Philip
  MARCH VIOLETS (TAR)     11/3/71
KEY WEST CONNECTION (Striker)
  (M*F)                      5/3/27
KICK START (Rutherford) (R)  3/3/43
*Kienzle, William X.*
  Clergy-Detectives (Cleary)  9/3/3-21
  DEADLINE FOR A CRITIC
    (R)                     10/3/68
  DEATH WEARS A RED HAT
    (R)                      4/2/41
  MIND OVER MURDER
    (M*F)                    5/4/22
  THE ROSARY MURDERS (M*F)
    (R)            3/5/40; 4/2/41

KIEV FOOTPRINT (Posey)
  (IAC)                      7/5/27
Kijewski, Karen
  KATWALK (TAR)          12/3/83-4
*Kiker, Douglas*
  DEATH AT THE CUT (TAR) 11/3/71
  Obituary (Lachman)       13/3/70-1
KIKI (Gill) (R)             3/6/48
*Kildare, Dr. Jimmy.* See Brand, Max
*Kilgerrin, Paul.* See Leonard, Charles L.
KILL 'EM WITH KINDNESS
  (Dickenson) (TBR)        12/4/63
KILL 3 (Shulman) (R)        7/4/34
KILL YOUR DARLINGS (Collins)
  (IAC)                    11/1/28
KILLED IN THE RATINGS
  (DeAndrea) (IAC) (TAR)
              5/6/30; 9/1/33; 11/2/68
KILLER'S INK (Karl) (TAR)
                  11/1/61; 11/2/73
KILLERS OF STARFISH, THE
  (Gillis) (R)               1/6/43
KILLING CIRCLE, THE (Wiltz)
  (M*F)                      6/3/34
KILLING FOR CHARITY, A (Kaplan)
  (M*F) (IAC)          P/27; 3/2/23
KILLING GIFT, THE (Wood)
  (R)                      11/4/95
KILLING IN ROME, A (Rostand)
  (R)                       2/3/51
KILLING IN SWORDS, A (Bretnor)
  (M*F)                     2/6/31
KILLING KIND, THE (West)
  (M*F)                     2/4/33
KILLING MAN, THE (Spillane)
  (R) (audio)     12/3/91-2, 92 & 93
KILLING OF KATIE STEELSTOCK,
  THE (Gilbert) (M*F)       4/5/30
KILLING TIME IN ST. CLOUD (Hill/
  Guest) (TAR)             11/1/59
KILLING ZONE, THE (Burns)
  (TAR)                    11/1/52
KILMAN'S LANDING (Judson)
  (R)                       2/5/40
Kim Philby, Master Spy in Fact and
  Fiction (Dukeshire)       3/6/14
  L: Floyd 3/4/60
Kimura, Jiro
  L: 7/1/48; 7/4/45; 13/2/96; 13/3/101-2
  THE SECOND INTERNATIONAL
    CONGRESS OF CRIME
    WRITERS PICTURE BOOK
    (MS)                    3/5/2

KINDLY DIG YOUR GRAVE AND
  OTHER WICKED STORIES (Ellin)
  (R)                         1/1/35
King, Betty J.
  L:                          4/1/43
King, C. Daly
  OBELISTS AT SEA (TBR)   11/3/66
KING EDWARD PLOT, THE (Hall)
  (R)                         4/2/46
King, Frank
  TAKE THE D TRAIN (TAR) 12/3/84
KING IS DEAD, THE (Queen)
  (R)                         7/3/34
KING OF TERRORS, THE: TALES
  OF MADNESS AND DEATH
  (Bloch) (R)                 1/6/43
King, Rufus
  THE CASE OF THE CONSTANT
    GOD (TBR)            13/2/69-70
  THE CASE OF THE DOWAGER'S
    ETCHINGS (TBR)       13/2/69-70
  DESIGN IN EVIL (TBR)    10/3/64
  MURDER BY THE CLOCK
    (R)                   12/1/48-9
  MUSEUM PIECE NO. 13
    (R)                       9/5/44
  THE STEPS TO MURDER
    (TBR)                    11/2/83
  A VARIETY OF WEAPONS
    (R)                    12/1/47-8
King, Stephen
  NIGHT SHIFT (R)            4/3/45
KINGSLEY'S TOUCH (Collee)
  (IAC)                      9/3/32
KINK, THE (Brock) (R)      12/1/44
Kinsley, Lawrence
  THE RED-LIGHT VICTIM
    (M*F)                    5/5/24
Kirby, Rip
  The Detective Hero in the Comics
    (Blom)                  6/1/8-15
Kirk, General. See Blackburn, John
Kirsch, Steven J.
  OATH OF OFFICE (TAR)   11/3/72
Kirst, Hans Helmut
  Obituary (Lachman)        11/3/53
KISS (Lutz) (TAR)   11/1/63; 11/2/75
KISS OF FIRE, A (Masako) (TAR)
                    11/1/68; 11/2/79
KISS OFF THE DEAD (Garrity)
  (M*F)                      6/2/35
KISS YOUR ELBOW (Handley)
  (M*F)                      3/6/37

KISSES LEAVE NO FINGERPRINTS
  (Fredman) (M*F)            4/5/32
KITCHEN CAKE MURDER, THE
  (Bush) (TBR)            13/1/42-3
Knickmeyer, Steve
  STRAIGHT (R) (M*F)  1/2/16 & 27
KNIFE WILL FALL, THE (Cumber-
  land) (M*F)               5/2/16
Knight, Clifford
  THE AFFAIR OF THE CORPSE
    ESCORT (M*F)            3/6/35
  THE AFFAIR OF THE FAINTING
    BUTLER (TBR)           10/3/54
Knight, Kathleen Moore. Also see
    Leonard, Charles L.
  Little Old Men (Nehr)    4/4/2-6
  TROUBLE AT TURKEY HILL
    (M*F)                   3/4/41
Knightley, Phillip; David Leitch, and
    Bruce Page
  THE PHILBY CONSPIRACY
    (IAC)                   6/4/31
KNOCKDOWN (Francis) (M*F) 1/3/40
Knott, Hal, and Marvin Lachman
  Pocket Books Checklist, 1–500
                         1/6/29-37*
Knowles, Barbara W.
  Encore! (McSherry)      12/1/9-22
Knox, Bill. Also see MacLeod, Robert
  LIVE BAIT (M*F)           3/6/30
  RALLY TO KILL (M*F)       1/5/36
  THE VIEW FROM DANIEL PIKE
    (w/Boyd) (R)            3/1/40
Knudson, Richard L.
  THE WHOLE SPY CATALOGUE
    (R)                     9/2/33
Koch, Jeffery
  Reviews:
    THE DREADFUL HOLLOW
      (Blake)               5/4/33
    THE EXTORTIONERS
      (Creasey)             5/6/47
    SCANDAL AT HIGH
      CHIMNEYS (Carr)       5/4/32
Koehler, Robert Portner
  THE HOODED VULTURE
    MURDERS (R)             3/3/47
Koenig, Joseph
  LITTLE ODESSA (TAR)      11/1/55
  SMUGGLER'S NOTCH
    (TAR)                  11/3/72
Koenig, Laird
  ROCKABYE (M*F)            6/2/34

Koepf, Michael
ICARUS (TAR)          11/1/56
*Koesler, Father Robert.* See Kienzle,
William X.
Kohler, Sheila
THE PERFECT PLACE
(TAR)          11/3/73
*Koontz, Dean R.*
HOW TO WRITE BEST SELLING
FICTION (R)          5/6/43
The Programmed Writing of Dean R.
Koontz (Kelley)          1/4/11-2
L: Hensley 2/4/59; Kelley 2/2/51
Kotzwinkle, William
FATA MORGANA (R)          1/4/46
*Kramer, Lt. Tromp.* See McClure, James
Krauzer, Steven
L:          3/1/53
KRIMINALITERATURE PA
SVENSKA 1749-1985 [CRIME
FICTION IN SWEDEN 1749-1985]
(Hedman) (R)          9/5/37
KRIMINALLITTERATUREN KAVAL-
KADE: KRIMINAL-OG DETEK
TIVHISTORIEN I BILLEDER OG
TEKST (La Cour/Mogensen)
(R)          7/6/35
L: Bleiler 8/2/42; Mogensen 8/1/41
*Kroeger, Berry*
Obituary (Lachman)          13/1/33
Kummer, F.A.
DESIGN FOR MURDER
(TBR)          12/2/50-1
Kurland, Michael
THE INFERNAL DEVICE (R) 3/3/45
Kutak, Rosemary
I AM THE CAT (TBR)          11/1/38
Kutzner, Carl
L:          2/5/58
KYD FOR HIRE (Harris) (R)          2/3/52
Kyle, Sefton
GUILTY, BUT— (IAC)          8/4/32

# L

La Barre, Harriet
THE FLORENTINE WIN
(TAR)          11/3/73
La Cour, Tage, and Harald Mogensen
KRIMINALLITTERATURENS
KAVALKADE: KRIMINAL-OG
DETEKTIVHISTORIEN I BIL-
LEDER OG TEKST (R)          7/6/35
LABYRINTH (Land) (R)          9/6/40

LABYRINTH (Pronzini) (M*F)
(R)          4/3/38 & 43
*Lachman, Marvin*
The Best Short Stories of 1986
          9/3/32
The Best Short Stories of 1987
          10/3/43-4
The Best Short Stories of 1989
          12/2/72-4
Bouchercon X: Two Views (w/
Grochowski)          3/5/11-3
Death of a Movie Detective
(Obituary)          8/3/29-30
Death of a Mystery Writer (Obitu-
aries) 6/1/29-30; 6/3/25-6; 6/4/33;
6/6/49; 7/1/35; 7/2/25-6; 7/4/23;
7/5/29-30; 8/1/21-2; 8/2/25;
8/3/28-9; 9/3/33-5; 9/4/38-9;
9/5/28; 10/1/66; 10/2/60;
10/3/44-6; 10/4/53; 11/1/36-7;
11/3/52-5; 11/4/55-6; 12/1/28-9;
12/2/70-2; 12/4/47-9; 13/1/30-34;
13/2/57-8; 13/3/69-73; 13/4/88-94
Death of a Mystery Writer's Friend
(Obituary)          8/3/29
Doom with a View (Film and TV
reviews) 10/1/64-6; 11/4/54-5;
12/1/25-28; 12/2/69-70; 13/3/73-4;
13/4/86-8
The EQMM Cover Murders
(fiction)          1/1/6-11
It's About Crime (column)
2/4/15-6; 2/5/3-4; 2/6/27-9,16;
3/2/21-5; 3/3/17-18,49,14;
3/4/23-4; 4/1/13-6; 4/3/31-3;
4/4/18-20; 4/5/24-6; 4/6/31-3;
5/1/17-9; 5/2/10-12; 5/3/22-6;
5/4/18-20; 5/5/17-9; 5/6/29-32;
6/1/27-30; 6/3/22-6; 6/4/30-3;
6/6/19-22; 7/1/32-5; 7/2/22-6;
7/4/20-3; 7/5/26-30; 8/1/16-22;
8/2/21-8; 8/4/29-33; 9/1/33-6;
9/2/24-30; 9/3/29-35; 9/4/35-9;
9/5/23-8; 10/1/61-4; 10/2/53-60;
10/3/39-46; 10/4/49-54;
11/1/22-37; 11/3/45-55;
11/4/47-56; 12/1/23-30;
12/2/63-74; 12/4/43-50;
13/1/27-34; 13/2/52-8; 13/3/65-74;
13/4/83-94
Lachman's Reviews in TMF
Volumes Two Through Four
(Doerrer)          5/2/6-9

Lachman, Marvin, continued
Lachman's Top Ten (Short Stories for
  1988)                    11/1/29-30
L: 1/1/42; 1/2/51; 1/4/58; 1/6/57;
  2/2/53; 2/5/48; 3/1/47; 3/3/59;
  3/4/57; 4/2/56; 4/5/44; 6/4/45;
  7/1/49; 7/4/50; 8/1/43; 8/3/48;
  9/3/45; 9/5/47; 10/1/97; 10/2/83;
  11/3/88
The Life and Times of Gideon
  Fell                      2/3/3-18
Miscellaneous Mystery Mish-Mash
  2/1/6; 2/2/19-20; 5/1/18-9; 5/2/12;
  5/5/18-9; 12/1/29-30; 12/2/70;
  12/4/49-50; 13/2/57-8; 13/3/68
The Mystery of Monboddo     8/4/33
Notes on Recent Viewing (Movie
  Reviews)                   8/1/20
Pocket Books Checklist, 1-500 (w/
  Knott)                  1/6/29-37*
President Nero Wolfe         5/3/22-6
Reviews:
  ANGEL EYES (Hunt)          1/4/51
  THE FILMS OF SHERLOCK
    HOLMES (Steinbrunner/
    Michaels)                3/3/43
  THE HARD-BOILED DETEC-
    TIVE: STORIES FROM
    BLACK MASK MAGAZINE
    (Ruhm, ed.)              1/2/34
  HOLLYWOOD DETECTIVE:
    GARRISON (Rovin)         1/1/34
  MYSTERY, DETECTIVE, AND
    ESPIONAGE FICTION: A
    CHECKLIST OF FICTION IN
    U.S. PULP MAGAZINES,
    1915-1974 (Cook/Miller)
                            11/1/75
  RETURN FROM VORKUTA
    (Hunt)                   1/4/51
  WHERE MURDER WAITS
    (Hunt)                   1/4/51
  WASHINGTON PAYOFF
    (Hunt)                   1/4/51
The Short Stop             13/45-52
The Short Story            11/1/29-36
Small Genre Department
                     13/2/55-7; 13/3/68-9
Television and film reviews in IAC
  5/1/18; 7/4/22-3; 7/5/29; 8/2/24-5
Wit and Wisdom of the Mystery
  Story: Quotations from the
  Mysteries—Part III P/3-10; Part
  IV 1/4/7-10

Lachman, Marvin, continued
L: Crider 2/6/45; Deeck 9/2/46;
  Nieminski 2/5/46, 4/6/40
Lachman's Reviews in TMF Volumes
  Two Through Four (Doerrer) 5/2/6-9
Lachman's Top Ten (Short Stories for
  1988) (Lachman)        11/1/29-30
Lacy, Ed
  SHAKEDOWN FOR MURDER
    (M*F)                     P/27
LADY FINGER, THE (Malcolm-Smith)
  (TBR)                      11/4/59
LADY IN BLACK, THE (Clarke)
  (M*F)                       2/5/30
LADY IN THE LAKE, THE (Chandler)
  (R)                         3/2/46
LADY IN THE MORGUE, THE
  (Latimer) (R)               9/4/42
LADY KILLER, THE (Togawa)
  (R)                        10/1/71
LADY LOVED TOO WELL, THE
  (Donahue) (M*F)             2/5/28
Lady Molly of Scotland Yard
  (Bargainnier)             7/4/15-9
LADY ON A TRAIN (movie)
  L: Schubert 8/1/44
LAIDLAW (McIlvanney) (IAC)  4/5/24
Laing, Patrick
  IF I SHOULD MURDER
    (TBR)                   12/2/47-8
LAKE OF DARKNESS, THE
  (Rendell) (M*F)             5/1/22
LAMAAR RANSOM—PRIVATE EYE
  (Galloway) (TBR)           10/2/64
Lamb, Hugh, ed.
  THE TASTE OF FEAR (M*F)   2/1/28
Lamb, Lynton
  DEATH OF A DISSENTER
    (TBR)                   13/4/81-2
Lambert, Mercedes
  DOGTOWN (IAC)             13/3/66-7
L'Amour, Louis
  Obituary (Lachman)         10/4/53
Land, Jon
  LABYRINTH (R)              9/6/40
Landrum, Larry N.; Pat Browne, and
    Ray B. Browne, eds.
  DIMENSIONS OF DETECTIVE
    FICTION (R)              1/4/50
Lane, Jeremy
  DEATH TO DRUMBEAT
    (TBR)                   13/3/50-1

Langham, James R.
SING A SONG OF HOMICIDE
(TBR)                    13/2/68-9
Langley, Bob
DEATH STALK (M*F)         3/6/27
Langton, Jane
THE MEMORIAL HALL MURDER
(M*F) (R) (IAC)
3/1/34; 4/1/29; 5/2/35; 5/4/19
THE MINUTEMAN MURDER
(R)              1/2/41; 5/2/36
MURDER AT THE GARDNER
(TAR)        11/1/62; 11/2/74
NATURAL ENEMY (R)         7/5/41
*Lansdale, Joe R.*
ACT OF LOVE (R)           5/3/36
L: 1/5/53; 2/3/61; 2/4/58; 2/5/47;
2/6/47; 3/1/56; 3/2/51; 3/3/51;
4/2/58
Reviews:
EXIT SHERLOCK HOLMES
(Hall)                3/5/44
FAT CHANCE (Laumer)    1/5/43
.44 (Breslin/Schapp)   3/5/43
THE HOLMES-DRACULA FILE
(Saberhagen)          2/6/36
THE INFERNAL DEVICE
(Kurland)             3/3/45
MURDER BY DECREE
(Weverka)             3/5/43
SHAMUS (Giles)         2/3/52
L: Crider 3/1/55
LaPorte, Karen
L:                        4/3/47
*Lariar, Lawrence*
DEATH PAINTS THE PICTURE
(TBR)                 11/1/43
Obituary (Lachman)     6/1/29-30
LaRosa, Linda J., and Barry Tanenbaum
THE RANDOM FACTOR
(M*F)                 3/1/33
*Larren, Simon.* See Charles, Robert
Larsen, Carl
L: 3/3/54; 4/1/46; 4/6/50; 5/1/46;
6/1/50
Old Time Radio Lives
4/5/18-20; 4/6/9-11; 5/6/3-6,9
Review: MURDER IN THE HELL-
FIRE CLUB (Zochert)    5/2/30
Larsen, Gaylord
DOROTHY AND AGATHA
(R)                   13/4/102

LASKO TANGENT, THE (Patterson)
(M*F)                    4/5/31
LAST COINCIDENCE, THE
(Goldsborough) (R)       12/3/95
LAST GOOD KISS, THE (Crumley)
(M*F)                    3/3/31
LAST HOUSEPARTY, THE
(Dickinson) (R)          8/2/39
LAST KILL, THE (Wells) (R)   4/1/30
Last of Gregory George Gordon Green,
The (Sampson)        13/2/18-22
L: Sampson 13/2/97-9
LAST OF THE HONEYWELLS, THE
(Gillespie) (TAR)    11/1/59; 11/2/70
LAST PAGE, THE (Fenster)
(IAC)                    11/4/49
LAST PLANE FROM NICE (Watson)
(TAR)                    10/4/47
LAST SEEN WEARING (Waugh)
(IAC)            6/4/30; 12/2/63
LAST WAR DANCE (Sapir/Murphy)
(R)                      1/3/48
LATE PHOENIX, A (Aird) (IAC)
(R)              5/2/11; 5/5/35
Latham, Brad
THE HOOK #1: THE GILDED
CANARY (M*F)          6/2/35
*Lathen, Emma.* Also see Dominic, R.B.
BY HOOK OR CROOK (R)   1/6/42
Can We Reach Agreement?
(Christopher)         8/1/14-5
GOING FOR THE GOLD (M*F)
(R)                5/3/32 & 34
GREEN GROW THE DOLLARS
(R)                   6/4/44
(IAC)                 6/6/20
WHEN IN GREECE (R)     7/1/41
*Latimer, Jonathan*
THE FIFTH GRAVE (TBR)  10/2/61
THE LADY IN THE MORGUE
(R)                   9/4/42
Obituary (Lachman)     7/5/30
(TBR)                 11/1/49
LATIMER MERCY, THE (Richardson)
(R)                   13/3/86-7
LAUGHING DOG (Lochte) (TAR)
11/1/62; 11/2/74
Laumer, Keith
DEADFALL (R)              5/5/43
FAT CHANCE (R)     1/5/43; 2/3/55
Laurance, Alice, and Isaac Asimov,
eds.
WHO DONE IT? (R)         4/4/48

Lauritzen, Henry
MY DEAR WATSON (MS)     7/3/4
Law, Janice
DEATH UNDER PAR (M*F)
(R)              5/3/32 & 39
GEMINI TRIP (M*F)       2/1/26
Law, Lawyers and Justice in the Novels
of Joe L. Hensley (Frauenglas)4/1/3-7
*Law School* (MS)           8/4/1-3
Townsend comment        8/6/47
Lawrence, Hilda
DEATH OF A DOLL (TBR)  11/2/84
LAW'S DELAY, THE (Woods)
(R)              1/4/48; 1/5/29
Layman, Richard
DASHIELL HAMMETT: A DE-
SCRIPTIVE BIBLIOGRAPHY
(R)                     3/6/49
A MATTER OF CRIME (w/Bruccoli,
ed.) (IAC)             11/1/33
SHADOW MAN: THE LIFE OF
DASHIELL HAMMETT
(M*F)                   6/1/32
LAZARUS MAN, THE (Lutz)
(R)                     3/5/44
*Le Carré, John*
CORRIDORS OF POWER: THE
WORLD OF JOHN LE CARRÉ
(Wolfe) (IAC)          10/2/55
The Fathers and Sons of John Le
Carré (Dawson)         5/3/15-7
Le Carré's Spy Novels (Banks/
Dawson)               2/5/22-5*
THE RUSSIAN HOUSE (TAR)
(R)           11/3/73; 12/4/76-7
(SSC)                  4/3/27*
Le Carré's Spy Novels (Banks/
Dawson)               2/5/22-5*
LEADEN BUBBLE, THE (Branson)
(R)                    10/1/78
LEAGUE OF FRIGHTENED MEN,
THE (Stout) (IAC)       7/1/33
*Leasor, James*
FROZEN ASSETS (TAR)   12/3/84-5
(SSC)                  4/4/16*
Leather, Edwin
THE DUVEEN LETTER (M*F)
                        4/5/33
THE MOZART SCORE (R)   4/1/34
LEAVENWORTH CASE, THE
(Green) (IAC)           6/6/21
*Lederer, Lillian Day*
Obituary (Lachman)     13/3/71

Lee, Austin
MISS HOGG AND THE MISSING
SISTERS (TBR)        13/2/62-3
*Lee, Gypsy Rose*
THE G-STRING MURDERS
(TBR)                  10/2/63
Who Really Wrote THE G-STRING
MURDERS? (Christopher)
                       8/3/18,20
LeFanu, J.S.
UNCLE SILAS: A TALE OF
BARTRAM-HAUGH (R)     2/1/45
*Legal Mysteries*
Antony Maitland and the Writings of
Sara Woods (Sarjeant)  10/4/3-40*
Law, Lawyers and Justice in the
Novels of Joe L. Hensley
(Frauenglas)           4/1/3-7
LEGEND, THE (Anthony) (M*F) 1/1/32
Leitch, David; Bruce Page, and Phillip
Knightley
THE PHILBY CONSPIRACY
(IAC)                   6/4/31
Lem, Stanislaw
THE CHAIN OF CHANCE
(M*F)                   3/5/35
Lemarchand, Elizabeth
DEATH OF AN OLD GIRL
(IAC)                   4/4/19
STEP IN THE DARK (M*F)  2/1/23
SUDDENLY WHILE GARDENING
(R) (M*F)       3/4/48; 3/6/27
UNHAPPY RETURNS (R)     7/5/44
Len Deighton Series, The (Banks/
Dawson)               3/1/11-3*
LENIENT BEAST, THE (Brown)
(IAC)                  11/3/46-7
*Leonard, Charles L.* [Kathleen Moore
Knight, q.v.]
DEADLINE FOR DESTRUCTION
(TBR)                  11/4/62
(SSC)                  4/4/17*
Leonard, Elmore
THE HUNTED (R)          2/1/35
THE SWITCH (M*F)        3/3/35
Leonid Andreyev and Jim Thompson: A
Comparison (Fellows)   11/2/59-61
Leslie Charteris and the Saint: Five
Decades of Partnership (Alex-
andersson/Hedman)      4/4/21-7
LESTER AFFAIR, THE (Garve)
(IAC)                   5/2/10

*Lester, Captain "Tiger."* See Betteridge, Don
Let the Public Decide: An Interview with Nicolas Freeling (Bakerman) 8/6/19-24
LET X BE THE MURDERER (Witting) (R) 2/4/43
 L: Shibuk 2/5/59
LET'S TALK OF GRAVES, OF WORMS, AND EPITAPHS (Player) (TBR) 13/1/41-2
Let's Hear It for Josephine Bell (Gottschalk) 11/2/47-56*
 L: Shibuk 11/3/85
LETTER FROM THE DEAD (Clarke) (M*F) (R) 5/5/21; 6/2/38
Letters. See Documents in the Case
*Letterzines* (MS) 9/1/6
LEVINE (Westlake) (R) 8/2/38
*Levinson, Richard*
 Obituary (Lachman) 9/3/34
LEW ARCHER, PRIVATE INVES-TIGATOR (Macdonald) (R) 2/4/47
Lewin, Michael Z.
 MISSING WOMAN (M*F) 5/6/39
 NIGHT COVER (M*F) 4/4/39
 OUTSIDE IN (M*F) 4/5/33
 THE WAY WE DIE NOW (M*F) 3/2/37
Lewis, Dave
 L: 6/6/49
*Lewis, Elliott*
 Obituary (Lachman) 12/4/47
*Lewis, Lucille Camps*
 Obituary (Lachman) 12/1/29
Lewis, Roy
 NOTHING BUT FOXES (M*F) 3/5/38
Lewis, Roy Harley
 A CRACKING OF SPINES (R) (M*F) 4/5/38; 6/3/43; 6/5/45
*Lewis, Steve*
 Mystery*File (column)
  P/23-31; 1/1/27-34; 1/2/23-8; 1/3/37-42; 1/4/37-40; 1/5/29-36; 1/6/38-41; 2/1/21-30; 2/2/33-35,32; 2/3/41-8; 2/4/30-6; 2/5/26-34; 2/6/30-5; 3/1/31-45,30; 3/2/36-41; 3/3/31-39; 3/4/38-41; 3/5/35-41; 3/6/27-41; 4/2/31-40; 4/3/34-41; 4/4/33-43; 4/5/27-36; 5/1/20-9; 5/2/13-25; 5/3/27-33; 5/4/21-7; 5/5/20-7; 5/6/33-41,48,53;

*Lewis, Steve,* continued
 Mystery*File (column) , continued
  6/1/31-8; 6/2/32-7; 6/3/30-7; 6/4/37-9; 6/5/41-5; 6/6/26-32
  (MS) 6/6/1
 Reviews:
  BIG BANG (Goulart) 7/3/37
  BLUE MASCARA TEARS (McKimmey) 7/5/45
  BY FREQUENT ANGUISH (Dean) 7/5/45
  THE COOKING SCHOOL MURDERS (Rich) 7/2/38
  CURTAIN FALL (Dewhurst) 7/4/31
  DAY OF WRATH (Valin) 7/4/32
  GOLDEN RAIN (Clark) 7/5/46
  THE HARD-BOILED DETEC-TIVE: STORIES FROM BLACK MASK MAGAZINE (Ruhm, ed.) 1/2/35
  MURDER COMES FIRST (Lockridge) 7/2/38
  REVEREND RANDOLLPH AND THE HOLY TERROR (Smith) 7/3/38
  SCATTERSHOT (Pronzini) 7/3/37
 L: Banks 2/4/54, 2/6/43, 5/4/41; Breen 2/1/54; Dillon 2/6/51; Ralph 1/6/55
Liddy, G. Gordon
 OUT OF CONTROL (R) 3/6/44
LIE DIRECT, THE (Woods) (R) 7/6/37
Liebow, Ely
 DR. JOE BELL: MODEL FOR SHERLOCK HOLMES (MS) 6/1/1; 7/2/23
 In Memorium: John Nieminski 9/2/3-6
LIES (Neely) (M*F) 2/5/29
LIFE, ADVENTURES, AND OPINIONS OF A LIVERPOOL POLICEMAN AND HIS CONTEMPORARIES
 The Policeman: A Victorian Novel (Bleiler) 6/2/7-10
Life and Times of Gideon Fell, The (Lachman) 2/3/3-18
 L: French 2/4/59
LIFE AND TIMES OF MISS JANE MARPLE, THE (Hart) (IAC) 10/2/58
LIFE OF RAYMOND CHANDLER, THE (MacShane) (IAC) 2/4/15

LIFE OF SIR ARTHUR CONAN
  DOYLE, THE (Carr) (IAC)    10/2/59
Lifson, David S.
  HEADLESS VICTORY (M*F) 3/3/38
LIFT AND THE DROP, THE (Galwey)
  (TBR)                 13/4/75-6
Light and Sound by Joseph Hansen
  (Alderson)               8/3/12-7
LIGHT THICKENS (Marsh)
  (IAC)                    9/5/25
LIGHTNING (McBain) (R)      8/3/45
LIGNY'S LAKE (Courtier) (R)   5/5/42
  An Australian Bibliomystery
  (Tolley)               10/3/37-8
Lilly, Jean
  DEATH THUMBS A RIDE
  (TBR)                 13/4/78-9
LIME PIT, THE (Valin) (M*F)   4/4/35
Lincoln, Victoria
  Obituary (Lachman)         5/5/18
Lindsey, David L.
  IN THE LAKE OF THE MOON
  (TAR)                   11/1/56
Lindsey, Robert
  A GATHERING OF SAINTS
  (R)                    13/2/90-1
Line-Up, The                2/1/20
Line-Up, The (Albert)        4/5/9-12
  L: Loeser 4/6/46
Line-Up, The (Briney)         P/22
Line-Up, The (Rall)          1/1/38
Linington, Elizabeth. Also see Egan,
  Leslie; Shannon, Dell
  NO EVIL ANGEL (R)         3/2/44
  Obituary (Lachman)       10/3/45-6
  L: Schubert 12/1/65
LINK OF FIRE (Hamilton)
  (MS)                    12/3/7-8
Linzee, David
  DEATH IN CONNECTICUT
  (M*F)                    1/5/33
  DISCRETION (R)            3/3/47
LIPSTICK CLUE, THE (Goyne)
  (TBR)                 12/3/76-7
LISTEN FOR THE CLICK (Breen)
  (IAC)            7/3/32; 8/1/16
LISTENER, THE (DuBois)
  (IAC)                    3/2/24
Lister, Stephen
  DELORME IN DEEP WATER
  (TBR)                 13/2/72-3

LITERARY DETECTION: HOW TO
  PROVE AUTHORSHIP AND
  FRAUD IN LITERATURE AND
  DOCUMENTS
  His Own Desert (Bleiler)    3/4/11,15
LITTLE CLASS ON MURDER, A
  (Hart) (R)               12/1/42
Little, Constance and Gwenyth
  THE BLACK SHROUDS
  (TBR)                   10/3/55
  GREAT BLACK KANBA
  (TBR)                   13/4/77
LITTLE LESS THAN KIND, A
  (Armstrong) (IAC)         11/4/48
LITTLE LOCAL MURDER, A
  (Barnard) (IAC)      8/3/26; 9/3/30
LITTLE MAN BLUES (Mathis)
  (TAR)                   10/4/44
LITTLE MISS MURDER (Avallone)
  (IAC)                    12/1/24
LITTLE ODESSA (Koenig)
  (TAR)                    11/1/55
Little Old Ladies I Have Known and
  Loved (Nehr)             3/4/3-7
  L: Gottschalk 4/1/39; Nehr 3/5/50
Little Old Men with Whom I'm Only
  Slightly Acquainted (Nehr) 4/4/2-6
  L: Lachman 4/5/44; Nevins 4/5/45
LIVE BAIT (Knox) (M*F)        3/6/30
LIVE BAIT (Wood) (IAC)        8/4/33
LIVING IMAGE (Gallant)
  (M*F)                    3/1/35
LIZZIE (Hunter) (R)          8/3/44
Llewellyn, Caroline
  THE MASK OF ROME
  (TAR)                   11/1/56
Llewellyn, Sam
  BLOOD ORANGE (TAR)     11/3/74
  DEAD RECKONING (TAR)   11/1/57
  DEATH ROLE (MS)          12/1/2
  (MS)                     11/1/2
LOBBY CARDS: THE CLASSIC
  FILMS (RM)               9/5/30
Lochte, Dick
  LAUGHING DOG (TAR)
                  11/1/62; 11/2/74
  SLEEPING DOG (IAC)        9/3/30
Lock and Key Library, The
  L: Bakerman 2/3/71
LOCKED ROOM MURDERS AND
  OTHER IMPOSSIBLE CRIMES
  (Adey)
  L: Deeck 13/1/87

*Locked-Room Mysteries*
  L: Adey 1/3/51
LOCKED ROOM PUZZLES (Green-
  berg/Pronzini, eds.) (IAC)    11/1/33
*Locken, Mike.* See Rostand, Robert
*Lockridge, Richard*
  DEAD RUN (R)         P/36; 1/1/28
  Obituary (Lachman)        6/4/33
  THE OLD DIE YOUNG (M*F)
    (R)            5/1/25; 5/3/39
  L: Broset 6/4/48
*Lockridge, Richard and Frances*
  Looking Glass Detection
    (Isaac)            8/5/18-22
  Mr. and Mrs. North (Davis)  1/1/21-6
  MURDER COMES FIRST
    (R)                 7/2/38
  MURDER OUT OF TURN
    (IAC)             13/1/28-9
LODGER, THE (Simenon) (IAC) 8/1/20
*Loeser, Bill*
  The Curmudgeon in the Corner
              3/2/3-12,20; 3/4/16-8
  L: 3/2/58; 3/4/59; 4/1/43; 4/6/46;
    5/1/47
  (MS)                 3/2/1-2
  L: Ballinger 4/1/44; Breen 3/3/52,
    3/4/53; Doerrer 3/3/55; Gottschalk
    3/3/59; Lachman 3/3/59; Mos-
    kowitz 3/3/61; Wooster 3/4/56
*Loew, Mildred Falk*
  Obituary (Lachman)        12/4/49
*Lofts, Norah*
  Obituary (Lachman)        8/1/21
LONDON DEAL, THE (Crisp)
    (R)                 3/4/47
*Lone Wolf, The.* See Vance, Louis
  Joseph
LONELY PLACE TO DIE, A
  (Ebersohn) (R)           4/1/35
LONELY SILVER RAIN, THE
  (MacDonald) (R)          8/4/45
LONELY WAY TO DIE, A
  (Bourgeau) (M*F)          4/5/29
LONG CHASE, THE (Eshleman)
  (TBR)              13/4/68-70
Long, Manning
  SHORT SHRIFT (TBR)     12/3/72-3
LONG SHORT CUT, THE (Garve)
  (R)                 2/5/35
LONG WINDOW, THE (Eshleman)
  (TBR)              13/4/68-70

Look at W. Adolphe Roberts, A
  (Lybeck)             11/1/3-6
  L: Deeck 11/3/96
LOOK BACK ON DEATH (Egan)
  (M*F)                3/3/36
LOOKING FOR RACHEL WALLACE
  (Parker) (M*F) (R) (IAC)
            4/3/34; 5/5/36; 9/4/35
  Looking for Rachel Wallace
    (Kelley)            4/3/29-30
  Looking for Rachel Wallace and Ginger
    North (Kelley)       4/3/29-30
  Looking Glass Detection: The Norths
    and Bill Weigand Speak
    (Isaac)            8/5/18-22
  L: Deeck 9/1/45
LOOKING GLASS MURDERS, THE
  (Lore) (M*F)            4/5/29
LOOPHOLE: OR HOW TO ROB A
  BANK (Pollock) (R)        2/1/44
LOOSE CONNECTION, A (Meek)
  (TAR)              12/3/87-8
*Lorac, E.C.R.*
  I COULD MURDER HER (R) 9/3/43
  PLACE FOR A POISONER
    (R)                 5/3/37
  A Scot at Scotland Yard
    (Sarjeant)          10/2/3-23*
LORD MULLION'S SECRET (Innes)
  (M*F)                6/1/38
LORD PETER (Sayers) (IAC)     9/2/25
Lore, Phillips
  THE LOOKING GLASS
    MURDERS (M*F)         4/5/29
*Lorre, Peter*
  THE FILMS OF PETER LORRE
    (Youngkin/Bigwood/Cabana)
    (R)                10/3/71
  MASTERS OF MENACE:
    GREENSTREET AND LORRE
    (Sennett) (R)          7/2/37
LOST GALLOWS, THE (Carr)
  (IAC)                9/1/36
LOST KING, THE (Sabatini)
  (R)               12/4/94-9
Lovallo, Lou, and Dennis Sanders
  THE AGATHA CHRISTIE COM-
    PANION: THE COMPLETE
    GUIDE TO AGATHA CHRIS-
    TIE'S LIFE AND WORK
    (IAC)                8/2/21
*Love, Dr. Jason.* See Leasor, James

LOVE KILLS (Greenburg) (M*F)
(R)                          3/1/31 & 42
LOVE TALKERS, THE (Peters)
(R)                          5/5/33
Lovell, Marc
  THE BIG TRENCHCOAT IN THE
    SKY (TAR)               10/4/43
LOVELY IN HER BONES (McCrumb)
  (IAC)                     13/3/65-6
LOVELY NIGHT TO KILL, A
  (Morgan) (TAR)       11/1/64; 11/2/76
LOVES MUSIC, LOVES TO DANCE
  (Clark) (TAR)             13/3/76
Lovesey, Peter
  THE BLACK CABINET (IAC)
                           12/2/67
  A CASE OF SPIRITS (R)     1/6/48
  THE DETECTIVE WORE SILK
    DRAWERS (R)             6/2/42
  THE FALSE INSPECTOR DEW
    (R)                     10/3/69
  ON THE EDGE (TAR)         11/3/74
  SWING, SWING TOGETHER
    (M*F)                   1/1/27
  WAXWORK (M*F) (R)
                       2/6/32; 6/2/43
Low, Ivy
  HIS MASTER'S VOICE (R)    5/3/40
Luard, Nicholas
  The Books of Nicholas Luard
    (Dukeshire)             4/1/12
LUCINDA (Rigsby)
  L: Crider 6/3/47; Goode 7/2/47;
    Shibuk 6/1/49
LUCK RUNS OUT, THE (MacLeod)
  (R)           4/1/34; 4/2/49; 5/5/37
LUCKY STIFF, THE (Rice) (R)  2/5/43
Ludlum, Robert
  THE GEMINI CONTENDERS
    (R)                     3/1/42
  THE ROAD TO GANDOLFO
    (IAC)                   8/5/30
Luhr, William
  RAYMOND CHANDLER AND
    FILM (IAC) (RM)    7/2/24 & 30
Luke, Keye
  Obituary (Lachman)        13/1/34
LUNATIC FRINGE, THE (DeAndrea)
  (M*F)                     5/1/24
Lupoff, Richard A., and Robert E.
  Howard
  THE RETURN OF SKULL-FACE
    (R)                     2/2/21-4

LURE, THE (Picano) (R)       4/4/46
Lutz, John
  BONEGRINDER (M*F) (R)
                    2/4/36; 6/4/22 & 29
  BUYER BEWARE (R) (M*F)
                       1/3/43; 1/4/37
  DANCER'S DEBT (R)         10/4/57
  JERICHO MAN (R)           4/5/37
  KISS (TAR)          11/1/63; 11/2/75
  THE LAZARUS MAN (R)       3/5/44
  THE RIGHT TO SING THE
    BLUES (R)           8/4/43 & 44
  THE SHADOW MAN (R)        5/5/29
  TROPICAL HEAT (R)         9/2/41
LUXEMBOURG RUN, THE (Ellin)
  (M*F) (R)          2/3/44; 2/5/36
Lyall, Gavin
  SHOOTING SCRIPT (IAC)     3/2/23
  UNCLE TARGET (TAR)        11/3/74
Lybeck, Alvin H.
  L:                        11/1/82
  A Look at W. Adolphe Roberts
                           11/1/3-6
  The Private Eye of Fred MacIsaac
                          10/2/29-42
  The Rise and Fall of Gillian
    Hazeltine               9/4/3-16*
  Tracking with Major Eagle 11/2/3-16*
Lyles, Bill
  L:                        3/4/58
LYING LADIES, THE (Finnegan)
  (TBR)                     13/1/41
Lynch, Jack
  BRAGG'S HUNCH (M*F)       6/5/41
Lyon, Dana
  Obituary (Lachman)        7/2/25
Lyons, Arthur
  CASTLES BURNING (M*F)     5/1/27
  THE DEAD ARE DISCREET
    (M*F)                   P/29
  HARD TRADE (M*F)          5/4/24
  OTHER PEOPLE'S MONEY
    (TAR)                   11/3/75

# M

Maartens, Maarten
  Chance and Illogic (Bleiler)   2/1/8
  L: Wooster 2/4/55, 2/5/53
MacBride/Kennedy Stories in Black
  Mask
  Some Very Tough People (Sampson)
                           8/5/7-17*

MacDonald, Charles
L:                                    5/2/39
*MacDonald, John D.*
  BRIGHT ORANGE FOR THE
    SHROUD (R)                       6/2/44
  CINNAMON SKIN (M*F)                6/6/27
  DEAD LOW TIDE (M*F)                1/3/40
  THE EMPTY COPPER SEA
    (M*F)                            3/6/38
  FREE FALL IN CRIMSON (M*F)
    (R) (IAC)        5/4/23 & 31; 12/4/44
  THE GOOD OLD STUFF (R)    8/1/18
  JOHN D. MacDONALD (Geherin)
    (IAC)                            7/2/23
  John D. MacDonald and the Real
    Murders (Cleary)       11/3/19-22
  THE LONELY SILVER RAIN
    (R)                              8/4/45
  NIGHTMARE IN PINK (R)       1/3/48
  Obituary (Lachman)               9/3/34
  ONE FEARFUL YELLOW EYE
    (R)                              2/4/47
  THE QUICK RED FOX (R)       6/2/44
  SLAM THE BIG DOOR (IAC) 9/4/37
  Sorry, John D., But... (Apostolou)
                                 11/3/15-8
  L: Shine 5/6/51, 6/3/47
MacDonald, Philip
  THE CRIME CONDUCTOR
    (TBR)                        13/3/56-7
  DEATH & CHICANERY (R)    3/4/50
  ESCAPE (R)                       3/4/50
  MYSTERY AT FRIAR'S PARDON
    (R)                              9/5/37
  THE NOOSE (IAC)                  2/6/29
  PERSONS UNKNOWN (R)       9/5/38
  SOMETHING TO HIDE (R)   10/1/88
  WARRANT FOR X (R)            8/4/46
*Macdonald, Robert.* See Lorac, E.C.R.
*Macdonald, Ross*
  THE BLUE HAMMER (R)         1/2/38
  THE CHILL (IAC)                  7/4/21
  The "I" in the Private Eye
    (Saylor)                        9/1/23-7
  LEW ARCHER, PRIVATE
    INVESTIGATOR (R)             2/4/47
  Obituary (Lachman)               7/5/29
  THE ZEBRA-STRIPED HEARSE
    (IAC)                           10/3/41
  L: Briney 5/5/45; Floyd 5/4/43
Mace, Merlda
  MOTTO FOR MURDER
    (R)                          12/1/49-50

MacGowan, Alice, and Perry Newberry
  THE MILLION-DOLLAR SUIT-
    CASE (TBR)                   13/4/73-4
*MacHarg, William*
  THE AFFAIRS OF O'MALLEY
    (TBR)                           11/3/60
  William MacHarg's O'Malley
    (Dove)                         8/6/14-8
*Machen, Arthur*
  Vincent Starrett vs. Arthur Machen
    (Bleiler)                      3/6/11-4
  L: Goldstone 1/1/46
*MacInnes, Helen*
    (IAC)                            4/5/25
  THE VENETIAN AFFAIR
    (IAC)                            4/1/15
*MacIsaac, Fred*
  The Private Eye of Fred MacIsaac
    (Lybeck)                    10/2/29-42*
Mackay, Amanda
  DEATH ON THE ENO (M*F) 6/1/36
MacKenzie, Donald
  BY ANY ILLEGAL MEANS
    (TAR)                           12/3/86
  DEATH IS A FRIEND (M*F)  1/5/34
  RAVEN AND THE KAMIKAZE
    (M*F)                            2/4/36
  A SAVAGE STATE OF GRACE
    (TAR)                           10/4/43
MACKIN COVER, THE (Shah)
    (M*F)                            2/2/34
MacKinnon, Allan
  DANGER BY MY SIDE (R)     3/4/49
*MacLean, Alistair*
  ATHABASCA (R)                    4/5/40
  Obituary (Lachman)               9/3/34
  L: Reilly 5/2/45
*MacLeod, Charlotte*
  Bloody Balaclava (Bakerman)
                                   7/1/23-29
  CHRISTMAS STALKINGS (ed.)
    (R)                          13/4/49-50
  THE LUCK RUNS OUT (R)
                      4/1/34; 4/2/49; 5/5/37
  MISTLETOE MYSTERIES (ed.)
    (IAC)                           12/2/67
  THE PALACE GUARD (M*F) 5/5/26
  THE RECYCLED CITIZEN
    (TAR)                           10/4/43
  REST YOU MERRY (M*F)
    (R)                      3/5/36; 4/2/48
  THE SILVER GHOST (TAR)
                          11/1/63; 11/2/75

MacLeod, Charlotte, continued
  VANE PURSUIT (TAR)      11/3/76
  THE WITHDRAWING ROOM
    (R)                   4/6/38
  WRACK AND RUNE (M*F)  6/3/31
MacLeod, Robert
  (SSC)                  4/5/22*
MacMurray, Fred
  Obituary (Lachman)      13/4/93
Macomber, Elisha. See Knight, Kathleen
  Moore
MacShane, Frank
  THE LIFE OF RAYMOND
    CHANDLER (IAC)       2/4/15
  SELECTED LETTERS OF RAY-
    MOND CHANDLER (ed.)
    (M*F) (IAC)     6/1/32; 10/2/58
MAD HATTER MYSTERY and the
  Tower of London, THE: Some
  Thoughts on the Tower and a
  Suggestion for the Dates
  (Keirans)             13/3/23-30
MAD HATTER MYSTERY, THE
  (Carr) (IAC)          11/4/52
MADAME MAIGRET'S RECIPES
  (Courtine) (IAC)      10/4/52
Madden, David. See Disney, Doris
  Miles
Maddock, Stephen [James Morgan
  Walsh, q.v.]
  (SSC)                  7/4/14*
MADE FOR MURDER (McGrew)
  (TBR)                12/3/70-1
MADNESS OF THE HEART, A
  (Neely) (R)            3/3/42
Mado, George. See Tute, Warren
Madsen, David
  U.S.S.A. (R)          13/1/70-1
Mae West: Mistress of Mystery?
  Almost... (Barton)      6/6/2,18
MAFIA FIX (Sapir/Murphy) (R)  1/6/52
Magazines. Also see Black Mask;
    Cream of Queen; Detective
    Story Magazine; Pulps
  Alfred Hitchcock's Mystery Magazine
    (IAC)                3/3/49
  The Armchair Detective
    (TCITC)            3/2/3-12,20
  Favorite Magazine Issues
    (Banks)             4/6/7-8
  (IAC)                  8/4/29

Magazines continued
  MONTHLY MURDERS: A CHECK-
    LIST AND CHRONOLOGICAL
    LISTING OF FICTION IN THE
    DIGEST-SIZE MYSTERY
    MAGAZINES IN THE UNITED
    STATES AND ENGLAND (MS)
    (M*F) (Cook)    6/2/5; 6/4/37
  THE SAINT MAGAZINE INDEX
    (Nieminski) (IAC)     4/3/31
  L: Harwood 3/5/49
MAGIC MIRROR (Friedman)
    (TAR)                11/1/54
Magill, Sheriff Moss. See Gardiner,
  Dorothy
Maguire, Michael
  SCRATCHPROOF (M*F)    1/6/38
Mahon, Thomas
  THE FANDANGO INVOLVE-
    MENT (M*F)         6/2/33-4
Mahoney, Ed
  L:                    5/1/46
MAIGRET & THE BLACK SHEEP
    (Simenon) (R)        1/5/44
MAIGRET AND THE HOTEL
    MAJESTIC (Simenon) (R)   2/5/40
Maigret, Jules (IAC)       10/4/52
Mail Order
  Murder by Mail (Albert)  3/5/7-10,16
MAINE MASSACRE, THE (van de
    Wetering) (R)        3/2/42
Maio, Kathi
  Review: THE OTHER SHOE
    (McMullen)          5/4/37
Mair, George B.
  (SSC)                 4/4/16-7*
Maitland, Antony. See Woods, Sara
MAJOR INQUIRY (Henderson) (M*F)
    (R)           1/1/27; 8/4/40
MAKASSAR STRAIT CONTRACT,
    THE (Atlee) (M*F)    1/3/40
MAKE MINE MURDER (Bowen)
    (TBR)               13/4/72
MAKE OUT WITH MURDER
    (Harrison) (R)       1/2/45
MAKING HATE (Wilson) (M*F) 2/6/33
Malcolm, John
  MORTAL RUIN (TAR)    11/1/57
  THE WRONG IMPRESSION
    (TAR)               13/2/44

Malcolm-Smith, George
  THE LADY FINGER (TBR)  11/4/59
  THE TROUBLE WITH FIDELITY
    (TBR)  11/4/59
MALICE IN WONDERLAND (Blake)
  (IAC)  9/1/40
Maling, Arthur
  THE RHEINGOLD ROUTE
    (R)  3/5/42
  SCHROEDER'S GAME
    (M*F)  1/5/29
  WHEN LAST SEEN (ed.)
    (M*F)  2/2/33
Malone, Michael
  TIME'S WITNESS (TAR) (MS)
    11/3/78; 12/1/4
MALTESE FALCON, THE (Hammett)
  (M*F)  5/3/31
*Maltese Falcon Society, The* (MS)  6/3/4
Malzberg, Barry N., and Bill Pronzini
  ACTS OF MERCY (R)  2/5/37
  THE RUNNING OF BEASTS
    (R)  1/1/17
MAMMOTH BOOK OF PRIVATE
  EYE STORIES, THE (Pronzini/
  Greenberg, eds.) (IAC)  11/1/33
MAN CALLED SCAVENER, A
  (Greenaway) (R)  5/4/33
MAN FROM THE SEA, THE (Innes)
  (IAC)  7/1/32
MAN IN A BLACK HAT (Thurston)
  (TBR)  11/3/60
MAN IN MY GRAVE, THE (Tucker)
  (TBR)  11/4/65
MAN IN THE BROWN SUIT, THE
  (Christie) (TBR)  13/2/63-4
MAN OF TWO TRIBES (Upfield)
  (R)  3/4/51
MAN ON THE BRIDGE, THE (Black)
  (M*F)  2/1/27
MAN RESPONSIBLE, THE (Robinett)
  (R)  7/5/39
MAN WHO DIDN'T FLY, THE
  (Bennett) (R)  5/4/30
MAN WHO DIED TWICE, THE
  (Peeples) (M*F)  1/3/41
MAN WHO HEARD TOO MUCH,
  THE (Woods) (IAC)  8/1/20
MAN WHO KILLED HIS BROTHER,
  THE (Stephens) (M*F)  5/2/17
MAN WHO LOST HIS WIFE, THE
  (Symons) (R)  2/1/43

MAN WHO MET THE TRAIN, THE
  (Adams) (TAR)  11/2/63
MAN WHO MISSED THE PARTY,
  THE (Adams) (TAR)  11/4/73
MAN WHO MURDERED GOLIATH,
  THE (Homes) (R)  2/5/43
MAN WHO MURDERED HIMSELF,
  THE (Homes) (R)  2/5/42
MAN WHO WAS THERE, THE
  (Temple-Ellis) (TBR)  11/4/70
MAN WITH BOGART'S FACE, THE
  (Fenady) (M*F) (R)  1/3/39 & 44
MAN WITH FIFTY COMPLAINTS,
  THE (McMullen) (M*F)  3/5/36
MAN WITH NO FACE, THE
  (Armstrong) (TBR)  11/3/68
MAN WITH THE TATTOOED FACE,
  THE (Burton) (M*F)  4/4/41
MAN WITHOUT A NAME, THE
  (Russell) (M*F)  2/3/42
*Manciple, Gideon.* See Hopkins,
  Kenneth
*Manhunt* (magazine)
  Favorite Magazine Issues
    (Banks)  4/6/7-8
Mann, Daniel
  Obituary (Lachman)  13/4/93
*Mann, Jack*
  Four Gees (Sampson)  12/3/13-34
  The Last of Gregory George Gordon
    Green (Sampson)  13/2/18-22
  L: Briney 13/1/83-5; Sampson
    13/2/97-9
Mann, Jessica
  FUNERAL SITES (M*F)  6/6/29
*Mann, Tiger.* See Spillane, Mickey
*Manners* (MS)  2/5/2
MANTRAP GARDEN, THE (Sher-
  wood) (R)  9/6/36
Maps of Xiccarph (Sampson)  6/6/9-18
Mara, Barnard
  THIS GUN FOR GLORIA
    (M*F)  P/23
MARAUDERS, THE (Shirreffs)
  (M*F)  1/3/41
MARCH VIOLETS (Kerr)
  (TAR)  11/3/71
Marcott, James
  HARD TO KILL (M*F)  P/26
*Margery Allingham Society*
  L: Cleary 10/4/60, 12/2/89-90,
    13/3/98

Margolies, Edward
  WHICH WAY DID HE GO?
    (IAC)                    7/2/23
MARK OF DISPLEASURE, A (Hely)
    (TBR)                   11/3/67
MARK OF MURDER (Shannon)
    (IAC)                    8/5/31
Mark, Ted
  L: Banks 1/4/55
MARK TWAIN MURDERS, THE
    (Skom) (R)             11/2/102
Markstein, George
  TRAITOR (IAC)             6/4/31
  ULTIMATE ISSUE (IAC)      6/4/31
Marlowe, Dan J.
  Obituary (Lachman)        8/6/36
Marlowe, Philip. See Chandler,
  Raymond
Marmor, Arnold
  Obituary (Lachman)       11/1/37
Maron, Margaret
  CORPUS CHRISTMAS
    (TAR)                  12/3/86
Marquand, John Phillips
    (SSC)                 4/5/22-3*
Marric, J.J. [John Creasey, q.v.]
  GIDEON'S DRIVE (M*F)      2/1/28
Marriott, Anthony
  PUBLIC EYE: MARKER CALLS
    THE TUNE (R)            7/4/33
Marsh, Geoffrey
  THE FANGS OF THE HOODED
    DEMON (TAR)            11/3/76
Marsh, Ngaio
  BLACK AS HE'S PAINTED
    (IAC)                  10/4/49
  THE COLLECTED SHORT FIC-
    TION OF NGAIO MARSH
    (Greene, ed.) (R) (IAC)
                     11/4/85; 12/2/69
  DEATH AT THE BAR (R)
    (IAC)             2/1/40; 4/4/20
  DEATH IN ECSTASY (R)      2/1/37
  ENTER A MURDERER (R)      2/3/54
  GRAVE MISTAKE (IAC)       4/3/32
    (IAC)                 6/6/19-20
  LIGHT THICKENS (IAC)      9/5/25
  THE NURSING HOME MURDER
    (IAC)                   6/3/23
  Obituary (Lachman)        6/3/26
  OVERTURE TO DEATH
    (IAC)                  10/4/49

Marsh, Ngaio, continued
  PHOTO FINISH (M*F) (IAC)
                     5/1/26; 6/3/23
  SCALES OF JUSTICE (R)     2/1/38
MARSHAL AND THE MADWOMAN,
  THE (Nabb) (TAR)         11/3/82
Marshall, William
  OUT OF NOWHERE (TAR)     11/3/77
  SCI FI (R) 6/3/43
  WAR MACHINE (TNSPE)      10/2/51
Marston, Edward
  THE QUEEN'S HEAD (TAR) 12/3/87
Martin, A.E.
  A.E. Martin's Pel Pelham
    (Deeck)              9/5/3-6*
  L: Deeck 10/2/78
Martin, Ian Kennedy
  THE DEAL OF THE CENTURY
    (M*F)                   1/5/33
Martin, James E.
  THE MERCY TRAP (TAR)     11/3/77
Martin, Kiel
  Obituary (Lachman)       13/1/34
Martin, Lee
  HAL'S OWN MURDER CASE
    (R)                    12/1/38
  TOO SANE A MURDER (R)    8/6/39
Martin, Richard
  INK IN HER BLOOD (R) (IAC)
                  11/2/98-101; 12/1/23
Martin, Robert
  JUST A CORPSE AT TWILIGHT
    (TBR)                 12/2/41-2
Martin, Walker
  L:                 4/2/59; 9/1/47
Martyn, Wyndham
    (SSC)                  4/5/23*
Maryk, Michael, and Brent Monahan
  DEATHBITE (R)             4/2/43
MASK OF ROME, THE (Llewellyn)
    (TAR)                  11/1/56
Masliah, Michael L.
  L:                10/1/92; 11/1/88
Mason, A.E.W.
  MURDER AT THE VILLA ROSA
    (M*F)                   4/5/28
Mason, Hugh Van Wyck
    (SSC)                   4/6/4*
MASS MURDER (Drummond)
    (TAR)                 13/3/78-9
Masser, Helmut
  L:  2/2/60; 5/2/40; 9/4/46; 11/1/81-2
  Review: THE MAN WHO DIDN'T
    FLY (Bennett)           5/4/30
  L: Albert 2/3/64

MASTER MYSTERY, THE (Small)
(R) 9/6/44
MASTER OF THE MOOR (Rendell)
(R) 6/4/42
MASTER PLAN (Stuart) (R) 12/4/56-7
Masterman, J.C.
AN OXFORD TRAGEDY (R) 2/2/38
MASTERPIECES OF MYSTERY
(Queen, ed.) (R) 2/1/43
MASTERS OF MENACE: GREEN-
STREET AND LORRE (Sennett)
(R) 7/2/37
MASTERS OF MYSTERY: A STUDY
OF THE DETECTIVE STORY
(Thomson) (IAC) 2/6/27
(TCITC) 3/2/3-12,20
Masterson, Whit
HUNTER OF THE BLOOD
(M*F) 1/5/30
THE SLOW GALLOWS
(IAC) 4/1/15
Masur, Harold Q.
SEND ANOTHER HEARSE
(R) 8/4/45
Mather, Berkeley
(SSC) 4/6/4-5*
Mathewson, Joseph
ALICIA'S TRUMP (M*F) 5/2/15
Mathis, Edward
THE BURNED WOMAN
(TAR) 11/3/78
LITTLE MAN BLUES
(TAR) 10/4/44
Obituary (Lachman) 10/3/46
SEPTEMBER SONG
(TAR) 13/2/44-5
Matt Helm Series, The (Banks/
Townsend) 2/2/3-11*
L: Parnell 2/5/59
MATTER OF CRIME, A (Bruccoli/
Layman, eds.) (IAC) 11/1/33
MATTER OF DEGREE, A (Philbin)
(TNSPE) 10/2/49
MATTER OF NERVES, A (Hull)
(R) 2/4/42
MATTERS OF FACT & FICTION:
ESSAYS 1973-1976 (Vidal)
(R) 1/5/39
Maugham, W. Somerset
ASHENDEN (IAC) 2/6/28
Maxwell, Victor
The Professionals (Sampson)
6/1/16-20*

MAY YOU DIE IN IRELAND
(Kenyon) (IAC) 2/6/29
Mayo, Asey. See Taylor, Phoebe Atwood
Mayo, James
(SSC) 4/6/5*
Mayor, Archer
OPEN SEASON (TAR)
11/1/63; 11/2/75
McAleer, John J.
COIGN OF VANTAGE (TAR)11/3/75
JUSTICE ENDS AT HOME, AND
OTHER STORIES (Stout) (ed.)
(R) 3/5/43
L: 1/1/40
REX STOUT: A BIOGRAPHY
(MS) (IAC) 2/2/64; 2/4/16
REX STOUT: AN ANNOTATED
PRIMARY AND SECONDARY
BIBLIOGRAPHY (w/Townsend/
Sapp/Schemer) (R) 5/2/29
ROYAL DECREE (R) 8/3/40
McAllister, Pam, and Dick Riley
THE BEDSIDE, BATHTUB &
ARMCHAIR COMPANION TO
AGATHA CHRISTIE (R) (IAC)
4/1/43; 4/3/31
McAuliffe, Frank
THE BAG MAN (R) 5/5/40
McBain, Ed [Evan Hunter, q.v.]
DEATH OF A NURSE (R) 1/4/44
EVEN THE WICKED (R)
1/4/44; 1/5/40
THE HOUSE THAT JACK BUILT
(TAR) 11/3/76
An Interview with Ed McBain
(Skinner) 13/4/3-11
(IAC) 5/6/31
LIGHTNING (R) 8/3/45
POISON (R) 9/5/35
TEN PLUS ONE (R) 1/4/47
VESPERS (TAR) 12/3/85
WHERE THERE'S SMOKE
(R) 1/5/40
McCafferty, Taylor
PET PEEVES (TAR) 13/2/42
McCahery, James R.
L: 2/5/55; 3/4/53
(MS) 12/3/6-7
McCarthy, Paul
Reviews:
THE BODY OF A GIRL
(Gilbert) 3/4/48
HENDON'S FIRST CASE
(Rhode) 4/4/44

McCarthy, Paul, continued
Reviews continued:
THE LONDON DEAL
(Crisp)                     3/4/47
MASTERPIECES OF MYSTERY
(Queen, ed.)                2/1/43
THE MOVING TOYSHOP
(Crispin)                   2/1/43
SUDDENLY WHILE GAR-
DENING (Lemarchand)  3/4/48
McCloy, Helen
BURN THIS (M*F)             4/4/42
THE CHANGELING CON-
SPIRACY (M*F)               1/6/38
THE IMPOSTER (M*F)          2/1/24
THE ONE THAT GOT AWAY
(R)                         9/5/45
McClure, James
Black and White and Dead
(Isaac)                   6/4/12-8
THE BLOOD OF AN
ENGLISHMAN (R)              5/2/37
SNAKE (R)                   1/1/35
McConnell, Frank (MS)      12/3/10
McCullough, David Willis, ed.
CITY SLEUTHS AND TOUGH
GUYS (IAC)                 12/2/66
McCullum, Karen Thomas, and Pamela
Granovetter
THE COPPERFIELD CHECKLIST
OF MYSTERY AUTHORS
(IAC)                      10/2/57
A SHOPPING LIST OF MYSTERY
CLASSICS (IAC)             10/2/56
McCrumb, Sharyn
LOVELY IN HER BONES
(IAC)                     13/3/65-6
McCutchan, Philip
(SSC)                      4/5/21*
McDermid, Val
REPORT FOR MURDER
(R)                       13/3/91-2
Mcdonald, Gregory
BUCK PASSES FLYNN (R)
(IAC)             6/1/40; 6/4/32
CONFESS, FLETCH (R)         1/5/37
FLETCH (M*F) (R)     1/3/37; 1/5/37
FLETCH AND THE WIDOW
BRADLEY (M*F) (R) 6/1/36 & 40
L: Briney 1/6/56
McFarland, Orin S.
L:                          1/1/40

McFarlane, Leslie
GHOST OF THE HARDY BOYS:
AN AUTOBIOGRAPHY
(R)                         7/3/36
McGARR AND THE SIENESE CON-
SPIRACY (Gill) (M*F)        3/1/32
McGARR ON THE CLIFFS OF
DOVER (Gill) (M*F)          3/3/39
McGee, David
Reviews:
THE MEMORIAL HALL
MURDER (Langton)     4/1/29
MY NAME IS NORVAL
(White)                 4/1/29
McGerr, Pat
DEATH IN A MILLION LIVING
ROOMS (TBR)             11/4/58
PICK YOUR VICTIM (R)    10/1/89
THE SEVEN DEADLY SISTERS
(R) (M*F)       2/2/38; 3/5/38
McGinley, Patrick
BOGMAIL (M*F) (R)   5/5/21 & 29
McGivern, William P.
BUT DEATH RUNS FASTER
(R)                     10/1/89
Obituary (Lachman)          7/1/35
REPRISAL (M*F)              4/2/34
VERY COLD FOR MAY
(IAC)                       9/3/30
McGown, Jill
MURDER AT THE OLD
VICARAGE (R)            12/1/36
McGraw, Lee
HATCHETT (M*F)              1/2/26
McGrew, Fenn
MADE FOR MURDER
(TBR)                 12/3/70-1
TASTE OF DEATH (TBR)    12/3/70
McGuire, Paul
THE BLACK ROSE MURDER
(TBR)                 13/1/44-5
McIlvanney, William
LAIDLAW (IAC)               4/5/24
McInerny, Ralph
BISHOP AS PAWN (M*F)        3/5/35
BODY AND SOIL (R)          11/4/85
Clergy-Detectives (Cleary)  9/3/3-21
FRIGOR MORTIS (TAR)     12/3/85-6
(IAC)                       4/4/19
THE SEARCH COMMITTEE
(TAR)                  13/2/43-4
McIntyre, John Thomas
A Few Kind Words for Ashton-Kirk
(Sampson)                 7/6/3-12

McKimmey, James
BLUE MASCARA TEARS (R) 7/5/45
McKinney, Robert L.
DEATH IN A SMALL SOUTHERN
TOWN (MS)                    9/5/2
McLeish, Dougal
THE TRAITOR GAME
(TBR)                    13/4/72-3
McMullen, Mary
A COUNTRY KIND OF DEATH
(R)                          4/2/46
DANGEROUS FUNERAL (R) 4/2/45
THE MAN WITH FIFTY
COMPLAINTS (M*F)         3/5/36
THE OTHER SHOE (R)       5/4/37
UNTIL DEATH DO US PART
(R)                          8/3/38
McQUAID IN AUGUST (Rifkin)
(M*F)                        3/6/29
*McQuay, Mike*
Some Recent Hybrids (Kelley)
6/2/16-8
McSherry, Frank D., Jr.
Encore!                  12/1/9-22
L: 2/1/52; 9/5/47; 11/3/84; 13/1/86;
13/2/101-2
The Morals of Parker     8/2/2-8
The Real Originality of Dashiell
Hammett              11/2/25-35
The Real Originality of Ian
Fleming              11/4/35-45
Reviews:
THE BLACK BAT'S INVISIBLE
ENEMY (Jones)        11/4/98
THE KILLING GIFT (Wood)
11/4/95
THE LOST KING (Sabatini)
12/4/94-9
A Study in Invisibility  11/3/23-43
*Mean Streets* (magazine) (MS)  12/4/1
MEANS OF EVIL (Rendell)
(M*F)                        4/3/34
Mearson, Lyon
PHANTOM FINGERS (TBR) 10/3/61
*Medical Doctors*
The Medical Practitioner in the
Writings of Raymond Chandler
(Skinner)            11/2/37-46
Meek, M.R.D.
A LOOSE CONNECTION
(TAR)                    12/3/87-8
A MOUTHFUL OF SAND
(TAR)                    11/3/79

*Meek, M.R.D.,* continued
THE SPLIT SECOND (R)
13/4/99-100
THIS BLESSED PLOT (TAR)13/2/45
A WORM OF DOUBT (TAR)10/4/44
MEET NERO WOLFE (movie)
L: Shibuk 5/6/52
*Melies, Georges* (RM)            6/6/23
Meltzer, Edmund S.
L:                           1/4/60
*Melville, James.* Also see Charles,
Hampton
A SORT OF SAMURAI (R)    6/6/34
THE WAGES OF ZEN (R)     5/6/45
L: Kimura 7/1/48
MEMORIAL HALL MURDER, THE
(Langton) (M*F) (R) (IAC)
3/1/34; 4/1/29; 5/2/35; 5/4/19
Memories of a Haunted Man
(Nevins)                 8/3/2-11
MEN ON THE DEAD MAN'S CHEST,
THE (Raymond) (M*F)      2/5/32
MENACE WITHIN, THE (Curtiss)
(IAC) (R)            3/2/24; 3/5/42
Menendez, Albert J.
THE SUBJECT IS MURDER: A
SELECTIVE SUBJECT GUIDE
TO MYSTERY FICTION (IAC)
(MS)                 8/4/30; 9/1/7
THE SUBJECT IS MURDER: A
SELECTIVE SUBJECT GUIDE
TO MYSTERY FICTION (MS)
(R)              12/1/3; 12/4/87-91
*Mental-Institution Settings*
(TBR)                    12/4/72
L: Deeck 13/1/87
MERCY TRAP, THE (Martin)
(TAR)                    11/3/77
*Meredith, John.* See Gerard, Francis
MERMAID (Millar) (M*F)       6/2/36
MERRY CHRISTMAS, MURDOCK
(Ray) (TAR)              12/4/54
Mersereau, John
MURDER LOVES COMPANY
(R)                          9/4/41
Mertz, Stephen. Also see Brett,
Stephen
In Defense of Carroll John
Daly                 2/3/19-22*
L:      2/3/58; 2/4/59; 2/5/49; 3/5/46
Reviews:
THE BIG STIFFS (Avallone)
2/5/39

*Mertz, Stephen,* continued
  Reviews continued:
    THE DEADLY KITTEN
      (Brown)           3/2/47
    DEATH IS LIKE THAT
      (Spain)           2/4/44
    THE DOCTOR'S WIFE
      (Avallone)      3/1/43
    DONAVAN'S DELIGHT
      (Brown)           3/6/47
    FIND THIS WOMAN
      (Prather)        2/1/47
    THE GEMINI CONTENDERS
      (Ludlum)         3/1/42
    THE LADY IN THE LAKE
      (Chandler)      3/2/46
    MURDER CAN'T STOP
      (Ballard)        3/4/42
    SAY YES TO MURDER
      (Ballard)        2/3/53
    THE SEVEN SISTERS
      (Ballard)        2/5/39
    STATE DEPARTMENT
      MURDERS (Ronns)   2/1/48
    THE TWISTED THING
      (Spillane)      3/1/38
    YOU CAN'T KEEP THE
      CHANGE (Cheyney)  2/4/44
METHOD IN HIS MURDER (Warriner)
  (TBR)               12/4/64-5
METZGER'S DOG (Perry) (IAC) 8/1/16
MEXICAN ASSASSIN, THE
  (Hartshorne) (M*F)    2/6/30
Meyer, Lawrence
  A CAPITOL CRIME (IAC)  3/2/22
Meyers, Martin
  SPY AND DIE (M*F)    1/2/24
Meyers, Richard
  TV DETECTIVES (IAC)   6/4/32
Meyerson, Jeffrey
  The Avon Classic Crime Col-
    lection        1/5/19-20*
  L: 1/1/45; 1/2/48; 1/3/56; 1/4/58;
    1/5/55; 1/6/57; 2/2/46; 2/3/69;
    2/4/54; 2/5/54; 2/6/48; 3/1/57;
    3/2/53; 3/4/60
  Reviews:
    THE AFFAIR OF THE BLOOD-
      STAINED EGG COSY
      (Anderson)      1/5/42
    THE AMBUSHERS (Hamilton)
                  1/2/38-9

*Meyerson, Jeffrey,* continued
  Reviews continued:
    BRIGHTLIGHT (Bernard)  2/1/31
    THE CAVANOUGH QUEST
      (Gifford)        1/3/44
    CIRCLE OF FIRE (Sadler) 1/3/47
    CONFESS, FLETCH (Mcdonald)
                  1/5/37
    THE CROOKED HINGE
      (Carr)          1/4/41
    CUTTER AND BONE
      (Thornburg)     1/4/43
    DEATH OF A NURSE
      (McBain)       1/4/44
    EVEN THE WICKED
      (McBain)       1/4/44
    FLETCH (Mcdonald)   1/5/37
    THE FRENCH KEY MYSTERY
      (Gruber)        1/5/47
    GUILTY BYSTANDER
      (Miller)        1/5/49
    THE HARDBOILED DICKS: AN
      ANTHOLOGY AND STUDY
      OF PULP DETECTIVE
      FICTION (Goulart, ed.)  1/2/37
    HEIST ME HIGHER (Ballinger)
                  1/4/52
    IN HOLY TERROR (Sapir/
      Murphy)        1/3/49
    LAST WAR DANCE (Sapir/
      Murphy)        1/3/48
    MAFIA FIX (Sapir/Murphy) 1/6/52
    MURDERERS' ROW
      (Hamilton)      1/5/50
    THE NAKED FACE
      (Sheldon)       1/3/47
    NIGHTMARE IN PINK
      (MacDonald)     1/3/48
    AN OXFORD TRAGEDY
      (Masterman)     2/2/38
    THE RAVAGERS
      (Hamilton)      1/2/38
    RAYMOND CHANDLER
      SPEAKING (Chandler)  1/6/45
    THE REMOVERS
      (Hamilton)      1/4/53
    RIM OF THE PIT (Talbot) 1/5/49
    THE SAINT IN NEW YORK
      (Charteris)      1/5/46
    SAM 7 (Cox)       2/3/50
    THE SINS OF THE FATHERS
      (Block)          1/2/22

*Meyerson, Jeffrey,* continued
  Reviews continued:
    THE SOUR LEMON SCORE
      (Stark)            1/6/51
    STORM WARNING (Higgins)
                    1/2/40
    STRAIGHT (Knickmeyer)  1/2/16
    A STUDY IN TERROR
      (Queen)           2/3/56
    A THREE-PIPE PROBLEM
      (Symons)        1/3/48
    THREE-TOED PUSSY
      (Burley)         1/6/52
    THE VALHALLA EXCHANGE
      (Patterson)      1/4/43
    WEDNESDAY THE RABBI
      GOT WET (Kemelman)  1/4/43
*Meynell, Laurence*
  Crime Novelists as Writers of Chil-
    dren's Fiction (Sarjeant) 13/1/23-6
  Obituary (Lachman)     12/1/29
MIAMI BLUES (Willeford)
  (IAC)              11/4/50
MICHAEL SHAYNE'S LONG
  CHANCE (Halliday) (M*F)  2/4/32
Michaels, Barbara. Also see Peters,
  Elizabeth
  WAIT FOR WHAT WILL COME
    (IAC)             2/6/29
Michaels, Melisa C.
  THROUGH THE EYES OF THE
    DEAD (TAR)      11/3/80
Michaels, Norman, and Chris Stein-
  brunner
  THE FILMS OF SHERLOCK
    HOLMES (R)      3/3/43
Mickey Spillane's Mike Hammer: The
  Great Cover-Up (Banks)  8/4/17-20
Middlemiss, Robert
  THE PARROT MAN (R)    2/2/39
MIDNIGHT LADY AND THE
  MOURNING MAN, THE
  L: Broset 2/5/56
MIDNIGHT SPECIALS: AN ANTHOL-
  OGY FOR TRAIN BUFFS AND
  SUSPENSE AFICIONADOS
  (Pronzini, ed.) (R)     1/6/46
MIKE DIME (Fantoni) (M*F)
  (R)         5/4/26; 6/1/43
MILKMAID'S MILLIONS, THE
  (Austin) (R)        9/5/39
Millar, Margaret
  ASK FOR ME TOMORROW
    (M*F)          1/4/37

*Millar, Margaret,* continued
  HOW LIKE AN ANGEL (IAC)
                    8/1/19
  MERMAID (M*F)     6/2/36
  THE MURDER OF MIRANDA (R)
    (M*F)      3/4/46; 3/6/29
  A STRANGER IN MY GRAVE
    (IAC)          8/1/19
*Miller, Don*
  Obituary (MS)       6/3/1
Miller, Rex
  SLOB (R)         9/6/40
Miller, Stephen T., and Michael L. Cook
  MYSTERY, DETECTIVE, AND
    ESPIONAGE FICTION: A
    CHECKLIST OF FICTION IN
    U.S. PULP MAGAZINES, 1915–
    1974 (R)       11/1/75
*Miller, Thorne*
  The Murder Cases of Pinklin West
    (Sampson)      8/1/3-7
Miller, Victor B.
  FERNANDA (R)     1/2/44
Miller, Wade
  GUILTY BYSTANDER (R)  1/5/49
MILLION-DOLLAR SUITCASE, THE
  (MacGowan/Newberry) (TBR)
                13/4/73-4
Mills, Osmington
  AT ONE FELL SWOOP (TBR)
                11/3/59
Milne, A.A.
  AUTOBIOGRAPHY (IAC)  8/5/31
  THE RED HOUSE MYSTERY (IAC)
    (R)      6/6/20; 8/5/38
Milton, David
  THE HYTE MANEUVER
    (TAR)        11/3/80
MIND OVER MURDER (Kienzle)
  (M*F)         5/4/22
MIND TO MURDER, A (James)
  (IAC)         9/2/24
MINISTRY OF DEATH (Bingham)
  (M*F)         2/5/26
MINOR MURDERS (Hensley) (R)
  (M*F)     4/1/32; 4/2/36
Minor, Valerie
  MURDER IN THE ENGLISH
    DEPARTMENT (R)   11/4/94
MINUTEMAN MURDER, THE
  (Langton) (R)   1/2/41; 5/2/36
MISADVENTURES OF SHERLOCK
  HOLMES, THE (Queen, ed.)
  (R)         3/3/40

Miscellaneous Mystery Mish-Mash
  (Lachman)
  2/1/6; 2/2/19-20; 5/1/18-9; 5/2/12;
  5/5/18-9; 12/1/29-30; 12/2/70;
  12/4/49-50
MISCHIEF IN MAGGODY (Hess)
  (TAR)                 11/1/61; 11/2/72
MISS HOGG AND THE MISSING
  SISTERS (Lee) (TBR)      13/2/62-3
Miss Julia Tyler: Detective Manqué
  (Deeck)                13/1/7-22*
Miss Marple She Isn't (Doerrer) 2/6/7-8
MISS MELVILLE REGRETS (Smith)
  (R)                      12/4/78-9
MISS MELVILLE RETURNS (Smith)
  (R)                        12/4/77
MISS SEETON AT THE HELM
  (Charles) (TAR)           13/1/53
MISSING MADONNA, THE (O'Marie)
  (TAR) (R)   11/1/64 & 78-80; 11/2/76
MISSING WOMAN (Lewin)
  (M*F)                       5/6/39
MISSION M.I.A. (Pollock) (R)   6/4/47
MISTLETOE MYSTERIES (MacLeod,
  ed.) (IAC)                12/2/67
MISTS OVER MOSLEY (Greenwood)
  (IAC)                     10/3/40
Mitchell, Gladys
  DEATH AT THE OPERA (R)    2/5/42
  WATSON'S CHOICE (R)       5/3/39
Mitchell, James
  DYING DAY (TAR)          11/3/81
  SMEAR JOB (M*F)           2/3/44
  (SSC)                    5/3/19-20*
MIZMAZE (Fitt) (M*F) (TBR)
                           5/3/28; 11/1/41
MODUS OPERANDI (Winks)
  (IAC)                      7/2/22
Moffatt, Len
  L:                         1/1/43
  Wilson Tucker's Charles
    Horne                  12/2/3-10
Mogensen, Harald
  KRIMINALLITTERATURENS
    KAVALKADE: KRIMINAL-OG
    DETEKTIVHISTORIEN I
    BILLEDER OG TEKST (w/La
    Cour) (R)                7/6/35
  L:                         8/1/41
  (MS)                       4/2/2
MOMENT OF FICTION, THE (Estow)
  (M*F)                      3/6/39

MOMENT OF TRUTH, THE (Blom)
  (R)                        1/4/45
MONA (Block) (M*F)           3/2/38
Monahan, Brent, and Michael Maryk
  DEATHBITE (R)              4/2/43
MONEY TO BURN (Hendricks)
  (TAR)                     12/3/82
Montalbano, William D., and Carl
  Hiaasen
  A DEATH IN CHINA (IAC)  11/4/47
Montand, Yves
  Obituary (Lachman)        13/4/93-4
Monteilhet, Hubert
  ANDROMACHE OR THE INAD-
    VERTENT MURDER (R)
                            13/2/76-7
Montgomery, Ione
  THE GOLDEN DRESS (TBR)
                            13/2/72
Montgomery, Yvonne
  SCAVENGERS (IAC)         12/4/43
MONTHLY MURDERS: A CHECK-
    LIST AND CHRONOLOGICAL
    LISTING OF FICTION IN THE
    DIGEST-SIZE MYSTERY
    MAGAZINES IN THE UNITED
    STATES AND ENGLAND (Cook)
    (MS) (M*F)          6/2/5; 6/3/37
  Closing the Gap: A Critique
    (Nieminski)          7/3/6-15,31
  L: Cook 5/2/48
MOOD FOR MURDER, THE (Siller)
  (TBR)                    12/3/73
MOONFLOWER MURDER, THE
  (Nichols) (TBR)          11/3/70
MOONLIGHT AT GREYSTONES
  (Bronte) (M*F)            1/1/31
MOONSTONE, THE (Collins)
  (IAC)                      6/6/21
Moore, Margaret
  DANGEROUS CONCEITS
    (TAR)                  11/3/81
Moore, Robin
  THE TERMINAL CONNECTION
    (R)                     1/5/41
Morals of Parker, The (McSherry)
                             8/2/2-8
MORBID TASTE FOR BONES, A
  (Peters) (M*F)            4/4/37
MORDIDA MAN, THE (Thomas)
  (M*F) (R)            5/6/34; 8/2/31
MORE CLASSICS OF THE HORROR
  FILM (Everson) (RM)       9/5/30

Morelius, Iwan
   L:                              12/2/98-9
Morgan, D. Miller
   A LOVELY NIGHT TO KILL
      (TAR)         11/1/64; 11/2/76
MORGUE THE MERRIER, THE
   (Truesdale) (M*F) (TBR)
                3/6/39; 13/1/39-40
*Morice, Anne*
   Ann Morice (Chouteau/Alderson)
                       6/6/5-8*
   DEAD ON CUE (R)       8/6/45
   DEATH IN THE ROUND (R)  5/5/36
   HOLLOW VENGEANCE (R)  6/3/40
   MURDER BY PROXY (R)   8/1/36
   MURDER POST-DATED (R)  8/1/36
   PUBLISH AND BE KILLED
      (R)                 8/6/46
   SCARED TO DEATH (M*F)  2/4/32
   SLEEP OF DEATH (R)    7/2/34
Morland, Nigel
   THE CLUE IN THE MIRROR
      (TBR)             12/2/51-2
Morley, Christopher
   THE HAUNTED BOOKSHOP
      (IAC)              7/5/27
MORMON MURDERS, THE (Naifeh/
   Smith) (R)           13/2/90-1
MORNING FOR FLAMINGOS, A
   (Burke) (TAR)          13/1/51
MOROCCAN, THE (Haddad)
   (M*F)                 3/3/33
Morris, W.F.
   "G.B.": A STORY OF THE GREAT
      WAR (TBR)        11/3/64
Morrison, Arthur
   BEST MARTIN HEWITT DETEC-
      TIVE STORIES (R)     1/5/38
   CHRONICLES OF MARTIN
      HEWITT (TCITC)     3/4/17
*Morrison-Burke, Constance.* See Porter,
   Joyce
Morse, L.A.
   THE OLD DICK (M*F) (R) (IAC)
           5/6/40; 6/1/40; 6/6/20
MORTAL RUIN (Malcolm) (TAR)
                     11/1/57
MORTAL STAKES (Parker) (R)
   (IAC)          2/1/32; 2/6/28
*Mortdecai, Charlie.* See Bonfiglioli,
   Kyril

Mortimer, John
   RUMPOLE À LA CARTE
      (TAR)             13/2/45-6
   RUMPOLE AND THE AGE OF
      MIRACLES (TV) (IAC)   12/1/26
   "Rumpole and the Sporting Life"
      (R)                 9/1/31
   "Rumpole and the Younger
      Generation" (R)       9/3/28
*Morton, A.Q.*
   His Own Desert (Bleiler)  3/4/11,15
Mosier, Alan S.
   Deduction in Duplicate  7/2/19-21,30
   L:              7/1/50; 7/4/38
   Reviews:
      BANQUETS OF THE BLACK
         WIDOWERS (Asimov)  8/3/37
      THE BEETHOVEN CON-
         SPIRACY (Hauser)   9/2/44
      BILLINGSGATE SHOAL
         (Boyer)            6/3/39
      THE BROWNSTONE HOUSE
         OF NERO WOLFE (Darby)
                       7/6/32
      THE CASE OF THE KID-
         NAPPED ANGEL
         (Cunningham)       7/4/32
      CATCH A FALLING CLOWN
         (Kaminsky)        7/1/40
      C.B. GREENFIELD: NO LADY
         IN THE HOUSE (Kallen) 6/5/49
      C.B. GREENFIELD: PIANO
         BIRD (Kallan)      8/2/29
      CEMETERIES ARE FOR
         DYING (Story)      7/5/47
      THE DAISY DUCKS (Boyer)
                       9/1/43
      DEATH AT CHARITY'S POINT
         (Tapply)          8/3/36
      DEATH SCENE (Suyker)  6/5/50
      ICEBREAKER (Gardner)  7/3/39
      MURDER AT THE ACADEMY
         AWARDS (Hyams)   8/1/33
      NOT DEAD, ONLY RESTING
         (Brett)           9/3/40
      THE PENNY FERRY (Boyer)
                       8/3/37
      THE PRIVATE LIFE OF
         DOCTOR WATSON
         (Hardwick)        8/1/27
      THE SOAP OPERA
         SLAUGHTERS (Kaye)  7/4/32

*Mosier, Alan S.*, continued
  Reviews continued:
    THE SHERIFF OF BOMBAY
      (Keating)        8/3/37
    SOMEONE ELSE'S GRAVE
      (Smith)        9/3/40
    VALEDICTION (Parker)  8/2/30
    THE VIRGIN IN THE ICE
      (Peters)       7/5/47
    THE WIDENING GYRE
      (Parker)      7/3/39
Moskowitz, Dick
  L:      2/5/45; 3/3/61, 4/2/62
MOSLEY BY MOONLIGHT
  (Greenwood) (IAC)    10/3/40
Mosley, Walter
  DEVIL IN A BLUE DRESS
    (MS)        12/1/3-4
MOSS MYSTERY, THE (Wells)
  (TBR)        13/4/77-8
MOTHER SHADOW, THE (Howe)
  (R)        12/1/43
MOTIVE IN SHADOW (Egan)
  (M*F)      4/2/40
*Moto, Mr.* See Marquand, John Phillips
MOTOR CITY BLUE (Estleman) (R)
  (M*F)      4/4/46; 5/3/27
Motsinger, Thomas L.
  L:        2/6/47
  Reviews:
    SHALL WE TELL THE
      PRESIDENT? (Archer)  2/6/36
    TWICE DEAD (Names)  3/1/41
MOTTO FOR MURDER (Mace)
  (R)       12/1/49-50
MOUCHE (Demouzon) (M*F)  5/2/21
MOUNTAINS HAVE A SECRET,
  THE (Upfield) (R)    3/4/51
MOUSETRAP AND OTHER PLAYS,
  THE (Christie) (IAC)    3/3/18
MOUTHFUL OF SAND, A (Meek)
  (TAR)       11/3/79
Move Over Spenser—Here Comes
  Cuddy (Saylor)    10/2/43-7
*Movies.* Also see Cinecon; Cinevent;
    Doom with a View; Movies
    Reviewed; Reel Murders
  THE FILMS OF HOPALONG
    CASSIDY (Nevins) (IAC)
             13/4/87-8
  THE FILMS OF PETER LORRE
    (Youngkin/Bigwood/Cabana)
    (R)       10/3/71

*Movies* continued
  THE FILMS OF SHERLOCK
    HOLMES (Steinbrunner/Michaels)
    (R)       3/3/43
  GUIDE TO MOVIES ON VIDEO
    CASSETTE (Blades et al.)
    (IAC)      11/4/55
  I Remember...B-Movies (Banks)
             4/5/13-7
  LOBBY CARDS: THE CLASSIC
    FILMS (RM)    9/5/30
  MASTERS OF MENACE: GREEN-
    STREET AND LORRE (Sennett)
    (R)       7/2/37
  Miscellaneous Mystery Mish-Mash
    Part II (Lachman)    2/1/6
  MORE CLASSICS OF THE HOR-
    ROR FILM (Everson) (RM) 9/5/30
  RAYMOND CHANDLER AND
    FILM (Luhr) (IAC) (RM)
            7/2/24 & 30
  Raymond Chandler on Film (Pross)
      1/6/3-10*; 2/3/27-31,40*
  Raymond Chandler on Film:
    Addendum (Shibuk)    2/4/14
  Raymond Chandler Without His
    Knight: Contracting Worlds in
    THE BLUE DAHLIA and
    PLAYBACK (Brewer)  13/3/37-49
  Spade Trumps Unplayed (Banks)
            8/6/3-6
  TROUBLE IS THEIR BUSINESS:
    PRIVATE EYES IN FICTION,
    FILM, AND TELEVISION
    (Conquest) (MS)    11/4/2
  L: Briney 2/2/45; Doran 3/4/54;
    Samoian 4/6/48; Van Tilburg
    5/3/41
*Movies Reviewed.* Also see Reel
    Murders; Doom with a View;
    Lachman – Television and Film
    Reviews in IAC; Traylor – Judg-
    ments
  AMONG THE LIVING    10/3/48
  ARSENE LUPIN      8/4/35
  THE BAT       8/2/27
  THE BAT WHISPERS    10/3/49
  BEDLAM       11/4/55
  THE BIG COMBO    6/4/35
  BLUEBEARD      6/3/29
  THE CANARY MURDER CASE
            6/2/25
  THE CAT AND THE CANARY
            8/2/26

| | |
|---|---|
| BLUE VELVET | 9/1/37 |
| BOB THE GAMBLER | 9/2/31 |
| CRISS-CROSS | 12/1/27 |
| DEAD MEN DON'T WEAR PLAID | 6/4/34 |
| DEATH ON THE NILE | 3/1/45 |
| DEATHTRAP | 7/5/29 |
| DIVA | 6/4/34 |
| DR. JEKYLL AND MR. HYDE | 7/1/36 |
| DROLE DE DRAME | 6/2/26 |
| EVIL UNDER THE SUN | 6/3/28 |
| THE EXORCIST II | 7/5/33 |
| FIRST TRAIN TO BABYLON | 13/4/87 |
| FIVE-STAR FINAL | 11/4/54 |
| FOG ISLAND | 8/1/24 |
| FOOTSTEPS IN THE DARK | 9/5/30 |
| FORCED VENGEANCE | 8/1/23 |
| FREAKS | 9/1/38 |
| THE GAY FALCON | 13/4/88 |
| THE GLASS KEY | 6/2/26 & 27 |
| THE GRACIE ALLEN MURDER CASE | 8/4/35 |
| GRAND CENTRAL MURDER | 12/1/27 |
| THE HILLS HAVE EYES | 8/1/25 |
| INDIANA JONES AND THE TEMPLE OF DOOM | 8/3/32 |
| IT'S IN THE BAG | 8/4/30 |
| JANE EYRE | 6/2/22 |
| JINXED | 7/5/34 |
| JULIE | 7/2/26 |
| KID-GLOVE KILLER | 12/1/27 |
| THE KILLING | 7/4/24 |
| LADY ON A TRAIN | 7/5/29; 8/3/31 |
| THE KISS BEFORE THE MIRROR | 8/3/32 |
| LADY KILLER | 9/3/37 |
| LAW AND ORDER | 10/3/50 |
| LE CORBEAU | 6/6/25 |
| LEMORA, LADY DRACULA | 7/2/28 |
| THE LODGER | 8/3/32 |
| LOVE CRAZY | 10/3/50 |
| MAD LOVE | 8/3/32 |
| THE MALTESE FALCON | 8/6/3 |
| THE MARK OF THE WHISTLER | 8/3/31 |
| MASK OF DEMETRIOS | 8/2/27 |
| THE MASK OF FU MANCHU | 12/2/69-70 |
| MICHAEL SHAYNE, PRIVATE DETECTIVE | 8/4/35; 12/2/70 |

| | |
|---|---|
| MICKEY'S MAGICAL WORLD | 10/3/50 |
| MIRACLES FOR SALE | 6/6/24 |
| MURDER INK | 8/1/20 |
| MURDER IS EASY | 6/2/31 |
| MURDER ON THE BLACK-BOARD | 10/3/49 |
| NIGHT NURSE | 10/3/48 |
| ONE MORE RIVER | 7/1/38 |
| OPERATOR 13 | 12/1/26-7 |
| THE PHANTOM OF CREST-WOOD | 13/3/73-4 |
| THE PASSING OF THE OKLAHOMA OUTLAW | 8/3/31 |
| THE PENGUIN POOL MURDER | 9/3/36 |
| PENTHOUSE | 10/1/65 |
| PEEPING TOM | 6/3/29 |
| PHANTOM LADY | 6/4/36 |
| PHILIP MARLOWE, PRIVATE EYE | 7/4/22 |
| QUIET AS A NUN | 7/4/22 |
| THE RACKET | 10/1/65 |
| RAW DEAL | 6/4/35 |
| RECKLESS MOMENT | 7/3/30 |
| REMEMBER LAST NIGHT? | 6/2/24 |
| ROLLOVER | 6/2/30 |
| THE RULING CLASS | 8/1/24 |
| SECRET OF THE BLUE ROOM | 12/2/79 |
| THE SECRET SIX | 10/3/50 |
| SATAN IN PRISON | 6/2/23 |
| SHARKY'S MACHINE | 6/2/26 & 29 |
| SHE | 8/3/30 |
| SILENT RAGE | 6/3/27 |
| THE SINGING DETECTIVE | 10/1/64 |
| SMART MONEY | 12/2/79 |
| SMITHEREENS | 7/5/34 |
| THE SPIES | 6/2/23 |
| THE STORY OF TEMPLE DRAKE | 8/4/36 |
| SUPER SLEUTH | 10/3/49 |
| TALK OF THE TOWN | 8/3/32 |
| TAXI | 8/4/36 |
| THIS DAY AND AGE | 12/2/78 |
| THREE AGES | 8/3/32 |
| THREE ON A MATCH | 12/2/77-8 |
| THROW MOMMA FROM THE TRAIN | 12/1/28 |
| TOP SECRET | 8/3/30 |
| TRUE CONFESSIONS | 6/2/23 |

*Movie Reviews* continued
UNDERWORLD    6/2/24
THE UNHOLY THREE    9/3/38
THE UNKNOWN    8/4/35
THE WEB    12/1/27
WHERE EAST IS EAST    6/2/24
WITHOUT A TRACE    7/2/27
THE WRONG BOX    8/1/21
YOU ONLY LIVE ONCE    6/2/25
  L: Goode 6/3/46; Reineke 6/4/48;
  Shibuk 1/4/56; 6/3/44; Traylor
  6/3/44; Wilf 6/3/45
MOVING TOYSHOP, THE (Crispin)
  (R)    2/1/43
Moyes, Patricia
  BLACK WIDOWER (R)
    (M*F)    1/6/47; 2/4/35
  FALLING STAR (IAC)    10/3/41
  MURDER À LA MODE
    (IAC)    8/6/34
MOZART SCORE, THE (Leather)
  (R)    4/1/34
Mr. and Mrs. North, and Mr. and Mrs.
  Lockridge (Davis)    1/1/21-6
  L: Clark 1/2/50
MR. CALDER AND MR. BEHRENS
  (Gilbert) (IAC)    6/4/31
MR. CAMPION AND OTHERS
  (Allingham) (R)    10/1/75; 13/4/51
MR. CAMPION: CRIMINOLOGIST
  (Allingham) (R)    10/1/75
MR. DASS: A NOVEL OF PURSUIT
  AND PUNISHMENT (Atkey)
  (R)    2/5/37
*Mr. Keen, Tracer of Lost Persons*
  Old Time Radio Lives
  (Larsen)    4/5/18-20
  L: Nieminski 4/6/40
MR. PRESIDENT, PRIVATE EYE
  (Greenberg/Nevins, ed.) (IAC) 11/1/34
MRS. MEEKER'S MONEY (Disney)
  (R)    9/6/37
MRS, PRESUMED DEAD (Brett)
  (R)    11/4/93; 13/1/60-1
MS. HOLMES OF BAKER STREET:
  THE TRUTH ABOUT SHERLOCK
  (Sarjeant/Bradley) (MS)    11/3/2
*Muffin, Charlie.* See Freemantle, Brian
*Muggeridge, Malcolm*
  Obituary (Lachman)    13/1/32
MUGGER'S DAY (Bagby) (M*F)3/6/39

Mulholland, John, and Cortland
  Fitzsimmons
  THE GIRL IN THE CAGE
  (TBR)    11/4/57
Muller, Marcia
  THE CAVALIER IN WHITE
  (R)    8/4/39
  EDWIN OF THE IRON SHOES
  (M*F) (IAC)    2/3/48; 3/2/23
  THE SHAPE OF DREAD (R) 12/1/40
  THERE HANGS THE KNIFE
  (TAR)    11/1/65; 11/2/76
  THERE'S SOMETHING IN A
  SUNDAY (R)    13/4/97-8
MULTIPLE MAN, THE (Bova)
  (R)    2/1/35
MUM'S THE WORD (Cannell)
  (TAR)    13/1/52
MUM'S THE WORD FOR MURDER
  (Baker) (TBR)    13/2/64-5
Mundell, Elmore
  L:    4/6/49; 5/1/45
*Munsey Magazines*
  L: Harwood 3/5/49
MURDER (Adams) (M*F)    6/1/37
MURDER À LA MODE (Moyes)
  (IAC)    8/6/34
MURDER À LA RICHELIEU
  (Blackmon) (TBR)    12/4/64
MURDER ARRANGED, A (Pentecost)
  (IAC)    2/6/29
MURDER ARRANGED, A (Philips)
  (M*F)    3/3/37
MURDER AT CAMBRIDGE (Patrick)
  (R)    2/5/43
MURDER AT ELAINE'S (Rosenbaum)
  (M*F) (IAC)    3/5/39; 11/3/45
MURDER AT GOVERNMENT
  HOUSE (Huxley) (IAC)    11/4/50
MURDER AT HIGH TIDE (Booth)
  (M*F)    3/4/40
MURDER AT HOBCAW BARONY
  (Roosevelt) (R)    10/2/71
MURDER AT MARTHA'S VINE-
  YARD (Osborn) (TAR)    11/3/83
MURDER AT SAN SIMEON (Hall)
  (TNSPE)    10/2/50
MURDER AT THE ABA (Asimov)
  (R)    1/2/39
MURDER AT THE ACADEMY
  AWARDS (Hyams) (R)    8/1/33

MURDER AT THE GARDNER
(Langton) (TAR)  11/1/62; 11/2/74
MURDER AT THE MURDER AT
THE MIMOSA INN, THE (Hess)
(R)  10/3/69
MURDER AT THE NEW YORK
WORLD'S FAIR (Dana) (R)  9/6/37
MURDER AT THE OLD VICARAGE
(McGown) (R)  12/1/36
MURDER AT THE PTA LUNCHEON
(Wolzien) (R)  13/2/85-6
MURDER AT THE RED OCTOBER
(Olcutt) (M*F)  5/6/41
MURDER AT THE SMITHSONIAN
(Truman) (R)  7/6/36
MURDER AT THE U.N. (Perry)
(M*F)  1/1/33
MURDER AT THE VILLA ROSA
(Mason) (M*F)  4/5/28
MURDER AT WILLOW RUN
(Collins) (R)  7/5/40
MURDER BEGETS MURDER
(Jeffries) (M*F)  4/2/32
MURDER BY BURIAL (Casson)
(TBR)  10/3/62
MURDER BY DECREE (Weverka)
(R)  3/5/43
MURDER BY FORMULA (Wallis)
(TBR)  13/4/70-1
Murder by Mail: A Dealer Checklist
(Albert)  3/5/7-10,16*
L: Asdell 4/1/40; Doerrer 4/1/44;
LaPorte 4/3/47; Samoian 4/2/57;
Sandulo 4/1/39; Shaw 4/1/41
MURDER BY MAIL: THE HISTORY
OF THE MYSTERY BOOK
CLUBS WITH COMPLETE
CHECKLIST (Cook) (MS)  3/2/1
L: Cook 3/1/54
MURDER BY PROXY (Morice)
(R)  8/1/36
MURDER BY REQUEST (Nichols)
(TBR)  11/4/67
MURDER BY THE CLOCK (King)
(R)  12/1/48-9
MURDER CAN'T STOP (Ballard)
(R)  3/4/42
Murder Cases of Pinklin West, The
(Sampson)  8/1/3-7
MURDER COMES FIRST (Lockridge)
(R)  7/2/38
MURDER FOR CHARITY (Ponder)
(R) (M*F)  2/3/5; 2/4/31

MURDER FOR CHRISTMAS
(Godfrey) (IAC)  9/5/24
MURDER FROM THE EAST (Daly)
(R)  2/6/40
MURDER GONE MINOAN (Clason)
(R)  3/3/46
MURDER IN A GOOD CAUSE (Sale)
(TAR)  13/2/48-9
MURDER IN CHURCH (Hughes)
(R)  9/5/43
MURDER IN E MINOR (Golds-
borough) (R)  8/6/37
MURDER IN FALSE FACE (Childer-
ness) (TBR)  10/3/63
MURDER IN JAPAN (MS)  9/1/7
MURDER IN PUBLIC (Crozier)
(TBR)  11/4/68
MURDER IN SILENCE (Selmark)
(TBR)  11/1/48
MURDER IN THE DOG DAYS
(Carlson) (R)  13/2/83-4
MURDER IN THE ENGLISH
DEPARTMENT (Minor) (R)  11/4/94
MURDER IN THE FAMILY (Ronald)
(TBR)  12/4/67-8
MURDER IN THE GILDED CAGE
(Spewack) (R)  1/5/48
MURDER IN THE HELLFIRE CLUB
(Zochert) (R)  5/2/30
MURDER IN THE MUSEUM (Heath)
(TBR)  11/3/63
MURDER IN THE O.P.M. (Ford)
(TBR)  13/4/79-80
MURDER IN THE ROUGH (Allen)
(TBR)  12/3/71-2
MURDER IN THE STATE
DEPARTMENT ("Diplomat")
(TBR)  12/2/49-50
MURDER IN THE TITLE (Brett)
(R)  7/6/41
MURDER IN THE WHITE HOUSE
(Truman) (R)  4/4/47; 5/5/31
MURDER INK (Wynn, ed.) (IAC)2/4/15
MURDER INK Cast of Contributors
L: Doerrer 2/6/59*
MURDER IS A GAMBLE (Barns)
(M*F) (R)  1/1/28; 9/4/44
MURDER IS ONLY SKIN DEEP
(Sims) (IAC)  10/1/62
MURDER ISN'T ENOUGH (Flynn)
(R)  8/1/37
MURDER KEEPS A SECRET
(Murphy) (TAR)  11/3/81

MURDER LOVES COMPANY
(Mersereau) (R)                    9/4/41
MURDER, MAESTRO, PLEASE
(Ames) (R)                         7/5/43
MURDER MAKERS, THE (Rossiter)
(M*F)                              1/6/39
MURDER: MEN ONLY (Cobb)
(TBR)                              13/3/62-3
MURDER MISREAD (Carlson)
(R)                                13/3/83-4
MURDER, MURDER, LITTLE STAR
(Babson) (M*F)                     4/3/34
MURDER MUST WAIT (Upfield)
(R)                                3/4/51
MURDER MYSTERY (Thompson)
(M*F)                              5/2/18
MURDER, MYSTERY AND MAY-
HEM (Carnell) (R) (TAR)
                    12/1/39; 12/2/57
MURDER MYSTIQUE, THE
(Freeman, ed.) (IAC)               7/2/24
MURDER '97 (Gruber) (R)            7/4/34
MURDER OF A MYSTERY WRITER
(Heath) (M*F)                      3/2/39
MURDER OF A NYMPH (Neville)
(TBR) (R)          11/3/67; 12/1/50-1
MURDER OF A SUICIDE (Ferrars)
(R)                                9/5/41
MURDER OF CROWS, A (Buchanan)
(M*F)                              1/1/28
MURDER OF MIRANDA, THE
(Millar) (R) (M*F)      3/4/46; 3/6/29
MURDER OF NAPOLEON (Weider/
Hapgood) (IAC)                     8/1/16
MURDER OF THE MAHARAJAH,
THE (Keating) (M*F)                4/4/40
MURDER OFF MIAMI (Wheatley)
(IAC)                              4/1/15
MURDER ON CAPITOL HILL
(Truman) (R)                       5/6/47
MURDER ON CUE (Dentinger)
(R)                                7/6/40
MURDER ON DISPLAY (Hale)
(M*F)                              4/3/40
MURDER ON EVERY FLOOR
(Demarest) (TBR) (R)
                    11/1/45; 12/1/46-7
MURDER ON HIGH HEELS (Burke)
(TBR)                              13/4/76-7
MURDER ON LOCATION (Kennedy)
(R)                                7/6/36
MURDER ON MARTHA'S
VINEYARD (Roos) (M*F)              5/5/23

MURDER ON STILTS (Dean)
(R)                                9/5/41
MURDER ON THE AISLE (Clark)
(IAC)                              9/5/23
Murder on the Sunshine Coast: L.R.
Wright's Experiments with Theme
and Form (Bakerman)     11/4/3-10
MURDER ON THE YELLOW BRICK
ROAD (Kaminsky) (M*F)    2/6/32
MURDER OUT OF TURN (Lockridge)
(IAC)                              13/1/28-9
MURDER POST-DATED (Morice)
(R)                       8/1/36; 8/2/40
MURDER R.F.D. (Stephan)
(M*F)                              2/5/27
MURDER REHEARSAL (East)
(TBR)                              12/3/77-8
MURDER SO REAL (Bird)
(M*F)                              3/1/35
MURDER SONG (Cleary) (TAR)
                                   13/1/54
MURDER TRAPP (Franklin) (R) 5/5/42
MURDER UNDER THE SUN
(Christie) (IAC)                   6/3/25
MURDER UNRENOVATED (Carlson)
(R)                                10/3/70
MURDER WHILE YOU WAIT
(Corbett) (TBR)          13/4/66-8
'MURDER WILL OUT': THE
DETECTIVE IN FICTION
(Binyon) (R)                       12/1/31-3
MURDER WITH LOVE (Howard)
(M*F)                              5/6/37
MURDER WITH MALICE (Blake)
(IAC)                              9/3/31
MURDER WITHOUT CLUES (Bonney)
(TBR)                              11/2/84
MURDER WITHOUT REGRET
(Cushing) (TBR)                    11/2/85
MURDER WITHOUT WEAPON
(Davis) (TBR)                      10/2/66
MURDER WITHOUT WEAPONS
(Cunningham) (M*F)       3/2/40
MURDERCON (Putrill) (R)      7/3/40
MURDERED CLICHÉ, THE (Samuel)
(TBR)                              11/2/90
MURDERER'S CHOICE (Wells)
(TBR)                              12/2/46-7
MURDERERS' ROW (Hamilton)
(R)                                1/5/50

MURDERERS' ROW (Hitchcock, ed.)
(M*F) 1/1/33
MURDERESS INK: THE BETTER
PART OF THE MYSTERY (Winn,
ed.) (R) (IAC) 4/1/34; 4/3/31
MURDERS & ACQUISITIONS
(Murphy) (TAR) (R)
10/4/44; 12/3/101-3
MURDERS AT SCANDAL HOUSE
(Hunt) (TBR) 13/4/80-1
MURDERS OF RICHARD III, THE
(Peters) (IAC) 9/3/29
*Murdoch, Bruce*. See Deane, Norman
Murdoch, Derrick
THE AGATHA CHRISTIE
MYSTERY (R) 1/2/4
Murphy, Haughton
MURDERS & ACQUISITIONS
(TAR) (R) 10/4/44; 12/3/101-3
MURDER KEEPS A SECRET
(TAR) 11/3/81
Murphy, John
PAY ON THE WAY OUT
(M*F) 1/1/27
Murphy, Warren
THE DESTROYER #31: THE HEAD
MEN (w/Sapir) (M*F) 2/4/33
THE DESTROYER 37: BOTTOM
LINE (w/Sapir) (M*F) 3/6/31
DYING SPACE (M*F) 6/3/35
IN ENEMY HANDS (w/Sapir)
(M*F) 1/2/28
IN HOLY TERROR (w/Sapir)
(R) 1/3/49
LAST WAR DANCE (w/Sapir)
(R) 1 /3/48
MAFIA FIX (w/Sapir) (R) 1/6/52
TRACE (IAC) 8/4/32
Murray, Edwin
L: 1/1/45
Murray, Max
THE QUEEN AND THE CORPSE
(TBR) 12/4/61-2
THE RIGHT HONORABLE
CORPSE (TBR) 12/4/61-2
MUSEUM PIECE NO. 13 (King)
(R) 9/5/44
MUSIC TO MURDER BY (Hinkle)
(R) 2/5/44
MUSTER OF THE VULTURES, THE
(Fairlie) (IAC) 3/2/22
MY BROTHER, THE DRUGGIST
(Kaye) (R) 3/6/48

MY DEAR WATSON (Lauritzen)
(MS) 7/3/4
MY FOE OUTSTRETCH'D
BENEATH THE TREE (Clinton-
Baddeley) (R) (M*F) (R)
P/39; 3/1/37; 5/5/37
MY GUN IS QUICK (Spillane)
(M*F) P/28
MY LAUGH COMES LAST (Chase)
(R) 2/3/51
MY LIFE IS DONE (Woods)
(M*F) 1/4/38
MY LOVELY EXECUTIONER (Rabe)
(M*F) 6/3/32
MY NAME IS NORVAL (White)
(R) 4/1/29
MYSTERIES (Library of Congress)
(R) 12/1/35
Mysteries of the Pseudonymous
Professors, The (Barbato)1/4/3-6
L: Wooster 1/5/54
MYSTERIOUS DISAPPEARANCE, A
(Tracy) (TBR) 11/2/89
Mysterious John Dickson Carr, The
(French) 1/6/13-4
*Mysterious Press* (MS) 9/2/2
Mysteriously Speaking... Also see
Stilwell, Stephen A.; Townsend,
Guy
P/1-2,40-2; 1/1/1-2; 1/2/1-2;
1/3/1-2,12; 1/4/1-2; 1/5/1-2;
1/6/1-2; 2/1/1-2; 2/2/1-2,62-4;
2/3/1-2; 2/4/1-2,61; 2/5/1-2,61;
2/6/1-2,35; 3/1/1-2; 3/2/1-2; 3/3/1;
3/4/1-2; 3/5/1-2,34; 3/6/1-2;
4/1/1-2,16; 4/2/1-2; 4/3/1-2; 4/4/1;
4/5/1-2; 4/6/1-3; 5/1/1-2; 5/2/1-2;
5/3/1; 5/4/1; 5/5/1-2; 5/6/1-2,32;
6/1/1; 6/2/1-6; 6/3/1-4; 6/4/1-2;
6/6/17; 7/1/1; 7/2/1; 7/3/1-5;
7/4/1-2; 7/5/1-2; 7/6/1-2; 8/1/1-2;
8/2/1; 8/3/1; 8/4/1-8; 8/5/1-6;
8/6/1-2; 9/1/1-9; 9/2/1-2; 9/3/1-2;
9/4/1-2; 9/5/1-2; 9/6/1-4; 10/1/1-2;
10/2/1-2; 10/3/1-2; 10/4/1-2;
11/1/1; 11/2/1-2; 11/3/1-2;
11/4/1-2; 12/1/1-4; 12/2/1-2;
12/3/1-12; 12/4/1-2; 13/1/1-2;
13/2/1-4; 13/3/1-2; 13/4/1-2
MYSTERIUM AND MYSTERY: THE
CLERICAL CRIME NOVEL
(Spencer) (R) 12/1/33-5; 13/1/62-6
*Mystery* (magazine) (IAC) 4/1/16

MYSTERY AND DETECTIVE
FICTION: AN INTERNATIONAL
BIBLIOGRAPHY OF SECONDARY
SOURCES (Albert) (IAC)     8/4/30
*Mystery & Detective Monthly* (maga-
zine) (MS) 8/4/3-8; 8/6/1-2; 11/3/2
L: Isaac 8/4/50
MYSTERY AT FRIAR'S PARDON
(MacDonald) (R)              9/5/37
Mystery by the Yard (Mystery Mosts)
(Banks)
L: Shibuk 11/3/85
*Mystery Cruise*
L: Hensley 5/4/38
MYSTERY, DETECTIVE, AND
ESPIONAGE FICTION: A CHECK-
LIST OF FICTION IN U.S. PULP
MAGAZINES, 1915–1974 (Cook/
Miller) (R)                11/1/75
*Mystery Fancier, The.* Also see
Mysteriously Speaking...
Dying Gasps                 1/2/54
An Index of Books Reviewed in TMF
Volume I (Including the Preview
Issue) (Meyerson)          2/1/9-14
An Index of Books Reviewed in TMF
(Doerrer): Volume Two 3/1/26-9;
Volume Three 4/2/3-7; Volume
Four 5/2/3-5; Volume Five 6/1/2-7
An Index to TMF Volumes I-V
(Cook)                     6/5/1-40
Index to TMF (Deeck): Volume Six
10/4/61; Volume Seven 10/4/85;
Volume Eight 10/3/81; Volume
Nine 10/2/85; Volume Ten
11/1/85-104; Volume Eleven
12/1/69-104; Volume Twelve
13/1/89-104
Lachman's Reviews in TMF Volumes
Two Through Four (Doerrer)
                           5/2/6-9
L: Albert 1/1/42; Aucott 1/1/43;
Banks 1/2/51; 1/3/56; 6/4/46,
7/3/49, 7/4/41, 8/6/49, 9/4/48,
9/6/49, 10/2/83; Bleiler 6/3/48,
8/5/42; Bloch 1/1/40; Bradley
7/4/41; Briney 1/3/52, 2/6/53;
Butler 1/2/47; Christopher 7/2/47,
13/2/103; Cleary 9/4/47,
13/2/103-4; Cole 1/5/59; Deeck
9/1/45, 9/4/47, 10/1/98, 10/2/78,
10/3/80, 12/2/81-2; Fellows
10/2/81; Floyd 7/4/42, 8/5/40;

*Mystery Fancier, The,* continued
L: Goodrich 7/2/48; Gorman 2/2/48;
Greene 7/4/39; Halpern 1/1/40;
Hatch 10/1/94; Hay 13/2/096-7;
Herzog 7/4/43; Himmel 7/4/38;
Jaysnovitch 9/1/48; Martin 9/4/49;
Masser 9/4/46; Moskowitz 2/5/45,
3/3/61; Penzler 8/6/50; Quain
6/3/49; Randisi 7/4/37; Reilly
9/2/45; Reineke 6/4/48; Reynolds
7/3/46; Scott 1/1/41, 1/2/53;
Sharpe 8/5/42; Smith 13/2/102-3;
Stilwell 2/3/58; Thompson 1/2/47;
Wooster 1/2/49
Mystery*File (column) (Lewis)
P/23-31; 1/1/27-34; 1/2/23-8;
1/3/37-42; 1/4/37-40; 1/5/29-36;
1/6/38-41; 2/1/21-30; 2/2/33-35,32;
2/3/41-8; 2/4/30-6; 2/5/26-34;
2/6/30-5; 3/1/31-45,30; 3/2/36-41;
3/3/31-39; 3/4/38-41; 3/5/35-41;
3/6/27-41; 4/2/31-40; 4/3/34-41;
4/4/33-43; 4/5/27-36; 5/1/20-9;
5/2/13-25; 5/3/27-33; 5/4/21-7;
5/5/20-7; 5/6/33-41,48,53; 6/1/31-8;
6/2/32-7; 6/3/30-7; 6/4/37-9; 6/5/41-5;
6/6/26-32
*MYSTERY*FILE* (magazine) (MS) 12/3/6
MYSTERY GUILD ANTHOLOGY,
THE (R)                     5/2/38
MYSTERY HALL OF FAME, THE
(Pronzini/Greenberg/Waugh, eds.)
(R)                         8/2/33
MYSTERY INDEX: SUBJECTS,
SETTINGS, AND SLEUTHS OF
10,000 TITLES (Olderr) (R)  9/6/41
*Mystery Library, The*
L: Briney 5/2/42; Hubin 5/1/40
Mystery Mosts (Banks)
(Movie) Actress & Roles      10/1/66
All Alliteration             11/2/16
Alliteration—The Finishing
Stroke                       12/2/16
A Best-Selling Title Pattern 10/2/77
Bulldogs                     11/3/83-4
Comic Book Heroes Again      10/3/76
Comicbook Heroes             9/5/31
Crime and Rhyme, Another
Time                         12/2/35-6
Double Alliteration          11/2/35
EQ by the Numbers            12/2/32
EQ's Device                  12/4/104
The Eternal Question         11/3/103-4

*Mystery Mosts (Banks)* continued
Extreme Alliteration        11/4/45-6
Fanzine Article Writers        10/2/52
Favorite Titles        11/2/56-7
Fu Manchus        11/3/18
Hero Roles        9/6/34
Invoking Poe        11/2/96-7
Kemelman's Rabbi Title
  Pattern        11/3/44
L.O.C.s        10/2/47
Long Careers        9/2/8
Longest Media Series Titles
        12/3/64; 12/4/28
Longest Titles        9/5/22
Magazines        9/2/6
Most Continuing Mystery Roles,
  Radio & TV Combined        12/4/20
Most Performances (Movie, TV,
  radio)        9/2/7-8
Most Reviewed Authors        11/2/96
Most Revived Character on
  Radio        12/2/80
Most Revived Mystery Series on
  TV        12/2/40
Movie Sidekicks        11/2/98
Mr. Private Eye        12/3/44-6
Mystery by the Yard        11/2/61-2
Mystery/Crime TV Aimed at
  Kids        11/2/7-8
Participation in Most Continuing
  Casts of Radio Mystery
  Series        12/4/50
Philip Marlowe's Crime
  Statistics        12/2/104
Philo Vance        11/4/81-2
Plays        9/3/35
Poe's Key Word        9/4/39
Poe's Other Word (a.k.a. Our
  Generic Label)        10/2/24
Police Procedurals        11/2/95-6
Pop Films        1/4/71-2
Pop Movie Rentals        12/2/10
Pop Movies on TV        11/4/28
Prolificity        9/3/38
Radio Sidekicks        11/2/97-8
Repetitious Titles        9/4/54
Repetitious Titles        10/3/52
Repetitious Titles One Final
  Time        11/2/46
Saintly Statistics        12/2/27-8
Secretaries        11/2/62
Serials        10/1/54
Serials Revisited        10/2/84

*Mystery Mosts (Banks)* continued
Series Episodes        10/1/104
Sherlockian Stats        11/2/81-2
TCOT Title Pattern        9/3/49
Team Players        11/2/35-6
Van Dine's Pattern        11/3/55-6
What Rhymes! with Crimes 11/3/13-4
L: Apostolou 12/2/83; Banks 9/2/48,
  9/3/48, 10/1/96; Bradley
  12/1/58-60, 13/3/97; Briney
  12/2/102-3; Samoian 10/1/96;
  Shibuk 9/4/49
*Mystery News* (MS)        6/2/4-5; 8/5/22
Mystery of Monboddo, The
  (Lachman)        8/4/33
MYSTERY OF AGATHA CHRISTIE,
  THE (Robyns) (IAC)        4/1/13
MYSTERY OF EDWIN DROOD, THE.
  See Dickens, Charles
MYSTERY OF EDWIN DROOD, THE,
  and Harvard Magazine
  L: Bleiler 7/4/40
MYSTERY OF GEORGES SIMENON,
  THE (Bresler) (IAC)        8/2/23
MYSTERY OF THE ANGRY IDOL
  (Whitney) (M*F)        2/6/34
MYSTERY OF THE PRINCES, THE:
  AN INVESTIGATION INTO A
  SUPPOSED MURDER (Williamson)
  (IAC)        9/2/26
*Mystery Scene Press*
  The Short Stop (Lachman)  13/4/51-2
MYSTERY STORY, THE (Ball, ed.)
  (R)        1/2/29 & 32
  L: Ball 1/3/51; Scott 1/3/58
MYSTERY TIME 1990
  L: Banks 12/2/85-6
MYSTERY VILLA (Punshon)
  (M*F)        5/6/34

# N

Nabb, Magdalen
  THE MARSHAL AND THE
  MADWOMAN (TAR)        11/3/82
Naifeh, Steven, and Gregory White
  Smith
  THE MORMON MURDERS
  (R)        13/2/90-1
NAKED FACE, THE (Sheldon)
  (R)        1/3/47
NAKED VILLAINY (Woods)
  (R)        12/3/97-100

Names, Larry D.
TWICE DEAD (R)      3/1/41
Nancy Pickard: Arrived (Gotts-
chalk)      13/2/23-8
L: Breen 13/3/103-4
Napier, Robert S.
L:      5/1/34; 8/6/47
Wolfe a Howler!      5/5/7-10
Narcotics, Barred Windows, and
Murder: The Medical Practitioner in
the Writings of Raymond Chandler
(Skinner)      11/2/37-46
NARROWING CIRCLE, THE (Hill)
(R)      2/5/38
*Nash, Anne*
Little Old Ladies (Nehr)      3/4/3-7
Natsuki, Shizuko
THE THIRD LADY (R)      11/2/103
NATURAL ENEMY (Langton)
(R)      7/5/41
NEAPOLITAN STREAK, THE (Holme)
Crystal-Ball Stories (Strøm)
      12/3/47-52
*Nebel, Frederick*
THE ADVENTURES OF
CARDIGAN (R)      11/4/101
Some Very Tough People
(Sampson)      8/5/7-17*
L: Apostolou 12/2/83-4
NECKLACE OF SKULLS, THE
(Drummond) (M*F)      1/6/39
NEEDLES (Deverell) (R)      6/1/45
*Neely, Richard*
LIES (M*F)      2/5/29
A MADNESS OF THE HEART
(R)      3/3/42
NO CERTAIN LIFE (M*F)      2/5/31
L: Crider 2/6/44
NEGATIVE IN BLUE (Brown)
(R)      1/4/48
Neglected Detective Novel, A:
Bellamann's THE GRAY MAN
WALKS (Bayne/Fisher)      12/4/3-19
L: Shibuk 13/1/85
Nehr, Ellen
L: 2/3/75; 2/4/60; 2/6/43; 3/2/59;
3/3/54; 3/5/50
Little Old Ladies I Have Known and
Loved      3/4/3-7
Little Old Men with Whom I'm Only
Slightly Acquainted      4/4/2-6

*Nehr, Ellen,* continued
Reviews:
THE LUCK RUNS OUT
(MacLeod)      4/1/34
THE MOZART SCORE
(Leather)      4/1/34
MURDERESS INK (Winn,
ed.)      4/1/34
NEON FLAMINGO, THE (Philbrick)
(TNSPE)      10/2/48
NEON GRAVEYARD, THE (Baxt)
(M*F)      4/2/31
NEON MIRAGE (Collins) (TAR)11/2/66
NEON PREACHER, THE (Chambers)
(M*F)      2/3/45
NEON RAIN (Burke) (R)      10/3/73
Nero Wolfe Saga, The (Townsend)
Part I 1/3/13-36; Part II 1/4/25-36;
Part III 1/5/21-8; Part IV
1/6/15-28; Part V 2/1/15-19; Part
VI 2/2/25-32; Part VII 2/3/34-40;
Part VIII 2/4/19-29; Part IX
2/5/13-21; Part X 2/6/20-6; Part XI
3/1/21-5; Part XII 3/2/13-20; Part
XIII 3/3/22-30; Part XIV
3/4/25-37; Part XV 3/5/22-34; Part
XVI 3/6/15-26; Part XVII
4/1/17-28; Part XVIII 4/2/14-30;
Part XIX 4/3/3-21
(MS)      1/3/1-2,12
L: Frazier 1/6/55; Goldman 2/4/56;
McCahery 2/5/55; Meltzer 1/4/60;
Pross 1/5/58
NEVER CROSS A VAMPIRE
(Kaminsky) (M*F) (R) 5/1/21; 6/4/18
NEVER SAY DIE (Foote-Smith)
(M*F)      2/1/24
Neville, Margot
MURDER OF A NYMPH (TBR)
(R)      11/3/67; 12/1/50-1
Nevins, Francis M., Jr.
BUFFET FOR UNWELCOME
GUESTS: THE BEST MYSTERY
SHORT STORIES OF CHRIS-
TIANA BRAND (w/Greenberg,
ed.) (IAC)      8/2/22
Cornell Woolrich: The Last Years –
Part I 8/5/23-8; Part II
8/6/11-14,18; Part III 9/1/17-22;
Part IV 9/3/25-31; Conclusion
9/6/5-30

Nevins, Francis M., Jr., continued
CORRUPT AND ENSNARE (M*F)
(IAC)          3/1/31; 4/1/14
EXEUNT MURDERERS, THE BEST
MYSTERY STORIES OF AN-
THONY BOUCHER (w/
Greenberg, ed.) (IAC)     8/2/22
FILMS OF HOPALONG CASSIDY,
THE (IAC)          13/4/87-8
Great Lizzie Borden T-Shirt Media
Event and Mystery Quiz   5/6/7-9
L: 1/2/47; 1/3/55; 1/4/57; 2/5/50;
3/1/55; 3/2/59; 3/4/56; 3/5/46;
4/2/59; 4/5/45; 4/6/47; 5/1/44;
5/2/50; 5/3/46; 5/4/43; 6/1/49;
7/1/50; 7/4/45; 8/3/48; 9/2/47;
10/1/93; 12/2/91-2
Memories of a Haunted Man 8/3/2-11
MR. PRESIDENT, PRIVATE EYE
(w/Greenberg, ed.) (IAC)  11/1/34
THE 120-HOUR CLOCK
(IAC)              9/2/27
Reviews:
THE AMBER EFFECT
(Prather)          8/6/42
AS HER WHIMSEY TOOK HER
(Hannay, ed.)         3/5/45
THE BEDSIDE, BATHTUB &
ARMCHAIR COMPANION TO
AGATHA CHRISTIE (Riley/
McAllister)         4/1/43
BOGMAIL (McGinley)    5/5/29
THE BUGLES BLOWING
(Freeling)         1/5/44
BUYER BEWARE (Lutz)    1/3/43
THE CASE OF THE AMOROUS
AUNT (Gardner)        1/3/49
THE CASE OF THE BEAUTIFUL
BEGGAR (Gardner)      1/4/54
THE CASE OF THE BIGAMOUS
SPOUSE (Gardner)      1/1/37
THE CASE OF THE BLONDE
BONANZA (Gardner)     1/2/10
THE CASE OF THE CARELESS
CUPID (Gardner)       1/5/50
THE CASE OF THE DARING
DIVORCÉE (Gardner)    1/3/49
THE CASE OF THE FABULOUS
FAKE (Gardner)        1/5/51
THE CASE OF THE HORRIFIED
HEIRS (Gardner)       1/3/50
THE CASE OF THE ICE-COLD
HANDS (Gardner)       1/2/45

Nevins, Francis M., Jr., continued
Reviews continued:
THE CASE OF THE MISCHIE-
VOUS DOLL (Gardner)  1/2/45
THE CASE OF THE PHANTOM
FORTUNE (Gardner)     1/3/50
THE CASE OF THE QUEENLY
CONTESTANT (Gardner) 1/5/50
THE CASE OF THE RELUC-
TANT MODEL (Gardner) 1/1/37
THE CASE OF THE SHAPELY
SHADOW (Gardner)      1/1/36
THE CASE OF THE SPURIOUS
SPINSTER (Gardner)    1/1/36
THE CASE OF THE STEP-
DAUGHTER'S SECRET
(Gardner)          1/2/45
THE CASE OF THE TROUBLED
TRUSTEE (Gardner)     1/4/54
THE CASE OF THE WORRIED
WAITRESS (Gardner)    1/4/54
CHANDLERTOWN (Thorpe)
8/3/33
THE CHINESE FIRE DRILL
(Wolfe)            1/2/40
CLOAK-AND-DAGGER BIBLI-
OGRAPHY (Smith)       1/4/50
DANCER'S DEBT (Lutz) 10/4/57
DANCING BEAR (Crumley)
7/6/41
THE DARK SIDE OF GENIUS
(Spoto)            7/2/31
DASHIELL HAMMETT
(Layman)           3/6/49
DEAD LETTER (Valin)   5/6/46
THE DEAD SIDE OF THE MIKE
(Brett)            5/2/28
THE DEAD SLEEP LIGHTLY
(Carr) (Greene, ed.)  8/1/26
DEADFALL (Pronzini)   8/5/39
DEADLY PATTERN (Clark) 3/3/46
DEATH AND THE GOOD LIFE
(Hugo)             5/2/27
DEATH IN DONEGAL BAY
(Gault)            8/3/46
THE DETECTIVE IN HOLLY-
WOOD (Tuska)          2/4/38
DISCRETION (Linzee)   3/3/47
DOROTHY L. SAYERS
(Brabazon)         6/1/39
DOROTHY L. SAYERS
(Hone)             3/5/45

Nevins, Francis M., Jr., continued
  Reviews continued:
    ERLE STANLEY GARDNER
      (Hughes)        2/4/37
    THE EYES OF BUDDHA
      (Ball)        1/5/45
    ENCYCLOPEDIA OF FRON-
      TIER AND WESTERN
      FICTION (Tuska/Piekarski,
      eds.)        8/1/18
    FADEAWAY (Rosen)    9/2/43
    FINAL NOTICE (Valin)  5/2/29
    FREE FALL IN CRIMSON
      (MacDonald)    5/4/31
    THE GATHERING PLACE
      (Breen)      8/2/38
    THE GLITTER DOME
      (Wambaugh)    5/5/28
    GONE, NO FORWARDING
      (Gores)      4/2/51
    GOOD BEHAVIOR (Westlake)
                9/1/42
    GOODBYE, CHICAGO
      (Burnett)     5/3/38
    HARDBOILED AMERICA
      (O'Brien)     5/6/42
    HITCH (Taylor)    4/2/52
    THE HOODED VULTURE
      MURDERS (Koehler)  3/3/47
    INTIMATE MEMOIRS
      (Simenon)     8/3/33
    JERICHO MAN (Lutz)  4/5/37
    JUSTICE (Simenon)   8/4/43
    KENNEDY FOR THE DEFENSE
      (Higgins)     4/5/43
    KINDLY DIG YOUR GRAVE
      AND OTHER WICKED
      STORIES (Ellin)   1/1/35
    THE LAZARUS MAN (Lutz)
                3/5/44
    LEVINE (Westlake)   8/2/38
    LISTEN FOR THE CLICK
      (Breen)      7/3/32
    MAIGRET & THE BLACK
      SHEEP (Simenon)   1/5/44
    MINOR MURDERS (Hensley)
                4/1/32
    MURDER GONE MINOAN
      (Clason)     3/3/46
    MURDER IN THE WHITE
      HOUSE (Truman)   4/4/47
    MURDER ON CAPITOL HILL
      (Truman)     5/6/47

Nevins, Michael M., Jr., continued
  Reviews continued:
    NEGATIVE IN BLUE
      (Brown)      1/4/48
    NO QUESTIONS ASKED
      (Bleeck)     1/2/14
    NOTHING LASTS FOREVER
      (Thorp)      4/1/43
    OUTCASTS (Hensley)  5/2/26
    THE RAT ON FIRE (Higgins)
                5/2/26
    RAYMOND CHANDLER
      (Bruccoli)    3/6/49
    THE RIGHT TO SING THE
      BLUES (Lutz)    8/4/43
    THE RUNNING OF BEASTS
      (Pronzini/Malzberg)  1/1/17
    THE SHADOW SCRAPBOOK
      (Gibson)     4/2/51
    THE SPECIALTY OF THE
      HOUSE AND OTHER
      STORIES (Ellin)   4/5/42
    SUICIDE HILL (Ellroy)  9/2/42
    SWAN DIVE (Healy)  10/4/56
    THEN CAME VIOLENCE
      (Ball)        4/5/37
    THREE BY BOX (Box)  3/1/44
    TROPICAL HEAT (Lutz)  9/2/41
    TROUBLE FOR TALLON
      (Ball)        5/5/31
    WATTEAU'S SHEPHERDS
      (Panek)      4/3/44
    WHEN THE SACRED GINMILL
      CLOSES (Block)   8/4/42
    WHO DONE IT? (Laurance/
      Asimov, eds.)   4/4/48
  THE SOUND OF DETECTION:
    ELLERY QUEEN'S ADVEN-
    TURES IN RADIO (w/Stanish)
    (IAC) (R)     7/5/28; 10/2/74
  NEVSKY'S RETURN (Gat) (IAC)
                7/4/21
  NEW HARD-BOILED DICKS (Skinner)
    (MS)        8/5/22
  NEW LEASH ON DEATH, A (Conant)
    (R)        13/2/87-8
  New Rippers, The (Tolley)  12/3/57-63
  NEW SHOE, THE (Upfield) (R)
                1/2/32 & 33
  NEW YEAR RESOLUTION (Cairns)
    (IAC)        9/2/25

Newberry, Perry, and Alice MacGowan
  THE MILLION-DOLLAR
    SUITCASE (TBR)        13/4/73-4
Newman, Bernard. Also see Betteridge,
  Don
  (SSC)                  6/3/5,26*
Newman, G.F.
  YOU NICE BASTARD (R)    2/2/37
NICE CLASS OF CORPSE, A (Brett)
  (R)                    11/4/93
NICE MURDERERS, THE (Delman)
  (M*F)                  2/1/22
NICE WEEKEND FOR A MURDER
  (Collins) (R)          10/1/72
Nichols, Beverly
  THE MOONFLOWER MURDER
    (TBR)                11/3/70
  MURDER BY REQUEST
    (TBR)                11/4/67
  Obituary (Lachman)     8/1/21
Nielsen, Helen
  AFTER MIDNIGHT (M*F)    3/2/28
Nielsen, Torben
  AN UNSUCCESSFUL MAN
    (M*F)                1/3/38
Nieminski, John
  Bouchercon Scrapbook (w/
    Townsend)            4/6/19-30
  Closing the Gap: A Critique
                         7/3/6-15,31
  In Memorium: John Nieminski
    (Liebow)             9/2/3-6
  L: 2/5/46; 3/2/50; 3/3/51; 4/6/40;
    5/1/30
  (MS)                   4/6/1-2; 9/1/1-2
  Pow-Wow on the Potomac: A Report
    on Bouchercon XI      4/6/12-8
  THE SAINT MAGAZINE INDEX
    (IAC)                4/3/31
Niesewand, Peter
  FALLBACK (R)           6/6/38
NIGHT COVER (Lewin) (M*F)  4/4/39
NIGHT LORDS, THE (Freeling)
  (R)                    4/2/42
NIGHT MASTER, THE (Sampson)
  (MS)                   6/2/6
NIGHT MY FRIEND, THE (Hoch)
  (R)                    13/4/50-1
NIGHT OF ERRORS, A (Innes)
  (IAC)                  11/3/50
NIGHT OF HORROR (Soutar)
  (TBR)                  13/2/65-6

NIGHT OF THE JABBERWOCK
  (Brown) (M*F)          3/6/40
NIGHT PEOPLE, THE (Finney)
  (M*F)                  2/3/41
NIGHT PROBE (Cussler) (M*F) 6/5/44
NIGHT SHE DIED, THE (Simpson)
  (M*F) (R)              5/5/22 & 34
NIGHT SHIFT (King) (R)    4/3/45
NIGHTMARE IN PINK (MacDonald)
  (R)                    1/3/48
NIGHTRUNNERS, THE (Collins)
  (M*F)                  2/6/33
NIGHTWORK (Hansen) (R)    8/1/32
NINE DOCTORS AND A MADMAN
  (Curtiss) (TBR)        12/4/65-6
Nithologist, O.R.
  BEAK! (R)              1/3/47
NO BONES ABOUT IT (Wallis)
  (TBR)                  12/4/69-70
NO BUSINESS BEING A COP
  (O'Donnell) (M*F)      3/5/36
NO CERTAIN LIFE (Neely)
  (M*F)                  2/5/31
NO EVIL ANGEL (Linington)
  (R)                    3/2/44
NO FACE TO MURDER (Howie)
  (TBR)                  11/1/45
NO HIGHWAY (Shute) (R)    7/2/35
NO ONE KNOWS MY NAME
  (Harrington) (M*F)     6/2/36
NO QUESTIONS ASKED (Bleeck)
  (R)                    1/2/14
NO SECOND WIND (Guthrie)
  (M*F)                  4/3/36
NO WORD FROM WINIFRED (Cross)
  (R)                    8/5/37
NOBODY'S PERFECT (Westlake)
  (M*F)                  5/1/22
Noguchi, Thomas T.
  CORONER (IAC)          8/2/24
NOLAN #5: HARD CASH (Collins)
  (R)                    6/4/40
  L: Collins 6/1/47
Nolan, Jeannette Covert
  "I CAN'T DIE HERE" (TBR) 11/4/66
Nolan, William F.
  THE BLACK MASK BOYS
    (IAC)                9/5/24
Noon, Ed. See Avallone, Michael
NOOSE, THE (MacDonald) (IAC)2/6/29
North, Gil
  SERGEANT CUFF STANDS FIRM
    (IAC)                2/6/29

*North, Hugh.* See Mason, Hugh Van
  Wyck
*North, Mr. and Mrs.* See Lockridge,
  Richard and Frances
Norville, Barbara
  WRITING THE MODERN
    MYSTERY (R)    9/1/8
NOT AS FAR AS VELMA (Freeling)
  (R)    12/3/103-4
NOT DEAD, ONLY RESTING (Brett)
  (R)    9/3/40
NOT ENOUGH HORSES (Roberts)
  (TAR)    10/4/46
NOT SLEEPING, JUST DEAD
  (Alverson) (M*F)    2/2/34
Not So Private Eye, The (Jaysno-
  vitch)    10/2/48-52
*Not So Private Eye, The* (magazine)
  (MS)    6/4/2
  L: Jaysnovitch 6/3/50, 7/4/48
NOT THAT KIND OF PLACE (Fyfield)
  (R)    13/3/84-6
Nothdurft, John
  L:    13/1/82-3
NOTHING BUT FOXES (Lewis)
  (M*F)    3/5/38
NOTHING LASTS FOREVER (Thorp)
  (R)    4/1/43
NOVEL VERDICTS: A GUIDE TO
  COURTROOM FICTION (Breen)
  (IAC)    8/4/30
*Nuns as Detectives*
  Clergy-Detectives (Cleary)    9/3/3-21
NURSING HOME MURDER, THE
  (Marsh) (IAC)    6/3/23
Nusser, Peter
  DER KRIMINALROMAN [THE
    DETECTIVE NOVEL] (R)  7/3/40
Nusser, Richard
  WALKING AFTER MIDNIGHT
  (R)    13/1/67-8

# O

*Oakes, Brian "Boysie."* See Gardner,
  John
OATH OF OFFICE (Kirsch)
  (TAR)    11/3/72
OBELISTS AT SEA (King)
  (TBR)    11/3/66
OBIT (Paisner) (IAC)    13/1/30

*Obituaries.* Also see Death of a Mystery
  Writer, Death of a Mystery
  Writer's Friend; Death of a Movie
  Detective; French 3/1 cover; (IAC)
  5/2/12, 5/5/18-9, 5/6/31-2; (MS)
  5/2/1, 6/3/1, 7/2/1
  In Memorium: John Nieminski
    (Liebow)    9/2/3-6
  John Dickson Carr (1906–1977)
    (Carr)    1/3/3-4
*Obituaries, Individual*
  Abbey, Edward    11/3/52
  Adams, Harriet    6/4/33
  Altshuler, Harry    12/4/48-9
  Arrighi, Mel    8/6/36
  Bacon, Peggy    9/3/34
  Ball, John    11/1/36
  Ballard, W. Todhunter    8/1/21
  Bandy, Franklin    9/3/34
  Bannon, Barbara A.    13/3/
  Bardin, John Franklin    5/6/31-2
  Bargainnier, Earl    9/1/2-3
  Blankfort, Michael    7/4/23
  Bocca, Geoffrey    7/5/30
  Bond, Raleigh Verne    11/4/55
  Boyle, Andrew    13/3/69
  Brahams, Caryl    7/2/25
  Brand, Christiana    10/3/44-5
  Brandt, Carl E.    13/3/72
  Brickhill, Paul    13/3/69
  Brown, R.D.    13/1/30
  Brown, Zenith Jones    8/1/21
  Browne, Coral    13/3/72
  Brussel, James A.    6/6/49
  Burnett, W.R.    6/4/33
  Carey, Bernice    12/2/70-1
  Carr, Jess    12/4/47
  Carson, Robert    7/4/23
  Caspary, Vera    9/4/38
  Clarke, T(homas) E(rnest)
    B(ennett)    11/3/52
  Corley, Edward    6/3/25
  Cox, William R.    11/1/36
  Coxe, George Harmon    8/2/25
  Craig, Mary Shura    13/1/31
  Crosby, John    13/3/69
  Dahl, Roald    13/1/31
  Dannay, Frederic    6/6/49
  Davidson, Muriel    8/1/21
  Dean, Robert George    11/4/55
  Delacorte, George T.    13/3/72
  Deming, Richard    8/2/25
  Dennis, Robert C.    8/1/21

Diamond, I.A.L.   10/3/45
Dick, Philip K.   6/3/26
Dickenson, Fred   9/3/34
Dodson, Daniel   13/1/31
Drachman, Theodore S., M.D.   11/1/37
Dûerrenmatt, Friedrich   13/1/31-2
Duff, Howard   12/4/49
Du Maurier, Daphne   11/3/52
Eden, Dorothy   6/3/26
Elston, Robert   10/1/66
Emshwiller, Ed   12/4/49
Epstein, Jon   13/1/33
Fish, Robert L.   5/2/1 & 12
Fox, James M.   11/3/53
Franciscus, James   13/3/72
French, Larry L. (Cover)   3/1
Garrett, Randall   10/3/45
Gilbert, Elliot L.   13/3/69
Giroux, Leo   12/2/71
Gordon, Milton A.   12/4/49
Greene, Graham   13/3/69-70
Guthrie, A.B.   13/3/70
Hart, Jeanne   13/1/32
Hay, Sara Henderson   9/4/38
Haycraft, Howard   13/4/90
Head, Lee   7/5/30
Hellman, Lillian   8/3/29
Holman, [Clarence] Hugh   6/1/29
Horan, James P.   6/1/29
Household, Geoffrey   11/1/37
Hurwood, Bernhardt   9/3/34
Huston, John   9/4/38
Iams, Jack   12/1/28
Jessup, Richard   6/6/49
Johns, Veronica Parker   10/3/45
Johnson, Jean   12/1/28
Johnson, Pamela Hansford   5/5/18
Kantor, Leonard   8/3/28
Kauffmann, Lane   10/4/53
Keith, Carlton   13/3/70
Kiker, Douglas   13/3/70-1
Kirst, Hans Helmut   11/3/53
Kroeger, Berry   13/1/33
L'Amour, Louis   10/4/53
Lariar, Lawrence   6/1/29-30
Latimer, Jonathan   7/5/30
Lederer, Lillian Day   13/3/71
Levinson, Richard   9/3/34
Lewis, Elliott   12/4/47
Lewis, Lucille Camps   12/1/29
Lincoln, Victoria   5/5/18
Linington, Elizabeth   10/3/45-6

Lockridge, Richard   6/4/33
Loew, Mildred Falk   12/4/49
Lofts, Norah   8/1/21
Luke, Keye   13/1/34
Lyon, Dana   7/2/25
MacDonald, John D.   9/3/34
Macdonald, Ross   7/5/29
MacLean, Alistair   9/3/34
Mann, Daniel   13/4/93
Marlowe, Dan J.   8/6/36
Marmor, Arnold   11/1/37
Marsh, Ngaio   6/3/26
Martin, Kiel   13/1/34
Mathis, Edward   10/3/46
McGivern, William P.   7/1/35
Meynell, Laurence   12/1/29
Miller, Don   6/3/1
Montand, Yves   13/4/93-4
Muggeridge, Malcolm   13/1/32
Nichols, Beverly   8/1/21
O'Rourke, Frank   11/3/53
Philips, Judson   11/3/53-4
Phillips, James Atlee   13/3/71
Popkin, Zelda   7/4/23
Powell, Michael   12/2/71
Powell, William   8/3/29-30
Rabe, Peter   12/4/47-8
Rand, Ayn   6/3/26
Richlin, Maurice N.   13/1/32
Ritchie, Jack   7/4/23
Roos, Audrey   7/2/25
Roosevelt, Elliott   13/1/32-3
Ross, Zola Helen   11/4/55
Sapp, Judson   7/2/1
Schaefer, Jack   13/1/34
Schisgall, Oscar   8/3/28-9
Schuetz, Dennis   11/3/54
Seton, Anya   13/1/33
Shaginyan, Marietta S.   6/3/26
Siegel, Benjamin   13/3/71
Siegel, Donald   13/3/72-3
Simenon, Georges   11/3/54
Skaaren, Warren   13/1/33
Sklar, George   10/3/46
Smith, Terrence Lore   11/1/37
Sneary, Rick   13/1/33
Spewack, Bella   12/2/71-2
Starr, Jimmy   12/4/48
Steeger, Henry   13/1/34
Steeves, Harrison   6/1/29
Sullivan, Eleanor   13/3/71-2
Swinnerton, Frank   7/1/35

*Obituaries, Individual,* continued
Taylor, Dwight                          9/3/34
Tidyman, Ernest R.                      8/3/29
Tierney, Gene                           13/4/94
Toomey, Regis                           13/3/73
Traver, Robert [John D.
  Voelker]                              13/2/58
Tryon, Tom                              13/3/72
Walz, Audrey Boyers                     7/2/25
Warren, Charles M(arquis)               12/4/48
Waterhouse, Howard                      4/2/1
Weist, Dwight                           13/3/73
Wheeler, Hugh [Callingham] 9/4/38-9
Whittington, Harry                      11/3/55
Wibberly, Leonard                       8/2/25
Willeford, Charles      10/2/60; 10/3/46
Wolff, Julian, M.D.                     12/2/72
Wollheim, Donald A.                     13/1/34
Wright, Lee                             9/3/35
O'Brien, Geoffrey
  HARDBOILED AMERICA: THE
    LURID YEARS OF PAPER-
    BACKS (R) (M*F)  5/6/42; 6/1/31
Obstfeld, Raymond
  THE GOULDEN FLEECE
    (M*F)                               3/6/34
OCork, Shannon
  END OF THE LINE (M*F)    6/3/34
OCTOBER CABERET, THE (Quest)
  (M*F)                                 3/6/41
ODD JOB MAN, THE (Crisp) (R)4/1/30
Odlum, Jerome
  THE MIRABILIS DIAMOND
    (R)                                 2/5/43
O'Donnell, Jim
  L:                          4/2/62; 4/4/49
O'Donnell, Lillian
  CASUAL AFFAIRS (R)        8/6/41
  THE CHILDREN'S ZOO (R)    6/2/39
  A GOOD NIGHT TO KILL
    (TAR)                               11/3/82
  NO BUSINESS BEING A COP
    (M*F)                               3/5/36
*O'Donnell, Peter*
  DEAD MAN'S HANDLE (R)  8/6/41
  Immoderate Homage to Modesty
    (Banks)                      4/2/8-10*
  THE IMPOSSIBLE VIRGIN
    (R)                                 1/6/54
OF MICE AND MURDER (Whitaker)
  (TBR)                          13/3/60-1

*Offord, Lenore Glen*
  Obituary (Lachman)        13/4/90
  THE SMILING TIGER (TBR) 11/2/86
  WALKING SHADOW (R)    12/1/51
OGILVIE, TALLANT & MOON
  (Yarbro) (M*F)                        1/4/39
OH, BURY ME NOT (Wren)
  (M*F)                                 2/5/32
Olcutt, Anthony
  MURDER AT THE RED OCTOBER
    (M*F)                               5/6/41
OLD BONES (Petersen) (TBR)   11/2/89
OLD CONTEMPTIBLES, THE
  (Grimes) (R)                  13/1/77-8
Old Man in the Corner, The
  (Bargainnier)                  7/6/21-3
  L: Bleiler 8/1/39, 8/2/42; Deeck
    8/1/38
Old Time Radio Lives (Larsen)
          4/5/18-20; 4/6/9-11; 5/6/3-6,9
  L: Bleiler 4/6/42; Nieminski 4/6/40;
    Shibuk 4/6/44
OLD DICK, THE (Morse) (M*F) (R)
  (IAC)          5/6/40; 6/1/40; 6/6/20
OLD DIE YOUNG, THE (Lockridge)
  (M*F) (R)                   5/1/25; 5/3/39
OLD SILENT, THE (Grimes)
  (R)                                   12/3/96-7
Olderr, Steven
  MYSTERY INDEX: SUBJECTS,
    SETTINGS, AND SLEUTHS OF
    10,000 TITLES (R)          9/6/41
Olsen, D.B. Also see Birkley, Dolan
  CATS DON'T SMILE (TBR)
    (R)              11/2/93; 12/1/51-2
Olson, Donald
  IF I DON'T TELL (M*F)      P/27
  SLEEP BEFORE EVENING
    (M*F)                               4/2/35
*O'Malley, Patrick.* See MacHarg,
  William
*Omar, Prince Abduel*
  Detection by Other Means
    (Sampson)                    7/1/7-17
*O'Marie, Sister Carol Anne*
  ADVENT OF DYING (R)      9/1/41
  Clergy-Detectives (Cleary)  9/3/3-21
  THE MISSING MADONNA (TAR)
    (R)      11/1/64 & 78-80; 11/2/76
On Fans and Bouchercon (Townsend)
                                        5/5/11-3
ON ICE (Dean) (R)                       10/1/83

ON NOT BEING GOOD ENOUGH:
WRITINGS OF A WORKING
CRITIC
L: Kelley 4/2/57
ON THE EDGE (Lovesey) (TAR)
11/3/74
*Once in a Blue Moon* (letterzine)
(MS) 9/1/6
ONCE UPON A CRIME (Chaber)
(M*F) P/23
ONE ANGEL LESS (Roden) (TBR)
(R) 11/1/40; 12/1/54-5
ONE CORPSE TOO MANY (Peters)
(M*F) 4/4/34
ONE DEAD DEAN (Crider)
(TAR) 11/2/68
ONE DEAD DEBUTANTE (Gould)
(M*F) 1/2/23
ONE DIP DEAD (Stein) (M*F) 3/6/35
ONE FEARFUL YELLOW EYE
(MacDonald) (R) 2/4/47
120-HOUR CLOCK, THE (Nevins)
(IAC) 9/2/27
One in Two: Some Personality Studies
by Ruth Rendell (Bakerman)
5/6/21-8, 32
ONE OF US IS WRONG (Holt) (IAC)
(R) 8/6/33; 8/6/40
ONE TEAR FOR MY GRAVE
(Roscoe) (M*F) 2/5/33
ONE THAT GOT AWAY, THE
(McCloy) (R) 9/5/45
ONE WREATH WITH LOVE
(Roffman) (M*F) 3/3/31
ONE-MAN SHOW (Innes) (IAC) 9/5/27
*O'Neill, Jim.* See Disney, Doris Miles
*O'Neill, Russell*
Obituary (Lachman) 13/4/90-1
ONLY IN L.A. (Sinclair) (M*F) 6/6/27
Onomastics of Sherlock, The
(Fleissner) 8/3/21-4
OPEN SEASON (Mayor) (TAR)
11/1/63; 11/2/75
OPEN SHADOW, THE (Solomon)
(M*F) 3/6/27
OPERATION APRICOT (Haddad)
(R) 2/4/45
OPERATION TEN (Scott) (IAC) 6/6/21
OPIUM FLOWER (Cushman)
(M*F) P/25
Oppenheim, E. Phillips
THE GREAT IMPERSONATION
(R) 2/3/49

*Orczy, Baroness Emmuska*
Lady Molly of Scotland Yard
(Bargainnier) 7/4/15-9
The Old Man in the Corner
(Bargainnier) 7/6/21-3
ORGANIZATION, THE (Anthony)
(R) 3/4/47
ORIGINAL CARCASE, THE (Bagby)
(M*F) 2/4/34
Oriol, Laurence
SHORT CIRCUIT (R) 5/5/39
Ormerod, Roger
AN ALIBI TOO SOON
(TAR) 10/4/45
FAREWELL GESTURE
(TAR) 13/2/46
*Ormiston.* See Walsh, James Morgan
*O'Rourke, Frank*
Obituary (Lachman) 11/3/53
*Orton, Joe*
Joe Orton's and Tom Stoppard's Bur-
lesques (Bargainnier) 7/1/18-22
Osborn, David
MURDER AT MARTHA'S
VINEYARD (TAR) 11/3/83
Osborn, Pauline M.
L: 5/2/45
OTHER PEOPLE'S MONEY (Lyons)
(TAR) 11/3/75
OTHER SHOE, THE (McMullen)
(R) 5/4/37
OUT (Rey) (R) 9/2/38
OUT OF CONTROL (Liddy) (R) 3/6/44
OUT OF NOWHERE (Marshall)
(TAR) 11/3/77
OUT OF THE WOODPILE: BLACK
CHARACTERS IN CRIME AND
DETECTIVE FICTION (Bailey)
(R) 13/2/91-3
OUTCASTS (Hensley) (R) 5/2/26
OUTLINE OF SANITY, THE (Dale)
(IAC) 7/2/25
OUTSIDE IN (Lewin) (M*F) 4/5/33
OVER THE EDGE (Kemp)
(M*F) 3/6/37
OVERDRIVE (Gilbert) (IAC) 11/1/23
OVERTURE TO DEATH (Marsh)
(IAC) 10/4/49
OXFORD TRAGEDY, AN (Masterman)
(R) 2/2/38
Ozaki, Milton K.
THE DUMMY MURDER CASE
(TBR) 10/3/57

# P

P.G. Wodehouse as Reader of Crime
Stories (Sarjeant)          9/5/7-19
L: Nevins 10/1/93; Shibuk 10/1/91
*P.I. MAGAZINE*
L: Banks 12/2/85-6
Pachter, Josh, ed.
TOP CRIME (R)          8/2/33
PACKET OF TROUBLE, A (Ashford)
(M*F)          5/4/25
Padgett, Lewis
THE BRASS RING (TBR)     11/3/62
Page, Bruce; David Leitch, and Phillip
Knightley
THE PHILBY CONSPIRACY
(IAC)          6/4/31
Page, Emma
EVERY SECOND THURSDAY
(R)          8/4/39
PAGODA (Phillips) (R)          3/1/39
Paisner, Daniel
OBIT (IAC)          13/1/30
PALACE GUARD, THE (MacLeod)
(M*F)          5/5/26
*Palfrey, Dr. Stanislaus Alexander.* See
Creasey, John
PALINDROME (Wood) (TAR) 13/2/50-1
Palmer, Stuart
THE PUZZLE OF THE SILVER
PERSIAN (R)          9/4/43
Panek, Leroy Lad
AN INTRODUCTION TO THE DE-
TECTIVE STORY (IAC)     10/2/54
WATTEAU'S SHEPHERDS: THE
DETECTIVE NOVEL IN
BRITAIN, 1914–1940 (R)
(IAC)          4/3/44; 4/4/18
PANIC IN BOX C (Carr) (IAC)  9/2/28
PAPER CHASE (Bayer) (TBR)13/2/67-8
PAPER PHOENIX (Friedman)
(R)          8/4/38
PAPER THUNDERBOLT, THE (Innes)
(IAC)          9/4/36
PAPERBACK PRICE GUIDE, THE
(Hancer) (IAC) (M*F)
4/6/32; 5/1/28
L: Napier 5/1/34
*Paperback Quarterly* (MS)      6/3/2-3
PAPERBACKS, U.S.A.: A GRAPHIC
HISTORY, 1939–1959 (Schreuders)
(M*F)          6/1/31
PAPERBAG (Russell) (M*F)     4/2/32

PARADE OF COCKEYED CREA-
TURES, A, OR DID SOMEONE
MURDER OUR WANDERING
BOY? (Baxt) (R)          3/4/42
PARCEL OF THEIR FORTUNES, A
(Byfield) (M*F)          4/2/38
Paretsky, Sara
BEASTLY TALES (ed.)
(IAC)          12/2/66-7
BLOOD SHOT (TAR)
11/1/65; 11/2/77
DEADLOCK (R)          8/2/36
A WOMAN'S EYE (ed.)
(R)          13/4/47-8
PARIAH, THE (Wilcox) (TAR) 10/4/48
*Parker*
The Morals of Parker (McSherry)
8/2/2-8
Parker, Robert
PASSPORT TO PERIL (M*F) 1/4/40
*Parker, Robert B.*
CEREMONY (M*F) (R) 6/3/36 & 39
CRIMSON JOY (TAR)
11/1/65; 11/2/77
GOD SAVE THE CHILD (R)
(M*F)          1/1/26; 3/4/39
Introduction to UNKNOWN
THRILLER: THE SCREENPLAY
OF PLAYBACK (IAC)     9/4/35
THE JUDAS GOAT (M*F)
(IAC)          3/3/37; 9/4/35
LOOKING FOR RACHEL
WALLACE (M*F) (IAC)
(R)     4/3/34; 5/5/36; 9/4/35
Looking for Rachel Wallace
(Kelley)          4/3/29-30
MORTAL STAKES (R)
(IAC)          2/1/32; 2/6/28
(MS)          12/3/2-6
PERCHANCE TO DREAM
(TAR)          13/2/46-7
POODLE SPRINGS (w/Chandler)
(IAC)          11/4/49
Professor Without a Pseudonym
(French)          2/2/12-14
PROMISED LAND (M*F)     1/1/32
A SAVAGE PLACE (M*F)     5/5/25
TAMING A SEA-HORSE (R)  8/4/37
VALEDICTION (R)          8/2/30
THE WIDENING GYRE (R)
7/3/39; 8/2/30
WILDERNESS (M*F)          4/2/33
Parnell, Patricia
L:          2/5/59

*Parrish, Frank*
  BIRD IN THE NET (TAR)    10/4/45
  DEATH IN THE RAIN (IAC) 11/3/49
  (IAC)    7/5/26
  STING OF THE HONEYBEE
    (M*F)    4/2/31
PARROT MAN, THE (Middlemiss)
  (R)    2/2/39
PARTY FOR LAWTY, A (Sarsfield)
  (TBR)    13/1/36
PARTY TO MURDER, A (Underwood)
  (R)    8/1/31
PASSENGER FROM SCOTLAND
  YARD, THE (Wood) (M*F)    2/5/30
PASSING STRANGE (Aird)
  (M*F)    5/4/21
PASSION PLAY (Blain) (TAR)12/2/56-7
PASSPORT TO PERIL (Parker)
  (M*F)    1/4/40
PAST MURDER IMPERFECT (Barton)
  (M*F)    6/1/35
PATCHWORK MAN, THE (Harper)
  (R)    2/5/44
Patrick, Andrew
  BARETTA (R)    2/1/40
Patrick, Q. Also see Wheeler, Hugh
  COTTAGE SINISTER (TBR)
    (R)    11/1/44; 12/1/52-3
  MURDER AT CAMBRIDGE
    (R)    2/5/43
Patterson, Harry. Also see Fallon,
  Martin; Higgins, Jack
  THE VALHALLA EXCHANGE
    (R)    1/4/43
Patterson, James
  THE SEASON OF THE MACHETE
    (M*F)    2/4/31
  THE THOMAS BERRYMAN
    NUMBER (M*F)    1/5/33
Patterson, Richard North
  THE LASKO TANGENT
    (M*F)    4/5/31
Paul, Barbara
  THE FOURTH WALL (R)    7/4/27
PAY ON THE WAY OUT (Murphy)
  (M*F)    1/1/27
*Payne, Laurence*
  Birkett and Saunders in Action
    (Sarjeant)    10/1/17-37*
*Peachy, St. George. See Starnes,*
  Richard

Peebles, Niles N.
  BLOOD BROTHER, BLOOD
    BROTHER (M*F)    4/2/37
*Peel, Judge Joseph A.*
  Twice-Told Tale of Murder
    (Floyd)    6/1/21-6
PEEPER (Estleman) (R)    12/4/99-100
Peeples, Samuel A.
  THE MAN WHO DIED TWICE
    (M*F)    1/3/41
PEKING DUCK (Simon) (M*F)  3/6/32
PEKING MAN IS MISSING, THE
  (Taschdigian) (M*F)    2/2/33
*Pelham, Pel. See Martin, A.E.*
*Pelazoni, Lexey Jane. See Head, Lee*
Penal Economy: A Lesson from Leo
  Tolstoy (Tolley)    12/2/33-5
Penchenat, Jean-Guy
  L:    11/3/94
*Penguin Books* (MS)    2/2/62
PENNY FERRY, THE (Boyer)
  (R)    8/3/37
PENNY MURDERS, THE (Black)
  (M*F) (R)    5/1/23; 5/5/37
Pentecost, Hugh. Also see Philips,
  Judson
  BEWARE YOUNG LOVERS
    (M*F)    4/3/40
  THE CANNIBAL WHO OVERATE
    (IAC)    12/4/45
  DEATH AFTER BREAKFAST
    (M*F)    5/2/20
  DIE AFTER DARK (M*F)    1/3/38
  A MURDER ARRANGED
    (IAC)    2/6/29
  RANDOM KILLER (M*F)    3/6/29
  THE STEEL PALACE (M*F)  3/1/32
*Penzler, Otto*
  THE ENCYCLOPEDIA OF MYS-
    TERY AND DETECTION (w/
    Steinbrunner, ed.) (R)    P/13
  GREAT DETECTIVES (ed.)
    (IAC)    2/4/15
  L:  5/2/45; 8/6/50; 9/3/44; 12/4/103-4
  (MS)    9/2/2
  PRIVATE LIVES OF PRIVATE
    EYES, SPIES, CRIME FIGHT-
    ERS, AND OTHER GOOD GUYS
    (IAC)    2/4/15
  WHODUNIT? HOUDINI? (ed.)
    (M*F)    P/31
  L: Reineke 5/1/40

PEOPLE NEXT DOOR, THE (Crane)
(TAR)                          11/2/67
PEOPLE'S REPUBLIC, THE (Amor)
(TAR)                          12/2/55
PEPPER PIKE (Roberts) (TAR)
                       11/1/66; 11/2/78
PERCHANCE TO DREAM (Parker)
(TAR)                         13/2/46-7
PERFECT CORPSE, THE (Wright)
(R)                             1/4/47
PERFECT PLACE, THE (Kohler)
(TAR)                          11/3/73
PERFECTIONIST, THE (Kauffmann)
(TBR)                          11/2/91
Perowne, Barry
   RAFFLES OF THE ALBANY:
      FOOTPRINTS OF A FAMOUS
      GENTLEMAN CROOK IN THE
      TIMES OF A GREAT DETEC-
      TIVE (R)                 4/3/44
Perry, Anne
   THE FACE OF A STRANGER
      (R)                    13/1/76-7
Perry, Ritchie
   (SSC)                      4/6/5-6*
   L: Doerrer 5/1/37
Perry, Robin
   WELCOME FOR A HERO
      (M*F)                     1/1/31
Perry, Thomas
   THE BUTCHER'S BOY (IAC)
      (R)                 8/1/16; 8/3/43
   METZGER'S DOG (IAC)        8/1/16
Perry, Will
   MURDER AT THE U.N. (M*F)
                                1/1/33
Perseverance Press
   (MS)          10/2/2; 11/2/2; 12/1/3
   L: Phillips 11/3/101
PERSON SHOULDN'T DIE LIKE
   THAT, A (Goldstein) (TBR)
                             13/3/59-60
PERSONS UNKNOWN (MacDonald)
   (R)                         9/5/38
PET PEEVES (McCafferty) (TAR)
                               13/2/42
Peter Rabe's Daniel Port
   (Tuttle)                   9/5/20-2
Peterman from the Old School
   (Sampson)                   5/4/2-4

Peters, Elizabeth. Also see Michaels,
   Barbara
   THE DEEDS OF THE DISTURBER
      (R)                     11/4/87
   THE LOVE TALKERS (R)      5/5/33
   THE MURDERS OF RICHARD III
      (IAC)                    9/3/29
Peters, Ellis
   A MORBID TASTE FOR BONES
      (M*F)                    4/4/37
   ONE CORPSE TOO MANY
      (M*F)                    4/4/34
   A RARE BENEDICTINE (R) 12/1/39
   THE SANCTUARY SPARROW
      (R)                      8/1/33
   THE VIRGIN IN THE ICE
      (R)              6/6/33; 7/5/47
Petersen, Herman
   OLD BONES (TBR)           11/2/89
Peterson, Keith
   THE RAIN (TAR)            12/4/51
Petievich, Gerald
   SHAKEDOWN (TAR)           10/4/45
PETROVKA 38
   L: Blom 6/6/41
Pettee, Florence Mae
   Doctor Wonderful (Sampson)
                             5/6/13-8*
PHANTOM FINGERS (Mearson)
   (TBR)                      10/3/61
Philbin, Tom
   A MATTER OF DEGREE
      (TNSPE)                 10/2/49
Philbrick, W.R.
   THE CRYSTAL BLUE PER-
      SUASION (TNSPE)         10/2/49
   THE NEON FLAMINGO
      (TNSPE)                 10/2/48
PHILBY CONSPIRACY, THE (Page/
   Leitch/Knightley) (IAC)     6/4/31
Philby, Kim
   Master Spy in Fact and Fiction
      (Dukeshire)              3/6/14
PHILIP MARLOWE: A CEN-
   TENNIAL CELEBRATION
   (Preiss, ed.) (TAR)        11/4/75
Philips, Judson. Also see Pentecost,
   Hugh
   BACKLASH (M*F)               P/31
   FIVE ROADS TO DEATH
      (M*F)                    2/5/31
   A MURDER ARRANGED
      (M*F)                    3/3/37
   Obituary (Lachman)       11/3/53-4

*Philips, Judson,* continued
REMEMBER TO KILL ME
(IAC)                          11/1/28
WHY MURDER? (M*F)              3/6/34
*Philis.* See Perry, Ritchie
Phillips, David Atlee
THE CARLOS CONTRACT
(R)                            4/2/50
*Phillips, James Atlee.* Also see Atlee,
Philip
The Joe Gall Series (Kelley/
Banks)                         3/2/26-35*
Obituary (Lachman)             13/3/71
PAGODA (R)                     3/1/39
L: Lachman 4/2/56
Phillips, Kathy
L:                             10/3/78
*Phillips, Meredith*
L:                             11/3/101
(MS)                           12/1/1,3
Reviews:
"C" IS FOR CORPSE
(Grafton)                      8/4/38
THE CAVALIER IN WHITE
(Muller)                       8/4/39
DEAD ON TIME (Keating)
                               13/3/89-91
DEAD UPON THE STICK
(Upton)                        8/5/34
THE GOING DOWN OF THE
SUN (Bannister) (R)   13/4/96-7
MURDERS & ACQUISITIONS
(Murphy)                       12/3/101-3
PAPER PHOENIX (Friedman)
                               8/4/38
RECKLESS ABANDON
(Salinger)                     13/4/100-1
REPORT FOR MURDER
(McDermid)                     13/3/91-2
THE SPLIT SECOND
(Meek)                         13/4/99-100
TAMING A SEA-HORSE
(Parker)                       8/4/37
THERE'S SOMETHING IN A
SUNDAY (Muller)       13/4/97-8
PHILLY STAKES (Roberts)
(TAR)                          12/4/55-6
PHOENIX NO MORE (Gage)
(M*F)                          3/1/36
PHOTO FINISH (Marsh) (M*F)
(IAC)            5/1/26; 6/3/23
L: Rapp 5/1/43

Picano, Felice
THE LURE (R)                   4/4/46
PICK YOUR VICTIM (McGerr)
(R)                            10/1/89
L: Lachman 10/2/84
*Pickard, Nancy*
Nancy Pickard: Arrived
(Gottschalk)                   13/2/23-8
SAY NO TO MURDER
(IAC)                          12/4/44
PICTURE PERFECT MURDERS, THE
(Adler/Chastain) (R)   12/4/91-4
PICTURE MISS SEETON (Carvic)
(M*F)                          1/4/38
Piekarski, Vicki, and Jon Tuska, eds.
THE DETECTIVE IN HOLLY-
WOOD (R)                       2/4/38
ENCYCLOPEDIA OF FRONTIER
AND WESTERN FICTION (IAC)
(R)                     8/1/18 & 29
Pierce, David N.
DOWN IN THE VALLEY
(TAR)                          12/4/51-2
Piercing the Closed Circle: The Tech-
nique of Point of View in Works by
P.D. James (Bakerman)          1/5/3-16
Pierson, Eleanor
THE GOOD NEIGHBOR MURDER
(TBR)                          13/2/74
Piesman, Marissa
UNORTHODOX PRACTICES
(R)                            12/1/41
PIGEON PROJECT, THE (Wallace)
(R)                            3/3/44
Pike, Barry A.
CAMPION'S CAREER: A STUDY
OF THE NOVELS OF
MARGERY ALLINGHAM (R)
(IAC)    9/2/2; 10/1/67-71; 10/2/55
*Pinkerton* (MS)               6/3/4
PINT OF MURDER, A (Craig)
(M*F)                          4/4/42
PIOUS AGENT, THE (Braine)
(R)                            2/3/52
PIOUS DECEPTION (Dunlap)
(R)                            12/1/41-2
Piper, Peter
THE CORPSE THAT CAME BACK
(TBR)                          11/3/57
Pirates in Candyland (Sampson)
                               6/3/7-13*
PISTOLS AND PEDAGOGUES (Evans)
(TBR)                          11/1/48

PLACE FOR A POISONER (Lorac)
(R)                                5/3/37
PLACE OF THE DEVILS, THE (Blair)
(R)                                2/1/37
*Plagiarism*
Abandoned Queens (Strøm) 9/1/10-6
Platt, Kin
THE PRINCESS STAKES MURDER
(IAC)                              5/2/10
THE SCREWBALL KING MURDER
(M*F)                              2/6/33
Player, Robert
LET'S TALK OF GRAVES, OF
WORMS, AND EPITAPHS
(TBR)                           13/1/41-2
PLAYING FOR KEEPS (Waterhouse)
(IAC)                             10/1/63
*Plays*
Joe Orton's and Tom Stoppard's
Burlesques (Bargainnier) 7/1/18-22
THE MOUSETRAP AND OTHER
PLAYS (Christie) (IAC)            3/3/18
PLOT IT YOURSELF (Stout)
(M*F)                               P/23
*Plotkin, Sylvia.* See Baxt, George
Plum, Mary
STATE DEPARTMENT CAT
(TBR)                             11/4/61
Pocket Books Checklist, 1–500 (Knott/
Lachman)                       1/6/29-37*
L: Lachman 1/6/58
*Poe, Edgar Allan*
L: Fisher 7/4/46, 11/1/84
POINT OF MURDER, THE (Yorke)
(R)                                5/2/33
POISON (McBain) (R)                9/5/35
POISON FOR ONE (Rhode) (R) 9/3/39
POISON IN THE PARISH (Kennedy)
(TBR)                             11/4/63
POISONED CHOCOLATES MYS-
TERY, THE (Berkeley) (IAC)   6/6/20
*Poisoned Pen, The* (magazine)
(MS)                               6/4/2
*Police Procedural*
Birkett and Saunders in Action
(Sarjeant)                   10/1/17-37*
THE POLICE PROCEDURAL
(Dove) (IAC)                      7/2/23
The Rural Policeman (Dove) 8/4/21-3
Thomas Chastain and the New Police
Procedural (French)           2/4/17-8
The Weevil in Bencurd, Or, The Cop
Abroad (Dove)         2/6/17-19, 16
William MacHarg's O'Malley
(Dove)                         8/6/14-8

POLICE PROCEDURAL, THE (Dove)
(IAC)                              7/2/23
L: Blom 6/6/41
Policeman, The: A Victorian Novel
(Bleiler)                        6/2/7-10
Polk, Beth
L:                                 7/4/39
*Pollifax, Emily.* See Gilman, Dorothy
Pollock, J.C.
MISSION M.I.A. (R)              6/4/47
Pollock, Robert
LOOPHOLE: OR HOW TO ROB A
BANK (R)                       2/1/44
POLO ANYONE? (Kennealy)
(TNSPE)                          10/2/51
*Polsky, Thomas*
Thomas Polsky's Curtains Trilogy
(Deeck)                     12/4/21-33*
Ponder, Patricia
MURDER FOR CHARITY (R)
(M*F)                 2/3/55; 2/4/31
*Pontivy, Francis (Papa).* See Newman,
Bernard
POODLE SPRINGS (Chandler/Parker)
(IAC)                             11/4/49
POOL OF TEARS (Wainwright)
(M*F)                              2/3/43
POOR DEAD CRICKET (Duncan)
(IAC)                             11/1/24
POOR OLD LADY'S DEAD, THE
(Scott) (TBR)                     10/3/57
POOR PRISONER'S DEFENSE
(Sheldon) (TBR)                 12/3/74-5
*Popkin, Zelda*
DEATH WEARS A WHITE
GARDENIA (R)                12/1/55-6
Obituary (Lachman)             7/4/23
*Popular Culture Society*
L: Bakerman 7/3/46
Popular Library Paperback Checklist,
1–200 (Butler)                 1/3/5-8*
PORK CITY (Browne) (TNSPE) 10/2/50
*Port, Daniel.* See Rabe, Peter
PORT ARTHUR CHICKEN (Chiu)
(M*F)                              4/2/36
*Porter, Joyce*
DEAD EASY FOR DOVER
(R)                             4/1/31
DOVER AND THE CLARET
TAPPERS (TAR)              12/4/52
Miss Marple She Isn't
(Doerrer)                      2/6/7-8
L: Breen 2/3/66; Doerrer 2/3/63

Portser, Elinor
  L: 2/3/72
Portway, Christopher
  ALL EXITS BARRED (R) 2/3/52
Posey, Carl A.
  KIEV FOOTPRINT (IAC) 7/5/27
Post, Melville Davisson
  Special Review Article
    (Wooster) 2/5/9-12
POST NO BONDS (Biederman)
  (TAR) 11/1/51
Postgate, Raymond
  VERDICT OF TWELVE (IAC) 8/4/32
POUR THE HEMLOCK (Russell)
  (M*F) 1/3/37
Powell, Michael
  Obituary (Lachman) 12/2/71
  L: Shibuk 12/4/102-3
Powell, Richard
  (SSC) 4/6/6*
Powell, Talmage
  CORPUS DELECTABLE
    (TBR) 11/1/46
Powell, William
  Obituary (Lachman) 8/3/29-30
  (RM) 8/5/32
POWER PLAYS (Wilcox) (M*F) 3/6/29
Powers, Elizabeth
  ALL THE GLITTERS (IAC)
    12/4/43-4
Pow-Wow on the Potomac: A Report on
  Bouchercon XI (Nieminski)
    4/6/12-8
  L: Gottschalk 5/1/42
Practical Lawyer, The (magazine)
  L: Wright 11/3/100
PRACTISE TO DECEIVE (Bradshaw)
  (R) 7/1/42
Prather, Richard
  THE AMBER EFFECT (R) 8/6/42
  FIND THIS WOMAN (R) 2/1/47
PRECIOUS BLOOD (Haddam)
  (R) 13/4/103-4
Predictions and Detective Fiction
  Crystal-Ball Stories (Strøm)
    12/3/47-52
Preiss, Byron, ed.
  PHILIP MARLOWE: A
    CENTENNIAL CELEBRATION
    (TAR) 11/4/75
Prentice, Lt. Cmdr. John. See Sea-Lion
Prescott, H.F.M.
  DEAD AND NOT BURIED
    (R) 9/5/46

President Nero Wolfe (Lachman)
    5/3/22-6
PRESIDENT'S PLANE IS MISSING,
  THE (Serling) (IAC) 3/2/22
PRESUMED INNOCENT (Turow)
  (TAR) 12/4/57-8
PRETTY PINK SHROUD, THE
  (Ferrars) (R) 2/6/41
Price, Anthony
  (SSC) 4/6/6*
PRICE TAG FOR MURDER (Dean)
  (R) 9/6/43
PRIME EVIL (Kelman) (IAC) 8/6/33
PRIME SUSPECT (TV) (IAC) 13/4/86
PRINCESS STAKES MURDER, THE
  (Platt) (IAC) 5/2/10
Printers, Computer
  Townsend comments 12/1/60-5
PRISON OF ICE (Axton) (R) 1/6/46
PRISONER OF THE DEVIL
  (Hardwick) (R) 6/4/36
Private Eye of Fred MacIsaac, The
  (Lybeck) 10/2/29-42
Private Eyes, Top 10
  L: Adey 7/4/44; Breen 7/3/50; Deeck
    7/6/44; Isaac 7/6/45; Lachman
    7/4/50; Randisi 7/2/41; Rice 7/6/49
PRIVATE LIFE OF DOCTOR
  WATSON, THE (Hardwick) (R)8/1/27
PRIVATE LIVES OF PRIVATE EYES,
  SPIES, CRIME FIGHTERS, AND
  OTHER GOOD GUYS (Penzler)
  (IAC) 2/4/15
PRO-AM MURDERS, THE (Cake)
  (IAC) 3/3/49
Probyn, Julia. See Bridge, Ann
Professionals, The (TV)
  Two from the Telly (Adey)
    5/6/19-20, 32
Professionals, The (Sampson) 6/1/16-20*
  L: Adey 6/1/47
PROFESSOR KNITS A SHROUD, THE
  (Van Arsdale) (R) 9/6/47
Professor Without a Pseudonym
  (French) 2/2/12-14
Professorial Sleuth of Roy Winsor, The
  (French) 2/1/3-4
Programmed Writing of Dean R.
  Koontz, The (Kelley) 1/4/11-2
  L: Briney 1/5/56; Wooster 1/5/54
PROMISED LAND (Parker)
  (M*F) 1/1/32

Pronzini, Bill. Also see Foxx, Jack;
    Saxon, Alex
    ACTS OF MERCY (w/Malzberg)
        (R)                          2/5/37
    Bill Pronzini Revisited (Kelley)
                                     2/5/5-6
    BLOWBACK (M*F)                   1/5/32
    BREAKDOWN (TAR)                  13/2/47
    DEADFALL (R)                     8/5/39
    THE EDGAR WINNERS (ed.)
        (IAC)                        4/4/18
    GAMES (R) (IAC) (R)
                     1/2/25; 3/2/22; 6/1/45
    GUN IN CHEEK (IAC)               7/2/23
    HOODWINK (M*F)                   5/5/27
    JACKPOT (TAR)                    12/4/52-3
    LABYRINTH (M*F) (R) 4/3/38 & 43
    LOCKED ROOM PUZZLES (w/
        Greenberg, ed.) (IAC)        11/1/33
    THE MAMMOTH BOOK OF
        PRIVATE EYE STORIES (w/
        Greenberg, ed.) (IAC)        11/1/33
    MIDNIGHT SPECIALS: AN
        ANTHOLOGY FOR TRAIN
        BUFFS AND SUSPENSE
        AFICIONADOS (ed.) (R)        1/6/46
    THE MYSTERY HALL OF FAME
        (w/Greenberg/Waugh, ed.)
        (R)                          8/2/33
    THE RUNNING OF BEASTS
        (w/Malzberg) (R)     1/1/17; 1/2/37
    SCATTERSHOT (MS) 6/2/37; 7/3/37
    SHACKLES (TAR) (IAC)
                     11/1/66; 11/2/78; 12/1/25
    SON OF GUN IN CHEEK
        (IAC)                        10/2/53
    The Suspense Novels of Bill Pronzini
        (Kelley)                     1/2/15-16
    TWOSPOT (w/Wilcox) (R)
        (M*F)                2/6/36; 3/1/36
    UNCOLLECTED CRIME (R)
                                     11/1/70-1
    UNDERCURRENT (R)                 7/3/40
    L: Frazier 2/6/53
Propper, Milton
    THE GREAT INSURANCE
        MURDERS (TBR)                10/3/59
Pross, Peter N.
    L:      1/1/46; 1/5/57; 2/1/57; 2/2/53
    Raymond Chandler on Film: An An-
        notated Checklist
                     1/6/3-10*; 2/3/27-31,40*

Proverbs in the Mystery
    L: Deeck 7/4/42
Pseudonyms
    The Mysteries of the Pseudonymous
        Professors (Barbato)         1/4/3-6
PUBLIC EYE: MARKER CALLS THE
    TUNE (Marriott) (R)              7/4/33
PUBLIC MURDERS (Granger)
    (M*F)                            4/3/35
PUBLISH AND BE KILLED (Morice)
    (R)                              8/6/46
Publishing. Also see Dover Publications;
    Magazines; Penguin; Pulps
    The Avon Classic Crime Collection
        (Meyerson)                   1/5/19-20*
    Brownstone Books (MS)
                     5/5/1-2; 8/5/22, 28, 33
    Cliffhanger Press (MS)
                     9/1/6; 9/2/2; 10/3/2
    Dell "Map Back" Checklist, 1–300
        (Butler)                     1/2/17-22*
    Five Star Mysteries (Deeck)
                                     11/2/17-23*
    The Gold Medal Boys (Tuttle)
                                     10/3/25-31
    (IAC)                            4/4/19-20
    PAPERBACKS, U.S.A.: A
        GRAPHIC HISTORY, 1939–1959
        (Schreuders) (M*F)           6/1/31
    Perseverance Press (MS)
                     10/2/2; 11/2/2
    Pocket Books Checklist, 1–500
        (Knott/Lachman)              1/6/29-37*
    Popular Library Paperback Checklist,
        1–200 (Butler)               1/3/5-8*
    The Saint Mystery Library
        L: Williams 3/3/50
    Vulcan Publications (Deeck)
                                     12/3/53-6*
    L: Adey 5/5/47; Broset 2/1/59; Crider
        5/5/44; Dueren 4/3/49; Grochowski
        2/3/66; Hubin 5/5/44; Mertz
        2/5/49; Samoian 5/4/40
Puckett, Andrew
    BED OF NAILS (TAR)               12/4/53
Pulps. Also see Black Mask; Detective
    Story Magazine; Magazines
    THE HARDBOILED DICKS: AN
        ANTHOLOGY AND STUDY OF
        PULP DETECTIVE FICTION
        (Goulart, ed.) (R)           1/2/37
    I Remember...Pulp Mysteries–Mystery
        Pulps (Banks)                3/4/19-22

*Pulps* continued
Maps of Xiccarph (Sampson) 6/6/9-18
MYSTERY, DETECTIVE, AND
ESPIONAGE FICTION: A
CHECKLIST OF FICTION IN
U.S. PULP MAGAZINES, 1915–
1974 (Cook/Miller) (R)     11/1/75
Peterman from the Old School
(Sampson)             5/4/2-4
The Professionals (Sampson)
                        6/1/16-20*
Some Very Tough People
(Sampson)             8/5/7-17*
Those Old Detective Pulp Magazines
(Thorpe)              1/3/9-11
L: Harwood 3/5/49
*Punctuation and Quotation Marks*
Townsend comments        2/6/52
L: Lyles 3/4/58; Stewart 3/3/50
Punshon, E.R.
INFORMATION RECEIVED
(TBR)                11/3/65
MYSTERY VILLA (M*F)    5/6/34
PURE SWEET HELL (Douglas)
(M*F)                    P/29
Putre, John Walter
DEATH AMONG THE ANGELS
(TAR)                13/2/47-8
Putrill, Richard
MURDERCON (R)           7/3/40
PUZZLE FOR FIENDS (Quentin)
(M*F)                   4/4/40
PUZZLE FOR FOOLS, A (Quentin)
(IAC)                    9/2/24
PUZZLE FOR PUPPETS (Quentin)
(IAC)                  11/4/48
PUZZLE IN PORCELAIN (Gresham)
(R)                    10/1/84
PUZZLE OF THE SILVER PERSIAN,
THE (Palmer) (R)         9/4/43

# Q

Quain, Dan
L:                       6/3/49
QUARK MANEUVER, THE (Jahn)
(M*F)                    1/5/31
QUEEN AND THE CORPSE, THE
(Murray) (TBR)        12/4/61-2
*Queen, Ellery*
Abandoned Queens (Strøm) 9/1/10-6
(TCITC)              3/2/3-12, 20
ELLERY QUEEN'S ANTHOLOGY
VOL. 41 (ed.) (R)        6/2/43

*Queen, Ellery,* continued
ELLERY QUEEN'S INTERNA-
TIONAL CASE BOOK
(TCITC)                  3/4/17
ELLERY QUEEN'S 1961 AN-
THOLOGY (ed.) (R)        6/2/42
Ellery Queen, Sports Fan
(Christopher)         10/3/3-24
THE FINISHING STROKE
(IAC)                  10/4/49
THE KING IS DEAD (R)    7/3/34
MASTERPIECES OF MYSTERY
(ed.) (R)                2/1/43
THE MISADVENTURES OF
SHERLOCK HOLMES (ed.)
(R)                      3/3/40
THE SCARLET LETTERS
(TBR)                  10/3/56
A STUDY IN TERROR (R)   2/3/56
THE TRAGEDY OF X (R)    2/4/40
L: Briney 3/1/46, 5/5/45; Cox 3/2/52;
Crider 3/3/52; Doerrer 3/3/55;
Doran 2/6/46; Lansdale 3/3/51;
Mertz 3/5/46; Meyerson 3/1/57;
Wooster 2/5/53, 2/6/50, 3/4/54
QUEEN'S HEAD, THE (Marston)
(TAR)                  12/3/87
*Quentin, Patrick* (IAC)        4/3/33
PUZZLE FOR FIENDS (M*F) 4/4/40
A PUZZLE FOR FOOLS
(IAC)                    9/2/24
PUZZLE FOR PUPPETS
(IAC)                  11/4/48
Query and a Note, A: Stewart's THOR-
NYHOLD (Gottschalk)   12/4/35-8
Quest, Erica
THE OCTOBER CABERET
(M*F)                    3/6/41
THE SILVER CASTLE (M*F) 3/3/36
QUESTION OF MAX, THE (Cross)
(R)                      2/5/44
QUESTION OF GUILT, A (Fyfield)
(R)          13/2/84-5; 13/3/84-5
QUICK RED FOX, THE (MacDonald)
(R)                      6/2/44
QUIET RIVER, THE (Hubbard)
(M*F)                    3/3/37
*Quill, Monica*
Clergy-Detectives (Cleary) 9/3/3-21
THE VEIL OF IGNORANCE
(R)                    11/1/78
*Quiller.* See Hall, Adam

Quiller Report, The (Banks/
  Dawson)                    4/1/8-11*
  L: O'Donnell 4/2/62
Quinn, Seabury
  THE ADVENTURES OF JULES DE
  GRANDIN (R)                1/2/42
QUINNEY'S ADVENTURES (Vachell)
  (TBR)                      12/3/76
Quintain, Richard
  (SSC)                      6/1/7*
Quotations
  Further Gems (Deeck)
  8/6/27-30; 9/1/28-30; 9/2/21-3;
  9/4/32-4; 9/6/31-4; 10/3/32-6;
  11/4/29-34; 13/2/29-35
  Literary Allusions in the Writings of
  Sara Woods (Sarjeant)  12/2/17-27
  Wit and Wisdom of the Mystery
  Story (Lachman) - Part III P/3-10;
  Part IV 1/4/3-7
  L: Gottschalk 12/2/94-6, 13/1/86,
  13/3/95-6; Hazen 12/2/101; Phillips
  11/3/101
QUOTH THE RAVEN (Fischer)
  (M*F)                      1/2/25
Qwilleran, Jim. See Braun, Lilian
Jackson

# R

Rabe, Peter
  AGREEMENT TO KILL
  (M*F)                      1/2/24
  MY LOVELY EXECUTIONER
  (M*F)                      6/3/32
  Obituary (Lachman)         12/4/47-8
  Peter Rabe's Daniel Port
  (Tuttle)                   9/5/20-2
Racina, Thom
  SWEET REVENGE (M*F)        2/4/30
Radio. Also see Mystery Mosts
  I Remember...Radio Mysteries
  (Banks)                    3/5/17-9
  Old Time Radio Lives (Larsen)
  4/5/18-20; 4/6/9-11; 5/6/3-6,9
  THE SOUND OF DETECTION:
  ELLERY QUEEN'S ADVEN-
  TURES IN RADIO (Nevins/
  Stanich) (R)        7/5/28; 10/2/74
  Spade Trumps Unplayed
  (Banks)                    8/6/3-6
  L: Harwood 4/1/41

Radley, Sheila
  THE CHIEF INSPECTOR'S
  DAUGHTER (M*F) (R)
                       5/2/22; 5/4/34
  DEATH IN THE MORNING
  (R)                        5/2/31
  FATE WORSE THAN DEATH
  (R)                        8/5/36
  A TALENT FOR DESTRUCTION
  (R)                        6/4/41
RAFFLES OF THE ALBANY:
  FOOTPRINTS OF A FAMOUS
  GENTLEMAN CROOK IN THE
  TIMES OF A GREAT DETECTIVE
  (Perowne) (R)              4/3/44
RAIN, THE (Peterson) (TAR)   12/4/51
RAISE THE TITANIC! (Cussler)
  (R)                        1/4/44
RAISING THE DEAD (Simon)
  (TAR)            11/1/67; 11/2/78
Rall, William J.
  L:                         2/151
  The Line-Up                1/1/38
RALLY TO KILL (Knox) (M*F) 1/5/36
Ralph, David C.
  L:                         1/6/55
Ramsdale, Lucy. See Dolson, Hildegarde
Rand, Ayn
  Obituary (Lachman)         6/3/26
Randisi, Bob
  THE BLACK MOON (w/Ashby, ed.)
  (R)                        12/4/81-2
  AN EYE FOR JUSTICE (ed.)
  (IAC)                      11/1/34
  L:                 7/2/41; 7/4/37
  SEPARATE CASES (TAR)       12/4/53
Randollph, The Rev. C.P. "Con." See
  Smith, Charles Merrill
RANDOM DEATH (Egan) (M*F) 6/3/32
RANDOM FACTOR, THE (LaRosa/
  Tanenbaum) (M*F)           3/1/33
RANDOM KILLER (Pentecost)
  (M*F)                      3/6/29
Ransome, Stephen [Frederick C. Davis,
  q.v.]
  THE UNSPEAKABLE (R)        3/3/45
Rapp, Howard
  L:                         5/1/43
  Review: PLACE FOR A POISONER
  (Lorac)                    5/3/37
RARE BENEDICTINE, A (Peters)
  (R)                        12/1/39

RAT ON FIRE, THE (Higgins)
(R)                                    5/2/26
RAT'S NEST (West) (TAR)    13/2/50
Rath, Virginia
  AN EXCELLENT NIGHT FOR A
    MURDER (M*F)                     3/6/36
RAVAGERS, THE (Hamilton)
(R)                                    1/2/38
Ravel, Claude. See Jones, Bradford
RAVEN AND THE KAMIKAZE
  (MacKenzie) (M*F)                 2/4/36
Raven House
  L: O'Donnell 4/4/49
Raven, Richard. See Griffin, John
Rawson, Clayton. Also see Towne,
  Stuart
  The Great Merlini (Dueren) 4/4/28-32
Ray, Becky (MS)                       3/6/1
Ray, Robert
  MERRY CHRISTMAS, MURDOCK
    (TAR)                             12/4/54
RAYMOND CHANDLER: A
  DESCRIPTIVE BIBLIOGRAPHY
  (Bruccoli) (R)                      3/6/49
RAYMOND CHANDLER AND FILM
  (Luhr) (IAC) (RM)          7/2/24 & 30
Raymond Chandler on Film: An
  Annotated Checklist (Pross)
                          1/6/3-10*; 2/3/27-31,40*
  L: Goodrich 2/1/56
Raymond Chandler on Film: Addendum
  (Shibuk)                           2/4/14
  L: Shibuk 2/5/59
RAYMOND CHANDLER SPEAKING
  (Chandler) (R)                     1/6/45
Raymond Chandler Without His Knight:
  Contracting Worlds in THE BLUE
  DAHLIA and PLAYBACK (Brewer)
                                     13/3/37-49
Raymond, Clifford
  THE MEN ON THE DEAD MAN'S
    CHEST (M*F)                      2/5/32
Reade, Bill
  THE IBIZA SYNDICATE
    (M*F)                            2/1/29
READER IS WARNED, THE (Dickson)
  (IAC)                              11/4/53
REAL COOL KILLERS, THE (Himes)
  (R)                                13/1/68-70
Real Originality of Dashiell Hammett,
  The (McSherry)                     11/2/25-35
  L: Shibuk 11/3/85; Lachman 11/3/89

Real Originality of Ian Fleming, The
  (McSherry)                         11/4/35-45
REAR WINDOW AND FOUR SHORT
  NOVELS (Woolrich) (IAC)           8/3/25
Reasoner, James M.
  Reviews:
    DEAD IN THE WATER
      (Wood)                         7/6/31
    DEAD MAN'S HANDLE
      (O'Donnell)                    8/6/41
    SHOOT THE WORKS
      (Ellington)                    7/6/31
    YESTERDAY'S FACES–VOL-
      UME I: GLORY FIGURES
      (Sampson)                      7/6/30
  TEXAS WIND (R) (M*F)
                          4/6/38; 5/5/26
Recent European Works on the
  Detective Story (Bleiler)    2/3/23-6
  L: Briney 2/4/52
RECKLESS ABANDON (Salinger)
  (R)                                13/4/100-1
RECLAMS KRIMINALROMAN-
  FUHRER (Arnold/Schmidt) (R) 7/2/36
RECOIL (Garfield) (M*F)             1/5/34
RECYCLED CITIZEN, THE (MacLeod)
  (TAR)                              10/4/43
RED ANGER (Household) (R)          2/2/40
RED BOX, THE (Stout) (IAC)         6/3/25
RED CASTLE MYSTERY, THE
  (Bailey) (M*F)                     1/5/35
RED HOUSE MYSTERY, THE (Milne)
  (IAC) (R)                 6/6/20; 8/5/38
RED IS FOR SHROUDS (Taylor)
  (M*F)                              5/4/21
RED-LIGHT VICTIM, THE (Kinsley)
  (M*F)                              5/5/24
RED RIGHT HAND, THE (Rogers)
  (R)                                2/5/42
RED THUMB MARK, THE (Freeman)
  (IAC)                              9/1/34
Reel Murders (column) (Albert)
    6/2/21-6; 6/3/27-9; 6/4/34-6;
    6/6/23-5; 7/1/36-8; 7/2/27-30;
    7/3/29-31; 7/4/24-6; 7/5/31-4;
    8/1/23-5; 8/2/26-8; 8/3/30-2;
    8/4/34-6; 8/5/32-3; 9/1/37-8;
    9/2/31-2; 9/3/36-8; 9/5/29-31;
    10/3/47-51; 12/2/75-9
  L: Albert 6/6/43; Goode 7/2/47
Rees, Idewald. See Mather, Berkley
Reeve, Arthur B.
  THE EAR IN THE WALL (IAC)
                                     13/2/54-5

Reference. See Bibliography; Secondary
 Sources
Reid, Robert Sims
 CUPID (TAR)                    13/2/48
Reilly, Helen
 DEAD MAN CONTROL (TBR)
  (R)                 11/3/64; 12/1/53-4
 DEATH DEMANDS AN AUDI-
  ENCE (TBR) (R) 11/4/68; 12/1/55
Reilly, John M.
 L:     5/2/45; 7/1/43; 8/1/43; 9/2/45
 TWENTIETH CENTURY CRIME
  AND MYSTERY WRITERS (ed.)
   The Body in the Library
   (Wooster)            5/1/11-4
 TWENTIETH CENTURY CRIME
  AND MYSTERY WRITERS,
  SECOND EDITION (ed.)
  (IAC)                         8/4/30
Reineke, Becky
 L:     4/5/46; 5/1/40; 5/3/41; 6/4/48
Reviews:
  THE REMBRANDT PANEL
   (Banks)                     4/6/37
  THE VIDOCQ DOSSIER
   (Edwards)                   5/3/36
Reiss, Bob
 SUMMER FIRES (R)              6/3/42
REMAINS TO BE SEEN (Butterworth)
 (M*F)                         2/4/35
REMBRANDT DECISIONS, THE
 (Badgley) (IAC)               3/2/24
REMBRANDT PANEL, THE (Banks)
 (R)                           4/6/37
REMEMBER TO KILL ME (Phillips)
 (IAC)                        11/1/28
REMOVERS, THE (Hamilton)
 (R)                           1/4/53
Rendell, Ruth
 THE BRIDESMAID (TAR)        12/4/54
 DEATH NOTES (M*F)            5/6/38
 A DEMON IN MY VIEW
  (M*F)                        1/3/37
 THE FALLEN CURTAIN (R)   3/4/45
 A GUILTY THING SURPRISED
  (R)                          3/4/44
 Humor, Horror, and Intellect
  (Bakerman)              5/4/5-10
 A JUDGEMENT IN STONE
  (R)                          3/4/44
 THE LAKE OF DARKNESS
  (M*F)                        5/1/22

Rendell, Ruth, continued
 MASTER OF THE MOOR (R) 6/4/42
 MEANS OF EVIL (M*F)         4/3/34
 One in Two (Bakerman)   5/6/21-8,32
 SHAKE HANDS FOREVER
  (R)                          3/4/45
 A SLEEPING LIFE (R) (M*F)
                   3/2/45 & 46; 3/3/38
 SOME LIE AND SOME DIE
  (R)                          3/4/44
 TO FEAR A PAINTED DEVIL
  (R)                          3/4/45
 THE VEILED ONE (R)     12/4/86-7
 WOLF TO THE SLAUGHTER
  (R)                          3/4/45
 The Writer's Probe (Bakerman)
                               3/5/3-6
RENDEZVOUS IN BLACK (Woolrich)
 (IAC)                         8/3/25
RENDEZVOUS, THE (Anthony)
 (R)                           2/1/39
REPORT FOR MURDER (McDermid)
 (R)                        13/3/91-2
Report from Scandinavia, A
 (Blom)                    8/2/19-20
Report on Bouchercon 7, A
 (Scott)                    P/18-21
Report on The Crime Writers Third
 International Congress, A
 (Hedman)                  5/6/10-2
Reprints
 L: Deeck 9/2/46; Lachman 9/3/45
REPRISAL (McGivern) (M*F)   4/2/34
Resnicow, Herbert
 L:                            9/1/48
 (MS)                         11/1/2
REST YOU MERRY (MacLeod) (M*F)
 (R)                  3/5/36; 4/2/48
Restaino, Katherine M.
 L:                            7/3/48
RETALIATORS, THE (Hamilton)
 (M*F)                         1/1/30
RETURN FROM VORKUTA (Hunt)
 (R)                           1/4/51
RETURN OF CHARLIE CHAN, THE
 (movie)
 L: Doran 3/4/54
RETURN OF MR. CAMPION, THE
 (Allingham) (TAR) (R)
                      13/1/48 & 58-60
RETURN OF SHERLOCK HOLMES,
 THE (Doyle) (IAC)            9/2/29

RETURN OF SKULL-FACE, THE
(Howard/Lupoff) (R)        2/2/21-4
RETURN TO SENDER (Cluster)
(TAR)        11/2/66
*Revealing Whodunit*
(TCITC)        3/2/3-12, 20
L: Adey 3/5/47; Albert 4/1/41; Bleiler
3/5/50; Breen 3/3/52; Doerrer
3/3/55, 3/4/62; Floyd 3/5/48;
Harwood 4/1/41; Lachman 3/3/59;
Loeser 3/4/59; Townsend
comments 3/3/56, 3/4/59; Wooster
3/4/56
*Revell, Louisa*
Miss Julia Tyler: Detective Manqué
(Deeck)        13/1/7-22*
REVEREND RANDOLLPH AND THE
AVENGING ANGEL (Smith)
(M*F)        2/6/30
REVEREND RANDOLLPH AND THE
FALL FROM GRACE, INC. (Smith)
(M*F)        3/4/38
REVEREND RANDOLLPH AND THE
HOLY TERROR (Smith) (R)        7/3/38
*Reviews.* See Armchair Reviewer; Back-
ward Reviewer; It's About Crime;
Mystery*File; Verdicts
L: Bleiler 2/5/46; Breen 2/1/54;
Broset 2/3/72; Doerrer 2/4/49;
Kelley 1/1/39; Lachman 1/4/58;
McFarland 1/1/40; Mertz 2/3/58;
Scott 1/2/53; Wooster 1/5/54,
2/4/56
(MS)        2/2/63
REX STOUT: A BIOGRAPHY (Mc-
Aleer) (MS) (IAC)        2/2/64; 2/4/16
L: Doerrer 2/4/49; Stilwell 2/3/58
REX STOUT: AN ANNOTATED PRI-
MARY AND SECONDARY BIBLI-
OGRAPHY (Townsend/McAleer/
Sapp/Schemer) (R)        5/2/29
Rey, Pierre
OUT (R)        9/2/38
Reynolds, Barbara Leonard
ALIAS FOR DEATH (TBR) 13/3/53-4
Reynolds, Melinda
L:        6/6/42; 7/2/48; 7/3/46; 7/6/45
RHEINGOLD ROUTE, THE (Maling)
(R)        3/5/42
Rhode, John
A.S.F. THE STORY OF A GREAT
CONSPIRACY (IAC)        3/2/21

*Rhode, John,* continued
THE DAVIDSON CASE
(IAC)        8/5/29
DEAD OF THE NIGHT (R)        9/6/43
FATAL DESCENT (w/Dickson)
(IAC)        9/5/26
HENDON'S FIRST CASE (R)        4/4/44
POISON FOR ONE (R)        9/3/39
THREE COUSINS DIE (M*F)        3/2/39
*Rice, Craig*
EIGHT FACES AT THREE
(IAC)        11/4/48
THE LUCKY STIFF (R)        2/5/43
THE SUNDAY PIGEON MURDERS
(R)        2/5/43
Who Really Wrote THE G-STRING
MURDERS? (Christopher)
8/3/18,20
L: Nevins 4/5/45
Rice, True
L:        6/3/49
RICH GET IT ALL, THE (Huston)
(M*F)        3/6/36
Rich, Virginia
THE COOKING SCHOOL
MURDERS (R)        7/2/38-9
RICH WAY TO DIE, A (Evans)
(M*F)        3/6/40
Rich, Willard
BRAIN-WAVES AND DEATH
(TBR)        13/1/35-6
*Richard III*        9/1/39; 9/2/26-7; 9/3/29
THE MYSTERY OF THE PRINCES:
AN INVESTIGATION INTO A
SUPPOSED MURDER
(Williamson) (IAC)        9/2/26
(MS)        8/4/1-5
Also see TO PROVE A VILLAIN
Richardson, Robert
BELLRINGER STREET (R) 13/3/87-8
THE BOOK OF THE DEAD
(TAR)        12/4/55; 13/3/88-9
THE LATIMER MERCY
(R)        13/3/86-7
*Richlin, Maurice N.*
Obituary (Lachman)        13/1/32
RIDDLE OF THE SANDS, THE
(Childers) (R)        1/6/49
RIDE THE PINK HORSE (Hughes)
(IAC)        10/3/40
Riefe, Alan
TYGER AT BAY (M*F)        P/26
TYGER BY THE TAIL (M*F)        P/29

Rifkin, Shepard
    McQUAID IN AUGUST
        (M*F)                          3/6/29
Riggs, John R.
    WOLF IN SHEEP'S CLOTHING
        (TAR)                          12/4/55
RIGHT HONORABLE CORPSE, THE
    (Murray) (TBR)                     12/4/61-2
RIGHT TO SING THE BLUES, THE
    (Lutz) (R)                         8/4/43 & 44
Riley, Dick, and Pam McAllister
    THE BEDSIDE, BATHTUB &
        ARMCHAIR COMPANION TO
        AGATHA CHRISTIE (R)
        (IAC)                          4/1/43; 4/3/31
Rilla, Wolf
    THE CHINESE CONSORTIUM
        (M*F)                          4/5/34
RIM OF THE PIT (Talbot) (R)            1/5/49
Rinehart, Mary Roberts
    THE CIRCULAR STAIRCASE
        (R)                            1/5/38
    IMPROBABLE FICTION: THE LIFE
        OF MARY ROBERTS
        RINEHART (Cohn) (IAC)          8/2/23
    THE YELLOW ROOM (R)                9/4/40
    L: Briney 1/6/56
Rings of Death (Sampson)             10/1/3-16
Riordan, Sergeant
    The Professionals (Sampson)
                                       6/1/16-20*
Rise and Fall of Gillian Hazeltine, The
    (Lybeck)                           9/4/3-16*
    L: Sampson 9/5/48
RISK (Francis) (R)                     8/1/17
Ritchie, Jack
    Obituary (Lachman)                 7/4/23
RITUAL MURDER (Haymon)
    (R)                                7/5/47
RIVERSIDE VILLAS MURDER, THE
    (Amis) (R)                         3/3/41
ROAD BLOCK (Waugh) (R) 13/2/79-80
ROAD TO GANDOLFO, THE
    (Ludlum) (IAC)                     8/5/30
ROAST EGGS (Clark) (R)
    (M*F)                              5/4/36; 5/6/36
ROBAK'S FIRM (Hensley) (IAC) 9/5/25
ROBAK'S RUN (Hensley) (R)
                                       12/4/79-80
Robert Rostand and Mike Locken
    (Dukeshire)                        2/4/4,14

Roberts, Gillian
    CAUGHT DEAD IN
        PHILADELPHIA (R)               10/4/55
    PHILLY STAKES (TAR)                12/4/55-6
Roberts, John Maddox
    SPQR II: THE CATALINE
        CONSPIRACY (TAR)               13/2/48
Roberts, Les
    FULL CLEVELAND (R)
        (TAR)                   12/1/38; 12/4/56
    NOT ENOUGH HORSES
        (TAR)                          10/4/46
    PEPPER PIKE (TAR)11/1/66; 11/2/78
Roberts, W. Adolphe
    A Look at W. Adolphe Roberts
        (Lybeck)                       11/1/3-6
Robeson, Kenneth
    THE EVIL GNOME (M*F)               P/24
Robinett, Stephen
    THE MAN RESPONSIBLE
        (R)                            7/5/39
Robyns, Gwen
    THE MYSTERY OF AGATHA
        CHRISTIE (IAC)                 4/1/13
ROCKABYE (Koenig) (M*F)                6/2/34
ROCKSBURG RAILROAD
    MURDERS, THE (Constantine)
        (IAC)                          10/1/60
Roddenberry, Gene
    Obituary (Lachman)                 13/4/91
Roden, H.W.
    ONE ANGEL LESS (TBR)
        (R)                     11/1/40; 12/1/54-5
    YOU ONLY HANG ONCE
        (TBR)                          13/3/58
Roden, Jess. See Cunningham, A.B.
Roeburt, John
    THE CORPSE ON THE TOWN
        (TBR)                          13/3/55-6
Roffman, Jan
    ONE WREATH WITH LOVE
        (M*F)                          3/3/31
Rogers, Joel Townsley
    THE RED RIGHT HAND (R)             2/5/42
ROGUE AGENT (Drake) (TAR) 13/3/78
ROGUE MALE (Household) (R)             2/2/40
Rogues for the New Century
    (Dueren)                           5/3/11-14
Rohmer, Sax. Also see Fu Manchu
    (SSC)                              5/1/2*
    L: Briney 5/2/42; Van Tilburg 5/3/41

ROLLING HEADS, THE (Stein)
(M*F)                           3/6/28
Ronald, James
    MURDER IN THE FAMILY
    (TBR)                       12/4/67-8
Ronns, Edward [Edward S. Aarons, q.v.]
    STATE DEPARTMENT MURDERS
    (R)                         2/1/48
*Roos, Audrey*
    Obituary (Lachman)          7/2/25
Roos, Kelley
    GHOST OF A CHANCE
    (TBR)                       11/3/58
    MURDER ON MARTHA'S
    VINEYARD (M*F)              5/5/23
*Roosevelt, Elliott*
    MURDER AT HOBCAW BARONY
    (R)                         10/2/71
    Obituary (Lachman)          13/1/32-3
Roper, L.V.
    HOOKERS DON'T GO TO
    HEAVEN (M*F)                1/2/26
*Roper, Steve, and Mike Nomad*
    The Detective Hero in the Comics
    (Blom)                      6/1/8-15
ROSARY MURDERS, THE (Kienzle)
    (M*F) (R)          3/5/40; 4/2/41
Roscoe, Mike
    ONE TEAR FOR MY GRAVE
    (M*F)                       2/5/33
Rosen, Richard
    FADEAWAY (R) (IAC)
                        9/2/43; 12/4/45
    SATURDAY NIGHT DEAD
    (IAC)                       12/4/45
Rosenbaum, Ron
    MURDER AT ELAINE'S (M*F)
    (IAC)               3/5/39; 11/3/45
*Ross, Angus*
    THE AMPURIAS EXCHANGE
    (M*F)                       2/1/25
    THE HAMBURG SWITCH (R)4/4/46
    (SSC)                       5/2/2*
Ross, Hal
    THE FLEUR-DE-LIS AFFAIR
    (M*F)                       1/1/30
Ross, Jonathan
    THE BURNING OF BILLY
    TOOBER (M*F)                P/28
ROSS MACDONALD (Bruccoli)
    (R)                         8/1/35
Ross, Philip
    TRUE LIES (TAR)             10/4/46

*Ross, Zola Helen*
    Obituary (Lachman)          11/4/55
Rossiter, John
    THE MURDER MAKERS
    (M*F)                       1/6/39
    THE VILLAINS (M*F)          1/1/28
*Rostand, Robert*
    A KILLING IN ROME (R)       2/3/51
    Robert Rostand and Mike Locken
    (Dukeshire)                 2/4/4,14
Rosten, Leo
    SILKY! (IAC)                4/5/25
*Roudybush, Alexandra*
    Introducing Alexandra Roudybush
    (Frazier)                   3/3/2-4
Roueché, Berton
    FAGO (M*F)                  2/3/43
ROUSE THE DEVIL (Weston)
    (M*F)                       1/1/29
Rovin, Jeff
    HOLLYWOOD DETECTIVE:
    GARRISON (R)                1/1/34
Roy, Archie
    DEADLIGHT (R)               2/5/42
    ROYAL DECREE (McAleer) (R) 8/3/40
Royce, Kenneth
    BUSTILLO (M*F)              1/3/38
*Royston, Colonel, and Peter Castle.* See
    Davison, G.
RUBBER BAND, THE (Stout)
    (IAC)                       6/3/25
RUBOUT AT THE ONYX (Jeffers)
    (M*F)                       5/6/37
Ruhm, Herbert, ed.
    THE HARD-BOILED DETECTIVE:
    STORIES FROM BLACK MASK
    MAGAZINE (R)        1/2/34 & 35
RULING PASSION (Hill) (M*F) 2/3/42
RUMPOLE À LA CARTE (Mortimer)
    (TAR)                       13/2/45-6
RUMPOLE AND THE AGE OF
    MIRACLES (TV) (IAC)         12/1/26
"Rumpole and the Sporting Life"
    (Mortimer) (R)              9/1/31
"Rumpole and the Younger Generation"
    (Mortimer) (R)              9/3/28
RUN AROUND, THE (Freemantle)
    (TAR)                       11/4/80
RUN IN DIAMONDS, A (Saxon)
    (M*F)                       1/6/40
Running Hot and Cold with Ron Faust
    (Kelley)                    5/4/11-2

RUNNING OF BEASTS, THE (Pron-
zini/Malzberg) (R)    1/1/17; 1/2/37
Rural Policeman in American Mystery
Fiction, The (Dove)        8/4/21-3
Ruse, Paul
    THE ALUMNI MURDERS
        (M*F)                5/2/23
Russell, A.J.
    POUR THE HEMLOCK (M*F)1/3/37
*Russell, Col. Charles.* See Haggard,
    William
Russell, Martin
    THE MAN WITHOUT A NAME
        (M*F)                2/3/42
Russell, Richard
    PAPERBAG (M*F)        4/2/32
RUSSIAN HOUSE, THE (Le Carré)
    (TAR) (R)        11/3/73; 12/4/76-7
Rutherford, Douglas
    KICK START (R)        3/3/43
*Ryan, Buck*
    The Detective Hero in the Comics
        (Blom)                6/1/8-15
*Ryan, Monsignor John Blackwood.* See
    Greeley, Father Andrew
Ryck, Francis
    SACRIFICIAL PAWN (R)        P/34

# S

Sabatini, Rafael
    THE LOST KING (R)        12/4/94-9
Saberhagen, Fred
    THE HOLMES-DRACULA FILE
        (R)                2/6/36
SABINE (Freeling) (M*F)        3/2/36
SACRIFICIAL GROUND (Cook)
    (TAR)                11/2/67
SACRIFICIAL PAWN (Ryck) (R)    P/34
Sadler, Mark
    CIRCLE OF FIRE (R)  1/3/47; 1/4/47
    TOUCH OF DEATH (R)    12/4/80-1
SAFE AT HOME (Gordon)
    (TAR)                13/3/81-2
SAINT AND THE TEMPLAR TREA-
    SURE, THE (Charteris) (M*F) 3/6/31
SAINT MAGAZINE INDEX, THE
    (Nieminski) (IAC)        4/3/31
*Saint Mystery Library, The*
    L: Williams 3/3/50
Saint of the North, The: Black John
    Smith of Halfaday Creek
    (Harwood)            3/6/3-7*
    L: Doerrer 4/2/54*

*Saint, The.* See Charteris, Leslie
SALAMANDER, THE (West) (R) 3/5/44
Sale, Medora
    MURDER IN A GOOD CAUSE
        (TAR)                13/2/48-9
*Salinger, J.D.*
    The Article I Couldn't Publish
        (Townsend)        1/1/18-20
Salinger, Sharon Singer
    RECKLESS ABANDON
        (R)                13/4/100-1
*Sallust, Gregory.* See Wheatley, Dennis
SAM 7 (Cox) (R)                2/3/50
Samoian, Robert
    L: 4/2/57; 4/6/48; 5/4/40; 8/2/48;
        10/1/96
    Review: SOME DAY I'LL KILL
        YOU (Chambers)        4/6/34
*Sampson, Robert*
    Amazing Grace            6/4/23-9
    DANGEROUS HORIZONS
        (MS)                13/1/2
    Detection by Other Means  7/1/7-17*
    Doctor Wonderful        5/6/13-8*
    The Fattest Man in the Medical
        Profession        7/3/16-22*
    A Few Kind Words for Ashton-
        Kirk                7/6/3-12
    Four Gees            12/3/13-34
    The Last of Gregory George Gordon
        Green            13/2/18-22
    L: 6/4/45; 8/2/48; 9/5/48; 10/1/96;
        11/3/94; 13/2/97-101; 13/3/100-1
    Maps of Xiccarph        6/6/9-18
    The Murder Cases of Pinklin
        West                8/1/3-7
    THE NIGHT MASTER (MS)    6/2/6
    Peterman from the Old School 5/4/2-4
    Pirates in Candyland    6/3/7-13*
    The Professionals        6/1/16-20*
    Rings of Death        10/1/3-16
    The Solving Sixth        5/5/3-6
    Some Very Tough People    8/5/7-17*
    That Pawn-Shop Gypsy    8/4/9-16
    YESTERDAY'S FACES—VOLUME
        I: GLORY FIGURES (R)    7/6/30
    L: Martin 9/1/47; Toole 7/2/45
Samuel, Joseph
    THE MURDERED CLICHÉ
        (TBR)                11/2/90
SAN FRANCISCO KILLS (Flinn)
    (TAR)                13/3/80

Sanchez, Thomas
THE ZOOT-SUIT MURDERS (M*F)
(IAC)          3/5/35; 4/5/24
SANCTUARY SPARROW, THE
(Peters) (R)          8/1/33
SAND DOLLARS (Terrall) (M*F)3/3/34
Sanders, Dennis, and Lou Lovallo
THE AGATHA CHRISTIE COM-
PANION: THE COMPLETE
GUIDE TO AGATHA
CHRISTIE'S LIFE AND WORK
(IAC)          8/2/21
*Sanders, Lawrence*
THE SECOND DEADLY SIN
(R)          3/4/43; 5/4/33
Sinning with Lawrence Sanders
(Kelley)          3/5/20-1
THE TANGENT FACTOR
(M*F)          2/5/30
THE TENTH COMMANDMENT (R)
(IAC)          4/5/39; 9/2/39
TIMOTHY'S GAME (R)          13/1/56-7
Sanders, Leonard
THE EMPEROR'S SHIELD
(TAR)          13/2/49
Sandford, John
EYES OF PREY (TAR)          13/2/49-50
Sandulo, Sandy
L:          2/2/56; 2/3/74; 3/2/61; 4/1/39
Sangster, Jimmy
HARDBALL (TAR)          11/1/66; 11/2/78
Saperstein, David
FATAL REUNION (IAC)          9/5/25
Sapir, Richard, and Warren Murphy
THE DESTROYER #31: THE HEAD
MEN (M*F)          2/4/33
THE DESTROYER 37: BOTTOM
LINE (M*F)          3/6/31
IN ENEMY HANDS (M*F)          1/2/28
IN HOLY TERROR (R)          1/3/49
LAST WAR DANCE (R)          1/3/48
MAFIA FIX (R)          1/6/52
*Sapp, Judson*
L:          3/5/50
Obituary (MS)          7/2/1
REX STOUT: AN ANNOTATED
PRIMARY AND SECONDARY
BIBLIOGRAPHY (w/Townsend/
McAleer/Schemer) (R)          5/2/29
L: Kimura 7/4/45
*Sapper*
(SSC)          4/5/22*

*Sapphire and Steel*
Two from the Telly (Adey)
5/6/19-20, 32
Sargent, Patricia
BLACK VALENTINE (IAC)          11/1/27
Sarjeant, William A.S.
Birkett and Saunders in Action: The
Police Novels of Laurence
Payne          10/1/17-37*
"Borrowed Jewels Well Display'd":
Literary Allusions in the Writings
of Sara Woods          12/2/17-27
Crime Novelists as Writers of
Children's Fiction
Manning Coles          12/1/5-8
John Creasey          13/2/36-42
Freeman Wills Crofts          12/3/67-9
Cyril Hare          12/4/39-42
Laurence Meynell          13/1/23-6
Dorothy L. Sayers          13/4/53-60
Sir Basil Thomson          13/3/31-6
Clifford Witting          12/2/37-9
The Household in Kempenfeldt
Square: Antony Maitland and the
Writings of Sara Woods 10/4/3-40*
P.G. Wodehouse as Reader of Crime
Stories          9/5/7-19
Review: CAMPION'S CAREER
(Pike)          10/1/67
A Scot at Scotland Yard: The Career
of Robert Macdonald, "A Very
Unusual Policeman"          10/2/3-23*
Sarsfield, Maureen
A PARTY FOR LAWTY
(TBR)          13/1/36
SATAN IN ST. MARY'S (Doherty)
(R)          11/4/88
SATURDAY NIGHT DEAD (Rosen)
(IAC)          12/4/45
*Saunders, Fred.* See Payne, Laurence
Savage, Ernest
TWO IF BY SEA (IAC)          6/6/22
SAVAGE PLACE, A (Parker)
(M*F)          5/5/25
SAVAGE STATE OF GRACE, A
(MacKenzie) (TAR)          10/4/43
SAVAGE WOMEN, THE (Curtis)
(R)          1/5/41
SAVARIN'S SHADOW (Goyne)
(R)          13/2/82-3
Saxon, Alex [Bill Pronzini, q.v.]
A RUN IN DIAMONDS (M*F)1/6/40

Saxon, Claude
L: 4/5/45
Some Notes on the Detective Element
in Western Fiction P/17
SAY IT AIN'T SO (Asinov) (M*F)
2/3/45
SAY NO TO MURDER (Pickard)
(IAC) 12/4/44
SAY YES TO MURDER (Ballard)
(R) 2/3/53
*Sayers, Dorothy L.*
AS HER WHIMSEY TOOK HER:
CRITICAL ESSAYS ON
DOROTHY L. SAYERS (Hannay,
ed.) (R) 3/5/45
The Complexity of THE NINE
TAILORS (Christopher) 7/4/3-9*
Crime Novelists as Writers of
Children's Fiction (Sarjeant)
13/4/53-60
DOROTHY L. SAYERS (Brabazon)
(R) 6/1/39
DOROTHY L. SAYERS: A
LITERARY BIOGRAPHY (Hone)
(R) 3/5/45
DOROTHY L. SAYERS: NINE
LITERARY STUDIES (Hall)
(IAC) 6/3/23
DOROTHY SAYERS: A REFER-
ENCE GUIDE (Hall) (IAC) 7/2/23
GAUDY NIGHT (IAC) 8/5/31; 9/5/26
HAVE HIS CARCASE (IAC) 9/5/26
LORD PETER (IAC) 9/2/25
STRONG POISON (IAC) 9/5/26
Three "Unknown" Stories
(Christopher) 11/1/15-21
Why Isn't There a Volume of
Dorothy L. Sayers' Letters?
(Christopher) 12/4/29-33
L: Christopher 8/2/43; Greene 8/3/49;
Nevins 8/3/48
Saylor, V. Louise
The "I" in the Private Eye 9/1/23-7
Move Over Spenser—Here Comes
Cuddy 10/2/43-7
Scaduto, Tony
A TERRIBLE PLACE TO DIE
(M*F) 3/1/35
SCALES OF JUSTICE (Marsh)
(R) 2/1/38
SCANDAL AT HIGH CHIMNEYS
(Carr) (R) 5/4/32

*Scandinavia.* Also see Sweden
Scandinavian Mystery Scene
(Blom) 8/4/24-6
Scandinavian Mystery Scene
(Blom) 8/4/24-6
SCARAB MURDER CASE, THE (Van
Dine) (IAC) 8/3/27
SCARED TO DEATH (Morice)
(M*F) 2/4/32
SCARLET LETTERS, THE (Queen)
(TBR) 10/3/56
SCARLET NIGHT (Davis) (M*F) 4/4/39
SCATTERSHOT (Pronzini) (MS)
6/2/37; 7/3/37
SCAVENGERS (Montgomery)
(IAC) 12/4/43
SCENT OF FEAR, THE (Yorke)
(R) 5/3/35
*Schaefer, Jack*
Obituary (Lachman) 13/1/34
Schapp, Dick, and Jimmy Breslin
.44 (R) 3/5/43
Schemer, Arriean; Guy M. Townsend,
John J. McAleer, and Judson C.
Sapp
REX STOUT: AN ANNOTATED
PRIMARY AND SECONDARY
BIBLIOGRAPHY (R) 5/2/29
*Scherf, Margaret*
THE BEADED BANANA (R) 3/1/31
IF YOU WANT A MURDER WELL
DONE (M*F) P/26
Little Old Ladies (Nehr) 3/4/3-7
Schier, Norma
THE ANAGRAM DETECTIVES
(R) 3/2/44; 4/1/32
DEATH GOES SKIING (IAC) 4/3/32
WHO'S ON FIRST (IAC) 6/3/22
*Schisgall, Oscar*
Obituary (Lachman) 8/3/28-9
Schleret, Jean-Jacques
L: 3/1/49
Schmidt, Joseph, and Armin Arnold
RECLAMS KRIMINALROMAN-
FÜHRER (R) 7/2/36
Schmolders, Claudia, and Christian
Strich, eds.
UBER SIMENON [ON SIMENON]
(R) 7/4/30
Schneider, Joyce Anne
DARKNESS FALLS (IAC) 11/3/49
SCHOLARS OF NIGHT, THE (Ford)
(TAR) 11/1/54

SCHOOL FOR MURDER (Barnard)
  (R)                          8/3/44
Schreuders, Piet
  PAPERBACKS, U.S.A.: A
    GRAPHIC HISTORY, 1939-1959
    (M*F)                      6/1/31-2
SCHROEDER'S GAME (Maling)
  (M*F)                        1/5/29
Schubert, Dick
  L:                     12/1/60 & 65-8
*Schuetz, Dennis*
  Obituary (Lachman)           11/3/54
Schultheis, Steve
  L:                           6/2/48
SCI FI (Marshall) (R)          6/3/43
Science and Technology in the Writings
  of Frederick Irving Anderson
  (Fisher)                     13/4/12-32
*Science Fiction*
  Some Recent Hybrids (Kelley)
                               6/2/16-8
Scot at Scotland Yard, A: The Career of
  Robert Macdonald, "A Very Unusual
  Policeman" (Sarjeant)        10/2/3-23*
Scott, Art
  Dumbfounded in Keelerland
                               1/1/12-17
  Further Excursions into the Wacky
    World of Harry Stephen Keeler
                               1/4/13-24
  L: 1/1/41; 1/2/53; 1/3/58; 6/4/47;
    8/3/48
  A Report on Bouchercon 7     P/18-21
  Reviews:
    THE BROWNSTONE HOUSE OF
      NERO WOLFE (Darby)       7/6/32
    THE ENCYCLOPEDIA OF MYS-
      TERY AND DETECTION
      (Steinbrunner/Penzler, eds.) P/13
    MAKE OUT WITH MURDER
      (Harrison)               1/2/45
    THE MYSTERY STORY (Ball,
      ed.)                     1/2/32
    THE NEW SHOE (Upfield) 1/2/33
    THE TOPLESS TULIP CAPER
      (Harrison)               1/2/45
Scott-Giles, C.W.
  THE WIMSEY FAMILY (IAC)3/4/23
Scott, Hardiman
  OPERATION TEN (IAC)          6/6/21
Scott, Jack S.
  A CLUTCH OF VIPERS
    (M*F)                      3/6/38

*Scott, Jack S.,* continued
  THE GOSPEL LAMB (M*F)  5/3/29
  THE POOR OLD LADY'S DEAD
    (TBR)                      10/3/57
  THE SHALLOW GRAVE (R)
    (M*F)                 2/4/45; 3/1/34
Scott, Ronald McNair, and T.H. White
  DEAD MR. NIXON (R)           3/2/43
Scott, Sutherland
  CRAZY MURDER SHOW
    (TBR)                      11/4/69
SCRATCH FEVER (Collins) (R)  6/3/41
SCRATCHPROOF (Maguire)
  (M*F)                        1/6/38
SCREAMING KNIFE, THE (Vardeman)
  (R)                          12/4/73-6
SCREAMING MIMI, THE (Brown)
  (IAC)                        11/3/46
Scremvin, Ansin F.
  Review: THE ANAGRAM DETEC-
    TIVES (Schier)             4/1/32
SCREWBALL KING MURDER, THE
  (Platt) (M*F)                2/6/33
SEA OF GREEN (Adcock) (TAR)
                               12/2/53
SEA OF TROUBLES (Smith)
  (MS)                         12/1/3
Seaberg, Lillian M.
  L:                           1/1/47
*"Sea-Lion"* [Geoffrey Masten Bennett]
  (SSC)                        7/4/14*
Seaman, Donald
  THE TERROR SYNDICATE
    (M*F)                      1/4/38
SEARCH COMMITTEE, THE
  (McInerny) (TAR)             13/2/43-4
SEASON OF THE MACHETE, THE
  (Patterson) (M*F)            2/4/31
SECOND BLACK LIZARD AN-
  THOLOGY OF CRIME FICTION,
  THE (Gorman, ed.) (IAC)      11/1/32
SECOND DEADLY SIN, THE
  (Sanders) (R)          3/4/43; 5/4/33
SECOND HORSEMAN OUT OF
  EDEN (Chesbro) (TAR)         11/4/76
SECOND INTERNATIONAL CON-
  GRESS OF CRIME WRITERS PIC-
  TURE BOOK, THE (Kimura)
  (MS)                         3/5/2
*Secondary Sources.* Also see
      Bibliography
  Bleeding the Fun Out (Isaac) 7/5/3-6
  The Body in the Library (Wooster)
                               5/1/11-4

Secondary Sources continued
A CATALOGUE OF CRIME
(Barzun/Taylor) (R)    11/4/83
CRIME AND MYSTERY: THE 100
BEST BOOKS (Keating) (IAC)
(R)    10/2/52; 11/1/71
ENCYCLOPEDIA OF FRONTIER
AND WESTERN FICTION
(Tuska/Piekarski, eds.) (IAC)
(R)    8/1/18 & 29
THE ENCYCLOPEDIA OF MYS-
TERY AND DETECTION, (Stein-
brunner/Penzler, eds.) (R)    P/13
THE ENCYCLOPEDIA SHER-
LOCKIANA (Tracey) (IAC) 4/1/15
German Secondary Literature
(Goode)    7/5/7-15
MASTERS OF MYSTERY: A
STUDY OF THE DETECTIVE
STORY (Thomson) (IAC)
(TCITC)    2/6/27; 3/2/3-12,20
'MURDER WILL OUT': THE
DETECTIVE IN FICTION
(Binyon) (R)    12/1/31-3
MYSTERIUM AND MYSTERY:
THE CLERICAL CRIME NOVEL
(Spencer) (R) 12/1/33-5; 13/1/62-6
MYSTERY INDEX: SUBJECTS,
SETTINGS, AND SLEUTHS OF
10,000 TITLES (Olderr) (R) 9/6/41
THE MYSTERY STORY (Ball, ed.)
(R)    1/2/29 & 32
NOVEL VERDICTS: A GUIDE TO
COURTROOM FICTION (Breen)
(IAC)    8/4/30
PRIVATE LIVES OF PRIVATE
EYES, SPIES, CRIME FIGHT-
ERS, AND OTHER GOOD GUYS
(Penzler) (IAC)    2/4/15
A SHOPPING LIST OF MYSTERY
CLASSICS (Granovetter/
McCullum) (IAC)    10/2/56
SNOBBERY WITH VIOLENCE
(Watson) (IAC)    10/2/59
THE SUBJECT IS MURDER, A
SELECTIVE SUBJECT GUIDE
TO MYSTERY FICTION (Men-
endez) (IAC) (R)    8/4/30; 9/1/7
THE SUBJECT IS MURDER: A
SELECTIVE SUBJECT GUIDE
TO MYSTERY FICTION (Men-
endez) (MS) (R) 12/1/3; 12/4/87-91

Secondary Sources continued
TROUBLE IS THEIR BUSINESS:
PRIVATE EYES IN FICTION,
FILM, AND TELEVISION
(Conquest) (MS)    11/4/2
TWENTIETH CENTURY CRIME
AND MYSTERY WRITERS
(Reilly, ed.)
The Body in the Library
(Wooster)    5/1/11-4
TWENTIETH CENTURY CRIME
AND MYSTERY WRITERS,
SECOND EDITION (Reilly, ed.)
(IAC)    8/4/30
WATTEAU'S SHEPHERDS: THE
DETECTIVE NOVEL IN
BRITAIN, 1914–1940 (Panek) (R)
(IAC)    4/3/44; 4/4/18
WHODUNIT? A GUIDE TO
CRIME, SUSPENSE AND SPY
FICTION (Keating, ed.) (R)
(IAC)    7/1/40; 7/2/24
SECOND CURTAIN, THE (Fuller)
(IAC)    13/4/83
SECRET ADVERSARY, THE (Christie)
(IAC)    9/2/29
Secret Agent X-9
The Detective Hero in the Comics
(Blom)    6/1/8-15
SECRET KILLS (Beechcroft) (TAR)
    11/2/64
SECRETS (Bailey) (M*F)    3/3/33
SECRETS OF THE WORLD'S BEST-
SELLING WRITER (Fugate)
(M*F)    5/2/13
SEE YOU AT THE MORGUE
(Blochman) (R)    10/1/76
Seeger, Mary A.
L:    2/6/50; 3/2/57; 5/6/53
Seeton, Miss Emily. See Carvic, Heron
SELECTED LETTERS OF RAY-
MOND CHANDLER (MacShane,
ed.) (IAC)    6/1/32; 10/2/58
SELECTED TALES OF GRIM AND
GRUE FROM THE HORROR
PULPS (Jaffery, ed.) (IAC)    11/1/35
Selmark, George
MURDER IN SILENCE (TBR)
    11/1/48
Selwyn, Francis
SERGEANT VERITY AND THE
BLOOD ROYAL (R)    3/6/48

*Selwyn, Francis,* continued
SERGEANT VERITY AND THE
  SWELL MOB (R)     6/4/29
  L: Breen 4/2/58
*Semi-Dual*
Detection by Other Means
  (Sampson)     7/1/7-17*
SEND ANOTHER HEARSE (Masur)
  (R)     8/4/45
Sennett, Ted
MASTERS OF MENACE: GREEN-
  STREET AND LORRE (R)  7/2/37
SEPARATE CASES (Randisi)
  (TAR)     12/4/53
SEPTEMBER SONG (Mathis)
  (TAR)     13/2/44-5
Seraphine, Kay
  L:     7/4/36
SERGEANT CUFF STANDS FIRM
  (North) (IAC)     2/6/29
SERGEANT RITCHIE'S CON-
  SCIENCE (Branston) (M*F)  3/5/35
SERGEANT VERITY AND THE
  BLOOD ROYAL (Selwyn) (R) 3/6/48
SERGEANT VERITY AND THE
  SWELL MOB (Selwyn) (R)  6/4/29
Serling, Robert J.
THE PRESIDENT'S PLANE IS
  MISSING (IAC)     3/2/22
SERN CHARTER, THE (Wyck)
  (M*F)     P/30
SERVICE OF ALL THE DEAD
  (Dexter) (M*F)     4/3/35
*Seton, Anya*
Obituary (Lachman)     13/1/33
*Seton, Graham*
  (SSC)     7/1/30*
SEVEN DEADLY SISTERS, THE
  (McGerr) (R) (M*F)  2/2/38; 3/5/38
SEVEN DIALS MYSTERY, THE
  (Christie) (R)     6/2/44
SEVEN DREAMERS, THE (St. James)
  (M*F)     6/3/32
SEVEN OF CALVARY, THE (Boucher)
  (R)     5/5/40
SEVEN SEATS TO THE MOON
  (Armstrong) (R)     3/1/39
SEVEN SILENT MEN (Behn)
  (R)     9/1/43
SEVEN SISTERS, THE (Ballard)
  (R)     2/5/39
SEVENTH MOURNER, THE
  (Gardiner) (TBR)     13/4/71-2

*Severance, Dr. Grace.* See Scherf,
  Margaret
Sewart, Alan
THE TURN-UP (R)     5/2/38
Seymour, Gerald
ARCHANGEL (R)     9/2/37
HARRY'S GAME (R)     2/1/44
SHACKLES (Pronzini) (TAR) (IAC)
     11/1/66; 11/2/78; 12/1/25
SHADOW KNOWS, THE (Johnson)
  (R)     7/5/42
SHADOW MAN, THE (Lutz) (R) 5/5/29
SHADOW MAN: THE LIFE OF
  DASHIELL HAMMETT (Layman)
  (M*F)     6/1/32
SHADOW MONEY (Effinger)
  (TAR)     11/1/53
SHADOW OF A BROKEN MAN
  (Chesbro) (R)     2/1/42
SHADOW SCRAPBOOK, THE
  (Gibson) (IAC) (R)  4/1/13; 4/2/51
SHADOWS IN BRONZE (Davis)
  (R)     13/4/101-2
SHADOWS ON THE MIRROR
  (Fyfield) (TAR)     13/3/80-1
*Shafer, Anthony*
  L: Adey 2/3/73
Shaffer, Peter
AMADEUS (IAC)     8/4/33
*Shaginyan, Marietta S.*
Obituary (Lachman)     6/3/26
  L: Shibuk 6/4/47
Shah, Diana K.
THE MACKIN COVER (M*F) 2/2/34
SHAKE HANDS FOREVER (Rendell)
  (R)     3/4/45
SHAKEDOWN (Petievich) (TAR)
     10/4/45
SHAKEDOWN FOR MURDER (Lacy)
  (M*F)     P/27
SHAKEDOWN, THE (Singer)
  (M*F)     1/2/27
*Shakespeare*
  L: Gottschalk 12/2/94-6, 13/1/86,
    13/3/96; Hazen 12/2/101; Phillips
    11/3/101
SHALL WE TELL THE PRESIDENT?
  (Archer) (R)     2/6/36
SHALLOW GRAVE (Scott) (R)
  (M*F)     2/4/45; 3/1/34
SHAMUS (Giles) (R)     2/3/52
*Shandy, Prof. Peter.* See MacLeod,
  Charlotte

Shane, Susannah
DIAMONDS IN THE DUMPLINGS
(M*F)                          3/4/39
SHANGHAI FLAME (Fleischman)
(M*F)                          2/4/30
Shankman, Sarah
IMPERSONAL ATTRACTIONS
(IAC)                          9/3/31
Shannon, Dell [Elizabeth Linington,
q.v.]
MARK OF MURDER (IAC)    8/5/31
SHAPE OF DREAD, THE (Muller)
(R)                            12/1/40
Shapiro, Stanley
A TIME TO REMEMBER
(IAC)                          11/1/26
*Shard, Simon.* See McCutchan, Philip
SHARDS (Bannister) (TAR)  13/1/49-50
SHARP PRACTICE (Farris) (R)  8/3/42
Sharpe, Howard W.
L: 2/1/52; 4/1/42; 7/2/40; 7/6/43;
8/5/42
*Shaw, Captain Joseph T.*
Captain Joseph T. Shaw's Black
Mask Scrapbook (Hagemann)
7/1/2-6
*Shaw, Commander Esmonde.* See
McCutchan, Philip
Shaw, Howard
DEATH OF A DON (M*F)     6/1/38
Shay, Frank
THE CHARMING MURDER
(R)                            9/6/45
*Shea, Douglas G.*
Obituary (Lachman)       13/4/91
Sheldon, Richard
POOR PRISONER'S DEFENSE
(TBR)                          12/3/74-5
Sheldon, Sidney
THE NAKED FACE (R)       1/3/47
SHE'LL HATE ME TOMORROW
(Deming) (M*F)                P/28
SHERBOURNE'S FOLLY (Barry)
(M*F)                          3/3/39
SHERIFF OF BOMBAY, THE
(Keating) (R)                 8/3/37
SHERLOCK HOLMES: MY LIFE AND
CRIMES (Hardwick) (IAC)   8/4/30
SHERLOCK HOLMES: THE PUB-
LISHED APOCRYPHA BY SIR
ARTHUR CONAN DOYLE AND
ASSOCIATED HANDS (Tracy,
ed.)
The Apocryphalization of Holmes
(Bleiler)                     4/5/3-5

*Sherlockon II* (MS)            9/1/6
Sherwood, John
THE MANTRAP GARDEN
(R)                            9/6/36
Shibuk, Charles
L: 1/2/50; 1/4/56; 2/2/55; 3/4/56;
4/5/44; 4/6/43; 5/1/30; 5/6/52;
6/1/49; 6/3/44; 6/4/47; 7/1/50;
9/1/47; 9/3/46; 9/4/49; 9/5/47;
10/1/90; 10/2/83; 11/3/85;
12/4/102-3; 13/1/85
Raymond Chandler on Film:
Addendum                      2/4/14
Reviews:
THE AGATHA CHRISTIE MYS-
TERY (Murdoch)            1/2/4
COLD BLOOD (Bruce)        1/1/34
THE CORPSE THAT WALKED
(Cohen)                   1/6/54
THE DISAPPEARANCE OF
ROGER TREMAYNE
(Graeme)                  1/2/41
FILE ON A MISSING REDHEAD
(Cameron)                 3/1/40
THE GIRL'S HEAD (Jepson)
1/3/43
LET X BE THE MURDERER
(Witting)                 2/4/43
A MATTER OF NERVES
(Hull)                    2/4/42
MR. DASS (Atkey)          2/5/37
MURDER IN THE GILDED
CAGE (Spewack)            1/5/48
THE NARROWING CIRCLE
(Hill)                    2/5/38
THE SEVEN DEADLY SISTERS
(McGerr)                  2/2/38
TOO GOOD TO BE TRUE
(Hutton)                  2/1/47
THE TRAIL OF FEAR
(Armstrong)               1/4/53
Shine, Jean & Walter
L:          5/6/51; 6/3/47; 8/1/42
SHIP THAT NEVER WAS, THE
(Spillane) (R)                8/1/28
Shirreffs, Gordon R.
THE MARAUDERS (M*F)       1/3/41
SHOOT THE WORKS (Ellington)
(R)                            7/6/31
SHOOTING SCRIPT (Lyall)
(IAC)                          3/2/23
SHOPPING LIST OF MYSTERY
CLASSICS, A (Granovetter/
McCullum) (IAC)               10/2/56

Shore, Viola Brothers
  THE BEAUTY–MASK MURDER
    (TBR)             11/4/70
SHORT CIRCUIT (Oriol) (R)    5/5/39
SHORT SHRIFT (Long) (TBR)
                       12/3/72-3
Short Stories. Also see Magazines
  The Best of 1986 (Lachman) 9/3/32-3
  Best Short Stories of 1987
    (Lachman)          10/3/43-4
  The Best Short Stories of 1989
    (Lachman)          12/2/72-4
  The Best Short Stories of 1991
    (Lachman)          13/4/45-7
  Detective Story Magazine (IAC)
                       11/1/30
  Ellery Queen, Sports Fan
    (Christopher)       10/3/3-24
  Encore! (McSherry)    12/1/9-22
  Hardboiled (IAC)       11/1/31
  (IAC)    3/3/18; 4/1/14-5; 4/3/33;
        7/4/21-2; 8/1/19; 12/2/64-9
  Lachman's Top Ten for 1988
    (Lachman)       11/1/29-30
  Notes on Recent Reading
    (Lachman)       11/1/29-36
  Rings of Death (Sampson) 10/1/3-16
  The Short Sheet (MS)     9/1/3-4
  The Short Stop (Lachman) 13/4/45-52
  The Social World in Dr. Gideon
    Fell's Shorter Cases (Christopher)
                      13/3/3-22
  Special Report—Fiction (magazine)
    (IAC)             11/1/31
  Three "Unknown" Stories by Dorothy
    L. Sayers (Christopher)  11/1/15
  L: Adey 3/5/47
SHOTGUN SATURDAY NIGHT
  (Crider) (IAC) (R)  10/1/63; 10/2/72
SHROUD FOR A NIGHTINGALE
  (James) (M*F)          P/24
SHUDDER PULPS, THE (Jones)
  (IAC)              3/4/23
SHUDDERS, THE (Abbot) (R)  9/5/38
Shulman, Milton
  KILL 3 (R)          7/4/34
Shute, Nevil
  NO HIGHWAY (R)      7/2/35
Schutz, Ben (MS)        9/1/7
SIDE EFFECTS (Allen) (IAC)  6/3/23
Siegel, Benjamin
  Obituary (Lachman)    13/3/71

Siegel, Donald
  Obituary (Lachman)    13/3/72-3
SILENCE AFTER DINNER (Witting)
  (TBR)             12/3/72
SILENT PARTNER (Kellerman)
  (R)              12/1/43
SILENT THUNDER (Estleman)
  (TAR)            11/4/79
SILENT WORLD OF NICHOLAS
  QUINN, THE (Dexter) (M*F) 2/2/34
Silk, Dorian. See Harvester, Simon
SILKY! (Rosten) (IAC)      4/5/25
Siller, Van
  THE MOOD FOR MURDER
    (TBR)           12/3/73
SILVER ARROW MURDER, THE
  (TBR)          13/3/58-9
SILVER CASTLE, THE (Quest)
  (M*F)           3/3/36
SILVER FALCON, THE (Anthony)
  (R)              2/6/42
SILVER GHOST, THE (MacLeod)
  (TAR)      11/1/63; 11/2/75
SILVER PIGS (Davis) (R)
              12/1/40-1; 12/4/83-4
  L: Gottschalk 13/1/86
Silverman, Robert
  THE CUMBERLAND DECISION
    (M*F)          2/3/47
Simenon, Georges
  INTIMATE MEMOIRS (R)    8/3/33
  (IAC)           10/4/52
  JUSTICE (R)        8/4/43
  THE LODGER (IAC)     8/1/20
  MADAME MAIGRET'S RECIPES
    (Courtine) (IAC)    10/4/52
  MAIGRET & THE BLACK SHEEP
    (R)            1/5/44
  MAIGRET AND THE HOTEL
    MAJESTIC (R)      2/5/40
  THE MYSTERY OF GEORGES
    SIMENON (Bresler) (IAC) 8/2/23
  Obituary (Lachman)    11/3/54
  L: Dillon 2/6/51
Simmel, Johannes Mario
  THE CAESAR CODE (M*F)  1/1/29
Simmons, Geoffrey I.
  THE Z PAPERS (R)      1/6/42
Simon, Njami
  COFFIN & CO. (TNSPE)   10/2/49
Simon, Roger L.
  PEKING DUCK (M*F)    3/6/32
  RAISING THE DEAD (TAR)
                11/1/67; 11/2/78

SIMPLE ACT OF KINDNESS, A
  (Estes) (R)                    2/3/56
Simpson, Dorothy
  DEAD BY MORNING (R) 13/1/57-8
  THE NIGHT SHE DIED (M*F)
    (R)                   5/5/22 & 34
  SIX FEET UNDER (R)         7/5/48
Sims, Dorothy Rice, and Valentine
    Williams
  FOG (TBR)                   11/3/69
Sims, L.V.
  MURDER IS ONLY SKIN DEEP
    (IAC)                     10/1/62
Sinclair, Murray
  GOODBYE, L.A. (TAR)
                     11/1/67; 11/2/79
  ONLY IN L.A. (M*F)          6/6/27
  TOUGH LUCK L.A. (M*F)      5/2/17
Sinclair, Upton
  (SSC)                      7/1/30*
SING A SONG OF HOMICIDE
  (Langham) (TBR)          13/2/68-9
Singer, Norman
  DIAMOND STUD (M*F)         1/2/28
  THE SHAKEDOWN (M*F)        1/2/27
SINGLED OUT (Whitney) (R)
  (M*F)              3/1/42; 3/3/32
Singular Miss Seeton, The
  (Chouteau)                 8/6/7-10
Sinning with Lawrence Sanders
  (Kelley)                   3/5/20-1
SINS OF THE FATHERS, THE (Block)
  (R) (M*F)          1/2/22; 2/4/30
SIR JOHN MAGILL'S LAST
  JOURNEY (Crofts) (R)        P/10
SIRENS SANG OF MURDER, THE
  (Caudwell) (TAR)           12/2/58
SISTERS IN CRIME 4 (Wallace, ed.)
  (R)                        13/4/47
SITTING DUCK, THE (Bagby)
  (M*F)                       6/1/35
SITUATION TRAGEDY (Brett)
  (M*F)                       6/3/35
SIX FEET UNDER (Simpson) (R)7/5/48
Skaaren, Warren
  Obituary (Lachman)         13/1/33
SKELETON IN THE GRASS, THE
  (Barnard) (TAR)            11/1/51
Skene Melvin Bibliography of Critical
    Writing, The (Albert)    5/3/5-10
  L: Briney 5/5/45

Skene Melvin, David and Ann,
    compilers
  CRIME, DETECTIVE, ESPION-
    AGE, MYSTERY, AND THRIL-
    LER FICTION & FILM: A COM-
    PREHENSIVE BIBLIOGRAPHY
    OF CRITICAL WRITING
    THROUGH 1979 (R)         5/2/30
Skinner, Robert E.
  Business Before Everything: The
    Hard-Boiled World of Matt
    Helm               10/1/39-53*
  A Gun-Toting Yankee in King
    Arthur's Court: The Violent World
    of Dempsey and Makepeace
                          8/6/25-6,30
  An Interview with Ed
    McBain                 13/4/3-11
  L:                      13/3/94-5
  Narcotics, Barred Windows, and
    Murder: The Medical Practitioner
    in the Writings of Raymond
    Chandler              11/2/37-46
  NEW HARD-BOILED DICKS
    (MS)                     8/5/22
  Reviews:
    COTTON COMES TO HARLEM
      (Himes)             13/1/68-70
    GRIM REAPER (De Noux)10/3/75
    THE HEAT'S ON (Himes)
                          13/1/68-70
    HEAVEN'S PRISONERS
      (Burke)               10/3/73
    NEON RAIN (Burke)      10/3/73
    NOT AS FAR AS VELMA
      (Freeling)          12/3/103-4
    PEEPER (Estleman)   12/4/99-100
    THE REAL COOL KILLERS
      (Himes)             13/1/68-70
    URGENT HANGMAN
      (Cheyney)          12/4/100-1
    WALKING AFTER MIDNIGHT
      (Nusser)            13/1/67-8
    U.S.S.A. (Madsen)      13/1/70-1
  "Tell It Like It Was": An Interview
    with O'Neill De Noux  13/2/5-17*
  Violence and Gunplay in Crime Fic-
    tion: From the Ridiculous to the
    Horrible                8/2/9-18
SKINWALKERS (Hillerman) (R)
  (IAC)          10/3/66; 12/1/24-5
Sklar, George
  Obituary (Lachman)         10/3/46

Skom, Edith
THE MARK TWAIN MURDERS
   (R)                          11/2/102
SKULDOGGERY (Flora) (R)      9/4/42
SKULL BENEATH THE SKIN, THE
   (James) (R)                   7/3/33
*Skullduggery* (magazine) (MS)    3/5/2
SKYROCKET STEELS (Goulart)
   (IAC)                         4/6/33
SKYSCRAPER MURDER, THE
   (Spewack) (TBR)           12/2/43-4
Skytte, Asbjørn
   The World of Nero Wolfe
                           7/2/11-12, 26
Sladek, John
   BLACK AURA (R) (M*F)
                           3/4/48; 4/2/37
SLAM THE BIG DOOR (MacDonald)
   (IAC)                         9/4/37
SLASHER, THE (Collins) (R)    2/1/42
SLAY THE MURDERER (Holman)
   (M*F) (TBR)           P/24; 11/1/47
SLEEP BEFORE EVENING (Olson)
   (M*F)                         4/2/35
SLEEP LONG, MY LOVE (Waugh)
   (IAC)                        11/4/51
SLEEP NO MORE (Taylor)
   (TBR)                        13/1/40
SLEEP OF DEATH (Morice) (R) 7/2/34
SLEEP WHILE I SING (Wright)
   (R)                          10/1/74
SLEEPERS OF ERIN, THE (Gash)
   (R)                           9/6/39
SLEEPING DOG (Lochte) (IAC) 9/3/30
SLEEPING LIFE, A (Rendell) (R)
   (M*F)              3/2/45 & 46; 3/3/38
SLEEPING MURDERS (Christie)
   (R)                           9/5/33
SLEEPING SPHINX, THE (Carr)
   (M*F)                         2/5/34
Slesar, Henry
   GRAY FLANNEL SHROUD
      (IAC)                      5/6/29
*Sleuth Journal* (magazine) (MS)  10/2/2
SLEUTHING IN THE STACKS
   (Altrocchi) (TCITC)          3/2/12
SLOB (Miller) (R)                9/6/40
SLOW DOWN THE WORLD (Ashford)
   (M*F)                         2/1/28
SLOW GALLOWS, THE (Masterson)
   (IAC)                         4/1/15
SLOWLY THE POISON (Drummond)
   (M*F)                         2/1/29

SLYPE, THE (Thorndike) (TBR) 12/4/71
Small, Austin J.
   THE MASTER MYSTERY (M*F)
      (R)                  3/2/41; 9/6/44
*Small, Rabbi David.* See Kemelman,
   Harry
SMALLBONE DECEASED (Gilbert)
      (IAC)                     11/1/22
   L: Fellows 12/2/91
SMEAR JOB (Mitchell) (M*F)    2/3/44
SMILING CORPSE, THE (Anonymous)
   (R)                           6/2/41
SMILING DEATH, THE (Grierson)
   (TBR)                       13/2/60-1
SMILING, THE BOY FELL DEAD
   (Delving) (R)                 1/6/50
SMILING TIGER, THE (Offord)
   (TBR)                        11/2/86
Smith, A.C.H.
   EXTRA COVER (R)              7/2/39
Smith, Alison
   SOMEONE ELSE'S GRAVE
      (R)                        9/3/40
*Smith, Black John*
   The Saint of the North (Harwood)
                                3/6/3-7*
*Smith, Charles Merrill*
   Clergy-Detectives (Cleary)  9/3/3-21
   REVEREND RANDOLLPH AND
      THE AVENGING ANGEL
      (M*F)                      2/6/30
   REVEREND RANDOLLPH AND
      THE FALL FROM GRACE, INC.
      (M*F)                      3/4/38
   REVEREND RANDOLLPH AND
      THE HOLY TERROR (R)    7/3/38
*Smith, David*
   L: Wilkerson 6/3/48, 6/4/48
*Smith, Denis Nayland.* See Rohmer, Sax
Smith, Evelyn E.
   MISS MELVILLE REGRETS
      (R)                     12/4/78-9
   MISS MELVILLE RETURNS
      (R)                       12/4/77
Smith, Gregory White, and Steven
   Naifeh
   THE MORMON MURDERS
      (R)                      13/2/90-1
Smith, Janet L.
   SEA OF TROUBLES (MS)      12/1/3
*Smith, Junius B.*
   Detection by Other Means
      (Sampson)                7/1/7-17

Smith, Kay Nolte
    COUNTRY OF THE HEART
      (TAR)                 10/4/46
Smith, Laurence Dwight
    FOLLOW THIS FAIR CORPSE
      (TBR)             13/2/61-2
Smith, Louie
    L:                  13/2/102-3
*Smith, Martin Cruz*
    Case in Point: Gorky Park
      (Dove)         6/4/9-11,18
Smith, Myron J., Jr.
    CLOAK-AND-DAGGER BIBLI-
      OGRAPHY: AN ANNOTATED
      GUIDE TO SPY FICTION (R)4/50
Smith, Shelley
    HE DIED OF MURDER!
      (TBR)             12/3/74
*Smith, Terrence Lore*
    Obituary (Lachman)     11/1/37
SMOKESCREEN (Francis) (IAC) 2/6/28
SMUGGLER'S NOTCH (Koenig)
    (TAR)               11/3/72
Smullyan, Raymond
    THE CHESS MYSTERIES OF
      SHERLOCK HOLMES
      (IAC)              4/4/18
SNAKE (McClure) (R)     1/1/35
*Sneary, Rick*
    Obituary (Lachman)    13/1/33
SNIPE HUNT (Dean) (M*F)   3/4/40
SNOBBERY WITH VIOLENCE
    (Watson) (IAC)      10/2/59
Snow, C.P.
    THE AFFAIR (R)       4/6/34
    DEATH UNDER SAIL (IAC)  3/3/49
SO MUCH BLOOD (Brett) (R)  1/5/37
SO THIS IS DEPRAVITY (Baker)
    (IAC)               6/3/23
SOAP OPERA SLAUGHTERS, THE
    (Kaye) (R)         7/4/32
Sobol, Donald J.
    ENCYCLOPEDIA BROWN AND
      THE CASE OF THE MIDNIGHT
      VISITORS (IAC)     4/5/24
Social World in Dr. Gideon Fell's
    Shorter Cases, The (Christopher)
                    13/3/3-22
*Society for Cinema Studies* (MR) 7/3/29
Solomon, Brad
    THE GONE MAN (M*F)   2/2/35
    THE OPEN SHADOW (M*F) 3/6/27
Solving Sixth, The (Sampson)  5/5/3-6

SOME DAY I'LL KILL YOU
    (Chambers) (R)       4/6/34
SOME DIE HARD (Brett) (R)  7/5/39
SOME LIE AND SOME DIE (Rendell)
    (R)                 3/4/44
Some Notes on the Detective Element in
    Western Fiction (Saxon)   P/17
    L: Sorrell 1/1/39
Some Recent Hybrids (Kelley) 6/2/16-8
Some Reminiscences of a Mystery
    Fancier (Fellows)    12/2/11-16
SOME RUN CROOKED (Hilton)
    (M*F)               3/1/34
Some Thoughts on Peacock Feet
    (Bleiler)         6/3/14-21
    L: Adey 7/1/49; Bleiler 7/2/44,
      6/6/45; Lachman 6/4/45, 7/1/49;
      Strom 7/1/48
Some Very Tough People (Sampson)
                    8/5/7-17*
SOMEONE ELSE'S GRAVE (Smith)
    (R)                 9/3/40
SOMETHING TO HIDE (MacDonald)
    (R)               10/1/88
SON OF GUN IN CHEEK (Pronzini)
    (IAC)              10/2/53
SONS OF SAM SPADE (Geherin)
    (IAC)               4/3/32
Soutar, Andrew
    NIGHT OF HORROR (TBR)
                   13/2/65-6
Sorrell, Martha
    L:           1/1/39; 1/5/53
Sorry, John D., But... (Apostolou)
                   11/3/15-8
SORT OF SAMURAI, A (Melville)
    (R)                6/6/34
SOUND OF DETECTION, THE:
    ELLERY QUEEN'S ADVENTURES
    IN RADIO (Nevins/Stanich)
    (R)       7/5/28; 10/2/74
SOUND OF MIDNIGHT, THE (Grant)
    (M*F)             3/3/37
SOUND OF MURDER, THE (Stout)
    (IAC)              7/4/20
SOUR LEMON SCORE, THE (Stark)
    (R)                1/6/51
*South Africa*
    Black and White and Dead
      (Isaac)         6/4/12-8
SOUTH STREET (Belsky) (R) 12/1/42
Southcott, Audley
    CROSS THAT PALM WHEN I
      COME TO IT (R)     5/2/38

Spade, Sam. See Hammett, Dashiell
Spade Trumps Unplayed (Banks) 8/6/3-6
   L: Shibuk 9/1/47
Spain, John
   DEATH IS LIKE THAT (R)      2/4/44
Spain, Nancy
   DEATH GOES ON SKIS
   (M*F)                      1/6/40
SPANKING GIRLS, THE (Brown)
   (R)                       11/4/92
SPEAK FOR THE DEAD (Burns)
   (M*F)                      3/1/34
SPEAK FOR THE DEAD (Yorke)
   (TAR)           11/1/69; 11/2/81
Speaking with Myself (Barton) 5/4/13-7
Special Report—Fiction (magazine)
   (IAC)                     11/1/31
Special Review Article: The Complete
   Uncle Abner (Wooster)      2/5/9-12
SPECIALTY OF THE HOUSE AND
   OTHER STORIES, THE (Ellin)
   (R)                        4/5/42
SPENCE AND THE HOLIDAY
   MURDERS (Allen) (M*F)      3/3/34
SPENCE AT THE BLUE BAZAAR
   (Allen) (M*F)              3/6/37
SPENCE IN PETAL PARK (Allen)
   (R)                        7/5/40
Spencer, William David
   MYSTERIUM AND MYSTERY:
   THE CLERICAL CRIME NOVEL
   (R)            12/1/33-5; 13/1/62-6
Spewack, Bella
   Obituary (Lachman)         12/2/71-2
   L: Shibuk 12/4/103
Spewack, Samuel
   MURDER IN THE GILDED CAGE
   (R)                        1/5/48
   THE SKYSCRAPER MURDER
   (TBR)                      12/2/43-4
SPHINX (Cook) (R)            3/6/46
SPIDER-ORCHID, THE (Fremlin)
   (M*F)                      2/6/30
Spiderweb (MS)               6/3/3
Spies. Also see Spy Series Characters
   CLOAK-AND-DAGGER BIBLI-
   OGRAPHY: AN ANNOTATED
   GUIDE TO SPY FICTION (Smith)
   (R)                        1/4/50
   THE WHOLE SPY CATALOGUE
   (Knudson) (R)              9/2/33
   WHODUNIT? A GUIDE TO
   CRIME, SUSPENSE AND SPY
   FICTION (Keating, ed.) (R)
   (IAC)            7/1/40; 7/2/24

Spillane, Mickey
   THE KILLING MAN (R) (audio)
                    12/3/91-2, 92 & 93
   Mickey Spillane's Mike Hammer
   (Banks)                    8/4/17-20
   MY GUN IS QUICK (M*F)      P/28
   THE SHIP THAT NEVER WAS
   (R)                        8/1/28
   Spillane's Hammer (Blom) 12/3/35-43
   The Tiger Mann Series (Banks)
                              2/3/32-3*
   THE TWISTED THING (R)      3/1/38
   The Violent World of Mike Hammer
   (Traylor)                  7/6/13-20
Spillane's Hammer (Blom)     12/3/35-43
SPINSTER'S SECRET, THE (Gilbert)
   (R)                        5/2/33
Spirit, The
   The Detective Hero in the Comics
   (Blom)                     6/1/8-15
SPLIT ON RED (Hughes) (M*F) 5/6/33
Sports
   Ellery Queen, Sports Fan
   (Christopher)              10/3/3-24
Spoto, Donald
   THE DARK SIDE OF GENIUS:
   THE LIFE OF ALFRED HITCH-
   COCK (R) (IAC)    7/2/31; 7/5/27
SPQR II: THE CATALINE CON-
   SPIRACY (Roberts) (TAR)    13/2/48
Sprenkle, Viola Alice
   L:                         2/6/60
Sprigg, C. St. John
   DEATH OF AN AIRMAN
   (TBR)                      12/3/79-80
SPLIT SECOND, THE (Meek)
   (R)                        13/4/99-100
SPY AND DIE (Meyers) (M*F)  1/2/24
SPY HOOK (Deighton) (TAR)
   (R)           11/4/78; 12/3/89-90
SPY LINE (Deighton) (TAR)
   (R)           12/2/60-1; 12/3/90-1
Spy Series Characters in Hardback (Van
   Tilburg): Part I 4/2/11-13*; Part II
   4/3/23-8*; Part III 4/4/16-7*; Part IV
   4/5/21-3*; Part V 4/6/4-6*; Part VI
   5/1/2*; Part VII 5/2/2*; Part VIII
   5/3/18-21*; Part IX 5/5/15-6*; Part X
   6/1/7,15*; Part XI 6/2/19-20*; Part
   XII 6/3/5,26*; Part XIII 7/1/30-1*;
   Part XIV 7/4/10-4*

Spy Series Characters in Hardback (Van
  Tilburg) continued
  L: Adey 5/1/31; Briney 5/2/42; Deeck
  7/6/43; Doerrer 6/1/46; Nieminski
  4/6/40; Sharpe 7/2/42; Shibuk
  4/6/44; Van Tilburg 6/1/50, 6/2/50,
  6/3/47, 8/1/44
SPY SINKER (Deighton) (TAR) 13/3/77
SS-GB (Deighton) (R)                3/4/50
St. James, Bernard
  THE SEVEN DREAMERS
  (M*F)                             6/3/32
St. John, David. See Hunt, E. Howard
STAB IN THE DARK, A (Block)
  (R)                               7/4/33
Stagge, Jonathan
  DEATH, MY DARLING
  DAUGHTERS (M*F)                   2/4/32
STALKING-HORSE (Delahaye)
  (TAR)                            11/1/53
STALKING THE ANGEL (Crais)
  (R)                              12/1/44
Stanich, Ray, and Francis M. Nevins,
  Jr.
  THE SOUND OF DETECTION:
  ELLERY QUEEN'S ADVEN-
  TURES IN RADIO (IAC)
  (R)                     7/5/28; 10/2/74
Stanley, Hagar. See Hume, Fergus
STAR LIGHT, STAR BRIGHT (Ellin)
  (M*F)                             4/3/38
STAR TRAP (Brett) (M*F)            2/5/27
Stark, Richard [Donald E. Westlake,
  q.v.]
  The Morals of Parker (McSherry)
                                   8/2/2-8
  THE SOUR LEMON SCORE
  (R)                               1/6/51
  L: Doerrer 2/4/50*; Meyerson 2/5/54
Starr, Jimmy
  Obituary (Lachman)              12/4/48
Starrett, Vincent
  (IAC)                             5/5/17
  Vincent Starrett vs. Arthur Machen
  (Bleiler)                       3/6/11-4
STATE DEPARTMENT CAT (Plum)
  (TBR)                           11/4/61
STATE DEPARTMENT MURDERS
  (Ronns) (R)                       2/1/48
STATE'S EVIDENCE (Greenleaf)
  (M*F)                             6/6/30
STEALING LILLIAN (Kenrick)
  (R)                               2/1/45

Steeger, Henry
  Obituary (Lachman)              13/1/34
STEEL PALACE, THE (Pentecost)
  (M*F)                             3/1/32
Steeves, Harrison
  GOOD NIGHT, SHERIFF
  (TBR)                           11/1/46
  Obituary (Lachman)               6/1/29
Stein, Aaron Marc
  THE CASE OF THE ABSENT-
  MINDED PROFESSOR
  (TBR)                         13/3/54-5
  COFFIN COUNTRY (M*F)             1/6/39
  DAYS OF MISFORTUNE (R)  1/6/52
  DEATH MEETS 400 RABBITS
  (M*F)                             5/1/27
  HANGMAN'S ROW (M*F)              6/3/32
  ONE DIP DEAD (M*F)               3/6/35
  THE ROLLING HEADS
  (M*F)                             3/6/28
  L: Meyerson 1/2/48; Nevins 1/2/48
Steinbrunner, Chris
  THE ENCYCLOPEDIA OF MYS-
  TERY AND DETECTION (w/
  Penzler, ed.) (R)                  P/13
  THE FILMS OF SHERLOCK
  HOLMES (w/Michaels) (R)  3/3/43
STEP IN THE DARK (Lemarchand)
  (M*F)                             2/1/23
Stephan, Leslie
  MURDER R.F.D. (M*F)              2/5/27
Stephens, Reed
  THE MAN WHO KILLED HIS
  BROTHER (M*F)                     5/2/17
STEPS TO MURDER, THE (King)
  (TBR)                           11/2/83
Sterling, Claire
  THE TIME OF THE ASSASSINS
  (IAC)                             8/2/24
Sterling, Stewart
  WHERE THERE'S SMOKE
  (R)                               9/2/40
Sterling, Thomas
  EVIL OF THE DAY (IAC)            5/6/30
Stevenson, Burton E.
  THE HOUSE NEXT DOOR
  (TBR)                           10/2/68
Stevenson, Richard
  DEATH TRICK (IAC)                9/1/33
Stevenson, Traill
  THE SILVER ARROW MURDER
  (TBR)                         13/3/58-9

Stewart, Enola
  L: 3/3/50
Stewart, Gary
  THE TENTH VIRGIN (R) 8/3/38
*Stewart, Mary*
  A Query and a Note (Gotts-
    chalk) 12/4/35-8
STIFF UPPER LIP, THE (Israel) (R)
  (M*F) 3/2/49; 3/4/38
STILL MISSING (Gutcheon) (R) 7/5/48
Stilwell, Stephen A.
  THE ARMCHAIR DETECTIVE
    INDEX (VOLUMES 1-10, 1967-
    1977) (MS) 4/3/1
  L: 2/2/50; 2/3/58; 5/4/41; 7/1/45;
    11/1/81; 11/3/99
  Mysteriously Speaking...
    8/1/1-2; 8/2/1; 8/3/1
  Review: WHAT ABOUT MURDER?
    (Breen) 5/4/28
STING OF THE BEE (Worrell)
  (R) 7/5/40
STING OF THE HONEYBEE (Parrish)
  (M*F) 4/2/31
*Stone, Grace Zaring*
  Obituary (Lachman) 13/4/91
*Stoppard, Tom*
  Joe Orton's and Tom Stoppard's Bur-
    lesques (Bargainnier) 7/1/18-22
STORM WARNING (Higgins)
  (R) 1/2/40
Story, William L.
  CEMETERIES ARE FOR DYING
    (R) 7/5/47
*Stout, Rex*
  BAD FOR BUSINESS (TBR)
    12/2/48-9
  BLACK ORCHIDS (IAC) 6/3/25
  THE BROKEN VASE (IAC) 6/3/25
  THE BROWNSTONE HOUSE OF
    NERO WOLFE (Darby) (R) 7/6/32
  THE DOORBELL RANG
    (R) 13/2/77-8
  Here Comes the Judge: The "Nero"
    Award (Crider) 3/6/8
  (IAC) 5/3/22-6
  JUSTICE ENDS AT HOME, AND
    OTHER STORIES (McAleer, ed.)
    (R) 3/5/43
  THE LEAGUE OF FRIGHTENED
    MEN (IAC) 7/1/33
  Nero Wolfe on TV: A Review
    (IAC) 5/1/18

*Stout, Rex,* continued
  The Nero Wolfe Saga (Townsend) –
    Part I 1/3/13-36; Part II 1/4/25-36;
    Part III 1/5/21-8; Part IV
    1/6/15-28; Part V 2/1/15-19; Part
    VI 2/2/25-32; Part VII 2/3/34-40;
    Part VIII 2/4/19-29; Part IX
    2/5/13-21; Part X 2/6/20-6; Part XI
    3/1/21-5; Part XII 3/2/13-20; Part
    XIII 3/3/22-30; Part XIV
    3/4/25-37; Part XV 3/5/22-34; Part
    XVI 3/6/15-26; Part XVII
    4/1/17-28; Part XVIII 4/2/14-30;
    Part XIX 4/3/3-21
  PLOT IT YOURSELF (M*F) P/23
  President Nero Wolfe (Lachman)
    5/3/22-6
  THE RED BOX (IAC) 6/3/25
  REX STOUT: A BIOGRAPHY (Mc-
    Aleer) (MS) (IAC)2/2/64; 2/4/16
  REX STOUT: AN ANNOTATED
    PRIMARY AND SECONDARY
    BIBLIOGRAPHY (Townsend/
    McAleer/Sapp/Schemer) (R) 5/2/29
  THE RUBBER BAND (IAC) 6/3/25
  THE SOUND OF MURDER
    (IAC) 7/4/20
  Wolfe a Howler! (Napier) 5/5/7-10
  The World of Nero Wolfe
    (Skytte) 7/2/11-12,26
  L: Breen 3/1/47, 5/2/46; Crider
    5/1/36; Doran 2/5/48, 3/4/54;
    Floyd 3/4/59, 5/6/49; Frazier
    1/6/55, 2/1/59; Gagnon 6/1/50;
    Jaysnovitch 6/1/47; Juri 1/5/53;
    Larsen 6/1/50; MacDonald 5/2/39;
    Nevins 3/5/46, 5/1/44; Toole
    5/2/50, 6/1/48, 6/4/49, 6/6/44,
    7/2/45, 9/1/46; Townsend comment
    5/2/39, 9/1/46
Strahan, Kay Cleaver
  DEATH TRAPS (TBR) 13/1/37-8
STRAIGHT (Francis) (MS) 12/1/4
STRAIGHT (Knickmeyer) (R)
  (M*F) 1/2/16 & 27
  L: French 1/6/58
STRANGE BEDFELLOWS (Burkholz)
  (TAR) 11/1/52
STRANGE CODE OF JUSTICE, A
  (Isely) (IAC) 11/3/45
Strange, John Stephen
  THE STRANGLER FIG (IAC)
    11/1/25

STRANGE MURDERS AT GREY-
STONES (Wright) (TBR)    11/2/87
STRANGE PLACE FOR MURDER, A
(Barroll) (M*F)    3/6/34
STRANGLER FIG, THE (Strange)
(IAC)    11/1/25
Stratton-Porter, Gene
Mistress of the Mini-Mystery
(Bakerman)    3/1/3-9
STRAWBERRY-BLONDE JUNGLE,
THE (Brown) (M*F)    3/6/35
STREETS OF FIRE (Cook) (TAR)
12/2/60
Strich, Christian, and Claudia
Schmolders, eds.
UBER SIMENON [ON SIMENON]
(R)    7/4/30
Striker, Randy
KEY WEST CONNECTION
(M*F)    5/3/27
STRIPPER, THE (Brown) (M*F) 1/5/34
Strøm, Ola
Abandoned Queens and Some Notes
on Unintentional Plagiarism
9/1/10-6
Crystal-Ball Stories    12/3/47-52
The Exit of Father Brown    13/4/42-4
Hammett Revisited: Or, The In-
scrutable Investigator    12/2/29-31
L:    7/1/48; 9/5/49; 12/2/99-100
Strong, Bill
L:    6/6/47
Strong, Harrington
WHO KILLED WILLIAM DREW
(IAC)    4/6/33
Strong, L.A.G.
ALL FALL DOWN (TCITC)    3/4/18
Struhsaker, Virginia L.
L:    7/2/42
Stuart, Anthony
Vladimir Gull (Dukeshire)    4/3/22
Stuart, Ian
MASTER PLAN (R)    12/4/56-7
L: Reilly 5/2/45
STUD GAME (Anthony) (R)
(M*F)    2/6/42; 3/3/35
"Study in Black, A" (McSherry)
L: McSherry 2/101-2
Study in Invisibility, A
(McSherry)    11/3/23-43
L: Adey 13/1/78-9
STUDY IN SCARLET, A (movie)
L: Bleiler 6/2/49

STUDY IN TERROR, A (Queen)
(R)    2/3/56
Stylometry
His Own Desert (Bleiler)    3/4/11,15
SUBJECT IS MURDER, THE: A
SELECTIVE SUBJECT GUIDE TO
MYSTERY FICTION (Menendez)
(IAC) (R)    8/4/30; 9/1/7
SUBJECT IS MURDER, THE: A
SELECTIVE SUBJECT GUIDE TO
MYSTERY FICTION (Menendez)
(MS) (R)    12/1/3; 12/4/87-91
SUCH STUFF AS SCREAMS ARE
MADE OF (Bloch) (R)    3/3/44
SUDDENLY WHILE GARDENING
(Lemarchand) (R) (M*F)
3/4/48; 3/6/27
SUICIDE HILL (Ellroy) (R)    9/2/42
SUICIDE SEAT (Carter) (M*F)    4/5/32
SUIT OF DIAMONDS, A (R)    13/4/49
SUITABLE VENGEANCE, A (George)
(TAR)    13/3/81
Sullivan, Eleanor
11 DEADLY SINS (ed.) (IAC)12/2/64
Obituary (Lachman)    13/3/71-2
SUMMER FIRES (Reiss) (R)    6/3/42
L: Goode 6/6/41; Lachman 6/4/46
SUNDAY PIGEON MURDERS, THE
(Rice) (R)    2/5/43
SUNK WITHOUT A TRACE (Devine)
(M*F)    4/2/31
Sunshine and Shadow in THE
MYSTERY OF EDWIN DROOD
(Fisher)    11/4/11-28
Supernatural
Detection by Other Means
(Sampson)    7/1/7-17
L: Adey 7/2/43; Deeck 10/1/98,
10/2/79; Townsend comment
10/1/99, 10/2/80
Suspense Novels of Bill Pronzini, The
(Kelley)    1/2/15-16
SUSPICIONS (Betcherman) (M*F)
4/4/38
Suyker, Betty
DEATH SCENE (R)    6/5/50
SWAN DIVE (Healy) (R) (TAR)
10/4/56; 11/1/54
Swan, Phyllis
FIND SHERRI! (M*F)    4/3/36
Sweden
The Crime Story in Sweden (Blom)
7/5/16-25

Sweden continued
  The History and Activities of Mystery
    Fans in Sweden (and Scandinavia)
    (Hedman)                    3/4/12,15
  Sweden's Commitment to Mystery
    Fiction (Bleiler)            2/5/7-8
Sweden's Commitment to Mystery
  Fiction (Bleiler)              2/5/7-8
SWEET DEATH, KIND DEATH
  (Cross) (R)                    8/2/37
SWEET REVENGE (Racina)
  (M*F)                          2/4/30
SWIFT TO ITS CLOSE (Troy)
  (IAC)                          6/4/30
SWING LOW, SWING DEAD (Gruber)
  (R)                            6/2/46
SWING, SWING TOGETHER
  (Lovesey) (M*F)                1/1/27
Swinnerton, Frank
  Obituary (Lachman)             7/1/35
SWITCH, THE (Leonard) (M*F)  3/3/35
Symons, Julian. Also see AGATHA
    CHRISTIE: THE ART OF HER
    CRIMES
  THE BLACKHEATH POISONINGS
    (M*F)                        3/5/37
  BLAND BEGINNING (IAC)      9/4/37
  THE BROKEN PENNY (IAC)
                                10/3/41
  CONAN DOYLE, PORTRAIT OF
    AN ARTIST (IAC)          10/2/56
  GREAT DETECTIVES (R)         6/3/41
  THE MAN WHO LOST HIS WIFE
    (R)                          2/1/43
  THE 31ST OF FEBRUARY
    (IAC)                        9/4/37
  A THREE-PIPE PROBLEM
    (R)                          1/3/48

# T

TAINTED JADE, THE (Blaine)
  (R)                          13/1/55-6
TAKE A STEP TO MURDER (Keene)
  (M*F)                          P/26
TAKE THE D TRAIN (King)
  (TAR)                        12/3/84
Talbot, Hake
  RIM OF THE PIT (R)           1/5/49
TALENT FOR DESTRUCTION, A
  (Radley) (R)                  6/4/41
TALENT TO DECEIVE, A (Barnard)
  (IAC)              4/6/31; 10/2/57

Tales As Like As Not (magazine)
  L: Banks 8/3/47
TALK SHOW MURDERS, THE (Allen)
  (M*F)                         6/3/30
TALL DARK MAN, THE
  (Chamberlain) (IAC)           8/4/31
TAMING A SEA-HORSE (Parker)
  (R)                           8/4/37
Tanenbaum, Barry, and Linda J.
    LaRosa
  THE RANDOM FACTOR (M*F)
                                3/1/33
TANGENT FACTOR, THE (Sanders)
  (M*F)                         2/5/30
TANNAHILL TANGLE, THE (Wells)
  (TCITC)                       3/2/12
Tannen, Jack
  Obituary (Lachman)          13/4/91
TANTALIZING LOCKED ROOM
    STORIES (Asimov/Waugh/Green-
    berg, eds.) (R)             7/2/33
Tapply, William G.
  CLIENT PRIVILEGE (TAR)     12/4/57
  DEAD WINTER (R)            11/4/95
  DEATH AT CHARITY'S POINT
    (R)                         8/3/36
TARGET OF OPPORTUNITY (Byrd)
  (TAR)                        11/2/65
TARTAN SELL, THE (Gash)
  (R)                           8/6/45
Taschdigian, Claire
  THE PEKING MAN IS MISSING
    (M*F)                       2/2/33
TASTE OF DEATH (McGrew)
  (TBR)                        12/3/70
TASTE OF FEAR, THE (Lamb, ed.)
  (M*F)                         2/1/28
TAURUS TRAP, THE (Dewey)
  (M*F)                         P/24
Taylor, Andrew
  FREELANCE DEATH (TAR)
                      11/1/67; 11/2/79
Taylor, Dwight
  Obituary (Lachman)           9/3/34
Taylor, John Russell
  HITCH: THE LIFE AND TIMES OF
    ALFRED HITCHCOCK (R) 4/2/52
Taylor, Mary Ann
  RED IS FOR SHROUDS
    (M*F)                       5/4/21
Taylor, Phoebe Atwood. Also see
    Dana, Freeman; Tilton, Alice
  Little Old Ladies (Nehr)     3/4/3-7
  Little Old Men (Nehr)        4/4/2-6

Taylor, Sam S.
   SLEEP NO MORE (TBR)   13/1/40
Taylor, Wendell Hertig, and Jacques
   Barzun
   A CATALOGUE OF CRIME
   (R)   11/4/83
Tedeschi, Frank
   Clergy-Detectives (Cleary)   9/3/3-21
Teilhet, Darwin
   HERO BY PROXY (R)   5/3/40
Television. Also see Mystery Mosts
   "The Arsenal Stadium Mystery"
   (IAC)   8/2/25
   Doom with a View (Lachman)
   12/1/26; 13/4/86-7
   A Gun-Toting Yankee in King
   Arthur's Court (Skinner)   8/6/25-6
   (IAC)   7/4/22-3
   Mickey Spillane's Mike Hammer
   (Banks)   8/4/17-20
   "Mike Hammer" (IAC)   8/2/24
   Nero Wolfe on TV: A Review
   (IAC)   5/1/18
   "A Talent for Murder" (IAC) 8/2/24-5
   TNT Cable Channel (RM)   12/2/75-6
   TROUBLE IS THEIR BUSINESS:
   PRIVATE EYES IN FICTION,
   FILM, AND TELEVISION
   (Conquest) (MS)   11/4/2
   TV DETECTIVES (Meyers)
   (IAC)   6/4/322
   Two from the Telly (Adey)
   5/6/19-20, 32
   Wolfe a Howler! (Napier)   5/5/7-10
   L: Adey 2/4/57, 4/3/49, 5/1/33,
   5/4/44, 9/1/47; Banks 12/2/85-6;
   Breen 5/2/46; Crider 5/1/36,
   5/2/41; MacDonald 5/2/39; Nevins
   5/1/44; Toole 5/2/50; Townsend
   comment 5/2/39
"Tell It Like It Was": An Interview with
   O'Neill De Noux (Skinner)13/2/5-17*
TELL YOU WHAT I'LL DO (Cecil)
   (R)   5/5/38
Telushkin, Joseph
   Clergy-Detectives (Cleary)   9/3/3-21
Temple-Ellis, N.A.
   THE MAN WHO WAS THERE
   (TBR)   11/4/70
TEN DAYS, MISTER CAIN? (Free-
   born) (M*F)   2/6/32
TEN PLUS ONE (McBain) (R)   1/4/47

TENANT FOR DEATH (Hare)
   (IAC)   5/5/18
Tension and Duality: Daphne du
   Maurier's "Don't Look Now"
   (Bakerman)   3/4/8-10
TENTH COMMANDMENT, THE
   (Sanders) (R) (IAC)   4/5/39; 9/2/39
TENTH VIRGIN, THE (Stewart)
   (R)   8/3/38
TERMINAL CONNECTION, THE
   (Moore) (R)   1/5/41
Terrall, Robert
   SAND DOLLARS (M*F)   3/3/34
Terrell, Timothy. See Maddock, Stephen
TERRIBLE PLACE TO DIE, A
   (Scaduto) (M*F)   3/1/35
TERROR AT COMPASS LAKE
   (Davis) (TBR)   12/4/66-7
TERROR SYNDICATE, THE (Seaman)
   (M*F)   1/4/38
TERRORIZERS, THE (Hamilton)
   (R)   1/6/48
TEXAS WIND (Reasoner) (R)
   (M*F)   4/6/38; 5/5/26
Tey, Josephine
   THE DAUGHTER OF TIME
   (IAC)   8/6/35
   (IAC)   10/4/50
   Little Old Ladies (Nehr)   3/4/3-7
   L: Hatch 10/1/94; Phillips 10/3/78;
   Townsend comment 10/3/79
   That Pawn-Shop Gypsy (Sampson)
   8/4/9-16
THEFTS OF NICK VELVET, THE
   (Hoch) (R)   2/6/39; 3/1/44
THEN CAME VIOLENCE (Ball) (M*F)
   (R)   4/3/39; 4/5/37
THERE ARE NO GHOSTS IN THE
   SOVIET UNION (Hill) (IAC) (R)
   11/1/31; 12/2/68-9l; 13/2/80-1
THERE HANGS THE KNIFE (Muller)
   (TAR)   11/1/65; 11/2/76
THERE'S SOMETHING IN A
   SUNDAY (Muller) (R)   13/4/97-8
THETA SYNDROME, THE (Trevor)
   (R)   2/1/34
THEY FOUND HIM DEAD (Heyer)
   (R)   1/6/42
THEY HUNTED A FOX (Campbell)
   (TBR)   11/4/60
THEY TALKED OF POISON (Ever-
   may) (TBR)   11/1/42

THIEF OF TIME, A (Hillerman)
  (R)             10/3/65
*Thieftaker Journals, The* (magazine)
  (Bishop, ed.) (MS)     7/3/5
Thielen, Bernard
  A CHARM OF FINCHES (TBR)
              12/3/78
THINK FAST, MR. PETERS
  (Kaminsky) (TNSPE) (TAR)
     10/2/51; 11/1/61; 11/2/73
THIRD LADY, THE (Natsuki)
  (R)          11/2/103
THIRTEEN CRIMES OF SCIENCE
  FICTION, THE (Asimov/Greenberg/
  Waugh, eds.) (R)     4/3/45
13 HORRORS OF HALLOWEEN, THE
  (Asimov/Greenberg/Waugh, eds.)
  (R)           8/1/17
13TH DIRECTORATE, THE (Chubin)
  (TAR)         11/2/65
30 FOR A HARRY (Hoyt) (M*F) 6/1/36
31ST OF FEBRUARY, THE (Symons)
  (IAC)         9/4/37
THIRTY-NINE STEPS, THE (Buchan)
  (R)          2/6/37
  L: Cox 3/1/54
THIS BLESSED PLOT (Meek)
  (TAR)         13/2/45
THIS DOWNHILL PATH (Clarke)
  (R)          5/5/33
THIS GUN FOR GLORIA (Mara)
  (M*F)         P/23
THOMAS BERRYMAN NUMBER,
  THE (Patterson) (M*F)   1/5/33
Thomas Chastain and the New Police
  Procedural (French)   2/4/17-8
Thomas, Craig
  WOLFSBANE (R)     3/4/49
Thomas, Dylan, and John Davenport
  THE DEATH OF THE KING'S
    CANARY (TBR)   12/2/44-5
Thomas, Jim
  CROSS PURPOSES (R)   2/6/41
Thomas, Leslie
  DANGEROUS DAVIES, THE LAST
    DETECTIVE (IAC)   6/6/20
Thomas, Murray
  BUZZARDS PICK THE BONES
    (TBR)        13/1/43
Thomas Polsky's Curtains Trilogy
  (Deeck)      12/4/21-33*
Thomas, Ross. Also see Bleeck, Oliver
  THE COLD WAR SWAP
    IAC)        10/3/39

*Thomas, Ross,* continued
  THE MORDIDA MAN (M*F)
    (R)     5/6/34; 8/2/31
Thompson, Estelle
  FIND A CROOKED SIXPENCE
    (M*F)       2/5/26
  HUNTER IN THE DARK
    (M*F)       3/6/28
Thompson, Gene
  A CUP OF DEATH (TAR)  10/4/46
  MURDER MYSTERY (M*F) 5/2/18
*Thompson, Jim*
  Leonid Andreyev and Jim Thompson
    (Fellows)     11/2/59-61
Thompson, Leslie M., and Jeff Banks
  When Is This Stiff Dead? Detective
    Stories and Definitions of
    Death      2/6/11-16
Thompson, Rik
  The EQMM Cover Story (fic-
    tion)       1/2/3-4
  L: 1/2/47
Thomson, H. Douglas
  MASTERS OF MYSTERY: A
    STUDY OF THE DETECTIVE
    STORY (IAC)    2/6/27
Thomson, June (IAC)    4/3/32
  DEATH CAP (M*F)   3/1/37
*Thomson, Sir Basil*
  Crime Novelists as Writers of
    Children's Fiction (Sarjeant)
           13/3/31-6
Thornburg, Newton
  CUTTER AND BONE (R)   1/4/43
Thorndike, Russell
  THE DEVIL IN THE BELFRY
    (TBR)      13/2/73-4
  THE SLYPE (TBR)    12/4/71
*Thorne, E.P.*
  (SSC)       7/1/30*
THORNE THEATER MYSTERY, THE
  (Willard) (TBR)    13/3/63
Thorne, Tony
  THE DICTIONARY OF CONTEM-
    PORARY SLANG (IAC) 13/4/84-5
Thorp, Roderick
  NOTHING LASTS FOREVER
    (R)        4/1/43
Thorpe, Dickson
  Those Old Detective Pulp Magazines
           1/3/9-11
  Will the Real Ken Crossen Please
    Stand Up    1/2/5-10*

Thorpe, Edward
  CHANDLERTOWN: THE LOS
    ANGELES OF PHILIP
    MARLOWE (R)    8/3/33
Those Old Detective Pulp Magazines
  (Thorpe)    1/3/9-11
THREE BY BOX (Box) (R)    3/1/44
THREE COUSINS DIE (Rhode)
  (M*F)    3/2/39
Three Gentle Men: Doris Miles Disney's
  Continuing Detectives (DeMarr)
    3/3/5-14
  L: Floyd 3/4/60; McCahery 3/4/53;
  Nevins 3/4/56
THREE HOSTAGES, THE (Buchan)
  (R)    6/2/43
THREE MINUTES TO MIDNIGHT
  (Davis) (R)    4/1/29
THREE MOTIVES FOR MURDER
  (Winsor) (M*F)    1/2/26
THREE-PIPE PROBLEM, A (Symons)
  (R)    1/3/48
THREE-TOED PUSSY (Burley)
  (R)    1/6/52
Three "Unknown" Stories—Two of
  Them Unpublished—by Dorothy L.
  Sayers (Christopher)    11/1/15-21
THREE WORLDS OF JOHNNY
  HANDSOME, THE (Godey)
  (R)    5/5/43
THROUGH THE EYES OF EVIL
  (Blair) (R)    8/3/43
THROUGH THE EYES OF THE
  DEAD (Michaels) (TAR)    11/3/80
Thurston, Temple
  MAN IN A BLACK HAT
    (TBR)    11/3/60
Tidyman, Ernest R.
  Obituary (Lachman)    8/3/29
Tierney, Gene
  Obituary (Lachman)    13/4/94
TIGER BY THE TAIL (Goldman)
  (M*F)    3/5/37
Tiger Mann Series, The (Banks)
    2/3/32-3*
  L: Banks 2/3/59, 2/4/53
Tilton, Alice [Phoebe Atwood Taylor,
  q.v.]
  Little Old Men (Nehr)    4/4/2-6
TIME AND AGAIN (Finney)
  (IAC)    2/6/28
TIME OF THE ASSASSINS, THE
  (Sterling) (IAC)    8/2/24

TIME TO MURDER AND CREATE
  (Block) (R)    8/3/41
TIME TO REMEMBER, A (Shapiro)
  (IAC)    11/1/26
TIME'S WITNESS (Malone) (TAR)
  (MS)    11/3/78; 12/1/4
TIMOTHY'S GAME (Sanders)
  (R)    13/1/56-7
Tinsman, Jim
  L:    7/1/50
Tippette, Giles
  WILSON'S GOLD (R)    4/3/42
TITAN GAME, THE (Busch)
  (TAR)    12/2/57
TNT Cable Channel (RM)    12/2/75-6
To Be and Not To Be (Bleiler)    6/6/3-4
TO DIE ELSEWHERE (Wilden)
  (M*F)    2/1/29
TO FEAR A PAINTED DEVIL
  (Rendell) (R)    3/4/45
TO KEEP OR KILL (Tucker)
  (M*F)    5/3/28
TO MAKE AN UNDERWORLD
  (Fleming) (M*F)    1/1/33
TO PROVE A VILLAIN (Townsend)
  (MS) (IAC) (R)
    8/5/1-5; 8/6/35; 9/1/39
  L: Lachman 9/3/45; Reilly 9/2/45;
  Townsend comment 9/2/45,
  10/1/94
TO RUN A LITTLE FASTER (Gardner)
  (R)    2/6/41
TO WAKE THE DEAD (Carr)
  (IAC)    11/4/52
Tod Hunter Question, The (Funct)
    6/4/3-8
Todd, Peter
  THE ADVENTURES OF HERLOCK
    SHOLMES (R)    2/5/41
Toepfer, Ray Grant
  ENDPLAY (M*F)    2/1/29
TOFF AMONG THE MILLIONS, THE
  (Creasey) (M*F)    3/2/36
Togawa, Masako
  A KISS OF FIRE (TAR)
    11/1/68; 11/2/79
  THE LADY KILLER (R)    10/1/71
Tolley, Michael J.
  An Australian Bibliomystery: Ligny's
    Lake    10/3/37-8
  Crime Fiction in Kenya    10/2/25-8
  L:    8/1/45; 8/2/43; 8/5/41
  The New Rippers    12/3/57-63

*Tolley, Michael,* continued
  Penal Economy: A Lesson from Leo
    Tolstoy          12/2/33-5
*Tolstoy, Leo*
  Penal Economy (Tolley)    12/2/33-5
TOO GOOD TO BE TRUE (Hutton)
  (R)              2/1/47
TOO LATE TO DIE (Crider) (R)
  (IAC)         8/5/29; 8/6/39
TOO MANY BONES (Wallis)
  (TBR)         12/4/69-70
TOO MANY DOORS (Crosby)
  (TBR)           13/3/62
TOO SANE A MURDER (Martin)
  (R)             8/6/39
Toole, Linda
  L: 4/3/48; 4/5/46; 5/1/43; 5/2/50;
    5/3/45; 5/4/41; 5/6/50; 6/1/48;
    6/3/45; 6/4/49; 6/6/44; 7/2/45;
    7/4/48
  Reviews:
    CRIME AND PUZZLEMENT
      (Treat)         6/5/50
    GREAT DETECTIVES (Symons)
                 6/3/41
    MURDERCON (Putrill)    7/3/40
    RITUAL MURDER (Haymon)
                 7/5/47
    REX STOUT: AN ANNOTATED
      PRIMARY AND SECON-
      DARY BIBLIOGRAPHY
      (Townsend/McAleer/Sapp/
      Schemer)       5/2/29
    ROYAL DECREE (McAleer)
                 8/3/40
    A STAB IN THE DARK (Block)
                 7/4/33
    UNDERCURRENT (Pronzini)
                 7/3/40
*Toomey, Regis*
  Obituary (Lachman)      13/3/73
TOOTH AND THE NAIL, THE
  (Ballinger) (TBR)      13/4/82
TOP CRIME (Pachter, ed.) (R)    8/2/33
TOP STORY MURDER (Berkeley)
  (M*F)             1/1/32
TOPLESS TULIP CAPER, THE
  (Harrison) (R)        1/2/45
TOUCH OF DEATH (Sadler)
  (R)             12/4/80-1
  L: Kimura 13/2/96
TOUGH GET GOING, THE (Bagby)
  (M*F)             2/6/33

TOUGH LUCK L.A. (Sinclair)
  (M*F)             5/2/17
Towne, Stuart [Clayton Rawson, q.v.]
  DEATH OUT OF THIN AIR
  (TCITC)           3/4/17
*Towns with Mystery Writers' Names*
  L: Banks 8/4/48
*Townsend, Guy*
  The Article I Couldn't Publish
                1/1/18-20
  Bouchercon Scrapbook (w/
    Nieminski)       4/6/19-30
  Dying Gasps           1/2/54
  Grise Notes       8/1/46, 15, 22
  L:           8/2/45; 8/3/50
  The Matt Helm Series (w/
    Banks)        2/2/3-11*
  Mysteriously Speaking...  P/1-2,40-2;
    1/1/1-2; 1/2/1-2; 1/3/1-2,12;
    1/4/1-2; 1/5/1-2; 1/6/1-2; 2/1/1-2;
    2/2/1-2,62-4; 2/3/1-2; 2/4/1-2,61;
    2/5/1-2,61; 2/6/1-2,35; 3/1/1-2;
    3/2/1-2; 3/3/1; 3/4/1-2; 3/5/1-2,34;
    3/6/1-2; 4/1/1-2,16; 4/2/1-2;
    4/3/1-2; 4/4/1; 4/5/1-2; 4/6/1-3;
    6/1/1; 6/2/1-6; 6/3/1-4; 6/4/1-2;
    6/6/1; 7/1/1; 7/2/1; 7/3/1-5;
    7/4/1-2; 7/5/1-2; 7/6/1-2; 8/4/1-8;
    8/5/1-6; 8/6/1-2; 9/1/1-9; 9/2/1-2;
    9/3/1-2; 9/4/1-2; 9/5/1-2;
    9/6/1-4;10/1/1-2; 10/2/1-2;
    10/3/1-2; 10/4/1-2; 11/1/1-2;
    11/2/1; 11/3/1; 11/4/1-2; 12/1/1-2;
    12/2/2; 12/3/1-12; 12/4/1-2;
    13/1/1-2; 13/2/1-2; 13/3/1-2;
    13/4/1-2
  The Nero Wolfe Saga - Part I
    1/3/13-36; Part II 1/4/25-36; Part
    III 1/5/21-8; Part IV 1/6/15-28;
    Part V 2/1/15-19; Part VI
    2/2/25-32; Part VII 2/3/34-40; Part
    VIII 2/4/19-29; Part IX 2/5/13-21;
    Part X 2/6/20-6; Part XI 3/1/21-5;
    Part XII 3/2/13-20; Part XIII
    3/3/22-30; Part XIV 3/4/25-37;
    Part XV 3/5/22-34; Part XVI
    3/6/15-26; Part XVII 4/1/17-28;
    Part XVIII 4/2/14-30; Part XIX
    4/3/3-21
  On Fans and Bouchercon    5/5/11-3
  Reviews:
    ARROW POINTING NOWHERE
      (Daly)           P/34

*Townsend, Guy,* continued
  Reviews continued:
    AN AUTHOR BITES THE DUST
      (Upfield)                    P/32
    ASIMOV'S MYSTERIES
      (Asimov)                    1/6/47
    BLACK LAND, WHITE LAND
      (Bailey)                    P/38
    BLACK WIDOWER (Moyes)
                                  1/6/47
    A CASE OF SPIRITS
      (Lovesey)                   1/6/48
    COMA (Cook)                   3/6/45
    DEAD EASY FOR DOVER
      (Porter)                    4/1/31
    DEAD RUN (Lockridge)          P/36
    DEADLY NIGHTSHADE
      (Daly)                      P/33
    DEATHBITE (Maryk/
      Monahan)                    4/2/43
    DEATH BY WATER (Innes)  P/31
    DEATH ON THE LIMITED
      (Denbie)                    P/38
    DEATH WEARS A RED HAT
      (Kienzle)                   4/2/41
    DESIGNS OF DARKNESS
      (Cooper-Clark)              7/5/35
    DIE LIKE A MAN (Delving)  P/37
    EXIT SHERLOCK HOLMES
      (Hall)                      1/5/51
    GOD SAVE THE CHILD
      (Parker)                    1/1/26
    THE GREAT IMPERSONATION
      (Oppenheim)                 2/3/49
    HAG'S NOOK (Carr)             P/35
    HOSTAGE: LONDON (House-
      hold)                       2/3/50
    THE INFILTRATOR (York)   P/16
    JOURNEY TO THE HANGMAN
      (Upfield)                   P/32
    THE KING EDWARD PLOT
      (Hall)                      4/2/46
    A LONELY PLACE TO DIE
      (Ebersohn)                  4/1/35
    RED ANGER (Household)  2/2/40
    THE RIDDLE OF THE SANDS
      (Childers)                  1/6/49
    ROGUE MALE (Household) 2/2/40
    SACRIFICIAL PAWN (Ryck) P/34
    SHALLOW GRAVE (Scott) 2/4/45
    SIR JOHN MAGILL'S LAST
      JOURNEY (Crofts)            P/10
    SO MUCH BLOOD (Brett)  1/5/37

*Townsend, Guy,* continued
  Reviews continued:
    SPHINX (Cook)                 3/6/46
    THE TERRORIZERS (Hamil-
      ton)                        1/6/48
    THE VICTORIAN UNDER-
      GROUND (Chesney)      P/34
    WATCHER IN THE SHADOWS
      (Household)                 2/2/40
    WAX APPLE (Coe)               P/20
  Reviews in Mysteriously Speaking...:
    DEATH IN A SMALL SOUTH-
      ERN TOWN (McKinney) 9/5/2
    MONTHLY MURDERS
      (Cook)                      6/2/5
    THE NIGHT MASTER
      (Sampson)                   6/2/6
    SCATTERSHOT (Pronzini) 6/2/37
    THE SUBJECT IS MURDER
      (Menendez)                  9/1/7
    WRITING THE MODERN
      MYSTERY (Norville)     9/1/8
  REX STOUT: AN ANNOTATED
    PRIMARY AND SECONDARY
    BIBLIOGRAPHY (w/McAleer/
    Sapp/Schemer) (R)           5/2/29
  TO PROVE A VILLAIN (R) (IAC)
                8/4/1; 8/6/35; 9/1/39
Toye, Randall
  THE AGATHA CHRISTIE WHO'S
    WHO (IAC)                     4/6/31
  TRACE (Murphy) (IAC)           8/4/32
  TRACES OF BRILLHART (Brean)
    (IAC)                        13/3/65
Tracey, Jack
  THE ENCYCLOPEDIA SHER-
    LOCKIANA (IAC)               4/1/15
  Tracking with Major Eagle (Lybeck)
                               11/2/3-16*
    L: Shibuk 11/3/85
*Tracy, Dick*
  The Detective Hero in the Comics
    (Blom)                       6/1/8-15
Tracy, Don
  HIGH, WIDE AND RANSOM
    (M*F)                         1/2/28
Tracy, Louis
  A MYSTERIOUS DISAPPEAR-
    ANCE (TBR)                   11/2/89
  TRAGEDY OF X, THE (Queen)
    (R)                          2/4/40
  TRAIL OF FEAR, THE (Armstrong)
    (R)                          1/4/53

TRAITOR (Markstein) (IAC)    6/4/31
TRAITOR GAME, THE  (McLeish)
   (TBR)                     13/4/72-3
TRANS-ATLANTIC GHOST, THE
   (Gardiner) (M*F)          3/5/41
Traver, Robert [John D. Voelker]
   Obituary (Lachman)        13/2/58
Traylor, Jim
   Judgments (More Movie Reviews)
                             6/2/27-32
   L:         6/3/44; 7/3/43; 8/5/43
   The Violent World of Mike
      Hammer                 7/6/13-20
   Reviews:
      THE BABY BLUE RIP-OFF
         (Collins)           7/1/39
      HARD CASH (Collins)    6/1/44
      HUSH MONEY (Collins)   5/6/45
      SCRATCH FEVER (Collins) 6/3/41
      THE SHIP THAT NEVER WAS
         (Spillane)          8/1/28
      WHODUNIT? (Keating, ed.) 7/1/40
TREASURE BY DEGREES (Williams)
   (M*F)                     2/5/26
TREASURY OF VICTORIAN GHOST
   STORIES (Bleiler, ed.) (MS)   6/1/1
Treat, Lawrence
   CRIME AND PUZZLEMENT
      (R)                    6/5/50
   CRIME AND PUZZLEMENT 2
      (R)                    7/4/33
TRENT'S OWN CASE (Bentley/Allen)
   (IAC)                     10/1/62
Trevanian
   L: Wooster 1/5/54
Trevor, Elleston. Also see Hall, Adam
   THE THETA SYNDROME (R) 2/1/34
TRIAL (Irving) (MS)          12/3/11-12
TRIAL AND ERROR (Berkeley)
   (IAC)             6/6/20; 8/6/43
TRIAL RUN (Francis) (M*F)    3/6/30
TROPICAL HEAT (Lutz) (R)     9/2/41
TROUBLE AT TURKEY HILL
   (Knight) (M*F)            3/4/41
TROUBLE FOR TALLON (Ball)
   (R)                       5/5/31
TROUBLE IS THEIR BUSINESS:
   PRIVATE EYES IN FICTION,
   FILM, AND TELEVISION
   (Conquest) (MS)           11/4/2
TROUBLE WITH FIDELITY, THE
   (Malcolm-Smith) (TBR)     11/4/59

Troy, Simon
   CEASE UPON THE MIDNIGHT
      (TBR)                  13/1/38-9
   SWIFT TO ITS CLOSE (IAC) 6/4/30
True Crime and Fiction
   The New Rippers (Tolley) 12/3/57-63
TRUE DETECTIVE (Collins) (R) 8/2/34
TRUE LIES (Ross) (TAR)       10/4/46
Truesdale, Jane
   THE MORGUE THE MERRIER
      (M*F) (TBR)    3/6/39; 13/1/39-40
Truman, Margaret
   MURDER AT THE SMITHSONIAN
      (R)                    7/6/36
   MURDER IN THE WHITE HOUSE
      (R)              4/4/47; 5/5/31
   MURDER ON CAPITOL HILL
      (R)                    5/6/47
Truss, Seldon. Also see Selmark, George
   ALWAYS ASK A POLICEMAN
      (TBR)                  11/2/90
   WHERE'S MR. CHUMLEY?
      (TBR)                  11/4/58
Tryon, Tom
   Obituary (Lachman)        13/3/72
TRYST, THE (Dibdin) (TAR)    12/2/61
Tubb, E.C.
   Some Recent Hybrids (Kelley)
                             6/2/16-8
Tucker, Wilson
   THE CHINESE DOLL (TBR)
                             13/4/74-5
   THE MAN IN MY GRAVE
      (TBR)                  11/4/65
   TO KEEP OR KILL (M*F)     5/3/28
   Wilson Tucker's Charles Horne
      (Moffatt)              12/2/3-10
   L: Briney 5/5/45
TUMBLEWEED (van de Wetering)
   (R)                       1/2/42
TURKISH WHITE (Arrighi)
   (M*F)                     2/1/23
Turnbull, Peter
   "McNaught's Obsession" (R)   9/2/20
TURN-UP, THE (Sewart) (R)    5/2/38
Turow, Scott
   PRESUMED INNOCENT
      (TAR)                  12/4/57-8
Tuska, Jon, and Vicki Piekarski, eds.
   THE DETECTIVE IN HOLLY-
      WOOD (R)               2/4/38
   ENCYCLOPEDIA OF FRONTIER
      AND WESTERN FICTION (IAC)
      (R)                    8/1/18 & 29

Tute, Warren
  (SSC)                              5/2/2*
Tuttle, George
  The Gold Medal Boys         10/3/25-31
  Peter Rabe's Daniel Port      9/5/20-2
TV DETECTIVES (Meyers) (IAC)
                                    6/4/32
Tweedale, Violet
  THE BEAUTIFUL MRS.
    DAVENANT (TBR)            12/3/79
TWELVE CRIMES OF CHRISTMAS
  (Asimov/Greenberg/Waugh, eds.)
  (IAC)                          6/3/22
TWENTIETH CENTURY CRIME AND
    MYSTERY WRITERS (Reilly,
    ed.)
  The Body in the Library (Wooster)
                                5/1/11-4
  L: Adey 5/4/44; Reilly 5/2/45; Bleiler
    5/3/44
TWENTIETH CENTURY CRIME AND
    MYSTERY WRITERS, SECOND
    EDITION (Reilly, ed.) (IAC) 8/4/30
  L: Toole 6/6/44; Reilly 7/1/43
TWENTY-THIRD WEB, THE
  (Himmell) (R)                  2/4/45
TWICE DEAD (Names) (R)          3/1/41
TWICE SHY (Francis) (M*F) (R)
                           6/3/39; 6/4/43
Twice-Told Tale of Murder
  (Floyd)                       6/1/21-6
TWISTED THING, THE (Spillane)
  (R)                            3/1/38
TWO GUNS FROM HARLEM: THE
    DETECTIVE FICTION OF
    CHESTER HIMES (Skinner)
  (MS)                           11/3/2
TWO IF BY SEA (Garve) (IAC)  8/4/31
TWO IF BY SEA (Savage) (IAC) 6/6/22
TWO IN THE BUSH (Bagby)
  (M*F)                           P/25
Two Short Chapters from Death of a
  .300 Hitter (Avallone)        P/11-12
TWOSPOT (Pronzini/Wilcox) (R)
  (M*F)                    2/6/36; 3/1/36
TYGER AT BAY (Riefe) (M*F)       P/26
TYGER BY THE TAIL (Riefe)
  (M*F)                           P/29
Tyler, Charles W.
  Peterman from the Old School
    (Sampson)                   5/4/2-4
  Pirates in Candyland (Sampson)
                                6/3/7-13
  L: Sampson 6/4/45

Tyler, Dennis. See "Diplomat"
Tyler, Miss Julia. See Revell, Louisa
Tynan, Kathleen
  AGATHA (IAC)                   4/1/13

# U

UBER ERIC AMBLER (R)            7/3/41
UBER SIMENON [ON SIMENON]
  (Schmolders/Strich, eds.) (R)  7/4/30
UCSD Mystery Quiz
  L: Nevins 6/1/49
Uhnak, Dorothy
  FALSE WITNESS (R)             6/1/41
  THE INVESTIGATION (R)         2/1/41
  THE INVESTIGATION: Fiction and
    Fact (Vicarel)              3/3/15-6
ULTIMATE ISSUE (Markstein)
  (IAC)                          6/4/31
UNBALANCED ACCOUNTS (Galli-
  son) (R) (IAC)          8/4/31; 8/6/40
UNBECOMING HABITS (Heald)
  (R)                            6/5/50
UNCLE SILAS: A TALE OF BAR-
  TRAM–HAUGH (LeFanu) (R) 2/1/45
UNCLE TARGET (Lyall) (TAR) 11/3/74
UNCOLLECTED CRIMES (Pronzini/
  Greenberg, eds.) (R)          11/1/70
UNDER COVER (Bonn) (IAC)   6/6/21
UNDERCURRENT (Pronzini) (R) 7/3/40
Underwood, Michael
  CROOKED WOOD (M*F)           3/3/36
  A PARTY TO MURDER (R)        8/1/31
UNFUNNY MONEY (Alexander)
  (TAR)                        12/2/53-4
UNHAPPY RETURNS (Lemarchand)
  (R)                            7/5/44
UNHOLY WRIT (Williams)
  (M*F)                          2/1/21
Unicorn (magazine) (MS)          3/5/2
University of Pittsburgh Press
  (IAC)                          8/2/23
UNKNOWN THRILLER: THE
    SCREENPLAY OF PLAYBACK
  (Chandler) (IAC)               9/4/35
UNORTHODOX PRACTICES
  (Piesman) (R)                 12/1/41
UNSPEAKABLE, THE (Ransome)
  (R)                            3/3/45
UNSUCCESSFUL MAN, AN (Nielsen)
  (M*F)                          1/3/38
UNSUITABLE JOB FOR A WOMAN,
  AN (James) (IAC)               7/1/32

- 158 -

UNTIL DEATH DO US PART
(McMullen) (R)                         8/3/38
UP AND COMING STAR, AN
(Branston) (M*F)                       2/1/25
*Upfield, Arthur W.*
   AN AUTHOR BITES THE DUST
      (R) (TCITC)              P/32; 3/2/12
   THE BATTLING PROPHET
      (R)                             11/4/87
   DEATH OF A LAKE (R)          3/4/50
   JOURNEY TO THE HANGMAN
      (R)                               P/32
   MAN OF TWO TRIBES (R)        3/4/51
   THE MOUNTAINS HAVE A
      SECRET (R)                     3/4/51
   MURDER MUST WAIT (R)         3/4/51
   THE NEW SHOE (R)       1/2/32 & 33
   VALLEY OF SMUGGLERS
      (R)                          13/2/78-9
   WINGS ABOVE THE DIAMAN-
      TINA (R)                       3/4/51
   L: Briney 1/1/45
Upton, Robert
   DEAD UPON THE STICK (R) 8/5/34
URGENT HANGMAN (Cheyney)
   (R)                           12/4/100-1
U.S.S.A. (Madsen) (R)            13/1/70-1

# V

V FOR VICTOR (Childress)
   (TAR)                            11/4/76
Vachell, Horace Annesley
   QUINNEY'S ADVENTURES
      (TBR)                          12/3/76
VALEDICTION (Parker) (R)         8/2/30
*Valentine, Daniel*
   Deadly Edges of the Gay Blade
      (Alderson)                  7/3/23-8*
VALHALLA EXCHANGE, THE
   (Patterson) (R)                  1/4/43
Valin, Jonathan
   DAY OF WRATH (R)               7/4/32
   DEAD LETTER (R) (M*F)
                             5/6/46; 6/6/26
   FINAL NOTICE (R) (M*F) (R)
                       5/2/29; 6/2/34; 7/4/28
   THE LIME PIT (M*F)             4/4/35
VALLEY OF FEAR, THE (Doyle)
   (IAC)                            3/2/21
VALLEY OF SMUGGLERS (Upfield)
   (R)                          13/2/78-9
Value of Gould, The (Fellows)   13/1/3-6

VAMPIRE'S HONEYMOON (Wool-
   rich) (IAC)                      9/1/36
Van Arsdale, Wirt
   THE PROFESSOR KNITS A
      SHROUD (R)                    9/6/47
Van de Water, Frederic F.
   HIDDEN WAYS (TBR)              11/1/39
van de Wetering, Janwillem
   THE BUTTERFLY HUNTER
      (R)                           7/3/42
   THE CORPSE ON THE DIKE
      (M*F)                         1/1/30
   DISTANT DANGER (IAC)    11/1/32
   THE JAPANESE CORPSE (M*F)
      (R)                     2/5/28; 2/6/41
   THE MAINE MASSACRE
      (R)                           3/2/42
   TUMBLEWEED (R)                 1/2/42
*Van Dine, S.S.*
   THE BENSON MURDER CASE
      (TCITC) (IAC)        3/2/10; 8/3/27
   THE SCARAB MURDER CASE
      (IAC)                         8/3/27
   THE WINTER MURDER CASE
      (TBR)                        13/2/68
   L: Breen 2/5/45
Van Greenaway, Peter
   A MAN CALLED SCAVENER
      (R)                           5/4/33
VAN, THE (Ball) (TAR)           11/4/73
Van Tilburg, Barry
   L: 4/2/59; 4/6/49; 5/1/46; 5/3/41;
      5/5/48; 6/1/50; 6/2/50; 6/3/47;
      8/1/44
   Spy Series Characters in Hardback:
      Part I 4/2/11-13*; Part II
      4/3/23-8*; Part III 4/4/16-7; Part
      IV 4/5/21-3; Part V 4/6/4-6*; Part
      VI 5/1/2*; Part VII 5/2/2*; Part
      VIII 5/3/18-21*; Part IX 5/5/15-6*;
      Part X 6/1/7,15*; Part XI
      6/2/19-20*; Part XII 6/3/5,26*;
      Part XIII 7/1/30-1*; Part XIV
      7/4/10-4*
Van Vogt, A.E.
   THE VIOLENT MAN (R)           8/4/41
*Vance, John Holbrook*
   L: Briney 2/1/56
*Vance, Louis Joseph*
   Fear and Loathing with the Lone
      Wolf (Kelley)             1/5/17-8*
VANE PURSUIT (MacLeod)
   (TAR)                           11/3/76

Vardemann, Robert E.
  THE SCREAMING KNIFE
    (R)                        12/4/73-6
VARIATION ON A THEME (Fisher)
    (M*F)                        5/6/38
VARIETY OF WEAPONS, A (King)
    (R)                        12/1/47-8
VEIL OF IGNORANCE, THE (Quill)
    (R)                        11/1/78
VEILED ONE, THE (Rendell)
    (R)                        12/4/86-7
VENETIAN AFFAIR, THE (MacInnes)
    (IAC)                        4/1/15
Vengeance Novels of Brian Garfield,
    The (Kelley)                2/1/5-6
  L: Banks 2/2/41
VERDICT OF 13 (IAC)           4/4/19
VERDICT OF TWELVE (Postgate)
    (IAC)                        8/4/32
VERDICT OF YOU ALL, THE (Wade)
    (IAC)                        4/5/25
Verdicts (Book Reviews)
  1/1/34-7; 1/2/29-46; 1/3/43-50;
  1/4/41-54; 1/5/37-52; 1/6/42-54;
  2/1/31-49; 2/2/36-40; 2/3/49-56;
  2/4/37-48; 2/5/35-44; 2/6/36-42;
  3/1/38-45,30; 3/2/42-9; 3/3/40-9;
  3/4/42-52; 3/5/42-45; 3/6/42-9;
  4/1/29-36; 4/2/41-53; 4/3/42-6;
  4/4/44-8; 4/5/37-3; 4/6/34-9;
  5/2/26-38; 5/3/34-40; 5/4/28-37;
  5/5/28-43; 6/1/39-45; 6/2/38-47;
  6/3/38-43; 6/4/40-4; 6/5/46-50;
  6/6/33-9; 7/1/39-42; 7/2/31-9;
  7/3/32-42; 7/4/27-34; 7/5/35-49;
  7/6/30-42; 8/1/26-37; 8/2/29-41;
  8/3/33-46; 8/4/37-47; 8/5/34-9;
  8/6/37-46; 9/1/39-44; 9/2/33-44;
  9/3/39-43; 9/4/40-5; 9/5/32-46;
  9/6/35-48; 10/1/67-90; 10/2/71-7;
  10/3/65-76; 10/4/55-7; 11/1/70-80;
  11/2/99-104; 11/4/83-104; 12/1/31-57;
  12/3/89-104; 12/4/73-101; 13/1/55-78;
  13/2/76-93; 13/3/83-92; 13/4/95-104
VERY COLD FOR MAY (McGivern)
    (IAC)                        9/3/30
VERY PARTICULAR MURDER, A
    (Haymon) (R)                12/4/85-6
(Very Temporary) Return of Skull-Face,
    The (Briney)                2/2/21-4
VESPERS (McBain) (TAR)        12/3/85

Vicarel, Jo Ann
  THE INVESTIGATION: Fiction and
    Fact                        3/3/15-6
  L:          2/2/55; 3/2/56; 5/5/48
VICE ISN'T PERFECT (Cleeve)
    (IAC)                        3/2/23
Vickers, Roy. See Kyle, Sefton
Victor, Sam
  CUBAN INFERNO (IAC)       6/3/22
  WHITE HOUSE MASSACRE
    (IAC)                        6/3/22
VICTORIAN UNDERGROUND, THE
    (Chesney) (R)                P/34
VICTORY SONG (Adams) (TBR)
                                13/3/61-2
Vidal, Gore. Also see Box, Edgar
  MATTERS OF FACT & FICTION:
    ESSAYS 1973-1976 (R)     1/5/39
VIDOCQ DOSSIER, THE (Edwards)
    (R)                        5/3/36
VIEW FROM DANIEL PIKE, THE
    (Boyd/Knox) (R)             3/1/40
VILLAINS, THE (Rossiter) (M*F)1/1/28
Vincent Starrett vs. Arthur Machen: or,
    How Not To Communicate over
    Eight Years of Correspondence
    (Bleiler)                   3/6/11-4
Violence and Gunplay in Crime Fiction:
    From the Ridiculous to the Horrible
    (Skinner)                   8/2/9-18
VIOLENT MAN, THE (Van Vogt)
    (R)                        8/4/41
Violent World of Mike Hammer, The
    (Traylor)                   7/6/13-20
VIRGIN IN THE ICE, THE (Peters)
    (R)                  6/6/33; 7/5/47
"VIRGIN" KILLS, THE (Whitfield)
    (M*F)                        5/5/24
VITAL STATISTICS (Chastain)
    (M*F)                        2/3/44
Vivian, E. Charles. See Mann, Jack
Vladimir Gull (Dukeshire)      4/3/22
  L: Doerrer 4/5/47
Vulcan Publications: An Annotated
    Checklist (Deeck)        12/3/53-6*

# W

Wade, Henry
  A DYING FALL (IAC)          5/6/30
  THE HANGING CAPTAIN (IAC)
    (M*F)                 6/1/29; 6/2/34
  THE VERDICT OF YOU ALL
    (IAC)                        4/5/25

Wager, Walter
  BLUE LEADER (R)                5/5/40
WAGES OF ZEN, THE (Melville)
  (R)                            5/6/45
Wainwright, John
  DEATH IN A SLEEPING CITY
  (R)                            7/4/34
  POOL OF TEARS (M*F)            2/3/43
WAIT FOR DEATH (Creasey)
  (IAC)                          8/5/30
WAIT FOR WHAT WILL COME
  (Michaels) (IAC)               2/6/29
WALDO (Kauffmann) (TBR)   11/2/91
Walker, Mark
  CASSIS...RESORT TO VENGE-
  ANCE (M*F)                     3/6/35
WALKING AFTER MIDNIGHT
  (Nusser) (R)                13/1/67-8
WALKING DEAD (Dickinson)
  (M*F)                          2/5/27
WALKING SHADOW (Offord)
  (R)                           12/1/51
Wallace, Edgar
  ANGEL ESQUIRE (IAC)          11/3/48
  FOUR JUST MEN (IAC)           9/1/36
  THE GREEN ARCHER (R)          9/6/47
Wallace, Irving
  THE PIGEON PROJECT (R)        3/3/44
Wallace, Marilyn
  A CASE OF LOYALTIES (R) 10/2/72
  SISTERS IN CRIME 4 (ed.)
  (R)                           13/4/47
Wallace, Robert
  AN AXE TO GRIND (TAR)   13/2/50
Walling, R.A.J.
  THE CORPSE WITH THE DIRTY
  FACE (M*F)                     3/6/33
Wallis, J.H.
  MURDER BY FORMULA
  (TBR)                       13/4/70-1
Wallis, Ruth Sawtell
  NO BONES ABOUT IT
  (TBR)                      12/4/69-70
  TOO MANY BONES (TBR)
                             12/4/69-70
Walsh, James Morgan. Also see Mad-
  dock, Stephen
  (SSC)                      7/4/10-1*
Walsh, Maurice
  L: Walsh 6/6/40; Wilkerson 6/3/48
Walsh, Robin S.
  L:                             6/6/40

Waltch, Lilla M.
  FEARFUL SYMMETRY (TAR)
                       11/1/68; 11/2/80
Walz, Audrey Boyers
  Obituary (Lachman)             7/2/25
Wambaugh, Joseph
  THE GLITTER DOME (R)          5/5/28
WANTON, THE (Brown) (M*F)    P/26
WAR MACHINE (Marshall)
  (TNSPE)                       10/2/51
WARRANT FOR X (MacDonald)
  (R)                            8/4/46
  L: Tolley 8/5/41
Warren, Charles M(arquis)
  Obituary (Lachman)            12/4/48
Warriner, Thurman
  METHOD IN HIS MURDER
  (TBR)                      12/4/64-5
Washburn, L.J.
  Reviews:
    ONE OF US IS WRONG
    (Holt)                       8/6/40
    TOO LATE TO DIE (Crider) 8/6/39
    TOO SANE A MURDER
    (Martin)                     8/6/39
    UNBALANCED ACCOUNTS
    (Gallison)                   8/6/40
Washburn, Mark
  THE ARMAGEDDON GAME
  (M*F)                          1/5/33
WASHINGTON PAYOFF (Hunt)
  (R)                            1/4/51
WATCHER IN THE SHADOWS
  (Household)                    2/5/29
WATCHER, THE (Wilcox) (M*F) 2/5/29
WATCHER WITHIN (Appel)
  (IAC)                          7/5/28
Waterhouse, Howard
  L:                             2/1/51
  Obituary (MS)                  4/2/1
  Review: THE VIEW FROM DAN-
  IEL PIKE (Boyd/Knox)           3/1/40
Waterhouse, Jane
  PLAYING FOR KEEPS
  (IAC)                         10/1/63
Watson, Clarissa
  LAST PLANE FROM NICE
  (TAR)                         10/4/47
Watson, Colin
  CHARITY ENDS AT HOME
  (M*F)                          2/6/34
  SNOBBERY WITH VIOLENCE
  (IAC)                         10/2/59

Watson, Hilary, ed.
WINTER'S CRIMES 12 (R)   6/2/46
WATSON'S CHOICE (Mitchell)
(R)                5/3/39
WATTEAU'S SHEPHERDS: THE
DETECTIVE NOVEL IN BRITAIN,
1914–1940 (Panek) (R) (IAC)
4/3/44; 4/4/18
Waugh, Carol-Lynn Rössel; Isaac
Asimov, and Martin H. Greenberg,
eds.
THE BIG APPLE MYSTERIES
(IAC)              6/4/32
TWELVE CRIMES OF CHRIST-
MAS (IAC)          6/3/22
Waugh, Charles G.
THE HUMAN ZERO: THE
SCIENCE FICTION STORIES OF
ERLE STANLEY GARDNER
(Gardner) (w/Greenberg, ed.)
(M*F)              5/2/13
THE MYSTERY HALL OF FAME
(w/Greenberg/Pronzini, eds.)
(R)                8/2/33
TANTALIZING LOCKED ROOM
STORIES (w/Asimov/Greenberg,
eds.) (R)          7/2/33
THE THIRTEEN CRIMES OF
SCIENCE FICTION (w/Asimov/
Greenberg, eds.) (R)    4/3/45
THE 13 HORRORS OF HALLO-
WEEN (w/Asimov/Greenberg,
eds.) (IAC)        8/1/17
Waugh, Hillary
BORN VICTIM (IAC)       3/3/18
LAST SEEN WEARING (IAC)
6/4/30; 12/2/63
ROAD BLOCK (R)     13/2/79-80
SLEEP LONG, MY LOVE
(IAC)              11/4/51
*Waves Press and Bookshop* (MS)   6/3/2
WAX APPLE (Coe) (R)        P/20
WAXWORK (Lovesey) (M*F)
(R)                2/6/32; 6/2/43
Way, Peter
DIRTY TRICKS (M*F)      2/4/31
WAY WE DIE NOW, THE (Lewin)
(M*F)              3/2/37
WAYS OF THE HOUR, THE (Cooper)
(R)                8/1/30
WE ALL KILLED GRANDMA
(Brown) (M*F)      1/2/24

*Webb, Jean Francis*
Obituary (Lachman)      13/4/91-92
Weber, Albrecht
DAS PHANOMEN SIMMEL: ZUR
REZEPTION EINES BEST-
SELLER-AUTHORS UNTER
SCHULEM UND IMLITER-
ATURUNTERRICHT (R)   7/5/44
Weber, Helen D.
L:                 3/1/60
Webster, Henry Kitchell
WHO IS THE NEXT? (M*F)
(IAC)              5/5/20; 6/1/29
Webster, Noah
AN INCIDENT IN ICELAND
(M*F)              4/2/32
WEDNESDAY THE RABBI GOT WET
(Kemelman) (R)     1/4/43
Weeks, Dolores
THE FRIDAY HARBOR MUR-
DERS (TAR)   11/1/68; 11/2/80
Weevil in Bencurd, The, Or, The Cop
Abroad (Dove)      2/6/17-19,16
L: Harwood 3/2/56; Meyerson 3/1/57;
Vicarel 3/2/56
Weider, Ben, and David Hapgood
THE MURDER OF NAPOLEON
(IAC)              8/1/16
*Weigand, Bill.* See Lockridge, Richard
and Frances
WEIGHT OF THE EVIDENCE, THE
(Innes) (IAC)      8/4/31
Weill, Gus
THE BONNET MAN (M*F)    3/5/36
A WOMAN'S EYES (R)      1/1/11
Wein, Anita
L:                 1/1/47
*Weinberg, Bob and Phyllis* (MS)
6/3/2; 6/4/39
Weiner, Henri
CRIME ON THE CUFF (TBR)
11/3/62
Weinman, Irving
HAMPTON HEAT (TAR)      10/4/47
Weisman, John
EVIDENCE (M*F)     5/6/39
*Weist, Dwight*
Obituary (Lachman)      13/3/73
WELCOME FOR A HERO (Perry)
(M*F)              1/1/31
*Welcome, John*
(SSC)              7/4/11-2*

Wells, Anna Mary
  MURDERER'S CHOICE
  (TBR)                    12/2/46-7
Wells, Carolyn
  THE CLUE OF THE EYELASH
  (R)                      12/1/56-7
  THE MOSS MYSTERY (TBR)
                           13/4/77-8
  THE TANNAHILL TANGLE
  (TCITC)                  3/2/12
Wells, Charlie
  THE LAST KILL (R)        4/1/30
Wenstrup, Dick
  L:                       5/1/45; 6/1/50
  Review: A CRACKING OF SPINES
  (Lewis)                  4/5/38
*Wentworth, Patricia* (IAC)   10/4/50
WEREWOLF, THE (Copper) (R) 2/4/46
West, Charles
  RAT'S NEST (TAR)         13/2/50
West, Elliot
  THE KILLING KIND (M*F)   2/4/33
*West, Mae*
  Mae West: Mistress of Mystery?
  Almost... (Barton)       6/6/2,18
West, Morris
  THE SALAMANDER (R)       3/5/44
*West, Pinklin*
  The Murder Cases of Pinklin West
  (Sampson)                8/1/3-7
West, Richard
  L:                       9/4/49
*Westerns*
  ENCYCLOPEDIA OF FRONTIER
  AND WESTERN FICTION
  (Tuska/Piekarski, eds.) (IAC)
  (R)                      8/1/18 & 29
  THE FILMS OF HOPALONG CAS-
  SIDY (Nevins) (IAC)      13/4/87-8
  Some Notes on the Detective Element
  in Western Fiction (Saxon)   P/17
  L: Banks 1/2/51; Lansdale 1/5/53;
  Nevins 1/3/55
Westlake, Donald E. Also see Stark,
  Richard
  DROWNED HOPES (TAR)      12/4/58
  GOOD BEHAVIOR (R)        9/1/42
  LEVINE (R)               8/2/38
  NOBODY'S PERFECT (M*F)   5/1/22
Weston, Carolyn
  ROUSE THE DEVIL (M*F)    1/1/29
Weverka, Robert
  MURDER BY DECREE (R)     3/5/43

WHALE'S FOOTPRINTS, THE (Boyer)
  (TAR)                    11/1/51
WHAT A BODY! (Green) (IAC) 5/6/29
WHAT ABOUT MURDER? (Breen)
  (IAC) (R)                5/4/18 & 28
WHAT NIGEL KNEW (Field)
  (M*F)                    6/1/34
WHAT OF TERRY CONISTON?
  (Garfield) (M*F)         1/2/25
WHAT WILL HAVE HAPPENED: A
  PHILOSOPHICAL AND TECH-
  NICAL ESSAY ON MYSTERY
  STORIES (Champigny) (R)  5/4/28
*Wheatley, Dennis*
  HEREWITH THE CLUES, THE
  FOURTH DENNIS WHEATLEY
  MURDER MYSTERY (R)       8/3/40
  MURDER OFF MIAMI (IAC) 4/1/15
  (SSC)                    5/3/18*
*Wheeler, Hugh [Callingham]. Also see*
  Patrick, Q.
  Obituary (Lachman)       9/4/38-9
WHEN IN GREECE (Lathen) (R) 7/1/41
When Is This Stiff Dead? Detective
  Stories and Definitions of Death
  (Thompson/Banks)         2/6/11-16
  L: Banks 3/1/51
WHEN LAST SEEN (Maling, ed.)
  (M*F)                    2/2/33
WHEN THE BOUGH BREAKS
  (Kellerman) (IAC)        8/4/32
WHEN THE CAT'S AWAY (Friedman)
  (TAR)                 11/1/58; 11/2/69
WHEN THE SACRED GINMILL
  CLOSES (Block) (R)       8/4/42
WHEN THEY KILL YOUR WIFE
  (Crowe) (M*F)            1/6/38
WHERE MURDER WAITS (Hunt)
  (R)                      1/4/51
WHERE SHADOWS FALL (Kelman)
  (IAC)                    11/1/25
WHERE THERE'S SMOKE (McBain)
  (R)                      1/5/40
WHERE THERE'S SMOKE (Sterling)
  (R)                      9/2/40
WHERE'S MR. CHUMLEY? (Truss)
  (TBR)                    11/4/58
WHICH WAY DID HE GO?
  (Margolies) (IAC)        7/2/23
WHILE THE BELLS RANG (Clifford)
  (M*F)                    5/3/30
WHIP HAND (Francis) (M*F) (IAC)
                          4/4/37; 5/2/11

WHISKEY (Estleman) (TAR)    13/3/79
Whitaker, Beryl
  OF MICE AND MURDER
    (TBR)                  13/3/60-1
WHITE HOUSE MASSACRE (Victor)
    (IAC)                    6/3/22
WHITE PRIORY MURDERS, THE
    (Dickson) (IAC)          6/4/31
White, T.H.
  DARKNESS AT PEMBERLEY
    (IAC)                     2/5/3
  DEAD MR. NIXON (w/Scott)
    (R)                      3/2/43
White, Terence de Vere
  MY NAME IS NORVAL (R)    4/1/29
White, Teri
  FAULT LINES (TAR)
              11/1/69; 11/2/80
  L:       7/3/48; 7/4/47; 8/1/42
Whitfield, Raoul
  THE "VIRGIN" KILLS (M*F) 5/5/24
Whitney, Phyllis A.
  MYSTERY OF THE ANGRY IDOL
    (M*F)                    2/6/34
Whitney, Steven
  SINGLED OUT (R) (M*F)
              3/1/42; 3/3/32
*Whittington, Harry*
  THE HUMMING BOX (R)      3/4/49
  Obituary (Lachman)       11/3/55
WHO DONE IT? (Laurance/Asimov,
    eds.) (R)                4/4/48
WHO IS TEDDY VILLANOVA?
    (Berger) (R)      1/4/46; 5/5/36
WHO IS THE NEXT? (Webster) (M*F)
    (IAC)            5/5/20; 6/1/29
WHO KILLED THE CURATE?
    (Coggin) (TBR)        13/2/66-7
WHO KILLED WILLIAM DREW
    (Strong) (IAC)           4/6/33
Who Really Wrote THE G-STRING
    MURDERS? (Christopher)  8/3/18,20
WHO'D HIRE BRETT? (Brett)
    (M*F)                    5/5/23
WHODUNIT? A GUIDE TO CRIME,
    SUSPENSE AND SPY FICTION
    (Keating, ed.) (R) (IAC)
              7/1/40; 7/2/24
  L: Adey 7/4/43
WHODUNIT? HOUDINI? (Penzler, ed.)
    (M*F)                     P/31
WHO'S ON FIRST (Schier) (IAC)
                             6/3/22

WHOLE SPY CATALOGUE, THE
    (Knudson) (R)            9/2/33
  L: Shibuk 9/3/46
Why Isn't There a Volume of Dorothy
    L. Sayers' Letters? (Christopher)
                          12/4/29-33
WHY MURDER? (Philips) (M*F)3/6/34
*Wibberly, Leonard*
  Obituary (Lachman)        8/2/25
*Wiber-Wood, H.F.*
  L: Adey 2/3/73
*Wickley, Mabel.* See Boniface, Marjorie
WIDENING GYRE, THE (Parker)
    (R)            7/3/39; 8/2/30
WIDOW, THE (Freeling) (R)    6/1/42
Wilcox, Collin
  BERNHARDT'S EDGE (TAR)
                            10/4/47
  A DEATH BEFORE DYING
    (TAR)                   12/4/59
  DOCTOR, LAWYER... (M*F)  2/1/23
  THE PARIAH (TAR)         10/4/48
  POWER PLAYS (M*F)         3/6/29
  TWOSPOT (w/Pronzini) (R)
    (M*F)          2/6/36; 3/1/36
  THE WATCHER (M*F)         2/5/29
*Wilde, Jonas.* See York, Andrew
Wilden, Theodore
  TO DIE ELSEWHERE (M*F)   2/1/29
WILDERNESS (Parker) (M*F)    4/2/33
WILDFIRE (Foxx) (M*F)        3/3/38
WILDTRACK (Cornwell) (MS)  12/1/4
Wilf, David J.
  L:                        6/3/45
Wilkerson, David
  L:            6/3/48; 6/4/48
WILL AND LAST TESTAMENT OF
    CONSTANCE COBBLE, THE
    (Forbes) (M*F)           4/3/37
Will the Real Ken Crossen Please Stand
    Up (Thorpe)         1/2/5-10*
  L: Briney 1/3/52
Willard, Joshua
  THE THORNE THEATER MYS-
    TERY (TBR)             13/3/63
*Willeford, Charles*
  MIAMI BLUES (IAC)        11/4/50
  Obituary (Lachman) 10/2/60; 10/3/46
William MacHarg's O'Malley:
  Transitional Cop (Dove)   8/6/14-8
Williams, David
  TREASURE BY DEGREES
    (M*F)                    2/5/26
  UNHOLY WRIT (M*F)         2/1/21

Williams, Richard and Jane (MS) 6/4/39
Williams, Robert M.
    L:          1/2/50; 1/5/57; 3/3/50
Williams, Valentine
    THE CURIOSITY OF MR. TREAD-
    GOLD (TBR)              11/4/61
    FOG (w/Sims) (TBR)      11/3/69
    (SSC)                   7/4/10*
Williamson, Audrey
    THE MYSTERY OF THE PRINCES:
    AN INVESTIGATION INTO A
    SUPPOSED MURDER
    (IAC)                   9/2/26
Williamson, Sherman
    THE GLORY GAME (M*F)    2/4/30
Wilmot, Robert Patrick
    BLOOD IN YOUR EYE (M*F)2/1/30
Wilson, G.M.
    I WAS MURDERED (TBR) 12/4/68-9
Wilson, Jacqueline
    MAKING HATE (M*F)       2/6/33
Wilson Tucker's Charles Horne (Mof-
    fatt)                   12/2/3-10
WILSON'S GOLD (Tippette) (R) 4/3/42
Wiltz, Chris
    THE KILLING CIRCLE (M*F)6/3/34
WIMSEY FAMILY, THE (Scott-Giles)
    (IAC)                   3/4/23
WIND BLOWS DEATH, THE (Hare)
    (M*F)                   6/6/31
WINDFALL (Bagley) (R)      8/3/39
WINGS ABOVE THE DIAMANTINA
    (Upfield) (R)           3/4/51
WINIFRED (Disney) (IAC)    10/4/51
Winks, Robin
    COLLOQUIUM ON CRIME (ed.)
    (R)                     11/4/89
    MODUS OPERANDI (IAC)    7/2/22
Winn, Dilys, ed.
    MURDER INK (IAC)        2/4/15
    MURDERESS INK: THE BETTER
    PART OF THE MYSTERY (R)
    (IAC)              4/1/34; 4/3/31
Winslow, Pauline Glen
    THE BRANDENBURG HOTEL
    (M*F) (R)          1/1/31; 1/2/42
    THE WITCH HILL MURDERS
    (M*F)                   2/1/22
Winsor, Roy
    The Professorial Sleuth of Roy
    Winsor (French)         2/1/3-4
    THREE MOTIVES FOR MURDER
    (M*F)                   1/2/26

Winsor, Roy, continued
    L: Adey 2/4/57; Albert 2/2/54; French
    1/6/58
WINTER MURDER CASE, THE (Van
    Dine) (TBR)             13/2/68
Winter, Rabbi Daniel. See Telushkin,
    Joseph
WINTER'S CRIMES 9 (Hardinge, ed.)
    (M*F)                   3/1/32
WINTER'S CRIMES 12 (Watson, ed.)
    (R)                     6/2/46
Wit and Wisdom of the Mystery Story:
    Quotations from the Mysteries
    (Lachman) – Part III P/3-10; Part IV
    1/4/7-10
WITCH HILL MURDERS, THE
    (Winslow) (M*F)         2/1/22
WITHDRAWING ROOM, THE
    (MacLeod) (R)           4/6/38
Witherall, Leonidas. See Tilton, Alice
Withers, E.L.
    DIMINISHING RETURNS
    (TBR)                   12/2/45-6
Withers, Hildegarde. See Palmer, Stuart
Witting, Clifford
    Crime Novelists as Writers of
    Children's Fiction (Sarjeant)
                            12/2/37-9
    LET X BE THE MURDERER
    (R)                     2/4/43
    SILENCE AFTER DINNER
    (TBR)                   12/3/72
WIZARD OF DEATH, THE (Forrest)
    (M*F)                   1/5/29
Wodehouse, P.G.
    P.G. Wodehouse as Reader of Crime
    Stories (Sarjeant)      9/5/7-19
WOLF IN SHEEP'S CLOTHING
    (Riggs) (TAR)           12/4/55
WOLF TO THE SLAUGHTER
    (Rendell) (R)           3/4/45
Wolfe a Howler! (Napier)   5/5/7-10
    L: Toole 5/6/50
Wolfe, Michael
    THE CHINESE FIRE DRILL
    (R)                     1/2/40
Wolfe, Nero. See Stout, Rex
Wolfe Pack
    Here Comes the Judge: The "Nero"
    Award (Crider)          3/6/8
    L: Toole 4/3/48

Wolfe, Peter
  BEAMS FALLING: THE ART OF
    DASHIELL HAMMETT
    (IAC)                          6/4/32
  CORRIDORS OF POWER: THE
    WORLD OF JOHN LE CARRÉ
    (IAC)                          10/2/55
Wolff, Julian, M.D.
  Obituary (Lachman)              12/2/72
WOLFNIGHT (Freeling) (R)           6/4/46
WOLFSBANE (Thomas) (R)             3/4/49
Wollheim, Donald A.
  Obituary (Lachman)              13/1/34
Wolzien, Valerie
  THE FORTIETH BIRTHDAY BODY
    (R)                          13/2/86-7
  MURDER AT THE PTA
    LUNCHEON (R)                 13/2/85-6
WOMAN AT BAY (Coxe) (M*F) 1/2/26
WOMAN IN THE DARK (Hammett)
    (R)                           11/1/73
WOMAN'S EYE, A (Paretsky, ed.)
    (R)                        13/4//47-8
WOMAN'S EYES, A (Weill) (R) 1/1/11
Women Fans
  L: Broset 2/2/42; Cramer 2/1/55;
    Frazier 1/6/55, 2/4/59; Glantz
    2/1/54; Goldman 2/4/56;
    Goldsmith 2/1/58; Juri 2/1/57;
    King 4/1/43; Nehr 2/3/75
Women Mystery Writers
  L: Adey 7/4/44; Callen 7/4/46;
    Christopher 7/4/35; Goldman
    2/4/56; Hill 7/1/50; Reynolds
    7/2/48; Rice 7/6/49; Toole 7/4/48;
    White 7/3/48, 8/1/42
Wood, Bari
  THE KILLING GIFT (R)           11/4/95
Wood, H.F.
  THE PASSENGER FROM SCOT-
    LAND YARD (M*F)               2/5/30
Wood, Stuart
  PALINDROME (TAR)             13/2/50-1
Wood, Ted
  DEAD IN THE WATER (R)
                            7/6/31; 8/1/37
  LIVE BAIT (IAC)                 8/4/33
Woodhouse, Martin
  (SSC)                          5/3/18*
Woods, Sara
  BLOODY INSTRUCTIONS
    (IAC)                        10/1/63
  The Household in Kempenfeldt
    Square (Sarjeant)         10/4/3-40*

Woods, Sara, continued
  THE LAW'S DELAY (R)
                          1/4/48; 1/5/29
  THE LIE DIRECT (R)              7/6/37
  Literary Allusions in the Writings of
    Sara Woods (Sarjeant) 12/2/17-27
  MY LIFE IS DONE (M*F)           1/4/38
  NAKED VILLAINY (R) 12/3/97-100
Woods, Stockton [Richard Forrest. q.v.]
  THE MAN WHO HEARD TOO
    MUCH (IAC)                    8/1/20
Woolery, Dale
  L:                             13/3/95
Woolrich, Cornell
  BLACK ALIBI (IAC)               7/1/34
  THE BLACK ANGEL (IAC)           7/1/34
  THE BLACK PATH OF FEAR
    (IAC)                         7/1/35
  THE BRIDE WORE BLACK
    (IAC)                         9/3/30
  Cornell Woolrich: The Last Years
    (Nevins) – Part I 8/5/23-8; Part II
    8/6/11-14,18; Part III 9/1/17-22;
    Part IV 9/3/25-31; Conclusion
    9/6/5-30
    (IAC)                       12/2/70
  Memories of a Haunted Man
    (Nevins)                    8/3/2-11
  REAR WINDOW AND FOUR
    SHORT NOVELS (IAC)            8/3/25
  RENDEZVOUS IN BLACK
    (IAC)                         8/3/25
  VAMPIRE'S HONEYMOON
    (IAC)                         9/1/36
Wooster, Martin Morse
  The Body in the Library: Twentieth-
    Century Crime and Mystery
    Writers and the Mystery World in
    Our Time                     5/1/11-4
  (TCITC)                     3/2/3-12,20
  L: 1/2/49; 1/4/56; 1/5/54; 2/4/55;
    2/5/53; 2/6/50; 3/4/54; 5/5/46
  (MS)                         2/4/2,61
  Reviews:
    THE ADVENTURES OF HER-
      LOCK SHOLMES (Todd) 2/5/41
    THE ADVENTURES OF JULES
      DE GRANDIN (Quinn)  1/2/42
    ASIMOV'S SHERLOCKIAN
      LIMERICKS (Asimov)   2/4/42
    THE CIRCULAR STAIRCASE
      (Rinehart)              1/5/38

Wooster, Martin Morse, continued
  Reviews continued:
    A COFFIN FOR DIMITRIOS
      (Ambler)        2/4/39
    THE COURTESY OF DEATH
      (Household)      4/3/45
    THE CROOKED HINGE
      (Carr)         1/4/41
    THE DETECTIVE WORE SILK
      DRAWERS (Lovesey)  6/2/42
    ELLERY QUEEN'S ANTHOL-
      OGY - VOL. 41 (Queen,
      ed.)          6/2/43
    ELLERY QUEEN'S 1961 AN-
      THOLOGY (Queen, ed.) 6/2/42
    FALLBACK (Nieswand)  6/6/38
    GREEN FOR DANGER
      (Brand)        2/6/38
    HOBGOBLIN (Coyne)   6/6/39
    THE IMPOSSIBLE VIRGIN
      (O'Donnell)      1/6/54
    THE INTRIGUERS (Hamilton)
                  4/3/46
    KEK HUUYGENS, SMUGGLER
      (Fish)         2/5/41
    THE KING OF TERRORS
      (Bloch)        1/6/43
    MURDER AT THE ABA
      (Asimov)      1/2/39
    THE MYSTERY STORY (Ball,
      ed.)          1/2/29
    THE NEW SHOE (Upfield) 1/2/32
    NIGHT SHIFT (King)    4/3/45
    THE PIGEON PROJECT
      (Wallace)      3/3/44
    RAFFLES OF THE ALBANY
      (Perowne)      4/3/44
    THE SEVEN DIALS MYSTERY
      (Christie)      6/2/44
    THE THEFTS OF NICK VELVET
      (Hoch)         2/6/39
    THE THIRTEEN CRIMES OF
      SCIENCE FICTION (Asimov/
      Greenberg/Waugh, eds.)  4/3/45
    THE THIRTY-NINE STEPS
      (Buchan)      2/6/37
    THE TRAGEDY OF X
      (Queen)        2/4/40
    THE THREE HOSTAGES
      (Buchan)      6/2/43
    WAXWORK (Lovesey)   6/2/43
  Special Review Article: The Com-
    plete Uncle Abner    2/5/9-12

Wooster, Martin Morse, continued
  L: Ball 1/3/51; Bleiler 2/5/46; Doerrer
    2/6/54; Doran 3/1/50; Lachman
    2/5/48; Lansdale 2/5/47; Mertz
    2/5/49; Meyerson 3/1/57; Nevins
    2/5/50; Nieminski 2/5/46, 3/3/51
WORKING MURDER (Boylan)
  (R)             11/4/86
World Mystery Convention. See
  Bouchercon.
WORLD OF CHAS ADDAMS, THE
  (Addams) (IAC)     13/4/84
World of Nero Wolfe, The (Skytte)
              7/2/11-12,26
WORM OF DOUBT, A (Meek)
  (TAR)         10/4/44
Worrell, Judith
  STING OF THE BEE (R)   7/5/40
Worts, George F.
  The Rise and Fall of Gillian Hazeltine
    (Lybeck)      9/4/3-16*
WRACK AND RUNE (MacLeod)
  (M*F)         6/3/31
Wren, M.K.
  OH, BURY ME NOT (M*F)  2/5/32
Wright, Charles Alan
  L:        11/3/100; 13/2/94-5
Wright, Elsie N.
  STRANGE MURDERS AT GREY-
    STONES (TBR)     11/2/87
Wright, L.R.
  A CHILL RAIN IN JANUARY
    (TAR)        12/4/59
  Murder on the Sunshine Coast
    (Bakerman)     11/4/3-10
  SLEEP WHILE I SING (R)  10/1/74
  THE SUSPECT (R)     9/5/32
Wright, Laurie Robeson
  THE PERFECT CORPSE (R)  1/4/47
Wright, Lee
  Memories of a Haunted Man
    (Nevins)       8/3/2-11
  Obituary (Lachman)    9/3/35
Wright, Stephen
  ADVENTURES OF SANDY WEST,
    PRIVATE EYE (IAC)   9/2/29
Writer's Probe, The: Ruth Rendell as
  Social Critic (Bakerman)  3/5/3-6
  L: Floyd 4/1/37
Writing
  L: Sampson 13/2/99-101
WRITING SUSPENSE AND MYS-
  TERY FICTION (Burack, ed.)
  (R)           2/2/39

WRITING THE MODERN MYSTERY
  (Norville) (R)                9/1/8
WRONG IMPRESSION, THE
  (Malcolm) (TAR)              13/2/44
WRONG TARGET (Kaye) (M*F) 5/6/35
Wyck, Francis
  THE SERN CHARTER (M*F)    P/30
WYCLIFFE AND THE SCAPEGOAT
  (Burley) (M*F)             3/6/38
WYCLIFFE AND THE SCHOOL-
  GIRLS (Burley) (M*F)        P/29
Wylie, Philip. See SMILING CORPSE,
  THE
*Wynne, Anthony*
  DEATH OF A BANKER
    (TCITC)                  3/2/11
  The Fattest Man in the Medical
    Profession (Sampson)   7/3/16-22*
  L: Adey 7/4/44

# X

X MARKS THE SPOT (Butterworth)
  (M*F)                      3/1/35
Xantippe
  DEATH CATCHES UP WITH MR.
    KLUCK (TBR)             11/2/92
XPD (Deighton) (M*F)         5/4/27

# Y

Yarbro, Chelsea Quinn
  OGILVIE, TALLANT & MOON
    (M*F)                    1/4/39
Yates, Donald A.
  Bouchercon, 1978: IX and
    Counting                3/1/15-20
  Film Review: DEATH ON THE
    NILE                     3/1/45
  Review: SEVEN SEATS TO THE
    MOON (Armstrong)         3/1/39
Yates, George Worthing. Also see Hunt,
  Peter
  THE BODY THAT WASN'T
    UNCLE (M*F)              3/5/39
YEAR'S BEST MYSTERY AND SUS-
  PENSE STORIES, 1987, THE (Hoch,
  ed.) (IAC)                 9/5/24
YEAR'S BEST MYSTERY AND SUS-
  PENSE STORIES, 1988, THE (Hoch,
  ed.) (IAC)                11/1/32
YEAR'S BEST MYSTERY AND SUS-
  PENSE STORIES 1989, THE (Hoch,
  ed.) (IAC)                12/2/65

YEAR'S BEST MYSTERY AND SUS-
  PENSE STORIES 1991, THE (Hoch,
  ed.) (R)                  13/4/47
YELLOW DOG PARTY (Emerson)
  (TAR)                     13/3/80
YELLOW ROOM, THE (Rinehart)
  (R)                        9/4/40
YESTERDAY'S ENEMY (Haggard)
  (M*F)                      1/4/37
YESTERDAY'S FACES—VOLUME I:
  GLORY FIGURES (Sampson)
  (R)                        7/6/30
YESTERDAY'S NEWS (Healy) (R)
  (TAR)              12/1/41; 12/3/82
*York, Andrew*
  THE FASCINATOR (M*F)      1/5/35
  THE INFILTRATOR (R)        P/16
  (SSC)                    5/3/18-9*
Yorke, Margaret
  THE COME-ON (M*F)         3/6/28
  THE COST OF SILENCE (R)  4/5/41
  DEAD IN THE MORNING
    (M*F)                   4/2/40
  DEATH ON ACCOUNT (R)     6/1/42
  DEVIL'S WORK (R)   7/5/49–7/6/50
  THE HAND OF DEATH (R)    7/5/42
  THE POINT OF MURDER (R) 5/2/33
  THE SCENT OF FEAR (R)    5/3/35
  SPEAK FOR THE DEAD (TAR)
                    11/1/69; 11/2/81
YOU BET YOUR LIFE (Kaminsky)
  (M*F)                      3/6/28
YOU CAN ALWAYS BLAME THE
  RAIN (Fredman) (M*F)      4/4/36
YOU CAN'T KEEP THE CHANGE
  (Cheyney) (R)             2/4/44
YOU MUST BE KIDDING (Chase)
  (R)                       3/6/44
YOU NICE BASTARD (Newman)
  (R)                       2/2/37
YOU ONLY HANG ONCE (Roden)
  (TBR)                     13/3/58
YOU'LL DIE TONIGHT (Grove)
  (IAC)                     4/5/26
Young Detective Kildare (Herzog)
                            7/2/2-10
  L: Herzog 7/4/43
Young, Edward
  THE FIFTH PASSENGER
    (IAC)                   6/1/29
Youngkin, Stephen; James Bigwood,
  and Raymond Cabana, Jr.
  THE FILMS OF PETER LORRE
    (R)                    10/3/71

YOUR DAY IN THE BARREL (Furst)
(M*F)                          P/28

# Z

Z PAPERS, THE (Simmons) (R)  1/6/42
Zackel, Fred
  CINDERELLA AFTER MIDNIGHT
    (M*F)                      5/1/23
  COCAINE AND BLUE EYES
    (R)                        7/5/40
ZEBRA-STRIPED HEARSE, THE
  (Macdonald) (IAC)          10/3/41

ZERO FACTOR, THE (Johnson)
  (IAC)                        4/3/33
Zochert, Donald
  ANOTHER WEEPING WOMAN
    (M*F) (R)          4/5/30; 6/4/41
  MURDER IN THE HELLFIRE
    CLUB (R)                   5/2/30
Zondi, Sergeant Mickey. See McClure,
  James
ZOOT-SUIT MURDERS (Sanchez)
  (M*F) (IAC)          3/5/35; 4/5/24

## About the Author

**William F. Deeck** was born in 1936. For many years a reader of crime fiction, he became active in mystery fandom in the 1980s and now has more than a score of articles and over 500 book reviews published in *The Armchair Detective, The Poisoned Pen, CADS, The Mystery Fancier, The Mystery Readers Journal,* and *The Criminal Record.* In 1989 he was Co-Fan Guest of Honor at the Philadelphia Bouchercon and in 1992 was Fan Guest of Honor at the Malice Domestic Convention. With Steven A. Stilwell, he compiled *The Armchair Detective Index (Volumes 1– 20),* published in 1992.

www.ingramcontent.com/pod-product-compliance
Lightning Source LLC
Chambersburg PA
CBHW030013290326
41934CB00005B/329